In Cold Pursuit

In Cold Pursuit

My Hunt for Timothy Krajcir—
The Notorious Serial Killer

By Lt. Paul Echols and Christine Byers

New Horizon Press
Far Hills, New Jersey

Echols, Paul and Byers, Christine
In Cold Pursuit: My Hunt for Timothy Krajcir—The Notorious Serial Killer
Cover design: Robert Aulicino
Interior design: Susan S. Sanderson

Library of Congress Control Number: 2010925080

ISBN 13: 978-0-88282-348-5
New Horizon Press

Manufactured in the U.S.A.

2015 2014 2013 2012 2011 / 5 4 3 2 1

Dedication

This book is dedicated to all of Tim Krajcir's victims and their families. Specifically, we dedicate this book to the families of Mary and Brenda Parsh, Sheila Cole, Virginia Witte, Joyce Tharp, Myrtle Rupp, Margie Call, Deborah Sheppard, Mildred Wallace and Grover Thompson. The murder victims have been identified, along with many of the rape victims, but there are others out there who were never found.

Authors' Note

This book is based on the experiences of the authors and reflects their perceptions of the past, present and future. The personalities, events, actions and conversations portrayed within this story have been taken from interviews, research, court documents, letters, personal papers, press accounts and the memories of some participants.

In an effort to safeguard the privacy of certain people, some individuals' names and identifying characteristics have been changed. Some characters may be composites. Events involving the characters happened as described. Only minor details may have been altered.

viii

Contents

Preface

Deborah Sheppard didn't have time to freshen up between her dancercise class and the championship intramural basketball game. But she didn't need to. She was beautiful even after a workout. It was a Thursday, one of two nights a week that Deborah religiously attended fitness classes. Heads turned as she walked into the basketball courts with her rust-colored jumpsuit with white stripes hugging her curves. The faint smell of chlorine lingered in the air from the Olympic-sized swimming pool near the basketball courts at Southern Illinois University's student recreation center. She was there to support her friends and roommate Anthony Smith as their all-black team "The Chosen Few" battled "The Saltons" for the title in a predominantly white league the night of April 8, 1982.

Summer break was about a month away for students. Deborah was about to graduate with a bachelor's of marketing degree. She planned to move back to the Chicago area after graduation to be near her family and had dreams of becoming as successful as her father. Her parents, Bernie and Hazel Sheppard, planned to make the six-hour trip down to Carbondale and spend Easter weekend with their firstborn. They hadn't seen her since Christmas. Her younger sisters looked forward to staying in Deborah's apartment to share some girl time while their parents stayed at a nearby hotel. Bernie decided against taking the girls out of school a day early to make the drive to Carbondale—it was a decision he would agonize over for the rest of his life. So instead of traveling that Thursday, the family planned to get an early start the next day, Good Friday.

Deborah didn't mind. The extra day gave her more time to clean up her apartment before their visit and time to go to the big game. She found a seat among some of her girlfriends, but it didn't take long for the first man to approach her. Randy Dickerson spotted her. The two had been in an on again, off again relationship since the year before. At the moment, it was on. He smiled when her eyes caught his. He got up and walked toward her just as the crowd erupted into applause for another basket scored by the Chosen Few.

"Hey, Deb, what's up?" Randy asked.

"Nothing much. You think they are going to win?" Deborah asked.

"Yes, they're hot tonight," he responded.

The pair watched the game, cheering for their friends as points were scored. Randy didn't want his moment with Deborah to end in the stands.

"Deb, would you like to go over to the Varsity Theater? *Richard Pryor Live on the Sunset Strip* is showing," he asked.

"Probably not. I am all sweaty and need to take a shower," she said. "I also need to pick up some stuff around my apartment. My parents are coming down tomorrow."

"Okay," Randy said.

Rejected.

Soon, a friend of Deborah's caught her attention and she moved to another spot on the bleachers to strike up a conversation. It was obvious the Chosen Few were going to have a good night. Deborah decided they didn't need her support as it was clear they were on their way to victory, so she got up to leave when an old friend, David "Goose" Canada, tried to stop her.

"How you doing, lady?" he asked.

Deborah looked at him with her big brown eyes but didn't flash a smile and didn't break stride on her way out of the building. He had tried courting her for something more than a friendship in the past. She told friends she would never date him, because she wasn't interested in him. David was not pleased with Deborah's cold reception. He mumbled something else to one of his friends about Deborah. She said something back. Their words got lost among the cheers of the crowd, which was focused on the game. And so did David's attention to Deborah.

About the same time, Randy noticed Deborah was gone. He assumed she had left for her apartment only a couple blocks away. He stayed and watched as the Chosen Few took the championship. Anthony beamed with pride as the photo was taken. The reward for the victory was modest: a T-shirt declaring them intramural league champions. Deborah watched from a doorway as the Chosen Few celebrated the victory. She called her friend Jo to tell her the good news.

"Hey, girl, they won!" Deborah said.

"For real? That's great. What are you doing for dinner? Do you want to grab something?"

"No, I have to go back and take a shower. My parents are coming tomorrow. I might call Murray and see if he'll bring me some tacos. Curt is supposed to come over later and go over what clothes I'm going to wear for that magazine shoot."

"Okay, that's cool. Talk to you later."

Murray Jones was like most of the men in Deborah's life: He would do any-thing for her. And she knew it. The previous summer, he asked her to go with him to his family reunion in Belleville, Illinois, just outside of St. Louis, Missouri. She agreed. He offered to give her a watch as a sign of their friendship, but Deborah took it as a sign that he wanted more. She rejected the gift. She did like him as a friend but wasn't attracted to his slightly overweight build. He now worked at a Mex-ican fast-food restaurant and didn't mind bringing leftovers to Deborah's apartment every chance he got.

His roommate was Curt Reichert, a photography major, who had taken pic-tures of Deborah before. She trusted him. He was busy taking pictures of the cham-pionship team as Deborah left for her apartment, only a few blocks away.

Anthony beamed with pride as Curt took the picture. The thrill of victory couldn't last long. He had to get ready for his job as a student janitor on campus. He got to the apartment he shared with Deborah around 7:30 P.M. Deborah was in the kitchen making something to eat. Soft music was playing from an eight-track player. She had changed into hot pink sweatpants and a V-neck top.

"Hey, Anthony. You guys played great tonight!" Deborah greeted him. "When are you going to get your T-shirt?"

"I'll pick it up tomorrow," Anthony said as he rushed into the apartment to gather his clothes and get ready for work. He only had about twenty minutes to get there.

"I need to take a quick shower before I go to work," he said.

"I do too, but I'll just wait until you're gone," she said.

Anthony glanced at the clock before he hastily left for work. It was 7:50 P.M. Deborah was still in the kitchen making red punch. She poured a glass for herself and put ice in it. She figured it would be nice and cold by the time she finished her shower and left it on her coffee table. She hung a note on her apartment door in case Curt, Murray or any of her other friends decided to stop by: "Knock hard; I'm in the shower." She got undressed in her bedroom.

Just before 11 P.M., Deborah's beautiful face began to haunt Randy. She had told him she was too busy to hang out that night, but he wanted to see her just one more time before her big weekend with her family and without him. First, he had to pick up his friend Kenny Bell at the recreation center. He had borrowed Kenny's car to go to a few parties that night. Randy climbed out of the car near his apartment after picking up Kenny. The friends said good-bye and Randy walked toward his apartment. He paused. *It really isn't that late*, he thought. *Why not visit Deborah?*

He couldn't resist. It was only a short walk across the alley to her apartment.

He walked into the foyer of her apartment building and turned to the right to knock on the front door. But it was already open. The note she always left on the door when she showered was on the floor just inside her apartment. He thought it was odd that she would leave the door ajar.

"Deborah, what's up?" he yelled as he peaked his head in the doorway.

There was no response. The television was on. So was a lamp near the window and a light in the bathroom. Deborah must be here, he thought.

"Deb?" he called cautiously as he took his first steps into her apartment.

Again, no response. He looked in the bathroom. The shower wasn't running. She wasn't there. He went to check her bedroom, wondering if she fell asleep. It was dark in the room. Randy felt the wall for the light switch and flicked it on when he found it. He looked for a lump under the covers of Deborah's bed and didn't see one; then his eyes dropped to the floor beside Deborah's bed. At first he thought he was seeing things. But there was Deborah's naked body. She was on her back. Her feet pointed toward the doorway where he stood. Her face turned away from him. He saw a red frothy substance on the floor in front of her face. A purple shirt was on the floor, just to Deborah's right. Fear consumed him. He dropped his book bag on the floor and rushed to Deborah's side.

"Deb! Deb! Are you okay?" he said in a rush.

There was no response. He shook her left leg. It was cool to the touch. Shock began to set in as he realized something was seriously wrong. He ran to the phone in the living room to call an ambulance. There was no dial tone. The phone line must have been cut. Randy grabbed his book bag and ran across the street toward Kenny's apartment. Kenny was still in his car, listening to one last song when Randy banged on his trunk and startled him. He looked back to see Randy crying and shouting words he could not understand at first.

"Kenny, something is wrong with Deborah!" Randy yelled, barely able to catch his breath. "Go get help!"

Then Randy ran into Kenny's apartment and yelled the same thing at Kenny's roommates, who were watching television.

"Somebody, please," he cried. "Call an ambulance!"

He raced out of the apartment and back to Deborah's, hoping he would wake from this nightmare.

1

"A Possible Homicide"

Just as Deborah Sheppard was finishing her shower, I was starting mine about two blocks away in a rented trailer across from the Carbondale Police Department. I had been hired just eight months before. Rookies usually get stuck working the midnight and weekend shifts. So as most people were preparing for the upcoming Easter weekend and settling in for the night, it was the beginning of the workweek for me. Living that close to the department was a convenient arrangement. My hometown friend, Dave Baker, was my roommate. We found the place after I was hired almost out of the blue by the Carbondale Police Department and after he decided to try his luck at attending Southern Illinois University. We grew up in Ullin, Illinois, a small town in Southern Illinois just thirty-five miles away from Carbondale.

After showering and putting on my tan and brown police uniform, I wrapped the black leather basket weave belt around my waist, secured it and reached for my stainless steel revolver. I slid the gun in the leather holster and tugged on it to make sure it was secure. The shiny steel gun against the black leather looked sharp. One last check in the mirror reminded me of how proud I was to be a police officer. It was something I wished my father, M. J. "Baldy" Echols, could have lived to see.

He had been a proud World War II Veteran who saw action in the South Pacific as well as my baseball coach and a full-time high school janitor. His work ethic was impeccable, but he always made time for community service. He was the fire chief and, for many years, police chief of our small town. My dad ruled the department like the television character Andy Taylor on *The Andy Griffith Show*. And Ullin was much like Mayberry. It really wasn't much of a police job, only paying fifty dollars per month. But he wasn't in it for the money. He did it because he liked helping people. He died of cancer at the young age of forty-eight. I was almost thirteen when he died. We were just getting really to know each other then. His death devastated our entire family.

I remember the excitement of going on patrol with him a couple times, starting when I was about eight. It was just a drive across town in our family station wagon. But with a red light on the dash and a siren mounted under the hood, as far as I was concerned it was the finest police cruiser money could buy! The car had a Citizens' Band Radio, so he could call my mother and she could summon help if something really did happen. I loved being his partner in those days, wrapping my plastic western gun belt around my waist and sliding my cap guns into their holsters. Fourteen years later, my dad was gone, the holster was leather and the gun was real.

My days off were in the middle of the week, which was okay with me. Most of the "action" was during the weekend and I did not want to miss a minute of that. I arrived for my ten-hour shift just before ten o'clock. Sergeant Johnny Knapp and officers Jim Temple, Margaret Winsauer, Debbie Smith and Leon Hamlin joined me on my shift. We gathered in the briefing room to receive our assignments and listened to Sergeant Knapp read from the logbook about what had occurred in the past twenty-four hours. I was assigned to patrol district 40, the northwest quadrant of Carbondale. At about eleven, it was time to hit the streets.

I was in my patrol car for fewer than twenty minutes when chatter started to buzz on my radio. The dispatcher's voice was calm. The call sounded fairly routine.

"3320, Carbondale."

"Go ahead, Carbondale," Officer Margaret Winsauer answered.

"3320, go to apartment number six at 418 South Graham to assist the ambulance with an unconscious female," the dispatcher ordered.

"10-4," Margaret responded.

I glanced at my watch. It was 11:09 P.M. I wondered if it was going to be a long night for Margaret. I knew exactly where the apartment in question was—just a couple blocks from our police station and, more importantly, near the campus of our town's lifeblood: the university. It sounded like other calls we had fielded when college students overestimated their ability to drink or, in some cases, overdosed on drugs. We usually just stood by to keep people away from the paramedics so they could treat the patients and take them to the hospital.

But this call was different.

The "unconscious female" in the apartment was Deborah Sheppard.

Jackson County Ambulance Service attendants Dottie Wilson and Arlen Kelley had already seen Deborah's body when Margaret arrived. Dottie knew it wasn't a medical emergency. It was a crime scene.

"Rigor mortis has begun to set in. She's been dead for a while. There's nothing we can do to help her," Dottie told Margaret.

Randy and two of Deborah's other friends were still in the apartment. Margaret forced them to leave. They gathered outside Deborah's open bedroom window, looking in to see what was going on. They were walking where the killer had walked only hours earlier. Deborah's bedroom window had been pulled out of its frame and was on the ground a few steps away.

Within minutes, I heard Margaret's call for the coroner and a supervisor. The dispatcher's voice became hurried. Flustered. It grew increasingly frantic as it echoed in my patrol car. I could now tell something major was going down on Graham Street. And I wanted in. I knew someone was dead. From what I could tell, the young woman's boyfriend had called paramedics after finding her unresponsive in her apartment. *Was it a rape? A murder?* I wondered, among about a dozen other scenarios that started playing out in my budding detective mind.

"8800 responding to Graham," the dispatcher said.

Wow, I thought. *That's Chief Ed Hogan's number.* Hearing his deep voice on the air was odd. I wondered why he was out so late at night. Later I learned he had been on his way home from a meeting when he heard the call for the coroner and decided to respond. I thought of the stress Margaret must be feeling right now. I knew any serious incident involving a student would automatically make it high profile. All I could do was stay glued to my radio and listen as more details emerged.

I felt it had to be a homicide. Why else would the chief go there at midnight? I wanted to be there. I wanted this to be my first homicide investigation. I wanted to turn on my cruiser's flashing lights and fly across town to the murder scene. But it wasn't my district and it would take many more years for me to gain the experience I needed to be part of the drama that began to unfold that night.

Instead, my mentors, the department's crime scene technicians, arrived to process the scene. Soon, detectives started rolling in. Dottie and Arlen waited nearby for permission to remove the body. Those on the scene debated whether the death was natural or a homicide. Bloody froth had pooled around the victim's nose and mouth postmortem. Dottie knew that sometimes happened when someone died from natural causes. And sometimes it happened after drug overdoses. She watched as the detectives searched but didn't find any drugs at the scene other than prescription allergy medications on Deborah's nightstand. She also noticed the window missing from Deborah's bedroom and the cut phone line leading to the living room phone. She couldn't believe there was any question of whether this was a homicide. But, like me, she too was a rookie in her field. She kept her mouth shut. To pass the time, she focused on the ice floating in a glass of red punch on Deborah's coffee table. She knew whoever did this was quick—even the ice hadn't yet completely melted in the young woman's late night drink. But Dottie wasn't lost in her thoughts for long. It was time to prepare the body for its solemn journey to the morgue.

The last gruesome task was the final crime scene photos. Dottie rolled Deborah onto her right side to expose her back to the detective's seemingly relentless flashes. She and Arlen loaded the body onto a stretcher and into their ambulance. Investigators did a final sweep of the scene. One last piece of evidence caught their eyes. When Dottie rolled the body over, the frothy substance from Deborah's mouth pooled onto the purple shirt near her body. They had meant to collect the shirt during a sweep of the scene, thinking it might have been used as a ligature if the woman had been murdered. But it had been hidden on the other side of her body and they forgot. Now, it had biological evidence on it. Into a brown paper evidence bag it went as the last piece of evidence to be collected from the scene.

Between catching speeders and checking homes on my house watch list that night, I listened to my radio as much as I could to hear what was unfolding. Dispatch called for backup to help control the small but growing crowd of Deborah's friends who had gathered outside the apartment. I knew our county's coroner, Don Ragsdale, would have to notify the victim's family. Telling parents of a child's death was never easy for him.

Randy told Don that Deborah's parents were planning to visit the next day. But this news couldn't wait. Don looked up the Sheppard's address. He didn't want to call them with news he felt would be best delivered in person by police officers. He called the police department in Olympia Fields, Illinois. Two officers who knew Bernie Sheppard were given the gloomy assignment. The drive to the Sheppard's home was short. Inside, the family had fallen asleep thinking about the trip they planned to take to visit their daughter and sister the next day. It was about 3 A.M. The house was dark. The officers rang the doorbell a couple times. A light finally turned on upstairs. The officers looked at each other knowing they were about to deliver the most devastating news a parent could ever hear. They knew it would change the family's life forever.

Bernie thought he was dreaming when he first heard the doorbell. Hazel nudged him and he headed to the door just ahead of her. Bernie opened the door and let the officers in his home.

"It's Deborah, isn't it? Something has happened to Deborah, hasn't it?" Hazel inquired as the officers filed into their kitchen.

"Hazel, let the men speak," Bernie said. "There's nothing wrong with Deborah."

The officers looked at each other. Their few seconds of silence validated Hazel's suspicions. Bernie's heart sank. His knees became weak.

"I am sorry, Mr. Sheppard," one of the officers said. "Your daughter Deborah has been found dead in her apartment in Carbondale."

Bernie stepped back. The officer's words knocked the wind out of him. His daughter's beautiful face flashed into his mind. At the same time, he heard a voice.

"Daddy, does that mean Debbie isn't coming home?"

He realized his two younger daughters were peering through the stairway banister taking in the whole scene. Hazel's cries were now audible as the grim reality of the situation began to sink in. The officers knew very little but gave Bernie the coroner's phone number. A moment later, they were gone.

Bernie rushed to the phone, hoping and praying this was all a mistake. Don was waiting for Bernie's call. He only confirmed the worst, but he couldn't say for sure how she died. Bernie knew his daughter had been murdered. His daughter's roommate, Anthony Smith, was the first suspect who came to his mind. He had telephoned his daughter the day before and was surprised when a young man answered. Bernie wasn't happy knowing his little girl was living with a man, even if they were strictly roommates. The grief-stricken father made a decision on the spot: he would go to Carbondale to find his daughter's murderer and kill him. He just needed someone to tell him who had done it.

But not everyone was as convinced as Bernie that Deborah had been the victim of a homicide. The morning after her death, Carbondale police issued a brief news release about the investigation, without Deborah's name. The *Southern Illinoisan* newspaper quoted the release in a short story inside its April 9 edition under the headline: "Woman found dead in Carbondale home." The article continued: "A police department news release stated, 'The incident at this time is being treated and investigated as a possible homicide until the cause of death can be determined.'"

Detectives worked the case through the night, interviewing Deborah's friends. Nobody knew who would want her dead. But a few curious statements became leads that detectives needed to follow up on. The autopsy was pertinent.

My shift ended at 8 A.M. I was curious about what was going on, but I was tired and realized my lack of experience would be of no value to the seasoned investigators. I went home and crashed. As I drifted off to sleep, Officer Larry Kammerer was meeting with Dr. Steven Nurenberger at St. Joseph's Hospital in nearby Murphysboro, Illinois. Dr. Nurenberger was a private company pathologist who had conducted autopsies on murder victims for the Jackson County Coroner's office for several years. He wasn't forensically certified but was respected for his expertise. He was very easygoing and talked to investigators as he conducted his autopsies, showing them what he found as he went through the process.

During Deborah's autopsy, Dr. Nurenberger first combed her beautiful black hair, capturing any debris and possibly foreign hair in the process. He did the same with her pubic hair. He then collected fingernail scrapings, hoping she might have scratched her killer during the attack. Then he swabbed Deborah's vagina, anus and oral cavity hoping the killer left semen behind if there was a sexual assault. He took the individual swabs and smeared them on microscopic slides for later examination. Usually, the swabs were also kept as evidence. But for whatever reason, only the microscopic slides were retained this time. Officer Kammerer recorded the items into police evidence.

Then Dr. Nurenberger proceeded with a typical autopsy, opening the body with a "Y" incision. He found some small petechiae, or pinpoint-sized red dots in the whites of her eyes, and a spot where her teeth had bruised her right upper lip—injuries typically found in victims who had seizures. Dr. Nurenberger told Officer Kammerer he could not find or see any obvious cause of death but pulmonary edema, or abnormal buildup of fluid, was present in the lungs. He would have to wait for toxicology results to eliminate any potential drug overdoses.

The lack of any definitive cause of death frustrated investigators. The only thing the autopsy told them was what did not kill Deborah. She was not shot, stabbed or beaten. There was no murder weapon to seek. They had no particular direction to follow.

After the autopsy and about twelve hours after Deborah's death, Chief Hogan met with his detectives. There was dissention among the group. Most of the detectives believed Deborah had been murdered and had continued their investigations so far as such. The chief, after consulting with some of the others who had been on the scene, did not think the evidence proved Deborah was the victim of a homicide. Chief Hogan released a statement to the media about a day and a half after Deborah's death:

> The deceased person discovered on April 8, 1982, has been identified as Deborah R. Sheppard, twenty-three years of age, a senior at Southern Illinois, Carbondale. A preliminary autopsy has been completed though tests requiring laboratory analysis have not been completed. Circumstances surrounding this incident do not indicate foul play. The death will be further investigated by the Carbondale and SIU Police Departments. The specific cause of death is, at this time, undetermined.

Bernie was waiting in Carbondale to claim his daughter's body when the statement went out. A friend and neighbor of Bernie's had flown Bernie and a few friends to Carbondale on his private plane. Deborah's distraught mother stayed home with their younger daughters.

Bernie went straight to the police station when he arrived, asking to speak with the detectives investigating his daughter's murder. By then, detectives Monica Joost and Mike Dismore had been assigned to the case. Bernie hoped the quality of the detectives exceeded the appearance of their building, which was a former college dormitory that had been converted into police headquarters. He had many questions for them. What about the cut phone cord in the apartment? What about the missing window pane? And most importantly, how did Deborah die?

The detectives told him they had no rational explanation for the phone cord and window and that the autopsy had not revealed a cause of death. They floated the idea that there could still be a medical reason for Deborah's death, although they did not really believe it. Bernie wasn't buying it either. He was convinced Deborah had been murdered and wanted the detectives to provide him a name—any name. He wanted revenge. At that moment, had the detectives hinted about whom they thought might have murdered Deborah, Bernie would have killed him. Unbeknownst to the detectives, Bernie was packing a loaded .32 caliber gun with him that day, which he planned to use to kill his daughter's murderer. Fortunately, the detectives did not provide the names of any suspects to him.

Bernie left the police station frustrated and set out to do some investigating on his own. Family friends of the Sheppard family had sent their son to SIU as well. Bernie trusted him and hoped he could tell him what he knew about what happened to Deborah.

"I need you to tell me what you know," Bernie said to the young man.

"Well, Mr. Sheppard, I know there were two dudes who had been hanging out at Deborah's apartment an awful lot lately. They're not students here. I heard through the grapevine that they might know something. I don't know their names, but I know where they live."

"Show me."

Bernie waited until it was dark to have the boy drive him to the apartment where the two men lived. He walked up to the door with the loaded .32 semiautomatic handgun tucked in his waistband underneath his coat. When one of the men answered the door, Bernie made his move and pushed his way in.

"Gentlemen, my name is Bernie Sheppard. I am Deborah's father."

"Sir, I'm so sorry about what happened— " one of the men began.

"If you harmed my daughter, I am going to blow your brains out now! There will be no trial. I am the judge, the jury and the executioner!" Bernie interrupted.

He didn't show the gun but held his hand to his waistband so the men knew he was armed.

"Sir, I am very sorry, but I don't know anything about Deborah's death," the first man began again.

"I wish I could tell you something, but I don't know a thing," the other added.

"If you know something, you better start talking now." Bernie was adamant.

"Mr. Sheppard, please, I'm telling you we don't know anything."

"If we did, we would tell you and the police. Deborah was our friend. We want to find out who did this just as bad as you," one insisted.

The men broke down into tears, likely fearing for their lives as well as feeling grief for the loss of their friend and seeing her father driven to an act of desperation. Just as quickly as he had burst into their lives, Bernie left. He was disappointed, having convinced himself he had the courage to kill, but didn't believe he had the evidence he needed to inflict the ultimate revenge at that moment. He wasn't convinced they were innocent, either, though. He met with Carbondale detectives the next day.

"I will give you $5,000 if you waste these guys if you figure out they killed Deborah," he told them, failing to mention his own interrogation of the two unidentified men the previous night.

Bernie took a plane back to Chicago on Easter Sunday. At the same time, a hearse carried his daughter's body back to Olympia Fields. That day, the *Southern Illinoisan* newspaper headline declared: "Student death now believed not foul play."

Bernie refused to believe it. He had an idea about how to prove his daughter had been murdered.

2

A Firestorm

The roots of Bernie's determination formed early in his life. Deborah became the first of three reasons why her father worked even harder to keep a vow he made never to return to the ghetto where he grew up in the Summerhill area of Atlanta, Georgia—about a mile north of Dr. Martin Luther King Jr.'s birthplace.

Bernie knew the King family and went to school with A.D. King, Martin Luther King Jr.'s younger brother. Bernie, too, dreamed of change for his family and all African-Americans. The neighborhood where the men grew up was home to the Atlanta Crackers, a minor league baseball team that later became the predecessor to the now famous Atlanta Braves. Bernie often passed time during his youth watching the Crackers play ball. Though he loved his time at the park, it was also a reminder to him of how far society was from reaching Dr. King's dreams of equality. He watched games from areas of the stadium reserved for black fans, in the outfield. By contrast, many years later, just a couple blocks away from Bernie's front porch, an African-American baseball player, Hank Aaron, hit his 715th home run, surpassing Babe Ruth's long-standing baseball record of 714 round trippers.

Bernie left the neighborhood at eighteen to join the Air Force. It was his ticket out of a lifestyle he knew would lead him to prison or an early grave, as it did to so many of his friends. He traveled the world as a member of the 22nd Bomb Wing of the Strategic Air Command. After he returned from the Korean War, he enrolled in college classes and went to work full time.

In his wife Hazel's eyes, it was God and a bit of flirting that brought her and Bernie together. The two met by accident around Christmastime when Bernie had moved from San Francisco, California, to Chicago to live with his aunt and uncle. Hazel, who was born in Columbus, Mississippi, had come to live with her uncle in Chicago as well. Bernie was riding back to the Great Lakes Naval Station with his cousin, who was in the Navy, when he spotted the most beautiful woman he had ever seen standing at a payphone at the 51st Avenue station. Hazel was a model for a national magazine, had been a bathing suit-clad centerfold and worked for a food company visiting local grocery stores and handing out freshly baked bread samples. Bernie looked pretty dapper himself, sporting a six-button camel hair overcoat that he had bought in London when stationed there. Bernie and his cousin boarded the train and took their seats, facing Hazel. Bernie couldn't resist flirting with her. He winked and puckered his lips at her. Hazel returned the gestures with a smile.

"I'm going to marry that girl," Bernie whispered to his cousin as he nodded toward Hazel.

"You're nuts," his cousin replied.

Bernie made his move and took a seat next to Hazel. Before they reached their destinations and departed, Bernie got her phone number. It's a number he remembers to this day. The couple married a year and a half later at city hall in Chicago. After their wedding day kiss, Bernie went back to selling subscriptions to the *Chicago American* newspaper and Hazel went to do the newlyweds' laundry at a local Laundromat. During the early years of their marriage, Hazel's beauty earned her a job as a hostess for a nightclub. But soon her husband's new career in insurance sales began to take off, as did the start of their family. Hazel quit her job to become a full-time housewife and mother to her firstborn, Deborah.

Bernie became involved in local politics and civil rights efforts in the Chicago area. The King family had moved into the slums of North Lawndale on Chicago's west side to attract attention to living conditions among the poor. Bernie met with a group of civil rights activists including Coretta Scott King. After the meeting, Mrs. King invited Bernie to meet her famous husband. It was the night before the civil rights march in Cicero, Illinois. They arrived just after midnight. Mrs. King went into the bedroom and told Dr. King that Bernie Sheppard, from the Summerhill area of Atlanta, Georgia, would like to meet him. Bernie sat nervously outside the room, wondering what he would say to the Nobel Peace Prize recipient. Before he knew it, Dr. King emerged from the bedroom dressed in a bathrobe and embraced Bernie.

"Homeboy!" Dr. King said.

The two men spent a few hours talking about Atlanta and issues they shared. Eventually, Bernie reminded Dr. King that he had a big day ahead of him and he should leave to let Dr. King get some rest. They shook hands and Bernie left. It was one of the highlights of Bernie's life.

As time passed, the young kid from the ghetto who was forced to take a back seat at minor league baseball games and had earned money as a hotel bellhop in downtown Atlanta found himself fulfilling the dream Dr. King had for all African-Americans. By then, Bernie and Hazel had welcomed two more little girls into their lives, Nicole and Bridgette. Bernie's hard work and dedication paid off as he went on to become a successful insurance salesman, representing more than thirty-five major life insurance companies in the Chicago area. The family built a new home in the affluent south suburban Chicago community of Olympia Fields. They were the second black family to move into the community. Life was good.

As Deborah prepared to pursue her education at college, Bernie balked at the thought of her leaving home to go to school. He wanted her to attend the University of Illinois after she graduated from Prairie State Junior College. He feared her sheltered upbringing might not have prepared her for a large university where students live on campus instead of commuting. But when Deborah's best friend Jo moved about six hours south of Chicago to go to Southern Illinois University-Carbondale, Deborah wanted to follow her.

Thousands of acres of rolling hills, creeks and recreational lakes mostly located in and around the Shawnee National Forest surround the town Deborah called home during her college years. Carbondale is six hours to the south of the hustle and bustle of Chicago. The city was founded in the 1850s as the Illinois Central Railroad was being built from the southern tip of the state in Cairo to the north in Chicago. Today, along what is now owned by the Canadian National Railroad, many freight and passenger trains still pass through the town with a population of about 27,000 residents—a number that nearly doubles when school at SIU is in session.

Hazel and Deborah kept the knowledge of just how far SIU was from Olympia Fields from conversation with Bernie. Hazel was very close to her oldest daughter and understood her desire to explore the world beyond the comforts of their suburban life. Comparing pictures of Hazel when she was her daughter's age with Deborah, they could have passed for twins. Mother and daughter did a good job of keeping Deborah's new hometown a secret from Bernie.

That fall, Bernie, Hazel and Deborah began their drive south on Interstate 57 headed for Carbondale. Bernie prepared to get off the interstate at the University of Illinois exit—almost a third of the way to Carbondale. The moment of truth had arrived. Hazel and Deborah confessed that Deborah was not enrolled there and Bernie had about four more hours to drive to get to SIU. He was furious. But there was not much he could do at that point. Deborah was officially an SIU Saluki. He had heard the school was known for partying. But he loved his daughter dearly and granted her wishes, although not happy with Hazel for keeping him in the dark. At first, Deborah lived in dormitories but eventually found her own apartment. Before long, time began to pass without any problems from Bernie. During breaks, Deborah always came home. Each time it was a celebration.

The Carbondale Police Department's news release declaring "No foul play suspected" and subsequent Easter Sunday news story bearing that headline sent Bernie into a rage. To him, if foul play wasn't suspected, that implied that Deborah had died of natural causes or a drug overdose. He knew his daughter better than that. He knew she prided herself on remaining physically fit, so a natural death or drug overdose was unacceptable. To him, he took it to mean that investigators thought Deborah had come from a poor black family in a Chicago ghetto without the resources to question what happened.

When Deborah's body arrived from Carbondale, Bernie called in a favor. A friend of Bernie's knew Cook County Medical Examiner Dr. Robert J. Stein. As Cook County's first medical examiner, Dr. Stein was forensically certified and had autopsied more than 20,000 cases in his career, including the thirty-three young boys slain by serial killer John Wayne Gacy. Dr. Stein was the best there was and Bernie would accept nothing less for his daughter. He needed answers. And he knew Dr. Stein would be the one to deliver at least some of them. Dr. Stein performed a second autopsy on Deborah. This one yielded more information. Bernie was right: Deborah had been murdered. Dr. Stein provided insight into her final moments and how she met her demise.

Dr. Stein found bruising in Deborah's neck tissues as well as evidence of a blow to the head. Cause of death: strangulation. Bernie and Hazel felt they were finally able to schedule a funeral service and bury their oldest daughter.

In the weeks that followed Deborah's murder, I watched as Chief Hogan landed in the middle of a racial firestorm once the story hit the media, especially in the Chicago area. I never did believe the chief had racial motivations for the way he handled the case. But the tall, white-haired Navy veteran was feeling the wrath.

Compared to large cities, crime in and around Carbondale had always been low. But during the next year the local newspaper used the word "murder" more than any other time in the city's history. A December headline in the *Southern Illinoisan* newspaper declared: "String of unsolved killings baffle Jackson County authorities." It started in March, when Marie Azevedo, an SIU employee, was found shot to death in her own car, gangland style, just outside Carbondale's northeast city limits. Then, in August, just one week after my first day on the job as a police officer, a twenty-one-year-old classmate of mine, Susan Shumake, was found raped and murdered along a wooded path between her dormitory and campus. In November, former SIU student Joan Wetherall was found naked in a mining strip pit just north of the city. The thirty-year-old had been abducted from "The Strip," a group of bars along South Illinois Avenue, beaten, raped and strangled. Just five weeks before Deborah's death, Sion Raveed, an associate professor in SIU's marketing department, was found murdered in the basement of his home.

No arrests had been made in any of these cases when Deborah was killed. Investigators believed some of the cases were likely connected but not all. Our police department had only sixty-two sworn officers. Our investigations unit consisted of only four investigators and two supervisors. Deborah's murder taxed an already exhausted group of investigators.

Residents and students once again feared for their safety after Deborah's murder. Parents who had sent their sons and daughters to SIU were alarmed. City fathers and university officials began to panic thinking how the murders would affect student enrollment and the economy of the city. The Carbondale Police Department was feeling the heat—and Bernie Sheppard was turning it up.

Confusion as to how Deborah died continued publicly when the Carbondale Police Department sent out another news release dated April 19 in response to Dr. Stein's autopsy results:

The death of Deborah Sheppard on Thursday, April 9, is being contin- ued as a major case. Investigators from both the Carbondale Police Depart- ment and the S.I.U. Police have been assigned to the case.

Pathology reports indicate the cause of death to be pulmonary edema. This condition can be brought on by many factors; however no specific factor has been isolated in this case. Toxicology reports reveal no drugs or other foreign substances which would have resulted in the edema. Follow-up investigations have developed no connection between this case and any other death in the city. There was no sign of a struggle at the crime scene and there were no marks, bruises or other wounds on the deceased. There is also no indication of rape. Crime scene processing has provided investigators with several leads indicating that someone was present at the time of death. Specific information regarding those leads is being withheld since exposing them would seriously diminish their investigative value. Anyone who has information regarding this case is requested to call the office of the chief. Any information provided will be held in the strictest confidence and if requested, anonymity will be maintained.

The words "homicide" and "murder" were not mentioned in the release state- ment. Dr. Nurenburger told detectives that the neck brace used in the first autopsy likely caused the bruising that Dr. Stein saw on Deborah's neck. But the toxicology results that Dr. Nurenberger was awaiting soon came back and brought with them a change of heart. They were all negative; Deborah's death had not been drug induced.

When Dr. Nurenberger completed his final report, another twist was added to the case. He noted the presence of "fine subcutaneous hemorrages on the superior and superior-lateral neck…" in his report, which he credited to Dr. Stein. Dr. Nurenberger also noted that Deborah had not consumed any alcohol or drugs the night she died. The vaginal and anal smears did not show any sign of sperm. But the oral smear did. Dr. Nurenberger conceded to the more senior and experienced pathologist's findings and concluded:

> The absence of any evidence of drugs in the deceased at toxicologic examination and the absence of medical history of epilepsy rules out drug overdose and any natural causes for the death of this girl. In summary, then, it appears from gross and microscopic findings that this young adult female was strangled from behind with a soft ligature and possibly the towel which was at the scene. Prior to her demise she had engaged in fellatio with a male who could produce sperm. There was no evidence of struggle with respect to bruises on the hands or body of the deceased apart from the bruising found in the neck and single bruise on her forehead. The manner of death is homicide.

Carbondale police waited until May 7 to tell the world in a press release that Deborah had been murdered: "Ms. Sheppard's death was treated as a homicide immediately upon its being reported…Investigators have a suspect in the case, but his identity is not being released at this time."

I asked Margaret about the suspect. She said he was one of Deborah's friends. Police conducted their first of many interviews with him only five days after Deborah's murder. He told investigators he had been home by himself during the time Deborah was likely murdered. He cooperated in later questioning.

I thought the news release with its hint at a suspect would signal the end of the controversy with Deborah's family. But it did little to soothe Bernie's feelings that our department had tried to keep his daughter's murder quiet. So, he called in another favor, this time to the media. The story appeared in the May 16 *Chicago Tribune* with a very sad picture of Bernie holding Deborah's senior portrait as his other daughters Nicole and Bridgette sat near his side. The article read:

> From the start, he said he knew that Deborah had been murdered and he has waged nothing short of war with the Carbondale Police and Jackson County Coroner to make them change their minds.
>
> "I want her murderer arrested, convicted and jailed," Sheppard said. "He's going to pay for what he's done. I don't care how much effort, money, time or heartache it takes to do it."

In the same article, Dr. Stein questioned Dr. Nurenberger's and Coroner Don Ragsdale's reports.

> Deborah Sheppard definitely did not die from natural causes. I feel she was strangled and received blows about the head. I saw discoloration inside and outside her throat. These bruises don't always show up immediately on black skin and may not have been recognizable to an inexperienced pathologist. The doctor who examined the body in Southern Illinois works in a hospital and is not a forensic pathologist. A beautiful, healthy young lady died for no apparent reason, yet they did not call in a more experienced man.

Ragsdale defended his Jackson County Coroner's office by stating that the press release announcing "no foul play suspected" did not originate from there.

Seeing the words in black and white in one of the nation's biggest, most influential newspapers was an important step, Bernie felt, in his quest for justice. But anger and rage rarely gave way to grief, except in rare moments that caught him off guard. Within days of the article, a package arrived at his doorstep. A Southern Illinois University logo adorned the return address window. He took it inside, put on his glasses and opened the wrappings near his dining room table. It was his daughter's degree, awarded posthumously. University officials kept Deborah's seat vacant during the graduation ceremony. Undoubtedly other parents, relatives or friends of another excited college student at the ceremony occupied the seats where Bernie and Hazel would have sat had they made it there as planned to see their first daughter graduate from a university. Bernie read each word on the diploma, even though his tears sometimes clouded his sight.

Southern Illinois University at Carbondale College of Business and Administration
On the recommendation of the President and Faculty,
The board of Trustees, by the virtue of the authority invested in it, has conferred on
DEBORAH RENEE SHEPPARD
The degree of Bachelor of Science Marketing
And has granted this Diploma as evidence thereof

Bernie sadly but proudly got up from his chair and placed the diploma on a shelf in his living room. As the weeks passed, he continued his efforts on his daughter's behalf. He talked by phone several times to Mike and Monica at the police department. He knew they still were working hard to find Deborah's killer despite what the administration had publicly released to the media. Bernie sent a handwritten letter to the chief as a gesture of his appreciation for the detectives' continued hard work.

Deborah's death was ruled a homicide at an inquest on May 12. I had just returned from my honeymoon. I had met my wife Sheila in Cape Girardeau, Missouri, just eighteen months before. We dated for nine months before I planned a camping trip to the Current River in southeast Missouri to propose to her. I'll never forget looking up to see a sign for the town of Van Buren, where the population was 714, as we floated in a raft along the river. It's a strange thing, but every time I have seen the numbers seven, one and four in some sequence throughout my life it has been like an omen telling me something good was about to happen. Sure enough, the omen didn't let me down. Sheila said yes. We were married less than a month after Deborah's murder.

The ruling meant Deborah's case officially earned a place among the murder investigations at our department. Detectives conducted dozens of interviews with Deborah's friends and her suitors, using polygraphs during most of them. They also collected head and pubic hair samples from Anthony Smith's and Deborah's beds, even though none were believed to belong to the suspect. Detectives kept watch over those who were being arrested in the area, especially those arrested for sex crimes.

The summer after Deborah's death, Carbondale detectives thought they had caught a break when a name noted in Deborah's file surfaced in a sexual assault case. He was one of about two dozen students who had gathered outside Deborah's apartment shortly after her murder. He had heard the commotion in the courtyard of Deborah's apartment complex along with Randy's cries for help. He told investigators that curiosity led him inside Deborah's apartment to see her body. He admitted to picking up Deborah's telephone to call for help, but he noticed the cord had been cut. The man said his fingerprints might be on Deborah's bedroom window, too, because he had waited outside there as police investigated the scene and his footprints might even be on the ground below her window where he had been standing that night after her murder. He said he was friends with Deborah but had not been in her apartment before that night since the previous December.

When he was arrested for raping an SIU student at gunpoint in her apartment, it ignited suspicion of him in Deborah's case once more. He had spent the night partying with friends and had broken into the victim's apartment through her window, just as investigators suspected Deborah's killer had. Investigators found his fingerprints on the window that he forced open. The victim's apartment was about eight blocks away from Deborah's. But police still lacked evidence to tie the man to Deborah's murder. He denied any involvement. Investigators were beginning to wonder if Deborah's killer could ever be identified.

Even detectives in other areas touched base with our department on occasion to report cases of sex offenses involving suspects known to have frequented Carbondale. Almost a year later, in April, Sergeant Tim Moss, who later became my boss, got a call from a detective in Allentown, Pennsylvania, saying they had just arrested a former Carbondale man for several rapes and believed he could be the perpetrator in other cold rape cases where he had lived. His name was Timothy Wayne Krajcir. With no other evidence and still theorizing that Deborah's killer probably was someone she knew, investigators did not pursue the lead any further. Despite their best efforts, a few months later detectives were still not any closer to finding the killer than they were after the first day.

The trail in Deborah's case had grown cold.

3

Picking Up the Trail

Working nights during my rookie years kept me away from the top brass at the police station. I tried to keep up with details about the department's ongoing murder investigations through the grapevine and occasional entries that detectives made in the logbook.

I couldn't forget Deborah's case, but I had a lot on my mind.

My wife and I had moved to Carbondale and settled into a mobile home across from the police station. Knowing there was a killer still out there, I worried about leaving her alone at home every time I left for my night shift. Even though our home was so close to the department, I knew the proximity of the police hadn't deterred Deborah's killer. He had broken into her apartment and taken her life just a few blocks from the station.

That summer, our department once again made heated efforts to bring closure to Deborah's case as well as those of Susan Schumake and Sion Raveed. It seemed to slow to a simmer in the wake of what many thought were some key arrests during the next year. Many believed a man arrested for a Jackson County Sheriff's case was also the perpetrator of Susan's murder. We arrested one of Sion's marketing students in his case. And I heard talk that a serial rapist we had arrested might be Deborah's killer.

All seemed to be going well for our department—or so it appeared to a rookie working midnights. The draw I felt to the forensic side of police work grew stronger during my days on patrol. The department had street-level crime scene technicians who were there to assist patrol officers by photographing and collecting evidence in simple crime scenes. Homicides, arsons and other high-profile and difficult crime scenes were left for the department's elite Crime Scene Specialist. The technician position was voluntary or an addition to an officer's duties that was not compensated. Veteran officers scoffed at it. Administrators loved it. A few officers worked as technicians, but most couldn't understand why a new officer like me would volunteer to do something extra. For me, the perks more than made up for the lack of a raise despite the added responsibilities. For one, I would get to use the department's photography equipment and darkroom. My mother Doris introduced me to photography as a child and I saw this as my chance for some formal training. The technician position also would bring me training in evidence recognition and crime scene processing, things that definitely caught my interest.

The man to ask about becoming a street-level crime scene technician was Lieutenant Bill Rypkema. Bill, an easygoing man with a husky voice, approved my request to be trained. He scheduled me to meet with Don Johnson and Larry Kammerer, who had processed Deborah's crime scene. A few days later, I got a key to the crime scene technician room and a fully-equipped latent fingerprint kit as well as a pat on the back from Bill.

"Good luck, kid," he said.

Through the first few years, I processed a few hundred crime scenes during my shift as a crime scene technician. I responded to everything from car break-ins to home burglaries and misdemeanors to felony theft scenes as well as some sexual assault cases. For me, it was more exciting than pulling over drivers for traffic violations and responding to domestic disturbances. Some officers thrive on the adrenaline they get when handling those situations, the "gotcha" moment and the chase. My adrenaline rushes came when I lifted fingerprints from crime scenes, wondering if they would identify a suspect. Many times, they did. My work was getting me some attention. The department soon named me police officer of the year.

Three years later all was going well in my career when Investigations Commander Lieutenant Larry Hill stopped me at the end of my shift.

"Hey, Echols, can I talk to you for a minute?"

"Yes, sir."

I assumed it had to do with a report I had written somewhere along the line. Larry was a quick-witted Vietnam veteran. I began thinking of the reports I had recently taken as we stepped deeper into the lobby of the police station, away from the other officers, so we could talk.

"Are you aware that Detective Bill Brandon, our full-time crime scene technician, is leaving?" he said.

"No, sir."

"Well, he is going to be leaving us to become a crime scene technician for the Illinois State Police. Basically, I want you to take over for Brandon."

"Sir, I don't know what to say," I said, feeling the blood rush to my face and a smile begin to stretch. "There are a lot of others who are more experienced than I am for the job."

"I know that, but you are my choice. We'll get you the training you will need. Think about it and give me an answer next week."

"Yes, sir."

I wanted to accept the job, but I felt like I needed to think it over and talk to my wife. Sheila was all for it. For her it would end the days of worrying about me engaged in the occasional high speed chase, responding to domestic disturbances, encountering shots fired and performing routine traffic stops that could turn deadly. For me it meant I would be one giant step closer to finally being able to investigate the case I couldn't forget and what had really happened the night Deborah was killed.

Larry told me I had a week to think about it. And a week was all I got. While on patrol, the dispatcher summoned me to see Chief Hogan. I thought, *This can't be good. Did someone file a complaint against me? Did I write a ticket to the wrong person?* Before long, I was in the chief's office. He closed the door behind me. I held my breath.

"I understand Lieutenant Hill has asked you to take Detective Bill Brandon's position as crime scene technician."

"Yes, sir," I answered, finally breathing more easily.

"Well, have you made a decision?"

"Yes, I have sir. I will accept it."

"Good. You'll report to Investigations on Monday so you can work alongside Detective Bill Brandon for the next few months as he prepares for his new job with the state police."

He shook my hand and sent me on my way. I couldn't believe how my career had completely changed, just like that. The next day, the chief sent out a memo announcing my selection as the new full-time crime scene technician.

There was barely time for small talk and introductions during my first day on the job with Bill. Larry sent us to investigate an accidental shooting involving a SIU student. Two friends had been watching television in their apartment. One of them was pretending to shoot people on the screen with a .357 revolver. During one of the imaginary shots, he brought the gun back over his right shoulder, imitating recoil. With his finger on the trigger, the gun discharged over his right shoulder, striking his friend in the face and killing him instantly. We combed the scene for clues thoroughly. We examined and photographed the victim's face to determine the range of the fatal shot. It was a very sad case, but it appeared to be accidental, influenced by poor judgment and alcohol. We later met with the parents and explained our findings. I felt sorry for them, but they told us how comforting it was to know the truth.

My days of riding with and learning from Bill were over when he left the department. I got my own office on the first floor of the department and just a few steps away from the evidence room. It was intentional and it was perfect. I found myself drawn to the evidence room often. Boxes of evidence lined the shelves with bold black letters yelling the victims' names at me along with their case numbers.

Theresa Clark, Murder—Case #75-0127-0834
Kathleen McSharry, Murder—Case #76-0712-0612
Susan Schumake, Murder—Case #81-2729
Deborah Sheppard, Murder—Case #82-0108-2309

They became etched in my mind. I delved into Deborah's case file. I had always been impressed with the work Monica Joost and Mike Dismore did during the first hours, days and months after Deborah's murder. The more I read, the more I became convinced that her killer's name was staring back at me from the list of suspects. Several perked my interest.

One of the first notes in the case file that caught my eye involved a double rape about eight blocks away from Deborah's apartment. It had happened a little more than a year after her murder. In that case, the suspect broke into an apartment where two women lived. He tied up one victim on a couch, the other on a bed. He repeatedly sexually assaulted each of them until one of their boyfriends returned home and interrupted the attack. He and the suspect wrestled as the suspect grabbed his clothes and escaped. A few days later, an anonymous phone call tipped investigators to a Carbondale man named Arron Snowden. Mike Dismore and Bill Brandon interviewed Arron and he eventually confessed to more than fifteen home invasions and sexual assaults in Carbondale as well as in Hawaii where he had served in the military.

This case was one I had heard talk of in the hallways at the department. I remembered how Mike, a war veteran like Lieutenant Hill and others at the department at the time, couldn't help but wonder if Arron could be the killer he had hunted in Deborah's case. I never knew just how convinced Mike was of a connection to Deborah's case until I read it for myself. In one of the rape cases to which Arron confessed, Mike thought the details were eerily similar to Deborah's murder. About a year prior to Deborah's death, Arron had broken into a home through an unlocked door and attacked a female he knew in her home by hitting her and choking her from behind until she was unconscious. Arron had said he was intoxicated and high on marijuana when he had intercourse with the woman and that she was barely breathing when he left. While the details were not identical to Deborah's case, Mike had wondered if Arron had either purposely or accidentally mixed some of the details of the many rapes he had committed. Mike checked the timing. It jibed. Arron was in Carbondale at the time of Deborah's murder. Arron gave detectives the name of the other victim, but when they interviewed her, she denied being raped. Mike and Bill again pondered if he was their man in Deborah's murder.

When they confronted him about it, Arron denied knowing, raping or killing Deborah but confirmed that he knew about her murder. He also threatened to end his cooperation if detectives continued to pester him about her murder. His defensive attitude perked Mike and Bill's investigative instincts. But with no other evidence to hold against Arron in Deborah's case, they decided it was better to back off and maintain his cooperation to clear the others. Mike and Bill had been lauded for getting a serial rapist to confess, but the seasoned investigators couldn't help but wonder if they might have solved Deborah's case.

Deborah's case stayed in the back of my mind. Along with reading Deborah's file, I also began to read and hear about a new development in the forensic science community called DNA fingerprinting. There were so many unknown factors involved with this new process. Courts had yet to accept it. The amounts of biological material needed for processing would exclude many cases. Still, I began researching what this new science might do for us, in our cold cases especially.

The go-to guy for DNA technology was serologist Andy Wist at the Illinois State Police Crime Lab. The soft-spoken and intelligent man was one of the first in the state to be trained in DNA science. In July, I packed the microscopic slides containing sperm from Deborah's killer into a brown paper bag and carried them to the laboratory where Andy worked, just a few doors down from our police station. Andy was familiar with the evidence from Deborah's case; he had examined it when it was first submitted.

"Do you think you could confirm whether there is even DNA material here?" I asked.

"Sure, I can take a look," Andy replied, "but we're not ready to process evidence for DNA here yet, Paul. You're going to have to send it to a private lab if there is something here."

A few moments later, Andy had an answer for me.

"Well, there's a small amount of DNA here, but I don't think there's enough here to profile with the methods we have right now. I wouldn't spend the money to send it to a private lab either at this point. Honestly, I would just return these slides back to the evidence room and wait for technology to progress. Right now they are building a DNA database, but without that and without a suspect's DNA, there will be nothing with which to compare it."

"Well, thanks so much for taking the time to look at this, Andy and for your advice. Back to the drawing board, I guess." I returned to my office.

While disappointed, I was still optimistic that someday the evidence would be the key to resolving the cases. Meanwhile, I had a new personal and forensic frontier to travel for myself: the birth of my first child along with latent fingerprint analysis. My son, Jarrod Paul Echols, had been born. Along with learning to become a father, I also learned how to become a fingerprint examiner. The Illinois State Police began an Automated Fingerprint Identification System, which served as a statewide database for fingerprints. It seemed revolutionary at the time to be able to enter an unknown fingerprint into a system and have it send potential matches back. I was trained as a latent print examiner and provided latent fingerprints to state police examiners as they learned how to enter them into the system. Our department was one of only a few police departments in the state that trained officers to identify fingerprints. We had always been quite successful at identifying fingerprints from crime scenes.

I kept many unidentified fingerprints in a file located in my desk, including prints from Deborah's crime scene. Officers lifted the best prints from the faucets on Deborah's bathtub. I ran them against the database, but no matches came back. I compared them to the two previous suspects, just as others had done before me, but they didn't match. I realized how compromised the crime scene had become that April night. So many friends, officers, supervisors, detectives and commanders had entered Deborah's apartment and had to provide fingerprints just to be eliminated. It was a worst case scenario for a crime scene technician. I believed the unidentified prints on the faucets were important, because there was an unexplained smear of dirt found in the bathtub where Deborah had showered. I was disappointed about not making an identification, but technology was evolving. I wondered if a breakthrough might be over the horizon.

In early 1990, another detective, Lynn Trella, was also looking at the evidence in Deborah's murder. She stacked what were now several hundred pages of reports behind her desk and read them every chance she got. She, too, became focused on Arron. By this time, he had been in prison for several years and had attended group therapy sessions. Lynn wondered if he had ever mentioned anything that might be related to Deborah's death during one of those sessions. She started digging for information and found some of the inmates who had been in his therapy group. A few had since been paroled. She thought they might talk.

Her hunch led her to the Chicago area to meet with an inmate named James. Detective Mike Osifcin, whom most everyone called Moe, went with Lynn to interview James, who had been in one of the group therapy sessions in the Psychiatric Ward of the Menard Correctional Center near Chester, Illinois. The facility, tucked in the southwestern corner of the state, is where most offenders were held. James was now out on parole and he confirmed that the man with whom he'd been in therapy had mentioned during one of their therapy sessions that he had killed a woman, but James couldn't recall any other details. The information was vague and once again led detectives nowhere.

The failed effort left investigators stranded once more. I was becoming more convinced that the forensic evidence was our only hope at catching Deborah's killer. In June of that year, I heard about a crime scene and mass disaster symposium at the FBI Academy near Quantico, Virginia. I applied, thinking there was no way a crime scene investigator from a small police department would have any chance. I was wrong. That summer, I was one of only two selected from Illinois to attend. It was my first time aboard a commercial jetliner.

After an hour-long ride south from Washington, D.C., the chartered bus pulled through the security gate of the FBI Academy. Suddenly a series of brick buildings emerged from the heavily wooded area. It reminded me of a small college campus. We unloaded our bags. I looked at the door ahead of me and thought of all the law enforcement officers who had passed through those doors. It was an honor to be among them.

During the week that followed I listened to numerous presenters, like forensic expert Dr. Henry Lee, from all over the world talk about their experiences. I was in awe. Some topics included the space shuttle Challenger disaster, the bombing of Pan Am Flight 103, the Mount St. Helens' eruption, the damage to Charleston, South Carolina, from Hurricane Hugo, the Laurie Dann school shooting in Winnetka, Illinois, and a host of other highly interesting subjects. I was like a sponge absorbing every detail, getting more and more excited that Deborah's case, too, might someday be solved. Time flew by and I wondered if I would ever get the chance to return.

Two years later, I did. This time, it was to attend a course in Administrative Advanced Latent Fingerprints. For three weeks, I learned about latent palm and fingerprint examination and development. During one of the sessions, an instructor spent some time discussing DNA fingerprinting. My ears perked up, as I remembered my conversation with Andy about the DNA evidence I had in Deborah's case.

"The FBI is taking an active role in partnering with state crime labs to ensure everyone is on the same page," the instructor said.

Wow. This is great, I thought. That had not been the case when the fingerprinting database emerged. Each state picked its own system. That led to a series of different systems across the nation that could not communicate with one another. I was so relieved to hear that was not going to be the case with this new DNA system.

"I've got to tell you folks, this new science is going to revolutionize crime scene processing and suspect identification as we know it by matching a suspect's genetic code from material left at crime scenes. If you have questions, just call our DNA unit."

I took him up on that offer as soon as I got home. They told me to refrigerate the evidence in a couple of cases, including Deborah's case, until DNA processing procedures and the database advanced far enough for the evidence to be tested. I took their advice and put the slides from Deborah's case in a refrigerator. I left several other items collected from Deborah's crime scene inside a brown paper bag, including a towel and the purple shirt. Both had been tested for the presence of semen after the crime and nothing showed up. So they remained hidden deep within the evidence room.

Over the years my assignment as a crime scene specialist led me to the crime lab often. Some coworkers even joked that I should get a lab coat and name tag. The working relationship I developed with some of the nation's best forensic scientists there, especially Andy, was priceless. I asked him to look at Deborah's slides again two years later. He let me peer into a high-powered microscope to see what he had been staring at every time I brought the slides to him. Although not many, I saw the sperm collected from Deborah's killer. It was strange to think I was looking at genetic material that belonged to her killer. I felt so close to her murderer it gave me goose bumps. Yet, I was still so far from knowing his identity.

Andy suggested I put Deborah's slides back in the box again. It was a bittersweet moment. I felt optimistic that someday the evidence would catch her killer. Then I thought of how Deborah's family must be feeling. I wondered if they would ever know just how much we cared and were trying to bring justice to her. I contemplated whether to call them and let them know all that we still were doing to solve the case. But it didn't seem like we were going to get a break anytime soon and I did not have the authority to make that call. Even if I did take the chance to contact them, I felt it would only drag up more emotions. The microscopic slide was my only chance—or so I thought.

I turned back to my only other option: her case file. I took the names of the suspects and checked to see where they were living and if anything new had popped up on their criminal histories. After much reconsideration all the leads once again led to dead ends, although some remained possible suspects.

It was all a moot point for the moment. We still did not have a DNA profile for the killer. Nevertheless, I hoped to have samples handy from most of the suspects in Deborah's case, ready for the day technology finally would allow us to catch up with her killer.

But my biggest break came in another case first: Susan Schumake. She was a twenty-one-year-old broadcast journalism major when she was found raped and murdered along a walking path near campus about eight months before Deborah's murder. She was a beautiful petite Italian, with long black hair that cascaded to the middle of her back. We had had an administrative science class together one spring at SIU and we had many friends in common. I was the same age as Susan and had just started my second week of police training when she was murdered.

Both Susan and Deborah were seniors at SIU. I often referred to them as "sister cases." No one believed their murders were linked. They were too different. Susan was found partially clothed in a wooded area near the railroad tracks. Deborah was found nude inside her apartment. Susan had been raped. Deborah had been sexually assaulted orally. Susan was white. Deborah was black. FBI profilers suspected Deborah's killer was someone among her circle of friends and there was a list of suspects that matched that theory. In Susan's case, investigators began with the basics of any murder investigation: interviewing any and all sex offenders in the area. There were two: Timothy Wayne Krajcir and John Paul Phillips. Investigators didn't think Tim was as good a suspect as John. They didn't really see Tim as a killer. Pervert, yes, but killer? No. John had been born and raised in Carbondale and was well-known for being the town's bad boy. John's alibi was weak during the time Susan was killed, just as it was when two other young white women were murdered. The detectives feared they were beginning to see a pattern.

But, just to be sure, Detectives Don Strom and John Kluge interviewed Tim Krajcir. He had been paroled a few months earlier after serving time for molesting his landlord's daughter. They approached his mobile home sandwiched between two houses on the southwest side of town and pounded on his door.

"Mr. Krajcir, Carbondale Police. Please open up."

He appeared in the doorway. His dark eyes and black bushy eyebrows looked at the detectives innocently. They could barely hear him, because his voice was so soft.

"Yes? Can I help you?"

"We just have some questions for you. Do you mind if we come in?" Detective Strom told him.

"No, come on in." He moved aside and the detectives followed him inside.

They quickly sized up the small living quarters, scanning the room for any signs of evidence, drugs or anything else out of place. All looked to be in order.

"Mr. Krajcir, where were you on the afternoon of Monday, August 17?"

"Um, let's see. I was actually studying at Morris Library on campus. I was there until they closed at 5:30 P.M."

"Okay, Mr. Krajcir. Thanks for your time."

Detectives had no reason to think he was lying. The library had held summer hours that day, which ended at 5:30 P.M. as he had stated. He was not nervous. He was very polite and cooperative with the detectives. There were no injuries on his hands or face or any other signs that he had been in a struggle of any kind. Besides, they had a much stronger suspect in mind.

John Paul Phillips had been paroled about four months earlier after serving time for unlawful restraint and the attempted murder of a couple of young lovers who were camping near a lake called Devil's Kitchen. They also suspected John of the murder of Joan Wetherall and thought it was similar to Susan's case. Both women had been beaten. Both had been strangled. Both were raped. Both were found outside. Both were from the Chicago suburbs. And both had connections to the university. I was working the day shift when a fisherman found Joan's body in the shallow water of a strip pit just north of the city limits.

Investigators also suspected John had killed twenty-two-year-old Theresa Clark, whose roommate found her body floating in their bathtub. She had been sexually assaulted, beaten and stabbed multiple times. Kathleen McSharry's roommate found her body on her bedroom floor. The twenty-four-year-old had been bound, gagged, sexually assaulted and stabbed multiple times. Her bathtub was filled with water. Her killer didn't have time to put her in it.

But I questioned John's guilt in this case. To me, the evidence at Susan's scene told a different story. The consistent factor in the murders of Joan, Theresa and Kathleen that was missing in Susan's was water. All of their murders happened under the cover of night. Susan's happened during the daytime. However, John's inconsistent statements about his whereabouts on the day of Susan's attack and scratches on his face had investigators convinced.

I knew I had to eliminate the number one suspect in Susan's case before I could get permission to pursue her real killer. I had no choice but to resort to extreme measures to eliminate him. He had died in prison of a heart attack while on death row for Joan's murder. In 2001, I exhumed his body. I helped remove his right femur. As I suspected, DNA results eliminated him as Susan's killer.

I dove back into her case file to start with the list of suspects once more. I sent packets of information to three police departments where the suspects lived. Two of the suspects agreed to give DNA samples. The one who didn't was Daniel Woloson. His prescription bottle was found six blocks from Susan's crime scene. He was now working in Detroit, Michigan, at an automobile salvage yard. With the help of the Washtenaw County Sheriff's Department, we collected a cigarette butt from a car he sold. It had enough DNA on it to prove he killed Susan. He was convicted in March 2006.

It was the biggest achievement in my career so far. My reputation was growing.

I interviewed for a promotion to become lieutenant but didn't get the job. I knew one of the reasons I had been passed over was because I had not "paid my dues" as a patrol sergeant. I didn't like it, but I understood it. My career had been atypical. Most officers earn their way through the ranks by spending time supervising patrol. It was time to do something radical if I were ever to get a shot at Deborah's case. So, after eighteen years of working day shifts with weekends off, I marched into the chief's office and asked to return to patrol as a shift supervisor.

I was reassigned to the midnight shift, the same one I had worked the night Deborah was murdered. After the first few days, fatigue was setting in. As much as I tried, I couldn't sleep during the day. I also hated leaving my family at night and coming home to an empty house after they all had started their days. I wondered if I had done the right thing. I could have stayed in my old position for the rest of my career. Instead, I had gambled and now felt like I was losing. I contemplated quitting the force entirely. But I wasn't old enough to draw a pension and I knew I would have difficulty finding another job and probably in a field that didn't interest me.

Informally, I interviewed with the Illinois Department of Corrections for a captain position in the local boot camp. I gave it some serious thought but ultimately stayed with the police department. Little by little, my experiences on the midnight shift got more interesting. I liked being back in the trenches with the men and women of the night shift. I felt like part of the team again. It renewed my sense of purpose as a police officer and reminded me of what brought me into this career in the first place. I also accepted that I might never be promoted and could spend the rest of my career as a patrol sergeant.

Solving Susan's case continued to bring considerable attention to our department. Two cable television crews, *Cold Case Files* and *Life Focus*, came to town to produce shows about it. They named their shows "Exhuming the Truth" and "Trail to the Truth." It was flattering to be a part of bringing a bit of celebrity among forensic science fans to our department. The experience also brought attention to the crime lab experts, especially Suzanne Kidd. She worked at the Illinois State Police Crime Laboratory just a few doors from our department. The crew set up their lights and mounted their cameras inside the lab where she had confirmed that the DNA profile recovered from Susan's body matched Daniel Woloson's DNA profile. They sat us at the corner of a table.

"We're not going to be using any audio from this, but we want you to talk to each other as if you are reviewing Susan's file," the director said.

We looked at each other and smirked, trying to think of something to say to each other while the film crew stared at us.

"You know, we have another DNA case that we might be able to resolve," I said. "But there is just not much DNA there. It happened in April 1982. Her name was Deborah Sheppard. The suspect forced her to perform oral sex before strangling her and leaving her nude body on the floor of her apartment. She was only twenty-three."

"I've heard Andy Wist mention it," she said. "Why don't you come over sometime and let's talk about it."

"I will, but I am working midnights, so it may be tough. Let me see if they will let me come in on my day off."

"Okay, that's a wrap," the producer chimed in.

The footage of Suzanne and I sitting and talking about Susan's case apparently landed on the cutting room floor. But the moment had served its purpose. I wanted to take Suzanne up on her offer to look at Deborah's case. A few weeks later, I asked Deputy Chief Calvin Stearns for permission to reopen Deborah's case from a forensic perspective, thinking the conclusion of Susan's case might have earned me some points. I hoped it might influence the department to make an exception and let me, a patrol sergeant, work on a cold case. The timing of my request was not good. Internal winds were shifting at the department. The chief had just resigned. Bob Ledbetter was trying to manage his duties as deputy chief as well as serve as acting chief. My request made it to Bob's desk. A week later, I had just finished my night shift and was walking back to my locker when Calvin pulled me into his office.

"Your request to reopen the Sheppard case has been denied. You're not part of Investigations and you need to concentrate on your current assignment. Maybe we can revisit it later."

"Okay, sir."

I had gone from the incredible high of the conclusion of Susan's case to another low in Deborah's. I wondered how Deborah's parents were doing. I thought about how they had essentially been told to wait for another indefinite period of time for justice in their daughter's case without them even knowing it. I wondered if Deborah's killer had struck again. It was clear that the lieutenant promotion to Investigations was what it was going to take to get the answers. But the chances of that happening looked very bleak.

4

Where Are They Now?

In early November 2006, Bob Ledbetter was named police chief after serving as the interim chief for seven months. Within one month I was promoted to lieutenant. It validated my decision to voluntarily return to patrol two years before but was unexpectedly bittersweet. I had become acclimated to the night shift and enjoyed working with a great group of young men and women. I had learned to sleep using little mental tricks and occasional over-the-counter sleep aides. I had even traded shifts with another sergeant when it came time to rotate, just so I could continue working nights. The officers told me they had enjoyed working for me and hated to see me go. They made me feel like a real street cop again, but I still wanted to become the lieutenant in charge of the Investigations Unit and get to the case that largely drove me there to begin with: Deborah's murder.

I sent an e-mail to Calvin asking for permission to reopen Deborah's case. Years before, Calvin and I had been hired at about the same time and worked the street together. He had been my lieutenant in Investigations. His dad was a Carbondale police officer but had been killed in a farming accident when Calvin was little. Having lost my father at a young age, I felt we had a bond. I knew Calvin would support my request, but Chief Ledbetter would have to as well. So, I sent the letter.

Cal,

About a year ago, I inquired about permission to look into re-submitting some of the Deborah Sheppard murder forensic evidence. I was told to wait. Several things have changed since then and I wanted to revisit this request. I am very busy right now and am not lacking of things to do. But the first steps I want to take will not be very time consuming. I am already familiar with the case and was the person who submitted the evidence the last time around. There have been some advances in forensic science since the DNA evidence was submitted in 1992. I have already discussed this with the lab a year ago and was advised to re-submit it. I also know it will take several months for the crime lab to get to this once it is submitted for re-testing. So once again, I would like permission to open this case back up from the forensic perspective. The first steps will be very simple: completing lab sheets for re-examination of the DNA material using today's advances in an attempt to gain a DNA profile for the killer. I will need to look back through the crime lab reports to determine exactly what I want to re-submit and maybe consider some new items we have not submitted before. If given the green light, I will try to get this done in the next few weeks when time permits. I hope this is the first step of many towards resolving this case. I am not looking for permission to seek out old suspects at this time, although if things go right, that would be the next step. As in the Schumake case, it is kind of like playing the lottery: you can't win if you don't play… I look forward to your response.

—Paul

Calvin responded the next day with his consent and an order to delay starting until all the accreditation files were completed.

Since I was a former accreditation manager myself, I understood where he was coming from. Being accredited by the Commission on Accreditation for Law Enforcement Agencies, Inc., or CALEA, means a lot in the law enforcement business. It's basically a seal of approval showing your department has met hundreds of rigorous standards. It also brings with it certain benefits of professionalism, limited liability and limited risk exposure, hopefully keeping us away from costly lawsuits. During the next few weeks, I spent most of my time on accreditation paperwork. I finished the work in record time.

As soon as I was done, I decided to seek out a familiar friend: Deborah's case file. It had been in the detective sergeant's office for years. I waited until no one was around one day, took the file off the shelf and wiped the dust off of it. I was not officially assigned to the Investigations Unit yet, so I didn't want the investigators knowing I was reopening the case. The covert move quickly proved unnecessary. The chief unexpectedly moved me to the investigations commander position.

I was right where I wanted to be, in the one position I had coveted my whole career. I moved upstairs across from the office I had left just a little more than two years earlier. Once I got settled, I quickly picked up my review of Deborah's case almost where it had left off. Four three-ring binders were stacked on a shelf just above my new desk. I stayed late nights and took the reports home with me over the weekends. I couldn't quench my thirst for the details in the documents. Many of the officers involved in the case were gone. Some had passed away. In some ways, it was like looking into a window of the past.

I also reviewed again the forensics we had in the case. I knew DNA would likely be the key, but I also knew I had very little with which to work. It was time to call in favors. DNA experts were no doubt overworked and underpaid, so it helped to have some connections—especially when your case had to do with a twenty-five-year-old otherwise forgotten murder. Making an arrest in Susan's case proved key in approaching DNA experts with Deborah's. My reputation among them was excellent.

I decided to call Taylor Scott at the DNA laboratory in Springfield. I met Taylor when he worked at the lab near our department and had stayed in touch with him through the years. I even had supper at his home in Springfield while I was there for some training classes several years earlier. Taylor, a very soft-spoken and extremely intelligent guy, was a great source for information about DNA. He was on top of all the latest developments in his field. And lucky for me, he always welcomed my calls. I tried not to take advantage of the rapport I had with him, so I limited my call to only what I considered the most serious and important issue: Deborah's murder case. I knew if anyone could direct me on what to do with the limited evidence we'd accumulated, it would be Taylor.

"All I've got in this case are the microscopic slides," I told him. "They have a few sperm fragments on them, but that's about it."

"Well, I really don't think we would be able to get a DNA profile with that, but we can advise you with the case. William Frank, who is in research and development, is working with a new process that might help you. It has the potential to work with limited and old DNA evidence. I think they call it mini-STR. Sounds like your case might be a good candidate. We can't do it since we are not ready yet, but there are a few private labs that might. Whatever lab you use, make sure it has the proper certifications that would be needed if you get a match and the case lands in court."

"Okay, I'll look into it. Thanks, Taylor."

It was just like Taylor to be thinking ahead. We talked for a few more minutes about our children and how old they were getting. How old we were getting. We said good-bye, but he told me to keep him posted on the case. I took his advice and found a private lab in San Diego, California, that would try to profile the slides using the technique Taylor had suggested. But I needed someone with DNA expertise to confirm they had the necessary certifications. So, I suggested Suzanne. They offered to fly her to California so she could witness the process. I knew getting permission to spend the money to bring the slides to a private lab would take some time. And I had to call Suzanne to see if she was willing to go.

"Hey, Suzanne, it's Paul. Do you remember discussing the Deborah Sheppard case when *Cold Case Files* was there taping us for the Schumake case?"

"Yeah, you mean the show that cut me out, leaving me on the editing floor?" she joked.

"Well, the time has come. Can I come over and meet with you to discuss the evidence I have? I also need to talk to you about sending the microscopic slides to a lab in San Diego."

"Sure. Why don't you come over next week and we will talk?"

"Great."

A week later, I met with Suzanne and hair and fiber expert Glenn Schubert. I brought Deborah's crime scene photos, evidence receipts and processing reports so we could discuss the materials with which we had to work. We focused on three items: a green towel, a purple shirt and microscopic slides containing smears taken from Deborah's body during her autopsy.

Investigators had found the towel tossed on Deborah's roommate's bed the night of her murder. It appeared as if Deborah went into her roommate's room after her shower and left the damp towel behind. Her house shoes had been scattered about on his bedroom floor in front of his bed.

The purple shirt was lying next to her body on the floor. Even though they weren't sure how Deborah died initially, investigators thought the shirt may have been used to strangle her. Later, a pathology report noted that a soft ligature may have been the murder weapon. Looking at the crime scene pictures, I doubted that theory because of one simple observation: the shirt still had a neat fold in one of the sleeves. It seemed impractical to me that the killer would have used it to strangle Deborah and taken the time to fold it neatly and lay it on the floor next to her. To me, it looked like it had just fallen off the bed. I wondered if it had been bumped off the bed during the struggle or when the suspect entered through the window. Illinois State Police Crime Lab experts had examined the shirt, because it had Deborah's blood on it, but didn't find any semen on it. Just to be sure, I asked Suzanne to take another look.

The best evidence I thought we had was the oral smears that had sperm fragments on them. Nothing had changed since the last time Andy Wist looked at them, but I wanted Suzanne's opinion as well. It was the evidence that proved Deborah had been orally assaulted. I couldn't totally eliminate the fact that Deborah could have voluntarily performed oral sex on someone before her death. It seemed strange not to find sperm on the vaginal slides. In most rape cases I had worked, I never remembered finding sperm only on oral slides or swabs. But after spending hours learning about her, it seemed highly unlikely that this evidence came from a voluntary encounter: In Deborah's circle of friends, oral sex was considered taboo.

Along with testing the three pieces of evidence, Suzanne also agreed to call the lab in California to find out more about the new DNA process Taylor had talked about. I knew Suzanne wouldn't get to test the items immediately, so I told her I'd gather the pieces during the next few weeks and get them to her. Maybe I could first get lucky looking into where the primary suspects were. *Maybe they want to talk,* I theorized. I had to find out where they were and what, if any, crimes they had committed. It was somewhat repetitive of what I had done several years before. This time around, I wanted to find Deborah's roommate Anthony. Even though Anthony and Deborah appeared to be just roommates, he was the last person to see her alive.

But the next call I knew I had to make was to Deborah's family. I needed to learn more about her life beyond what I had read about her last night alive. Meeting Susan Schumake's family had had such a profound impact on me as an investigator and as a person. I wanted to make that connection with Deborah's family. I didn't even know if Deborah's parents were still alive. I searched for the last known address we had for them and found that they were both alive and well and still living in the same home with the same phone number in Olympia Fields. It had been almost twenty-five years since our department had made contact with them and I had not forgotten how Bernie felt about our department in the early stages of this investigation. I found the *Chicago Tribune* article in Deborah's case file. Once again, the centerpiece of the article, a photo of Bernie holding a picture of Deborah flanked by his younger daughters, struck me. I wasn't sure he would talk to me.

The morning of May 3, 2007, I decided it was time to make the call. I shut my office door and stared at the phone on my desk for a few minutes, pondering what I would say should someone answer at the Sheppard residence. I was also concerned that if it did not go well and resurrected Bernie's issues with our department, it would blindside Chief Ledbetter, who had no idea I was calling Bernie that day. My heart was racing. I took a deep breath and dialed.

"Hello?" a woman's voice asked.

Could this be Deborah's mother? I thought anxiously. *I better ask for Mr. Sheppard just to be sure.*

"Hello, is Mr. Sheppard there?"

"He's outside; just a minute…" There was a pause then I heard the woman call, "Bernie! You're wanted on the phone."

She put down the phone for a few moments. *This is good,* I thought. *I'm going to talk to Bernie for the first time in my career.*

Mrs. Sheppard's voice came back on the line, interrupting my thoughts. "He can't come to the phone at the moment. Who is calling?"

"Mrs. Sheppard, my name is Lieutenant Paul Echols. I am the investigations commander with the Carbondale Police Department."

A brief pause followed.

"Can you call back later this afternoon?" she asked.

"Yes, I will try to call back around one o'clock."

"Okay. Thank you."

I said good-bye, hung up the phone and sat back in my chair. Turning, I looked out the large window behind my desk. The sky was blue and I stared at it wondering whether I was doing the right thing. *Did I just get blown off? Or was he really busy?* I asked myself. Spring had arrived. Everything was turning green. So maybe Bernie really was outside enjoying the weather. I got busy on some other things and went for an afternoon run. Sergeant Heather Reno was my running partner. We averaged two to three miles during our lunch hours and tried to run three times a week. I didn't mention anything to her about the phone call during that day's run, but it was on my mind the entire time. I was still thinking that I might be doing the wrong thing, stirring up Deborah's family, but I had to try. I showered and went back to my office to eat my sack lunch. I wondered if Bernie was waiting for my call. *What would he be thinking?* I wondered. Once again, I shut my door and dialed his phone number.

"Hello?" a small boy answered.

"Is Mr. Sheppard there?"

"Grandpa!" the little boy yelled.

A nephew of Deborah's? I wondered.

About that time, someone else picked up the phone.

"Who is this?" a young female inquired.

"My name is Lieutenant Paul Echols. I am the investigations commander with the Carbondale Police Department."

Click.

"Hello?" I asked.

The drone of a dial tone soon echoed in my ear. I looked at the phone to make sure I had not accidentally hung up or pushed the wrong button. *Maybe the little boy accidently hung up the phone,* I thought. Puzzled, I picked up the phone and dialed again. This time, someone picked up the phone and hung up immediately. There was no mistake. Someone didn't want me to get through to Bernie. I sat there completely dumbfounded. It appeared that the Sheppards wanted nothing to do with me. Or maybe it was just too much for them to handle. I couldn't let my efforts to reach them end there, but I had no idea how to proceed. I called the one person whom I thought might be able to relate with what the Sheppards were feeling: Susan Schumake's brother John.

"I don't quite know how to proceed in this, John. Maybe it's too painful for them. Your family was in the same situation. Tell me: what are they thinking?"

John sort of chuckled at what seemed so obvious to him. "You mean, you guys haven't talked to them in almost twenty-five years?"

"I hate to admit it, but I don't think so. The last record of any conversation we had with them was twenty-five years ago."

"Well, if it were me, I don't know if I would talk to you or not. That's incredible that there was no effort to keep the family updated."

"John, I thought maybe I would just send Bernie Sheppard a letter and see if he gets it."

"Yes, do that. That way he can ponder if he wants to read it or not. I am betting that after all these years he'll wonder why you're trying to contact him. Curiosity will get the best of him."

"Okay, John, I will do that. Thanks for letting me bend your ear."

"No problem. Take care and give our best to Sheila and the kids."

"I will."

I sat at my computer trying to come up with the words that would undoubtedly reignite feelings that the family had likely suppressed so many years ago. Eventually, my thoughts came together and I wrote:

Dear Mr. and Mrs. Sheppard,

My name is Paul Echols. I am a lieutenant with the City of Carbondale Police Department. I am the new commander of the Carbondale Investigations Section. Among my other duties, I am responsible for follow-up in "cold cases." This includes your daughter Deborah's murder.

I attempted to contact you three times by phone on May 3, 2007, but was unsuccessful. I sense that you or someone in your house did not want to talk to me. The intent of this contact is not to cause you heartache but to bring you up-to-date on what has been done through the years in an attempt to find Deborah's killer.

I have included my card and hope you will call or write me and acknowledge receipt of this letter. I stand ready to answer any questions you might have.

Five days later, I heard Bernie's voice for the first time. He left a voicemail on my phone saying he wanted to talk. Once again, I shut my door. The same woman who had answered the first time I called picked up. This time, Bernie came to the phone.

"Mr. Sheppard, this is Lieutenant Paul Echols. I received your message and I'm glad you called."

"Yes, lieutenant, I did. I just want to say I'm very appreciative that you are taking the time to let me know all that has been done during the past twenty-five years in my daughter's murder investigation and about your intentions for the future of her case." Bernie's voice sounded sincere.

"Well, thank you, Mr. Sheppard. I wanted to talk to you about what you remember about the suspects in your daughter's case and about the second autopsy you had conducted."

"Well, there was this boy with whom Deborah was living," Bernie began. "I didn't know anything about it until I called there the day she was murdered and he answered the phone. Deborah did not tell me that she had a male roommate. I would not approve of such an arrangement. I heard he has since passed on. There was also this boy who really liked Deborah. I can't remember his name right now, but I know some folks in your department thought of him as their main suspect."

I knew Bernie was referring to Murray.

"Anyway," Bernie continued, "he called me after Deborah died. We talked very briefly. He called to assure me he had nothing to do with her death. He wanted me to know that he really liked Deborah and he offered his condolences. I was not sure what to make of it. I did not know if he was sincere or if he was trying to see what I knew. Some years later he killed himself."

We chatted for about an hour. He said no one had told him of my previous phone calls. I left it at that. I assumed the family's emotions about Deborah's murder and subsequent investigation ran deep. Bernie struck me as a man of integrity, with his cordial and formal way of speaking. He was straightforward and all business. He agreed to send me copies of what he had in a file that he kept about his daughter's murder. I wanted to find out if there were some swabs collected from Deborah's body during the second examination that might be stored on a shelf somewhere in Chicago. Bernie said he would go to the Cook County Medical Examiner's Office to see what he could find. Just as I had suspected, connecting with Deborah's family inspired me even more to solve her case.

Plans also were coming together to test the microscopic slides at the private lab in San Diego. I wasn't sure if I would be able to take them. One thing I knew for sure was that they would be hand-delivered one way or another. No way was I going to send the only DNA evidence we had in this case in the mail. I could just imagine trying to explain the box of microscopic slides to airport security agents. I hoped it would only be a short matter of time before that slide would yield a DNA profile and I wanted to have my top suspects' DNA ready to compare.

Bernie was right. Anthony had killed himself in 1997, after holding his girlfriend hostage in Menlo Park, California. His DNA was going to be difficult to obtain, since his body had been cremated. The only hope of getting his DNA was to swab a crack in the concrete floor where he shot himself. There was a slim chance of success but, luckily, when I contacted the case officer he agreed to try.

In the meantime, there was another suspect to consider, Murray Jones. So I called Murray's former roommate, Curt. He remembered that one of Deborah's friends, Jo, felt uneasy about Murray. Shortly after our conversation began, I realized why he was Margaret's main suspect.

"You know, lieutenant, all these years I have believed he did it. He asked Jo to lie for him and say he was at our apartment the night Deborah was killed. We were real good friends up until that point. But to be honest, I never spoke to him again after that."

"Well, thank you for your cooperation. Hopefully I'll have an answer soon one way or another on whether he did kill Deborah."

I had just found an address for Murray in Belleville, Illinois, just outside of St. Louis, when my bosses asked me to take an FBI cybercrime training course in Fairview Heights, Illinois. The timing couldn't have been better. I knew there would be Belleville detectives at the training, so I didn't feel like I was missing out on time investigating Deborah's case by attending. During one of our breaks, I sought out the Belleville detective there and briefed him about Deborah's case. I also told him about Susan's case and how the guys from Michigan helped get the DNA sample from the cigarette butt in the suspect's car. We exchanged cards and he told me to call him that next week. I was happy to have the contact secured if I needed it.

I was so fortunate to have so many people standing by to help me—not the least of whom was Suzanne. I needed to get the towel and shirt evidence to her so she could take another look at it. One Friday afternoon in early July 2007, Carbondale Police Evidence Technician Steve Michaels opened the door for me to the Major Case Evidence room. It felt a bit awkward signing a log, recording my visit there after eighteen years of walking freely inside as a supervisor. I went straight to the shelf where the boxes of Deborah's evidence were stored. Among them were others I recognized. It was as if I was visiting old friends. The other boxes displayed the names of Theresa Clark, Kathleen McSharry and Susan Schumake. Susan's case was now resolved, but we still had to keep the evidence in case of an appeal. I took the boxes bearing Deborah's name to the counter inside the intake room to search for the microscopic slides, the towel and the shirt.

A musty smell overwhelmed the area where I was standing as soon as I opened the boxes. It propelled my thoughts back to the night of Deborah's murder. The pictures of her crime scene flashed through my mind. I could see her body lying lifeless and nude on the floor of her apartment. Essentially, these objects were my only witnesses to the crime. I wondered if they might have more to tell me all these years later.

I found the purple shirt and green towel each inside its own wrinkled and nearly flattened brown paper bag. Red and yellow evidence tape adorned the bags. One color represented the crime scene technicians who had sealed the items in the bag at the crime scene; the other represented the crime lab expert who sealed them after his exam. Neither item had seen the light of day since 1982. Red, green, blue and yellow tape covered the Styrofoam box holding the microscopic slides. Each piece of tape recorded the dates and names of those who opened the box. It was a colorful display showing just how much effort had gone into resolving this case long before that moment. Most everyone was now retired or deceased. It was now my turn to try.

I signed out of the evidence room and carried the bags to the lab to hand them to Suzanne. I didn't expect to hear from her anytime soon. I knew her backlog of other cases was deep. Suzanne and her counterpart, Stacie Speith, were known for their thoroughness. If they couldn't find anything on the shirt or towel, it didn't exist. I was more optimistic that we would obtain a DNA profile from the microscopic slides than from the other two items. The towel and shirt had been stored at room temperature for more than two decades. But there was always hope.

I broke away from the intensity of the case on July 14, 2007, to meet up with my Century High School classmates for our thirtieth anniversary class reunion at the Giant City State Park Lodge. But my thoughts abruptly turned back to all that was going on at work as I parked my car and looked at the observation deck. I thought of the picture of Susan and her father standing together there. I also thought of Deborah. I knew she had graduated from Rich Township High School in Olympia Fields, Illinois, on the same day that I graduated along with the classmates I was about to see.

A couple weeks later, I was at the crime lab with one of my detectives submitting evidence in another case when unexpectedly I met Stacie. A smile beamed across her face.

"Have you talked to Suzy?" she asked.

"No, why?"

"Oh, well, uh, I better not say," she replied, her demeanor becoming more closed.

"Is it in reference to the Sheppard case?"

"Maybe...I better not say." Stacie tried to remain vague in her responses.

"Good news or bad news?" I pressed.

"I better let her tell you. She is on vacation until next week. But...it isn't bad news."

My mind was racing. *Maybe Suzanne had obtained a DNA profile.* All I kept hearing in my head was Stacie's voice: "It isn't bad news." Stacie loved to keep me guessing and once again, she had succeeded. I left feeling optimistic and eager to hear from Suzanne.

A few days later, I headed back to the crime lab to meet with an expert about another case when I saw Suzanne. I didn't see the same sense of excitement that Stacie had displayed, but their personalities were quite different. Suzanne was all business.

"I just wanted to let you know that I found a little spot of semen on Deborah's shirt. It's not much and I'm not sure if there is enough to get a profile, but I'm going to try," Suzanne told me.

"Really? That's incredible."

"Well, I wouldn't get too excited yet," she said. "Keep your fingers crossed."

"Don't worry, I will keep everything crossed. Call me when you know if you have something."

"Oh don't worry, I will."

I was stunned and puzzled. How did semen get onto the shirt? When I got back to my desk, I laid all of the crime scene photos in front of me. The story of the blood-stained shirt began to unfold. Initially, the purple shirt was lying next to Deborah's face. When the ambulance workers rolled Deborah's body onto her side for a photograph of her back, the shirt was still there. It was a mistake. Usually, any and all evidence near a body is collected before the body is moved. Lucky for us, someone had forgotten to pick up the shirt, letting fluid from Deborah's mouth flow onto the sleeve of the purple shirt. That's why in the next photo, blood had pooled on the shirt. In it was a tiny bit of semen from the oral sexual assault. *How ironic*, I thought. *Deborah may have caught her own killer!*

5

Profile of a Killer

About twenty-four hours after Suzanne told me of the new evidence from Deborah's shirt, my phone rang. My heart almost stopped when I heard Suzanne's voice. She didn't call me this quick when she found the evidence in the first place, but now she was calling me the day after we discussed it. *It has to be good*, I told myself.

"I've got a partial DNA profile from the semen stain on Deborah's shirt sleeve," she said in her usual matter-of-fact tone.

My heart felt like it stopped and I couldn't speak. Despite my stunned silence, Suzanne continued.

"The examiner must have missed it originally. But to be fair, it was very small. It was about the size of a BB. I used an alternative light source that helped me find it. They didn't have that in 1982. There are nine loci, or genetic markers, there. So we can do a search in the Illinois DNA database but not the national CODIS database, which requires ten loci."

"Well, that sucks. What if he's been arrested in another state?"

"Then we won't be able to find him."

The United States national DNA database, known as CODIS, or Combined DNA Indexing System, began in the late 1980s and became a national system in 1998. It is a hierarchical system that has local, state and national levels. CODIS currently is based on thirteen core genetic locations, also known as loci, along the twenty-three pairs of human chromosomes. A full profile includes results from all thirteen core loci as well as the X or Y gender chromosome. Each level of CODIS may set its own minimum number of loci required for inclusion and searching. Suzanne's testing of the old semen stain found on Deborah's shirt had only developed nine of the genetic loci, which allowed a search of only local and state databases. But having this profile was huge. It was the first big break in Deborah's case.

"Well, this is still great news. At least we know we have more than just the microscopic slides. When are you going to run it?"

"Probably in a couple days. You want to come over when we run it?"

"Absolutely."

"Okay, I'll call you at 10:30 A.M. Thursday and let you know when we will do it."

"I look forward to it."

Could lightning really strike twice? I wondered, remembering the DNA match in Susan's case. For more than two decades Susan's and Deborah's cases had remained mysteries. One had been resolved and now, in just a few days, the other might yield the evidence needed to solve it.

Suzanne wanted to run the DNA profile on Thursday, August 9, which was my twenty-sixth anniversary with the Carbondale Police Department. I thought it was a fitting way to celebrate. I had made it to another milestone, but I did not sleep well the night before, knowing what was ahead. I knew it might be a bust or a very memorable moment. I had a gut instinct about this one. I really felt like Thursday would mark the beginning of the end of Deborah's murder investigation. I didn't want to get overly confident, but I grabbed a small digital camera from home before I left, just in case. On my way to Carbondale, I glanced at the time. It was 7:14 A.M. The number sequence, my good omen, had surfaced again.

On my way in to work the mercury had already passed eighty degrees. Another very hot, humid Southern Illinois day was ahead. We held our usual Investigations Department meeting shortly after I arrived. I darted to my office afterward and didn't mention my pending visit to the lab to anyone. I stared at the clock waiting for 10:30 A.M. to come. By 10:40 A.M. I couldn't take it. I picked up the phone receiver and dialed.

"Hey, Suzanne, just wanted to make sure I didn't miss your call," I lied, as if my voicemail wouldn't have picked up the call.

"Stacie has been gone this morning, so I'll have to give you a call early this afternoon and have you come over then," she said.

My heart was pounding. Stacie didn't want to miss the moment either. Finally, at 1:15 P.M., the phone rang.

"We're ready. Why don't you come on over? I will wait for you at the door."

"I will be right there."

The hot humid air hit my face as I walked outside. It was a bit unprecedented for Suzanne to invite me to watch this process. After working closely with the crime lab experts for so many years, they now treated me as one of their own. My rapport with the experts in Carbondale and in other Illinois State Police crime laboratories was something I had worked hard to build. I trusted them and they trusted me. These men and women worked hard to bring justice into the world every day. Most of the time, they did so unnoticed. No matter the outcome of their research, they marched on each day, giving each case their best efforts. I had hoped and prayed for this day to arrive and finally we had a DNA profile to compare against suspects. I knew I would keep pressing forward even if there was no match in the database of Illinois offenders. At least I now had something with which to work. *Just who the hell could it be?* Maybe I would soon know. And at least I would know who didn't do it. Suzanne called to me from the third floor landing as soon as I walked in.

"Sign in and come on up," she said.

Wow, I thought. *This is déjà vu.* It was exactly the same way I had met Stacie on the day the match was made in Susan's case three years earlier. Stacie, Suzanne and another DNA expert, Eric Corey, were waiting for me inside the office. We looked at Deborah's crime scene pictures. I pointed out how the semen got on the purple shirt. They were fascinated. I was too. We walked into an adjoining room and I watched Suzanne and Stacie prepare to enter the partial DNA profile. After a few minutes, my excitement fizzled. It was apparent they were having computer problems. *Just my luck*, I thought.

It wasn't the database; it was a hardware problem with the computer. A short somewhere was interfering with Internet access. It was not the first time this had happened. Stacie went downstairs where the server and other computer hardware were stored to try and fix the problem.

"Did you jiggle the wire?" Suzanne asked Stacie over the phone.

"Yes, I jiggled it."

I found it amusing to listen to these extremely intelligent forensic experts try to fix a computer problem. Here I was in a multi-million dollar, state-of-the-art crime lab and it all had come down to jiggling a wire. Stacie wasn't getting anywhere, but she noticed the computer in the server room was working perfectly. We joined her there.

"All right, here we go," Suzanne said as she hit the *Enter* button, sending the codes to the DNA database.

We stood back and waited. In about five minutes a message popped up on the screen. I could tell by the looks on Suzanne and Stacie's faces that it had to be good.

"Paul, there's a match," Suzanne said.

"Who is it?"

"It will take several days to know the identity. The lab in Springfield has to verify it first and then they will send us a name."

"Well, we've waited twenty-five years—what's another two weeks, right?"

I had brought a camera with me to record history if it were to occur—and it had. I snapped a picture of Suzanne standing by the screen. She did the same for me. I also took a picture of the computer screen with the unknown killer's genetic codes, which were now side-by-side with the codes collected from the purple shirt. I wanted a copy of the codes, but because we were working on a different computer, they couldn't print one. I had no idea how important that picture would become nor how much trouble it would cause Suzanne and Stacie.

As I walked back to the police department, I thought I was dreaming. Lightning had struck twice. Just three years before, Stacie and I were sharing the same excitement over a DNA match in Susan's case. I barely noticed the heat, even though it was now over one hundred degrees. The excitement of finally gaining justice for Deborah was building. Would this evidence result in our finding out who the killer was? Only time would tell.

My next thought was to call Bernie. I wanted to prepare him for what might happen. But the call was going to have to wait, because Chief Ledbetter's command staff meeting was already beginning. I got that "You're late for my meeting" stare as soon as I walked in the meeting room.

"Sorry I'm late. But I've got great news. We have a DNA match in the Sheppard case."

"You can be late to all the meetings if you bring news like that each time." Calvin looked pleased.

I took some time explaining what had happened. Everyone was excited about what this might mean for solving Deborah's case. I couldn't wait to share the news with Bernie. No one answered when I called him after the meeting. I reached him that Sunday after church. I was in my car, so I found a quiet place to park and talk.

"I'm sorry to call you on a Sunday. Do you have a few minutes?"

"Yes, sir, I do."

"I wanted you to know we have a significant development in Deborah's case and it might lead to an arrest as early as next week."

There was a brief pause.

"Was it one of her friends?" Bernie inquired.

"I don't know yet. I'll know more next week, but I want you and your family to prepare for this," I explained to him.

"Lieutenant, I have been prepared for years. I will not be sharing any of this information with my family until you tell me you have made the arrest. I cannot express how we appreciate your efforts."

"Well, sir, we still have some hoops to jump through, but I'm hoping to meet you if we finally can solve her murder and bring justice to Deborah."

"That would be great. I just want you to know we really appreciate what you have done."

As I spoke with Bernie, the voices of his grandchildren echoed through the phone. All they knew of their Aunt Deborah was her name and picture. I knew my call had left Bernie numb. Reopening the case had torn open old wounds. The family had held onto the good memories of Deborah and pushed away the bad ones as best they could. I felt like I was dragging those bad memories back into their lives. But I knew above all they needed closure. They understood and were grateful.

Five days later, Stacie called.

"We have a name," she said. "Timothy Wayne Krajcir."

Memories revolved in my mind. I remembered he had been interviewed as a suspect in Susan's case. At that time, he was a convicted rapist who had recently been released from prison. The FBI profile of Deborah's killer hypothesized that her killer would be black and likely among her circle of friends. Tim was white and nowhere near her circle of friends.

"He's in the Big Muddy River Correctional Center. That's about all I know."

"Wow. Well, you guys have done it again!" I exclaimed. "Thanks so much for all your hard work again. I'll definitely be in touch."

Word of the DNA match spread quickly throughout the department. Sergeant Mike Osifcin, or Moe as most called him, brought Tim's mug shot to me.

"I remember this idiot," he said, as I got my first look at Tim's face from the black and white mug shot after his arrest for indecent exposure years before. His look was distinctive. He would not have blended in. He was balding with very pronounced black bushy eyebrows and matching mustache. "Kluge brought him down for molesting his landlord's daughter."

"No kidding," I said, now eager to talk to Kluge and others about their memories of Tim.

For the next few weeks, I immersed myself in learning everything I could about Tim before I planned to interview him. The more I researched, the more I was beginning to feel that my upcoming interrogation with him might not be the first time I had met him. Maybe we had crossed paths before.

He was born Timothy Wayne McBride in Allentown, Pennsylvania, to Fern Yost, a teenage mother, and Charles McBride, a World War II Marine. Tim's father split before he ever got a chance to know his son, but his mother didn't wait to find another man. He told doctors that she frequently went out, leaving young Tim among friends or other family members. He also told doctors that when he saw his mother wearing lingerie, it excited him and he felt guilty for his urges. He started acting out at the age of five by breaking into a neighbor's house while no one was there and urinating and defecating in the living room. At eight, Tim was on probation for stealing bikes. He told doctors that his peeping started in his mid-teen years. In school, Tim was a natural athlete. He excelled in basketball and baseball, something that would later get him through the dark days of prison.

Before he became a rapist, Tim became a sailor and a husband. At seventeen, he joined the Navy and was stationed at the Great Lakes Naval Base in Waukegan, Illinois. On the way to visit an uncle in nearby Milwaukee, Wisconsin, for a weekend, he met a girl while waiting for a train. The two kept in touch after their chance encounter and Tim began spending his weekend leaves with the girl. A few months later, she got pregnant. It was the happiest time of Tim's life. They were married in a simple wedding at a Milwaukee courthouse. But their marital bliss was short-lived. Only twenty-five days after their wedding night, Tim became a rapist.

That night, Tim's urge to peep into windows of unsuspecting women took over as he walked back to the naval base from a night out in downtown Waukegan. He saw a twenty-two-year-old mother of three in her nightgown through a window of a two-story home. But this time, just watching her wouldn't do. He had to have her. Tim went to the back porch of the house and found a pair of grass cutting shears. He forced the door open and found the woman standing, stunned, outside her bathroom. He grabbed her, dragged her into the bedroom, tore open her night-gown and forced her to perform oral sex on him as he continued to utter threats. All the while he ran the shears up and down her legs. Then he raped her.

The incident only made his hunger to hunt women grow. That April, he walked in through an unlocked back door of a home where he saw a twenty-seven-year-old mother of two. He tried to rape her but halted the assault to let her comfort her crying baby. When he turned to leave through the kitchen, a pair of ten-inch scissors caught his eye. Tim stood over the woman as she held her baby in her lap and told her to look away from him. As soon as she turned her head, he plunged the scissors into her back, puncturing her lung, and fled. She screamed out her window before passing out. Her father, who happened to live nearby, heard her and called police.

Waukegan Police finally caught Tim in May, literally with his pants down and moments before he attacked another unsuspecting woman in her home. A neighbor saw Tim crawl through the woman's basement window and called police. When officers arrived, they found Tim naked in her basement. After a few hours of interrogation, Tim finally cracked. He admitted he had raped the two women and stabbed the second. He told the court that the woman he stabbed had done all that he had asked. He offered no defense. During that crime, he cut the victim's phone line—just like he did in Deborah's attack. He also admitted to four burglaries in Waukegan, one burglary in North Chicago and fifteen burglaries near his hometown in Pennsylvania before joining the Navy. Tim told police he routinely broke into homes and stole women's underwear and peeped into the windows of about three dozen homes in the Waukegan area and masturbated while watching the women inside.

By June of that year, Tim was sitting in a Lake County Illinois jail cell as his new wife gave birth to their daughter. During one of Tim's many court appearances, she brought their daughter to the courthouse to meet her daddy. The moment was brief. Tim held his daughter for the first and only time. His wife filed for divorce shortly after he pled guilty to the rapes and was sentenced to twenty-five to fifty years in the Illinois Department of Corrections. He never saw his wife or daughter again.

Shortly after his sentence began, Tim was shipped downstate to the Psychiatric Ward at the Menard Penitentiary, along rocky bluffs overlooking the Mississippi River at Chester, Illinois. Soon, Tim began talking and acting his way out of Menard. He shined on the prison's basketball and baseball teams and enrolled in a study for inmates sponsored by Southern Illinois University at Carbondale. Prison psychologists rated Tim's IQ as superior intelligence. But for as well as Tim seemed to be doing in classes, he told doctors his time at Menard was the worst time of his life. I could only imagine what that really meant.

The hard times at Menard Psychiatric Ward ended for Tim a few years later. By then, he had earned his way, through good behavior and positive talks with counselors, to the Promised Land for inmates: the Vienna Correctional Center, a minimum security facility. There, inmates can sometimes get jobs. It's the next best thing to freedom. At one time, Tim served as a tour guide for visitors at the prison. I had visited the center as a junior high school student. I glanced at the time lines. It fit. Tim was likely my tour guide.

Aside from leading tours, Tim started training to become an emergency medical technician. His first job as a lifesaver was with a prison ambulance service that provided emergency response services to the economically depressed counties in Southern Illinois. While assigned to Cairo in Alexander County, Tim slept in the old St. Mary's Hospital obstetrics ward between shifts. It was the same hospital, the same OB ward, where I was born. He was later assigned to the Union County Hospital in Anna, Illinois—the same hospital to which I went after I broke my leg playing football. I wondered if we had seen each other then.

Also while at Vienna, Tim enrolled in classes offered by Shawnee Community College. On graduation day, Tim walked across the stage to receive his diploma, graduating with honors. At fourteen, I was in the audience that day, watching my sister graduate with her nursing certificate. Later I played baseball for, graduated from and taught night classes for Shawnee College. In 2006, I was selected as their Alumnus of the Year.

In September 1976, Tim's efforts as a model prisoner paid off. He was released back into society after serving just thirteen of his twenty-five to fifty-year sentence for the rapes in Waukegan and North Chicago. With his newfound freedom, Tim wanted to finish his college degree at SIU Carbondale—putting him on course to one day take Deborah's life.

6

Warning Signs

It was a turning point of sorts in Tim's life. Prison, it seemed, had prepared him well for life on the outside. With his ambulance experience, SIU hired Tim on the spot as a student EMT despite his criminal record. And the college credits that he had earned while he was incarcerated transferred to the university. It appeared as though Tim truly had all that he needed to start over.

He chose a bachelor's degree in administration of justice with a minor in psychology. I found his choice of a major interesting: Administration of justice is usually reserved for those pursuing a career in law enforcement or the legal field. I had taken one administration of justice class as an undergraduate and one as a graduate. Tim and I missed each other by one semester. I wondered what it must have been like for Tim to sit among future police officers after killing Deborah, listening to them discuss her murder.

He found a quaint apartment in downtown Carbondale, close to the university. While it was conveniently within walking distance from campus, Tim wanted something a bit quieter. Lucky for him, a coworker named Ted Thomas was looking for a new roommate. Ted lived in a little white trailer behind a home for about a year before his old roommate graduated and moved on. Likely built in the 1960s, the trailer outlasted most other mobile homes of its vintage. It was tucked away in a quiet residential neighborhood, occupied mostly by families rather than college students. The landlord's grandmother lived in the house in front of the trailer. Occasionally, the giggles of the landlord's young daughters could be heard as they played in their great-grandmother's yard.

By the time Tim moved in, the Jackson County board of trustees had formed the Jackson County Ambulance Service to replace the hodgepodge of ambulance services in our slice of Southern Illinois. At that time, undertakers and firefighters also served as ambulance workers, responding to emergencies wherever and whenever needed. Those who worked for the university's ambulance service, including

Tim and Ted, were given jobs with the county's new and more professional ambulance service. Even though they were coworkers, classmates and roommates, Ted and Tim rarely saw each other. They worked different shifts and had different class schedules. The arrangement left Tim with plenty of time alone.

The city's arrest logbooks revealed that it didn't take long for Tim to resurrect his old habits. During that period, police recorded daily crimes and happenings by handwriting the reports. The records section of the department maintained card files to search for old reports. By 2007, those cards were stored in a closet. Only a few of us even knew they existed and how to use them. When we decided to look at them, Moe found a series of cards filed under Tim's name:

December 5, 1978	Public Indecency
February 14, 1979	Indecent Liberties
March 12, 1979	Public Indecency
May 4, 1979	Public Indecency
June 11, 1979	Illegal Transportation
May 26, 1982	Auto Burglary-Victim

The card files and police logbooks from those dates provided only a few details and most of the reports were gone. However, with all the time he spent in Carbondale, I couldn't believe Deborah was Tim's only victim in our city. I searched the handwritten logbooks for unsolved rapes during the period Tim was in Carbondale. One stood out. It happened February 27, 1979, only two days after one of the worst snowstorms to hit Southern Illinois. A woman named Sarah claimed she had been forced to perform oral sex on a man, who ambushed her inside her home. I was sure it was Tim. It was only about 200 to 300 feet from the area of town where Tim had lived. Police tracked what they thought were the suspect's footprints in the snow north through the alley to an address I was very familiar with: It was mine from 1982 through 1987. I realized I had missed being neighbors with Tim by just a few years. The police eliminated the resident living there at the time, but it was odd to see my former address associated with a rape case that I felt sure Tim had done.

I chatted with several retired detectives who recalled both criminal and recreational encounters with Tim. He was a pick-up player for the Carbondale Police softball team and a standout softball player for the Jackson County Ambulance Service team. I spoke with a few officers, some of whom played various roles in the early days of Deborah's murder investigations, who remembered playing with Tim. Many thought he was the best player on the team. I realized I most likely saw Tim during one summer when I played for the Carbondale American Legion Baseball Team. It was common for the ambulance service to stand by during our games between calls. I wondered if I would get the chance to ask Tim if he ever remembered watching any of our games. It was pretty chilling to think he could have been standing there watching me.

The giggling and squealing of his landlord's young daughters must have caught Tim's ear not long after he moved into the trailer with Ted. He perched himself under the shade of a large tree in front of the trailer to watch them. It wasn't long before the girls noticed Tim. Each week they grew bolder, moving closer to him and smiling. Eventually, the two youngest ones, eleven and ten, found talking to Tim very interesting. At thirty, he was close to their dad's age. The older girl became infatuated. Neither she nor her parents were aware of Tim's history as a rapist. The situation was perfect for Tim and for the next couple years, he took advantage of it.

On a day normally reserved for lovers, February 14, 1979, the secrets of the little white trailer began to unravel. The girls' mother took both girls with her to the doctor because of a skin rash on her thirteen year-old daughter's face. The mother stayed in the waiting room with the younger girl as the doctor examined the older one. As part of a routine questionnaire, he asked the girl if she was having sex. She surprised him when she said she was involved in a sexual relationship with her thirty-three-year-old boyfriend. She lied to the doctor and said her mother knew about the relationship but her father didn't. The doctor sent her home with birth control pills. Once home, her mother found the pills. She confronted her daughter, who denied being sexually active. But her twelve-year-old sister told their mother that while the girls were home from school on a snow day, they had called Tim over to the house. They went into their father's bedroom where Tim fondled the younger one and had sex with the older one. The mother called the girls' father, who came home from work to report the crime to Carbondale Police. The mother brought the two girls to the station. The older girl told Detective John Kluge that she and her sister wore their cheerleading uniforms and performed their newest cheers for Tim before the assaults. The younger told detectives that when Tim began to show attention toward her in the bedroom, fondling her breasts, her sister got mad. Tim asked the younger to leave so he could talk to her older sister. The younger girl said that when she came back, Tim and her sister were having sex. The older girl told Kluge she had been having vaginal and oral sex with Tim for the past year or so.

Kluge took several days to gather evidence and prepare his reports. On February 20, Illinois First Judicial District Judge Richard E. Richman issued a warrant for Tim's arrest, charging him with two counts of indecent liberties with a child.

Tim denied having any involvement with the girls when Kluge grilled him. Moe talked to Kluge, who had long since retired. He remembered Tim admitted to having guns in his trailer—a felon in possession of a firearm was yet another violation of Tim's parole—so Kluge obtained a search warrant. He found two handguns in Tim's bedroom closet, right where Tim told him they would be. One was a five-shot .38 caliber revolver, the other a chrome .25 caliber handgun. Both were new and loaded. They found more ammunition for the guns in the trailer as well. Tim's admission to the guns struck Kluge as odd. It seemed he had nothing to hide and nothing to fear.

Tim was on duty with the ambulance service when police arrested him. Tim's ties with his coworkers ran deep. Most felt it was inconceivable that Tim could have done what his landlord's daughters said he did. He borrowed a shirt from a coworker to wear for his mug shot, because he didn't want to shame his uniform. Stunned, two of his fellow ambulance service workers paid his bail. One of them, a beautiful woman, posted $4,500 of the $5,000 bond. She also drove Tim back to his trailer after picking him up from jail. He walked out of jail after only two days. I theorized that it was probably during this time out on bond that Tim attacked Sarah in her home.

Although she was not among the contributors to his bail, I was shocked to learn one of Tim's coworkers was Dottie Wilson. She had come a long way since the day she responded to Deborah's murder: She was now the director of the Jackson County Ambulance Service. I decided to call her.

"Hey, Dottie, can I pick your brain about something that happened a long time ago?" I asked after she answered the phone.

"Sure, go ahead."

"Do you remember the Deborah Sheppard murder?"

"What do you want to know about it?"

"Well, what do you remember?"

Dottie told me all of her memories of that night as if it were yesterday and even recalled what the weather was like. After handling thousands of ambulance calls, some of them murders, I asked Dottie why she remembered this call so well.

"There was so much debate among the officers at the scene as to whether it was a murder or not," she explained. "I thought it was so obvious. Deborah was a very beautiful girl."

"Do you remember a guy named Tim Krajcir?" I asked.

"Oh, yes, I remember Timmy. I worked with him on the ambulance service. It was a long time ago. He was a really nice guy, but he got in trouble with the law."

"Was he working that night?"

"No, he was fired a few years before that for having an affair with a young girl."

"Do you recall seeing him at the scene that night?" I prodded.

"No, he was not there."

"Well," I paused, took a deep breath, let it out and then went on. "Tim is the guy who killed Deborah."

"Tim?" she said almost unbelievably.

"It's Tim, Dottie. I have a DNA match."

"Oh, my goodness."

"There's more, Dottie. I think you are partly responsible for catching him."

"How?" she wanted to know.

"Well, when you guys turned over her body, a small trickling of fluid spilled onto a shirt near her body. I got the DNA from the fluid on that shirt. The report reflects that you and Arlen Kelley were the ambulance service employees on the scene. One of the pictures shows the gloved hands of one of you turning the body for the pictures."

"Yes, that would be me. I remember turning her over so they could take the pictures."

"Your work helped catch her killer," I told her.

"Paul, this is hard to believe. Tim was so protective of me and the other young women in the ambulance service. We all felt comfortable enough to sleep in the same quarters as him. I remember him telling me not to work at the Menard Correctional Center, because the guys in there were no good."

"That's because he was one of them, Dottie."

"But how could he care about us and be a rapist and killer at the same time?" Dottie exclaimed.

"I don't know, but I'm going to try and find out."

"I don't mean to be rude," Dottie said slowly, "but I need some time to process this. Tim used to be one of my very good friends and Deborah's murder has haunted me since the day I responded to the scene. And now you are telling me Tim did it. It's hard to believe Tim was a killer."

"I know it's a lot to take," I said gently. "I'll keep you posted."

I could hardly believe it was Dottie who rolled Deborah's body over, providing the lynchpin to the case. *How ironic that a friend's seemingly mundane act later led to another friend's arrest for murder*, I thought.

After posting bail, Tim knew he had to move out of the trailer. He also had been suspended from the Jackson County Ambulance Service until further notice. He hadn't been home long before the phone rang. On the other end was a young voice he recognized. It was his landlord's older daughter. She had watched him come home from her window. Tim asked the girl to try talking her father into dropping the charges and not to tell anyone they had spoken. That was the last time she ever spoke with Tim. She later told Kluge she had called Tim, because she felt she was in love with him and needed to know he wasn't angry at her for talking to the police.

Knowing Tim was in need of a place to live, another coworker and friend, John Crosby, a kind-hearted and hard worker, called and offered to let Tim stay with him until he could find another home. Tim accepted the offer and moved into his trailer in the Carbondale Mobile Home Park. During the next six months, that trailer held more of Tim's secrets as Tim's attorney John Ryan of the Carbondale law firm FSMG and Associates kept Tim out of jail with continuances and several psychiatric evaluations on Tim.

Both of his landlord's daughters testified in the preliminary hearing in March 1979 and described all that took place in their home that February day. Tim's attorney argued to Judge Richman there were inconsistencies between the daughters' statements. Assistant Jackson County State's Attorney John Clemons argued that the inconsistencies were due to both girls being in the bedroom with Tim at different times. The judge denied Ryan's motion. Tim pled not guilty. Clemons reminded the court that Tim had been charged with two misdemeanors for having two guns in his trailer. Judge Richman accepted Tim's not guilty plea and allowed his $5,000 bond to cover the gun charges as well. Tim was once again allowed to walk away and get into more trouble. A few days later, he exposed himself to a woman in a Carbondale discount store parking lot.

Eventually, though, the molestation case caught up with Tim. He went back to prison in September 1979. In a negotiated plea, the judge dismissed the charges of indecent liberties with a child as long as Tim agreed to be classified as Jackson County's first sexually dangerous person (SDP). In determining that Tim was a SDP for the court that May, a Carbondale psychologist wrote:

> In the psychiatric interview Mr. Krajcir spoke openly and was cooperative. He admits to concern over his compulsion to masturbate and expose himself publicly and says that he does not understand why this is happening. There does seem to be an element of voyeuristic excitement in these actions also…During the interview Mr. Krajcir stated, "I'm scared by what I did and I know that I do need psychiatric help of some kind."
>
> …It is my opinion that there is unconsciously still much resentment and hostility toward women and that these issues were not resolved during his incarceration. His previous history of rape, attempted murder, voyeurism, transvestism, and exhibitionism, without basic change in his personality patterns or understanding of those feelings, would make the likelihood of future

actions of the same kind quite probable. This is particularly supported by the fact that he is again involved in compulsive sexual actions which in the past were a prelude to more severe and aggressive actions. Mr. Krajcir also feels these to be compulsions and "not normal" but does not know how to control his sexual and, by history, aggressive feelings in appropriate ways…My recommendation would be for rather intensive psychiatric treatment preferably in a setting sophisticated in dealing with patients with severe personality disturbances and sexual deviations. I see at the present time no need for institutionalization in a maximum security facility since he has functioned in a less restrictive environment (e.g. Vienna Correctional Center and on parole).

The SDP label required Tim to return to prison, but it also mandated counseling. Tim could see the light at the end of that tunnel. While in prison, Tim played the game and attended the required counseling sessions religiously. After a little more than a year, he had doctors convinced he was fit for society. With a yellow sticky note, I marked one particular psychiatric evaluation from the Illinois Department of Corrections dated January 28, 1981. I must admit, it upset me. The psychiatrist stated: "With the time he has served, the help we have offered and the supervision he will have available in the outside, he might no longer be sexually dangerous, however this cannot be proven as long as he remains incarcerated. As I reviewed in the above points, his risk for chronic behavior seems to be of very low order."

He couldn't have been more wrong. Then Jackson County State's Attorney John Clemons apparently saw it too. He doubted the credentials of the doctors who provided psychiatric care for inmates. But working with a rural county's limited budget, he couldn't provide any experts to refute the doctors' opinions. In June of 1981, he argued vehemently with the judge to keep Tim incarcerated. It was the same judge who two years before had let Tim's bond cover both his child molestation charges and weapons charges so Tim could enjoy a few more months of freedom. But Clemons' arguments were rejected. The judge released Tim with conditions and he returned to Carbondale to finish his bachelor's degree at SIU. Tim's release back into our community didn't go unnoticed by our department. I found another logbook entry dated June 23 from Detective Don Strom:

Timothy W. Krajcir has recently been released to the Carbondale area from the Department of Corrections. For those of you unfamiliar with Krajcir, he was most recently determined to be a sexually dangerous person and committed under the provisions of that statute. Krajcir is being released back into society so they can tell if he is cured. Krajcir is known to masturbate in his auto in parking lots, has had intercourse with young girls and served time for attempted murder and rape. He is definitely a sexually dangerous person and deserves to be watched. Krajcir is currently residing at the Carbondale Mobile Home Park and is starting work at Southern Manor Nursing Home. He is a former Jackson County ambulance attendant. Krajcir has a date of birth of 11-28-44. Krajcir will be required to report for mental health counseling and report to Jack Jones at the parole office.

This time, Tim moved into a trailer directly across the street from Mike Dismore, who later became one of the lead investigators on Deborah's case. As Mike spent long hours trying to find Deborah's killer, he didn't realize her killer was close by all along. I could just imagine them nodding to greet each other as neighbors often do. Tim also got a job working nights at the Southern Manor Nursing Home, just a short distance from the police department. He bathed helpless seniors, changed their diapers, fed them and even resuscitated them when needed.

He graduated with a degree in administration of justice and a minor in psychology from SIU in May 1982—one year after I graduated from the same school and one month after Deborah's murder. I thought about how Tim had probably passed Deborah on campus at some point. I wondered if she had caught his eye and how long he stalked her before breaking into her apartment that fatal night.

I also found a police report from that same year in which Tim was listed as the victim of a crime. Seven weeks after he had murdered Deborah, he called the police to report that his car had been burglarized, even though he knew they were working hard to find Deborah's killer. He had left his car unlocked and someone had taken a few items from his glove box. *How bold,* I thought.

Tim didn't stay around town after graduation. The Illinois Department of Corrections granted Tim's request to transfer his parole to Pennsylvania so he could move back to his mother's home in Laury's Station. He worked part-time at a home-care agency in Bethlehem, Pennsylvania, and then full-time at a nursing home in Nazareth, Pennsylvania. But it wasn't long before Tim got into trouble.

In December 1982, Tim's demons got the best of him. At about 4 A.M., he forced his way into an Allentown, Pennsylvania, home through a kitchen window where Rosa, her daughter Beth and her young son lived. Tim stealthily moved about the house, cutting some phone lines, and covered his face with a red bandanna. He hid inside Beth's room and watched her get up to get a drink. He ambushed her when she returned. She begged him not to rape her. He told her he was going to perform oral sex on her. If she didn't comply, he said he would kill her mother or little brother. Tim's threats were loud enough to rouse Rosa from her sleep. She heard the noise in her daughter's bedroom and called 911. When Tim heard her on the phone, he forced Beth into her mother's bedroom. He pointed a gun at Beth's head and ordered Rosa to hang up the phone. He forced both women to disrobe and fondled them as he masturbated and ejaculated onto Beth's buttocks. He stole some change on his way out before police arrived. Allentown Police recovered a suitable latent palm print from the kitchen window. I noted how he used the child as leverage in that case, just like he did in his earlier rapes.

Tim acted out again in January 1983, when he parked near a young woman's car in the Mountainville Shopping Center in Allentown. When she returned, Tim grabbed her butt. She asked him what his problem was and grabbed a pen and paper to write down his license plate. Tim drove off and the woman realized masking tape was covering his plate and the make of his car. She called police. While officers were taking her statement, Tim drove by again. The victim pointed him out and officers arrested him. He had already removed the masking tape from his license plate, but some of it was still on the back of his car. Officers booked and fingerprinted Tim. Soon, investigators matched his palm print to the sexual assault on Rosa and her daughter. He was charged with indecent assault, aggravated assault, reckless endangerment, robbery, burglary, theft by unlawful taking, terroristic threats and weapons offenses.

While awaiting trial at the Lehigh County jail, Tim met another rapist named John Grello. They devised a plan to escape. Around 10:30 P.M. on May 1 of that year, they launched it. They cut off the metal door stops on a door leading to a fire tower. From there, they made it to a recreation yard and to the north wall. John used several bed sheets tied together to descend the thirty-foot stone and mortar wall. Then, it was Tim's turn. He was not so lucky. A guard saw him on the rope and yelled. Startled, Tim lost his grip and landed on top of one of the guard's cars, breaking his leg. I couldn't help but chuckle at Tim's blunder and reminisce about what I was doing at that moment. It was my first wedding anniversary. As Tim was landing in a load of trouble, Sheila and I were eating the top layer of our wedding cake. John was caught a few days later. Tim ended up in surgery to repair his leg. He was charged with attempted escape, which only added to the mounting crimes against him. He was now classified as an escape risk.

I wanted to know more about Tim's time in Pennsylvania, so I called the Allentown Police Department. Detective Todd Rushate of their criminal investigations unit said he wasn't familiar with Tim, but he would do some research and fax me copies of their reports. He also said he would talk to some of the older investigators and have them call me. It didn't take long for Tim's name to ring a bell with someone. Retired Pennsylvania State Police Detective Joe Kocevar called me. He was a soft-spoken man who started his career as a police officer in Washington, D.C., the same year Tim was entering the Illinois Department of Corrections for his first rapes. Three years later Joe joined the Pennsylvania State Police—the same year of the *Miranda v. Arizona* decision, which required officers to read suspects their Miranda warning.

"I wasn't ready to retire, but when I turned sixty, it was mandatory," Joe told me. "One of the reasons I wasn't ready to retire was actually Tim. We had a murder in Lehigh County in November 1982. It was a young lady who had been shopping with her mother. She went home and did not report to work the next day. When someone went to check on her, they found her dead. It appeared the killer followed her home from the shopping mall. That and a few other details are very similar to some of Tim's past crimes, so it caught my attention.

"I interviewed Tim shortly after his arrest for the rapes and indecent exposure in Allentown, but he denied killing anyone. We also had a rash of rapes around then. The media dubbed the suspect 'The Southside Rapist.' Tim denied those rapes as well. I even gave him a polygraph, but the examiner said Tim showed no response at all. The damn needle didn't even flinch the whole time. It was the damndest thing the examiner ever saw. I pursued Tim for most of my career after that. In fact, after we caught Tim here, I spoke with someone from Carbondale about his criminal activities there as well."

"Did they respond?" I asked.

"Yeah, they mailed me copies of the reports. Matter of fact, I've still got them."

"Would you send them to me?"

"Sure. It will take me a while, though. I'll have to check and make sure it's okay to release the documents now that I'm retired and all," he explained.

"No problem, do what you have to do. I appreciate it."

The crimes in Pennsylvania also violated Tim's sexually dangerous person parole status in Illinois. John Clemons successfully petitioned the court to revoke Tim's parole to Pennsylvania. So, when Tim was done serving his time there, the Illinois Department of Corrections brought him back to Illinois. In accordance with his sexually dangerous person status, he had to undergo treatment for his sexually violent tendencies in order to be released. All he had to do was attend group therapy sessions and participate in counseling sessions, just like he did in 1981. But this time, something was different. Year after year, he refused to attend any therapy sessions, knowing he could not be paroled without them. I wanted to ask him why.

In 1988, just three days before my son was born, Tim returned to the Menard Psychiatric Center in Southern Illinois, a place with which he was familiar. He would stay there until 1995, when he was transferred to the Big Muddy Correctional Center, also in Southern Illinois. It was a relatively new prison, built to hold all of Illinois' sexually dangerous persons. I had been there a few times on other cases; maybe even saw Tim working out in the yard. But I really didn't have any solid contacts there. I knew I needed to find someone who wouldn't tell anyone why we would be coming to interview Tim. I knew it would take an ambush for us to be successful in getting a confession out of Tim and I couldn't risk losing that edge if a guard got wind of what we were doing and talk began to spread. I didn't want Tim to have time to think and come up with an alibi or another story, I called my cousin, who is a counselor at the Shawnee Correctional Center, about an hour south of the Big Muddy Prison. He put me in touch with a friend of his at Big Muddy, who then referred me to Internal Affairs Lieutenant Harold Schuler.

Lieutenant Schuler had worked at Big Muddy since November 1992. He graduated from Belleville East High School, a town not too far from St. Louis, Missouri. He joined the Air Force after high school and quickly found himself on the fringe of the Vietnam Era, serving two tours in Thailand. Between those tours, he married and had two daughters. He spent the next few decades working his way up to the rank of chief master sergeant, specializing in aircraft weapons and ordnance. He retired in 1992 and took a job as a prison guard. He was promoted to lieutenant in 1998 and moved to internal affairs in 2000. He was the best person to help me learn all I could about Tim.

"Holy cow, I know him," Lieutenant Schuler said when I asked about Tim. "He works over in our warehouse unloading trucks and inventorying supplies. He's a good worker, never causes trouble. He's a laidback, easygoing guy. But there is one thing he won't do and that is go to group therapy. Says he can't be honest in them, so he won't go."

"Well, that's very interesting," I replied. "I'll be in touch to let you know when we will be coming to pay Tim a visit. Once we pick a date, I will submit the paperwork through Springfield to get us through the door."

As I continued to read the reports, I found Lieutenant Schuler's comment about Tim's withdrawal from therapy was true. A periodic review report by the prison psychiatrist read:

> Mr. Krajcir indicated that he continues to avoid group [therapy] and he is of the firm belief that he is appropriately placed here. He has no desire to get out of here, because he is afraid that he might victimize others. He also indicated that he has difficulties in talking about his past.

In another report, the same psychiatrist stated:

> He is not attending any groups. He does not think there is anything they can teach him. He does not think he will ever go out and he knows he is going to spend the rest of his life behind bars. He stated "I won't let myself out. I

will spend the rest of my life here. I don't want to hurt nobody. I have made peace with myself. I spent five years with a psychiatrist in Pennsylvania. I have read books and know everything [about my condition]. I am a good athlete. I play sports, chess, and read extensively if I am depressed."

With all the knowledge about Tim that I had gathered, I felt I needed to communicate with Deborah's father Bernie about the man who murdered his daughter. I telephoned him.

"I wanted to give you the name of the man whom we think killed Deborah. Please keep it confidential for now. It's not one of Deborah's friends. He is a white male and his name is Timothy Wayne Krajcir. He was thirty-seven at the time of Deborah's murder and he is in his sixties now. He has been incarcerated since 1983."

"Well, I want him to die for killing my daughter. In fact, I want to be the one who puts the needle in his arm."

"Unfortunately, Mr. Sheppard, under 1982 law, the death penalty is not a possibility in this case. The best that the state's attorney can do is push for a maximum sentence of forty years or maybe a life sentence," I tried to gently explain.

"Then I want the life sentence."

It was déjà vu. Three years earlier, I had explained the same thing to John and Cynthia Schumake as to why Daniel Woloson, the man who had raped and killed their younger sister, wouldn't get anything more than a forty-year sentence.

"I understand. The state's attorney will be in contact with you after we do our interview and forward the case to him. He will explain the options when we get to that point."

"Well, Paul, I guess it is what it is. I'm telling you, he's lucky he's in prison. If he wasn't, I would find him and kill him myself. I said that was what I was going to do when I learned Deborah had been killed and those are still my intentions. When are you going to talk to him?" Bernie asked.

"Probably within the week. I'll call to let you know how it goes. Depending on if he's feeling chatty, we might get a confession so you won't have to go through a trial. If not…well, it's not going to be easy and it's going to take a while."

We talked for about an hour that day. I learned a lot I hadn't known about Bernie and his family. I learned a lot about Deborah too. My respect for Bernie grew with each minute of our conversation and at the end, he said, "Paul, I want you to know, with this news, I feel like a large burden has been lifted off my chest. Thank you!"

"The honor has been mine. Thanks."

The pressure I felt to get a confession from Tim Krajcir for the Sheppard family was immense. I didn't want to see Bernie's family go through a grueling trial like the Schumake family had.

Sergeant Mike "Moe" Osifcin decided it would be a good idea to see if we could walk through Deborah's former apartment before our interrogation with Tim to get a better feel for the layout than just what we could see from the crime scene pictures. It was great to have him there. He had come on the force two years before I did and knew Deborah's case. He called the property manager to get the keys. It was vacant. That was good. We really didn't want to have to explain ourselves to tenants.

Later I visited the apartment alone and brought the crime scene photos with me. I held them in front of me as I walked from room to room, trying to duplicate the crime scene in my mind. I was intrigued when I compared the pictures of how Deborah decorated the living room against the backdrop of the same walls. Nail holes were still visible on the wall where she had once hung wooden block letters that spelled out "Deborah." I walked into what had been Deborah's bedroom and over to the window where Tim had broken in. I jiggled it. Amazingly, it was still not secure. I shook my head at the irony that the window was still leaving unsuspecting ground-floor renters at risk. As I stared at the window, I could almost hear the shower running as I envisioned how Tim slipped quietly through the faulty window and into Deborah's bedroom. I thought of how I had been just two blocks away at that moment preparing to go to work with only eight months' experience on the force. Tim's selfish acts that night when he murdered Deborah had affected and changed so many lives. As I stood there, looking at the window, I realized his actions had also affected mine.

After I walked the same path Tim had taken through Deborah's apartment on that horrific night years before, I felt I was armed with firsthand knowledge of the crime scene. I had researched Tim's background. I was as ready as I was ever going to be to confront him. Given Tim's above average IQ, criminal psychology courses and his obvious ability to fool trained psychologists, I knew he wasn't going to be an easy person to crack. But I was going to give it everything I had. Never had I been so determined.

7

The Day of Reckoning

Beep…beep…beep rang the familiar and usually unwelcome sound of my alarm. It was 6 A.M. on August 21, 2007. *About time*, I thought. I had been awake for hours, waiting for the alarm to go off. Normally, my arm instinctively swung over to hit the snooze button a few times before nudging my wife out of bed and climbing out myself. Not today. I nearly leapt out of bed and into the shower. I shaved, got dressed and grabbed a breakfast bar washed down with a soda. Everything I did seemed to be rushed, although I had no reason to hurry. I had plenty of time before I was supposed to head to the Big Muddy Correctional Center where Tim Krajcir had no idea his past was about to catch up with him. But there was definitely a spring in my step. It was like the final chapter in a long book that I had been reading and I couldn't wait to find out how it ended. I jumped in my truck, then stopped to grab the newspaper out of my mailbox at the end of my rural driveway. *If only the police reporters knew what was going on today*, I thought. If things went well, I would soon be able to tell them all about it. It was a hell of a story, that's for sure. I noted the time. It was 7:14 A.M. I smiled when I saw the sequence of numbers. My good omen had appeared once more. It was a morale boost. It let me know I was on the right track. And I certainly needed it today.

The name Deborah Sheppard meant nothing to the younger guys at the station until about two weeks before when we received the DNA match linking Tim to the crime. It seemed like I could hardly walk through the hallways without one of the younger detectives wanting to hear the story. The few who saw me and Moe that morning wished us luck.

The ride to the prison Tim had called home for nearly a decade was relatively quiet. Moe and I were both lost in our thoughts. I noticed a few inmates out in the yard when we got there. I wondered if one of them was Tim. We had to lock our guns and cell phones in the trunk of our car. Giving up my gun and phone seemed totally unnatural. As we walked toward the main gate, we could feel the eyes watching us from the guard towers. We pinned visitor badges to our shirts and Internal Affairs Lieutenant Harold Schuler greeted us. It was the first time I was able to put a face with the distinctive deep mellow voice I had gotten to know on the phone. We followed him inside. A heavy metal door slammed behind us. We were now within the same walls as Tim.

We had obtained a court order to allow us to see Tim's prison records—we did not want any surprises. The documents were mostly dated. I was drawn to the dozens of prison mug shots included in his file. They reminded me of the school pictures my mother kept of me and my sisters, showing the progression of age and maturity as we advanced through school. The pictures of Tim showed a man aging in prison, progressing toward death. In a sense it was sad. We also reviewed old psychiatric reports and evaluations. No surprises there. Lieutenant Schuler then took us to meet Tim's psychologist. We learned Tim was not attending any counseling and met with the doctor only occasionally. Again, nothing surprising. It was almost time for the meeting for which I had been waiting so long.

Moe and I had planned the seating arrangements inside the twelve feet by twenty-four feet interrogation room. I was going to sit across from Tim. I wanted the killer's eyes on me. Moe was going to sit to my left. A single chair between the table and cinder block wall waited for Tim. We had been hunting for this man for decades. Now, a large wooden conference table would separate us from him by just a few feet.

Within minutes, Tim was standing before us.

His handshake was not what I expected of a man who had used his hands to strangle his victim to death. It was weak. Limp. Unassertive. And yet, I knew Tim was the man who had murdered Deborah. Long had I anticipated this moment when I finally could ask him why he did it. How he did it. And what he had to say about it. For me, it wasn't just about closing the cold case file that had sat inside the confines of our department for more than two decades. It was about confronting the man who robbed the Sheppard family of their beautiful daughter and left them with a void that they filled with guilt that nearly tore them apart.

As soon as we introduced ourselves as detectives with the Carbondale Police Department, I could tell Tim knew why we were there. Images of his fatal encounter with Deborah must have flashed in his mind. Of course, I could only imagine the other images that he had to mentally sort through to find the one of Deborah's naked body which he left lifeless at the side of her bed. Still, he stood there looking calm.

I, on the other hand, was anything but. I knew how crucial this interview could be. I didn't want to tell the Sheppard family to brace for a lengthy judicial process. This time, I wanted a confession. I had come up with several scenarios of the day.

Quickly, I went over them in my mind. The best-case scenario: Tim confesses to Deborah's murder when we confront him with the DNA evidence. Second-best scenario: Tim denies ever knowing Deborah, so he would have to explain to a jury how his DNA ended up in her mouth. Worst-case scenario: Tim says he had a consensual relationship with Deborah, which would explain why his semen was found in her mouth. In that case, he could be exonerated, assuming he could make a judge or jury believe him. It was my job to make sure this didn't happen. I knew he was smart. The question was, could I outsmart him?

Tim's arms swung carelessly at his sides as he cased the room. He eyed the camcorder over my right shoulder and the tape recorder on the table in front of him. His plastic prison photo ID card dangled from his collar.

"How're you doing, Tim?" I pretended to care.

"All right," he said.

His first words revealed a soft raspy voice. His cheeks sunk into holes where teeth were missing. I was struck by the seemingly feeble nature of the sixty-two-year-old man who had once masterfully crawled into Deborah's bedroom window, forced her to perform oral sex on him and strangled her. He looked much older than the mug shot Moe had found in the Carbondale police files, taken when Tim was arrested for exposing himself to a woman while sitting in his car in a grocery store parking lot. He was bald. His mustache, once black as coal, was now gray. It curled at the ends like horns. Tim's once thick black bushy eyebrows matched the salt-and-pepper hue of his facial hair. But one feature remained the same: I found myself drawn to Tim's eyes, hidden in the shadow of a dark blue baseball cap. His oversized prison-issued plastic-framed glasses magnified the seemingly endless black pools of darkness. Suddenly, my heart started to race. *Those were the last eyes Deborah saw before this man took her life.* Quickly, I shook the thought off, we all took our strategically placed seats and I focused on my objective.

"We have something that could be interesting, that you might want to hear," I began.

"Maybe not," Tim replied.

"I'm going to test your memory," I continued. "I'm gonna take you back many years. Maybe you can—"

"Go ahead," he interrupted.

"—help us out with something," I continued.

"Shoot," he said.

Tim had to have known this day would come. During his more than two decades in prison, he had read about DNA technology and how it was solving cold cases. The technique of comparing genetic codes from fluids found at crime scenes against DNA samples submitted by prisoners like Tim had practically been perfected as he sat in his cell. Through the years, he watched as fellow inmates arrived having just been convicted and given new sentences they never thought they would face so long after the crimes they committed. And he watched a few be released after DNA evidence exonerated them. Still, Tim sat, just another number on a long list of inmates, another face in the crowd, holding the answers to so many questions he left in so many minds. Tim knew the technology might catch up to him should a detective somewhere along his murderous path have evidence tested from his crime scenes. He didn't know that moment had just arrived—or did he?

I ran through the customary Miranda rights, hoping Tim wouldn't decide to lawyer up. Tim probably knew them better than I did. Tim signed the Miranda form after each point. *So far, so good,* I thought.

"We're gonna talk to you about a case that occurred several years ago. But… before I get into that, I just want to get a little background on you. In case, by the way, you may actually have information that can help us," I said.

"What year you talkin' about?" Tim asked.

"We're gonna go back to 1982. You…you were in Carbondale from what we understand."

"Oh, that was way back."

"You were released in '76? And that's when you came to Carbondale?"

"Yes. Right. Went to school…graduated in '82. Summer," he answered, his calm look not straying from his face.

"What was your degree in?"

"Administration of justice with a minor in psychology. I was tryin' to figure myself out."

"Did you get yourself figured out?" I asked.

"I did a piss poor job of that."

I changed the topic of conversation and made some small talk with Tim, running through the time line of his life, getting his mind further away from the Miranda warning. He recalled raping the women near Chicago and spending time in the Navy and talked a little of how he moved around a lot in his younger years because his stepfather's construction job took him and his two half-brothers around Pennsylvania.

"When you were in Carbondale, do you…do you remember any murders in Carbondale when you were a student there?"

"Two of them, yeah," he nodded. "There's one they questioned me about, by the railroad tracks or something. And they caught that guy."

My mind raced. *Has he heard about Daniel Woloson's conviction? Does he know who I am? Or does he still think John Paul Phillips was the killer?*

"Okay, that was Susan Schumake. Do you remember the name of the detective?"

"Yeah, yeah. That's all I really remember. I think it was Detective Kluge."

Wow. This guy is sharp, I thought, hoping my face didn't betray my surprise. *He just pulled Kluge's name out of nowhere after all these years.*

"Yeah, that's a…good recall," I said, trying to hide my amazement.

"Yes, it was," Mike said, equally impressed.

"He came over and asked me about it. There was two of 'em, but I remember Kluge."

"There was another murder which occurred in April 1982," I continued. "It was…a black female. Do you remember that? She was an SIU student. I figured since you were on the SIU campus, you might recall that."

"Vaguely," his memory conveniently faded.

"Do you know where South Graham is located?"

"Sure I do. Remember, I drove an ambulance. I know Carbondale pretty well."

"The murder was big news at that time. Carbondale had only a few murders and that one made the news headlines. Do you recall any details of the murder?"

"No," he said simply.

Our strategy for questioning Tim that day included a simple lie. A lie that an innocent man would know was a lie. I wanted at least our second-best scenario to come true. Confessions are so rare, unlike what most television shows depict, especially with a man who knows the system and how to manipulate it for his own good. Tim was smart and he knew how to work it. I wanted Tim to at least deny that he ever knew Deborah. I made up a story about a fictitious former coworker of Tim's. I told Tim that this coworker had agreed to identify Tim as Deborah's killer in order to get out of some charges he was facing. I based the story upon a real witness who said they saw a person looking in through Deborah's bedroom window the night she was killed. I mixed fact with fiction to make the story believable. It had worked for me in Susan's case as well as others before. The question was, would it work with this smart, evasive heinous criminal? I had tried to get Tim's employment records at the nursing home where he had worked, but they had long since been discarded. I couldn't be sure of whether Tim had worked with any black men, but the witness was black. So, I took a chance. I told Tim that our fictitious informant was black.

"Black male?" Tim asked, as his bushy eyebrows furrowed in confusion.

"But we're not sure if it's going to be you or him, because he's trying to get something out of it too. If you know where this address is at, I'm going to take you back to a Thursday night on April 8, 1982. You would've still been in Carbondale, because you were going to school."

"Yeah, I was still there," he agreed.

"Would you have had any reason to be over there?"

"A black female?"

"Yeah, it's a black female."

"No."

"So there's no reason that you would have been—"

"Black female?" he interrupted.

"—over in that area on foot walking?" I continued.

"I never worked with no black guy over there at the nursing home," Tim stated.

"You don't think so?"

"No."

Shit. Even though more than two decades had passed since Tim worked in that nursing home, he knew he didn't work with any black men. Or was he bluffing my bluff? At that moment, I feared I might lose credibility with him and if I did, my whole strategy would go down in flames. The mind game was on. It was me against him. I had to make Tim second guess himself, not let him do the same to me. Even though my nerves were on edge, I did my best to hide it. I knew Tim was reading my body language just as much as I was reading his.

"Well, he says he knew you. He said he didn't work there long."

"A black guy?"

"Well, let me go a little further. Maybe this will make a little more sense to you. On the night this young girl was murdered, he was visiting his girlfriend at the address on South Graham…at apartment five. The girl who was killed was in apartment six. Now, like I said, he's trying to get out of something, but he's provided this information. He doesn't like police. I mean, he never came to us with this information until now…But he's pretty adamant that he saw you in that area that night."

"I doubt it."

"Well, you doubt it or are you just not sure?"

"I doubt it. I had no reason to be over there in that area."

Gotcha, I thought. We had made the first chink in his armor. He didn't deny killing Deborah. He was leaving himself some wiggle room. *This is good.*

"Now, you've got pretty good recall and if you had friends or something over there, would you remember it?" I asked as my confidence began to build.

"Sure."

"Well, this girl's name was Deborah Sheppard. Does that mean anything to you?"

"No."

At this point, I could feel my heart beginning to beat a bit faster. He had just admitted that he had never been in Deborah's apartment building and didn't even know her. Even without a confession, that was big. He would now have to explain how his bodily fluids were found in a building he said he had never been in and on a woman he said he never even knew. I could tell his head was spinning. I had been down this road before. Denial always came first. The confession—if at all—second. I was focused on getting a denial so strong a jury could see he was lying and a good attorney would not be able to say Tim simply forgot about an affair he had with Deborah when we interviewed him and that was how his semen got on the shirt. Denial was the next best thing to a confession. I had to keep going with it.

"Well, did you…do you have many black friends that might have lived in that area? Because most of the people who lived in that area were black, I think."

"No."

"No? So, there's just no reason for you to have been in that area at all?"

"No."

"Would you have ever been inside an apartment over there at any time?"

"No."

Tim then admitted to dating a black woman with whom he worked at a nursing home.

"So you never went with her over there to visit anybody who would have lived there?" I asked, again reiterating his denial of ever stepping foot near Deborah's apartment.

"No." Tim's short answers returned.

"Now, not only did this guy say he'd seen you in the area, he says he saw you coming out of that particular apartment building where Deborah lived."

"Nah! He's crazy."

"Now, there's no chance that you would have been with him and you both went into this building and he's just ratting you out, is there?"

"No, I don't even know the guy. I can't even remember working with the guy."

"So, you would not have raped or murdered Deborah Sheppard?"

"No."

"Would your fingerprints be in the apartment?" I prodded.

"No way."

"So essentially, you've just never been in there."

"No."

"Now, you know, this guy is pretty believable. He's saying that not only did he see you outside the apartment and coming out the door, he actually saw you through the window inside that apartment."

"No, he's got the wrong man."

"I have the wrong man?"

"Yeah, I'd say he's feeding you a good line."

It was time to turn up the heat.

"Now, Tim, we actually have very, very good information since he brought this up and we've done some investigating and we know you killed Deborah Sheppard," I stated.

"No way," Tim said, letting out a nervous chuckle. "No way. Take a DNA test or something. Anything. I'm fine with all that."

"So your DNA would not be there?" I asked.

"No. My DNA is on file," Tim said.

"Yes, it is," Moe said, unable to resist drawing out the words to overemphasize the point. But I wasn't ready to show our hand just yet. I wanted Tim to dig himself in deeper. If he really did not think we had DNA, then he would keep denying ever being there.

"So," I said, "if we test anything with DNA in there, whether it be blood, semen or something you touched…"

"You can't find nothing from me," Tim said, his confidence eerily convincing.

"Nothing of yours is gonna be there?" I persisted.

"No."

"What if it was? How would you explain that?" I asked.

"It's not gonna happen. No way. That's an impossibility…You're barking up the wrong tree."

"Well, Tim, I know you've got a conscience and I know in the past, from what I understand, you've shown that."

"Wrong person."

"We know you did it."

"Ah, baloney. I'm telling you. You got the wrong person. You've got the wrong person."

Okay, I calculated my next move. *He has dug himself in deep enough. It's time to show our hand.*

"What if I told you that we have a DNA match?"

"You ain't got no DNA match, because there is no DNA match," Tim said simply.

"There is."

"No, there ain't."

"It came back to you, Tim," Moe said.

"Tim, why would we be here otherwise?" I asked.

"I have no idea."

"Well, it's because of the DNA match. Now, I mean, honestly, we need to get beyond that, because that's what happened. That's why we're here. We have matched your DNA to this murder."

"No, I don't believe you."

"Now…I want to tell you that your cooperation in this means a whole lot. You're already here. Obviously, you're probably never going anywhere anyhow."

"That's right. I'm never gettin' out."

"Your cooperation is about the only thing that you've got left here that can help keep you where you are at, to help us to put in good words to maintain where you are gonna stay. And it's my understanding that you'd like to stay here. I cannot make any promises, but what I can tell you is your cooperation will be reflected in our report and reflected with the state's attorney, who does have some leverage on what he suggests when he presents the case to a judge. So, you know, this young girl was killed and I don't know what happened. I don't know what went wrong. That wasn't your style. Yeah, you've raped. Yeah and way back you actually stabbed a girl and you've held knives before. I don't know what went wrong with this one. Her mother and father are still alive. They're elderly now. She has two sisters. She has grandnieces and nephews now. We want to bring an end to this. And this is your opportunity now to help us with this."

"Nah. It wasn't me," Tim continued his denial.

"Then how do we explain your semen being in her body?"

"I don't know how you can explain it. I don't…I don't believe it's the case."

"Well, it is."

"Well, you'd have to show me more evidence than that. I…I…I just don't believe you," Tim shifted in his chair.

"Did you bring the lab report?" Moe asked me.

"Let me see if I have it," I said as I searched for the report among the files and photos I had brought. I realized I had left it on my desk. I left the room to call Suzanne and have her fax me a copy. I had no idea why Tim was so confident that we didn't have the DNA match and I didn't expect him to ask for the proof. Moe took the opportunity to keep tugging at whatever conscience Tim might have.

"Tim, we're not here to make this up," Moe said. "We're just trying to get some closure for a family that's lost a daughter. You've got to kinda know what that's gonna be like. I mean, you know you're here forever."

"That's…that's true."

"A murder rap is not gonna get you any more time than what you've already got."

I came back to the room as I waited for the fax to arrive. "Well, Tim, if that's gonna make the difference, we will sit here until it gets faxed up here to me. If that's gonna make a difference to you…"

"It's not gonna make any difference to me. I didn't do it."

"Because I'm not lying to you. You know, like I said, I don't know what went wrong, but something went wrong. And you owe it to that family to explain to them what happened. You owe it to them. You know what? They have suffered twenty-five years without their daughter. Over twenty-five years…I assume you were out there peeping in the window. And I assume you saw her. You went in on her. She was getting out of the shower. You grabbed her. You raped her. And then somehow you killed her. And I want you to tell me what happened."

"Didn't happen."

"So we go back to the state's attorney and tell him to go ahead and file charges against you, because you're not gonna tell us what happened."

"If…it…if you've got DNA, that's gonna happen anyway, so…" Tim drifted off.

"That's right. It is."

"Cooperation is gonna matter more than anything. More than you can believe," Moe added.

"Wasn't me. Didn't do it."

"Well, I'm gonna have that report faxed while you're still here."

"Is that gonna change your mind?" Moe asked.

"Nah…Not gonna change my mind. It wasn't me."

"You know, you've been in here in corrections and from what I understand you've been doing well. We're not here to make things any worse than you are. You've already lost your freedom and I can't think of anything that's worse than that. You know we've talked to them to ask what would happen with you once this goes to court. And from what we understand is that…you'll likely stay here. Now, we don't know that for sure, because that's all up to the state's attorney and what references and suggestions he makes to the judge," I explained, knowing the only leverage we had with him was the prison he called home.

"You made a decision several years ago and probably it was a smart decision by deciding that this is where you need to stay, because you don't want to hurt anybody anymore," Moe said.

"That's true."

"That's a pretty good decision on your part. I mean, you could have lied and gave them a bunch of BS with all the testing and psychiatric evaluations and tried to get yourself out, but you were honest enough with yourself to know there was a problem.

And it was safer for everybody, including yourself, to be here forever. I commend you for that, because I'm sure there are a lot of guys who are trying to run the scam and are getting out, so they can do their thing again. But you figured it out. You weren't able to control or stop yourself and so you did a great job there," Moe said.

"And now's your opportunity to complete that circle. You've got to finish up what you did when you were out. You've got to bring closure to this," I interjected.

"Put it behind you. Get rid of it…" Moe continued. "Now, you know you had a daughter. I'm sure you didn't want the same thing to happen to her. I mean, those people have had to live with it the last twenty-five years, as you've had to live with it for the last twenty-five years. All they want is some closure."

"It didn't happen," he denied.

"Well, we know it did. You know it and we know it. We just didn't pick up your DNA and put it on the evidence. I know that after twenty-five years you kind of put it all behind you and thought it was all gone. But…it's not all gone anymore. It's here. Again, I commend you for keeping yourself locked up. That's gotta be tough. Because you know if you play the game, like you did the first time you got out: you convinced those people that you were okay. And they let you out. There's no controlling it really. You figured that out. At least you're keeping yourself away from anybody. Are you afraid of losing your privileges here or getting transferred out of here?" Moe said.

"Nah. What does it matter?"

"Tim, I want to show you a couple of pictures," I said, laying out Deborah's crime scene photos in front of Tim's face.

"Don't bother," he said, glancing at them.

"You don't want to see them?"

"Why would I want to see pictures like those?"

"We wouldn't be here if we didn't think you did it," I said.

"Well, you may think I did, but…that sure is not the case. I…if that guy is a real guy…I don't remember him at all. So…I think…"

"Forget the guy! We're talking about DNA. A DNA match. The science. It's black or white. It either is or it isn't. And in this case, it is."

"I don't think so."

Lieutenant Schuler knocked on the door, saying someone needed to talk to me from the crime lab. I left to take the call. As long as Tim was talking, Moe had to keep him going.

"In your estimation, how many rapes do you think you did? More than you can count?"

"No. Probably more than twenty-five or thirty."

"What set you off? What made you want to do it? Do you remember? Was it something inside—"

"It was…moods of depression…I've been acting out since I was like four or five years old. I…was screwed up as a toddler. A baby. A pup."

"Were you abused?" Moe asked.

"Not physically, no…Well, it was mostly…mostly emotionally. Just left alone too much. The first…I believe the first three or four years of my life I was just left alone way too much. No mother. No father."

"So you don't remember your dad?"

"Nah. My momma was sixteen. I don't remember my father at all. He was a Marine in the war. The only and first time I remember a guy in my life was when I was about six years old. When she got remarried. Most of the time I was alone all the time."

"Was that Krajcir?"

"Yeah and he was a hardworking man and fed and clothed us…But emotionally…there was no connection whatsoever."

"Like I say, it can be worse than physical abuse. Did you get along with your mom?"

"No, like I said, when…when she had me she was too young to have me to begin with. And…and then you know, when he left right away. I guess she was out looking for another guy and she was just never there."

"Did she leave you alone or did people babysit you?"

"Well, I was in a house of…full of people, but I was basically alone. I used to wander by myself all the time."

"No sexual abuse in your past?"

"No, no. He was a good provider."

"Did you start doing burglaries pretty early?"

"Probably around fourteen, fifteen, somewhere in there. Pretty young…It gives a rush. Well, I was looking for help, that's why I had emotional pain then, you know, you just…you had to find some kind of release somewhere. It went the wrong way."

"No drug abuse in your background though, is there?"

"No."

"Do you know what set you off on this one?" Moe interjected, hoping the rapid change of subjects would catch Tim off guard.

"It wasn't me."

Damn, Moe thought.

A few minutes later, the report arrived. I returned to the room and placed the matching DNA profiles in front of Tim. The proverbial ace had been pulled from the deck. He methodically and quietly examined the documents. I could tell he had no idea how we could have found DNA at Deborah's scene. Truth is, we almost didn't. There was such a small amount of semen, I doubted he had ejaculated. Maybe Tim was banking on that fact, thinking he would not leave anything behind. But there had been just enough. The evidence was damning and Tim knew it.

"You can't explain it, can you?" I asked.

"I still don't think it's a 100 percent match."

"It is. Tim, what I did the bulk of my career, for a fourteen-year period I was a crime scene technician. Of course they call it CSI today. I went away to the FBI academy and lots of other places and learned how to do fingerprints. I'm not a DNA expert, but I did learn how the science works. And they're even letting inmates out in cases where they have identified them, but where they didn't use DNA. You know this: that they get out, because the DNA didn't match them. And they had other evidence against them. So DNA evidence is very, very powerful. It either is or it is not. There's no down the middle here. In this case, it is you. And you know it's you. You've just got the big decision to make whether you want to fess up to it."

"No."

"What happened? What went wrong?"

"Not going there."

"What did this girl do wrong that she deserved to be killed? She wouldn't even have known you. There's no way she would have ever identified you. You didn't have to kill her."

"It wasn't me. I think we need to end this right now. This...I'll talk to an attorney. I ain't gonna continue this...this makes no sense to continue this. It wasn't me."

And with that, it was over, one hour and one minute after it began. Getting the denial was extremely important. But the more I thought about it later that night, the more I felt like I had failed the Sheppard family. They would have to endure a potentially long, drawn out court case. I dreaded the thought of calling Bernie, so I put off calling him until the morning. It was a good thing I did.

8

"I'm Twisted"

I went in to work early the next morning so I could prepare the probable cause statement I needed to take to the state's attorney to get a murder warrant for Tim. Moe and I went to our investigators meeting, where our fellow officers grilled us about the interview with Tim. They, too, were somewhat disappointed to hear we couldn't get Tim to crack entirely. Afterward it was time to call Bernie, but I noticed my voicemail light was blinking. I checked my messages. When I heard the voice on the other end, it was as if my prayer had been answered and the angel delivering the message was Lieutenant Schuler. I closed my eyes and listened.

Tim wanted us to come back. He wanted to confess. I called Lieutenant Schuler and told him Moe and I would be there soon. He was excited, too. I quickly gathered my recording equipment and called the state's attorney, Mike Wepsiec. With such an important case at stake, I wanted his input. Wepsiec told me to make sure we had Tim acknowledge on tape that he knew his rights and had chosen on his own to refuse his right to remain silent. I got off the phone and found Moe had gone to get his daily orange scone and coffee at the delicatessen nearby. When he walked back in the office, I told him to eat quickly.

"Why?" he asked between bites.

"Lieutenant Schuler at Big Muddy called. Tim wants to confess."

"Seriously?" Moe said, his eyebrows rising.

"Yes, seriously!"

"Let's get over there right away."

During the forty-five minute drive Moe and I talked the whole way, running through scenarios of what Tim might say, what we said that might have provoked Tim to talk, whether he would confess to everything. Arriving at the prison, we locked our guns and cell phones in the car again. Armed only with my recording devices, we went in. Everything was in place when the clunk of the heavy steel door echoed through the hallway signaling Tim's impending arrival. I could hardly believe we were standing there about to take his confession to a case so many had forgotten. A case most felt was hopeless. A case most thought lacked the evidence needed to solve it. And here I was, about to hear what happened from the mystery man who nearly got away with a murder on my shift so many years before.

"Hey, Tim, how're you doing?" I pretended to care once more.

"Under the circumstances, not so good. Been up most of the night, trying to think things through."

He waived his right to an attorney and signed the Miranda rights statement. Lieutenant Schuler put a paper cup of water in front of him.

"A stiff drink would be better," he quipped.

"We aren't able to get that for you, but, Tim, I understand you want to talk to us. What do you want to talk to us about?" I asked.

"Well, about yesterday…what does the state's attorney want?"

"He wants a confession. He wants to know if you killed Deborah Sheppard. He wants you to say you killed Deborah Sheppard. Did you kill Deborah?" I asked.

I wanted the damn confession as soon as possible before Tim changed his mind.

"Uh…then what happens? I'd like to know what's gonna happen here."

I explained to Tim that he would have to appear in the Jackson County Court but that his court appearances would be fewer if he pled guilty.

"I know all that," Tim said.

"Now, if you're concerned about publicity, I can't guarantee you anything as far as publicity…I really don't know what will happen. But even though this is a twenty-five-year-old case, I think it will be of interest to the public. And you can expect that it would."

"Well, I'd like to see it handled quickly. Quietly. And discretely as possible. The only reason I'm here…right now, is for the Sheppard family."

"A good decision," Moe said.

"It is a good decision. And I will guarantee you that it is important to the family. If it goes to trial, the family would have to go through all these things which would come out. And their memories would be even more traumatic," I said.

"I know. I know. So I'd be arrested today?"

"No."

"Well, I talked to Dr. Carich this morning," Tim said. "And I think he's the one who made the phone call. Like I said, I was up most of the night thinking about it. And…what I had…was planning ten or fifteen years down the road, as my health started to go and etcetera, etcetera, etcetera, I was going to disclose anyway."

"And there're no guarantees the family would be alive at that point."

"That's true. I think I'm doing the right thing. I told Dr. Carich this morning that all of the decisions I've made in the past ten or fifteen years have been for good things. And I've got to have enough courage to do this as a good thing. For the past fifteen years or so, all the guys in group have come to me and asked me how come I don't go to group. And I tell them I couldn't, because I couldn't tell the truth. And that I had made the decision to spend the rest of my life incarcerated, because I accepted the fact that I'm pretty twisted. And at some point in time, you have to accept responsibility of what you are and what you're not. And if I sit here and lie and lie and lie, well, I'm not doing that. So what's the last ten or fifteen years worth if I'm just gonna turn around and lie some more here. So I'm not gonna do that. I'm gonna…"

"Well, you started on the right path years ago by keeping yourself confined here, so…" Moe said.

"And you are doing the right thing," I added.

"I think so. So let's get on with it."

"Just simply, did you kill Deborah Sheppard?" I asked.

"Yes."

With that one word, a twenty-five-year-old murder mystery was over. It was the culmination of thousands of hours of investigative efforts by many police officers, especially Mike Dismore, Monica Joost and forensic science experts. Now it was time to find out why.

His voice was quiet and unemotional as he began talking about how his desire to touch Deborah that cold early spring night in 1982 was only hindered by Deborah's bedroom window. Tim had spied on her before and masturbated as he stood outside her bedroom window watching her. That night he could see her through a small gap in her curtains. From his perch outside the window and under the cover of darkness, he watched Deborah's roommate leave in a hurry to go to work. He knew she was all alone. He watched as Deborah gathered clothes to take to the bathroom. Tim had to get a better look. He couldn't take it anymore. He walked around the building and heard Deborah's shower begin to run. He thought of her naked body in the shower. Fantasies raced through his mind. Maybe tonight things would be different. Maybe tonight he would touch her. Maybe tonight she would do the pleasing instead of his pleasing himself.

Not many people were stirring about, but Tim wondered if her roommate would return. He also thought about the self-imposed rule he was about to violate: Never "hunt" in Carbondale—a place where people knew him. A place he called home. A place where he worked as an ambulance driver. A place where he fit in. He was on parole and knew if he was caught he would go back to prison. But this was not the time to rationalize. *Just do it*, he told himself.

He walked back to Deborah's bedroom window and reached for the glass with his gloved hands. He was pleasantly surprised when he found the lower glass window was loose. After manipulating it for a few seconds, the window and aluminum frame fell out into his hands and he laid it below the other bedroom window. His heart raced as he climbed in headfirst and slithered into the dark room. He had passed the point of no return. He pulled the curtains together to hide the missing glass. His weight had bent the curtain rod at the top of the window, but lucky for him, the curtains did not fall. Everything was going his way. He pulled a silver .25 automatic pistol from his pocket and pulled a blue bandanna over his face. He walked out of Deborah's bedroom quietly and looked around the apartment. He had guessed right. No one else was there. He cut her phone cord with a knife he always carried. There would be no interruptions. He walked into her roommate's bedroom and waited until he heard the shower stop. It was his signal to take up position in front of the bathroom door. His sexual excitement grew by the seconds. Deborah dried herself off with a green towel and wrapped it around her body. When she opened the bathroom door, Tim pointed a gun in her face. Terrified, she backed away from him.

"If you cooperate, I won't hurt you," he told her.

Remaining quiet, she continued to back away from him but tripped and fell into the tub, still clinging to the towel she had wrapped around herself. Tim stepped into the tub with one foot to lift her out. *That's where the muddy smudge they found on the tub came from*, I realized.

Knowing she had been in the shower and that she had a roommate who had left that night were two huge details that only the killer could know. My case was getting more and more solid as the conversation went on. Tim's matter-of-fact demeanor in reliving these details was chilling. He listed every detail for two hours as if he were telling us about the items on his commissary list. There was no emotion, no inflection in his voice, no remorse, no feeling. Just the horrifying facts.

"I was wearing a mask and as I was getting ready to leave, she pulled the mask off and I got scared. I was already under the SDP act so I knew that if, you know, I got arrested I was gone for the rest of my life. And I was fearful of being caught, so I killed Deborah," he stated simply.

"How did you kill her?" I asked, keeping the revulsion I felt from my tone.

"Strangled her. When she took my mask off my face, I just freaked because I knew. She went along with the program. I mean, she wasn't fighting, she wasn't arguing. Until I was getting ready to leave when she…like I said, I had a handkerchief on and she pulled it down. I had no intention of killing her."

"What kind of sexual assault was it?"

"Just, uh…intercourse and oral sex."

"It was vaginal intercourse as well?"

"Yeah."

"Did you ejaculate?"

"I don't think so."

He said that he had raped Deborah vaginally. I knew he preferred oral sex from his other assaults and the evidence supported an oral assault on Deborah. The limited amount of semen we collected seemed to confirm that he did not ejaculate. *Maybe the vaginal intercourse was very limited and no sperm was left behind that could be found?* I wondered. Still, it was hard to believe that she had been raped. There were no signs of bruising or other force that sometimes is seen on rape victims. But I wasn't about to interrupt Tim.

"Did you announce why you were there?"

"Well, I…I…like I say, you're talking about twenty-five years ago. I remember…you know…I took her in the bedroom and did what I did there. I don't remember what I said then. Usually at something like that, it's about having a feeling of power and control. And…you just say things. I couldn't tell you."

"But it was in that room when she reached up and pulled your mask down?"

"Yeah. I was getting ready to go. After she got my handkerchief, I wrestled her to the floor there and she fought me. I just overpowered her. A terrible thing. I think her hands were trapped in my legs. I was sittin' on top of her and she was struggling the best that she could."

"Did you realize that you had killed her when you left?"

"I wasn't sure, because it was really quick. You know, I…I…I didn't think. I held on to her that long. But…who knows? I was gone."

"When did you first know that you killed her?"

"I read it in…one of the papers."

"Okay. Do you remember anything about that? Things that you thought of when you read the articles?"

"No. Just that, uh…you know, over the years I have on several occasions thought about it in the sense that, uh…what the family was going through. One of the things I did to make myself stay inside was trying to see my victims' families. And then, so, I would see somebody on TV and what if that was your brother or that was your sister? I…try and put that in my head. But it…it didn't work, because ever since I was a little guy, I did something, got left out when I was growing up. And it was those kind of feelings. So, more for me to, uh…I…continue to have, uh…try and put that in my head, you know. What was the families thinking about?

That's what I say. Down the road, I was going to try and disclose that. But I was gonna wait until I got older and infirmed or whatever. It was…it's been on my mind several times."

"Well, this will absolutely help the family finally put it to rest. They'll know what happened. They'll know who did it."

"Did you feel pretty upset about it afterward?" Moe asked.

"Yes."

"What would you want me to convey to the family?"

"That Deborah was not at fault, in no way, shape or form. I don't know. I regret her death. As much as I'd like to say there was a lot of feeling there, I don't have that part in me. That's one of the terrible things about my situation. I wish I had those kind of feelings, but I've never had them since I was little. I tried to force those kind of feelings on myself, so I can see some of my victims' pain. And…I tried to do that like I said over the years. And, uh…I shouldn't have been out there… I mean, I already was an SDP. The sad part about it was that I was smart enough, like we was talking about yesterday, to fool the counselors…and the psychologists. I was just fooling myself, you know, in the long run."

"And you feel like you could do that again if you wanted, right?"

"Without a doubt."

"I mean, if you would have chosen to. If you would have made that decision in your life, you think you could have played the game and got back out with this?"

"Oh, without a doubt. Like you know, in '88 I had letters from two doctors saying that they would both recommend my release. One was from, uh…St. Joseph Peter's Institute in Philadelphia and the other was, uh…Dr. Canal, doctor of psychiatry, uh…worked at the prison in Grantsburg, Pennsylvania. And, uh…both of them said they would recommend my release, but through Dr. Canal's especially. Like, we had a lot of one-on-one sessions. And even though I never really disclosed to them, neither of them realized that I was a walking time bomb. And when I came out here and I got back in the SDP program and I could see, you know, that I should never have been put back on the street. Uh…that's, you know, I was a walking time bomb."

"Have you ever confessed this to anyone?"

"No. No."

"Never told a cell mate or one of the doctors?" Moe asked.

"No, we didn't talk about stuff like that. You try and put it out of your mind. Try not to think about it, but that's an impossibility. It keeps coming back to you. You think about it. Like I say, it's several times over the years I've thought about it."

"Do you still see her face? Do you remember it that well?"

"Yeah, I remember her," Tim replied. "She was a pretty girl. And, uh…I remember her. But I…I…you know, I remember with sadness, because like I say, I had no intention of harming that girl, other than the sexual assault."

"What did you think yesterday when you saw her picture for the first time in twenty-five years?"

"I just tried not to. I tried not to. Like I say, I was up all night, you know, thinking about it and, you know, do I have the courage of my convictions. I decided I had to say yes, so…that's why I am sitting here right now."

I pulled out some more pictures of the crime scene without Deborah's body in them so Tim could continue to verify all that he did that night.

"About how long, start to finish, from going through the window until you actually left through the door?"

"I'd say no more than twenty or twenty-five minutes."

"So it wasn't the fact that the curtains weren't in place that attracted you to that…so I have to assume, based on what you are saying, that you peeped in a lot of windows in that area?"

"Actually, it wasn't a lot. I…I was using that more or less so I could do other things. Trying to find outlets where I didn't have to hurt people, you know, to get off sexually. I…I…was, you know, looking in windows. I would make obscene phone calls and stuff like that. Trying to avoid, I even bought a lot of…you know… and paid them to do it, whatever. And I still…I just couldn't stop. And it would get worse and worse. And then when I moved out to Pennsylvania, it got even worse. I couldn't stop. I was going out every night. Ridiculous! That's when I finally got caught. It got to the point where it became an obsession. I mean, I go to a mall or shopping center someplace and I'd see a woman, I'd grab her on the ass. I mean, I just got terrible. And finally, one of those nights, they arrested me. Thankfully before anybody else got hurt."

"That was the night where you had masking tape on a license plate?"

"Yeah, yeah. I'd get off work and man, whew, I'd go out and I mean I couldn't stop. I'd go back to the same place. You know, uh…I think I was looking to get… get busted…"

"What brought it on so bad when you went to Pennsylvania? Was it moving back with—" Moe asked.

"I don't know. I was living by myself. Uh…I was sharing a place with my brother. I don't know what it was."

"Which brother did you live with at that—"

"My youngest brother."

"Was Deborah's murder a catalyst that motivated you to move back to Pennsylvania?"

"Yeah and I was afraid I might do something again."

"And plus you graduated about that time too, right?"

"In May yeah."

"Did you actually go through with the ceremonies for graduation?"

"No…no…I had it mailed to me."

"Okay, so you had never met Deborah Sheppard on campus either?"

"No. No. She was just in the wrong place at the wrong time and by luck, walked by. Basically, I shouldn't have been there to begin with. I should have been locked up."

He seemed to want to talk, so I took the opportunity to bring up the other unsolved sexual assault that happened in his neighborhood about three years before Deborah's murder. It was an ambush just like Tim pulled off in Deborah's case, surprising the victim inside her home. And it was a forced oral sex assault. But her attacker didn't kill her. Didn't even try.

"I'll just read the details and like I said, there…there are no charges here. If anything, we just want to clear the case and know it was you."

"I didn't do it. No other rapes," he snapped, way too quickly for me to believe.

I knew it had to be him. He admitted to masturbating frequently in mall parking lots and grabbing women as they walked past his car, but he stayed away from anything that remotely suggested any of his crimes ever escalated to the level of Deborah's attack.

"There're more things like that than there was actual assaults," Tim said, trying to make it seem like rapes were rare for him.

"So you didn't have anything to do with…I know you were masturbating. Was it the orgasm or was it actually, just mentally, something you just had the desire to do? What was it you got out of it?"

"I don't know. I think it has to go way…way…way…way back, when I was, like, little. Like, uh…uh…what better way to get some self-gratification than sexually? I mean, that's immediate gratification. I…I…I think it's evolved from when I was a youngster, like ten, eleven, twelve, thirteen, when I first started masturbating and I first started peeping in windows. I mean, like I said, I starting acting out when I was four years old. I mean and…and…as I grew older, it just got more and more and worse and worse and then I couldn't stop it."

"You don't remember any other sexual assaults?"

"No."

"Is that basically how you selected your victims, even when you went back to Pennsylvania: whether they were attractive? Or what process did you use for selecting?"

"Mostly looking for attractive women. I mean, it…it got to the point where a woman didn't have to be attractive. I mean, it was just that obsessive. You know, I just…I just couldn't say no. I couldn't stop. And probably had not…what…I don't know if I would have hurt anybody, because I think, like I said, I was in and out of therapy for years and years and years. And I think as the years went by, after a lot of this stuff had already happened, I think some of that therapy was having an effect. Because then I did notice that, you know, I moved out to Pennsylvania. I would get…my body would get so hyped up, adrenaline and sometimes…I…I I would lose control of my bowels. Sometimes, you know, I mean, I just…such a rush that I couldn't control myself. I'd be trembling, you know. And maybe subconsciously my body was trying to tell me to stop. You know what I'm saying? This…this…is my thought anyway. And I think over the years some of that therapy was sinking in. Sinking in. And, uh,,.kept me from hurting anybody, because I had all kinds of opportunities to hurt someone had I wanted to. And I didn't."

I felt like more confessions were on the tip of his tongue. There had to be more assaults in Carbondale. *Could he have only violated his rule once?*

"Were there a lot of rapes in Pennsylvania?" Moe asked.

"No. Again, I was spending a lot of money. But there were a couple. Let's see. Maybe four or five."

"Did they charge you with two of those?" Moe pressed.

"Um…I think I got charged with indecent assault, home invasion, carrying a firearm."

"I mean, you say there were, like, four…were you…"

"Well, no…no…no…that was…that was…that was, they had questioned me about some of them, but I never, uh…did any of them. They did come in there with a list this long and wanted me to confess to everything that happened, you know, for the past two years. I didn't."

"Were there some you did that you never confessed to?"

"Uh…like I say, I think there was three or four that I did that they never pressed me on. I guessed they figured they had enough charges on me as it was."

He went on to talk about raping an Asian woman in her home as her two little boys watched TV in the front room of the house, never knowing Tim had broken in through the kitchen and raped their mother. He also recalled forcing a black woman to perform oral sex on him inside her apartment after she and her son had just returned from the grocery store. He said a nosy neighbor interrupted an assault on an "older white gal" inside her apartment, so he ran out her back door before attacking her. He followed most of his victims home from parking lots. He ended each recollection by saying, "Didn't hurt nobody," even though he admitted to raping his victims or forcing them to perform oral sex. I wondered what his definition of "hurting someone" must be. He covered his face with a handkerchief during the attacks.

"It was a handkerchief, like a blue handkerchief, because they ended up calling me the bandanna rapist in the newspaper."

"Really? Because I would have thought that after the Deborah Sheppard incident you would have done something different, since it was so easy for her to pull it down."

"Well, you become so obsessed, you don't…you don't think. You don't think period. You just…you don't have control."

"A lot of these seem to be…there were kids," Moe said.

"Easy victims."

"Can you think of any others? Now, in Carbondale, though, Sheppard is the only one? I mean, obviously, it's kind of hard to believe, because, you know, you were having this issue."

"At the time, I was fighting it."

"You were fighting it?"

"Pretty hard. And it's just a losing battle."

"So the one case I described to you, you don't think there's any way that could have been you?"

"No, I had already left that area."

"Well, I mean, you were still in Carbondale, though; you were familiar with that area. I mean, I'd like to bring closure to that one too, if it's you. I mean, obviously if it's not…"

"If it was, I'd tell you. It wasn't me."

I backed off quickly, seeing that the question made him uneasy, so we turned the conversation back to his family life.

"In your travels to and from Pennsylvania, were there any incidents that you remember?"

"No, usually most of the time I had company. I would drive and I'd take some students with me and drop them off in Ohio or Jersey or Philadelphia wherever they were going. That would save gas and stuff like that."

I bet those students had no idea of the violence he was capable of, I considered. I continued trying to put together a time line of Tim's life in his own words, being sure to note every geographical area he had ties to during his lifetime. I wanted to follow up with police in those areas to check their cold case files. Conversation turned to his days as an ambulance driver for hospitals in Southern Illinois.

"I saw where you were credited for saving several lives during that period. Do you remember that?"

"Yeah, yeah. Those were good times. I delivered a couple…a couple of babies."

"Did you really?" I said, thankful I didn't have a mouthful of water when he said that.

"Yeah, then I taught for a while. Helped people. But all the time that shit was in my head but under a lot better control. Probably because I was so busy and active. I mean a lot of stuff would happen when I wasn't…you know, working or was keeping myself busy."

"So…it's been in your head your whole life essentially and you've dealt with it better at some times than others."

"Um, pretty much. I guess when I…when I first got out, it took me some time to get my stuff together pretty good. For, oh I'd say, I didn't do anything for like a year. I mean, I did pretty good. Then…then the peeping started. Then the phone calls. I started buying. And it went from bad to worse. But the whole time, like the first two and a half years, I was working on the ambulance service so I was really busy. Yeah, thankful for that. Because if I had a whole lot of downtime, I don't know, I probably would have started acting out earlier. I don't know. Who knows. Lucky that I hadn't hurt a lot more people."

"There were no other murders?" Moe asked.

"No."

"Nothing?" Moe pressed.

"No. And I can't think of no more rapes but those I mentioned. Like I say, a lot of simple assaults, a lot of indecent exposures."

"What about in the nursing homes you worked? Were there ever any issues there?"

"Oh, no. I took an oath to help people, but again…it's conflicting issues here."

"Well, can you understand why I would ask?"

"Oh, I can. I would never hurt people I was caring for. Sick, yes, but not quite that sick."

"So the Deborah Sheppard murder is the only murder with which you've ever been involved?"

"Yeah."

I didn't believe him, but I had to move on for now. We needed another DNA sample from him to compare to the partial profile from Deborah's body that we had already matched to the DNA sample that the Illinois Department of Corrections took from Tim in 1996. In 1989, Illinois began requiring sex offenders to submit DNA samples. No doubt Tim was tested then, but by the early 1990s, DNA profiling techniques had progressed and new samples had to be collected. Tim was in custody then, so he was tested again as corrections staff tried to catch everyone up. I told Tim how to put the swab between his cheek and gum and spin it around so enough skin cells would be collected. He seemed to get a kick out of it, as if he were amazed that such a simple procedure could bring him down for murder.

"Just thought I'd somehow, uh…the Sheppard family, I'd again, I sincerely regret her death and, uh…I had no intention of killing that girl when I went in there. I just freaked out when she pulled the mask off my face," he said, quickly changing the subject.

"And you're absolutely sorry for what happened."

"Absolutely, because, I mean, I don't have big feelings of remorse or anything, because if I did, then I wouldn't have done it to begin with."

"Good point."

"But I'm trying to be honest. And, uh…but I made myself regret what I did. And I sincerely do regret her death. That was never my intent. Never. I just hope we can handle the rest of this discreetly and quietly as possible, though I know that's not going to be easy either."

I was struck by Tim's obsession about the thought of his case hitting the media. I assumed it was because he didn't want to shame his family. I'm still not convinced that thought didn't cross his mind, but there turned out to be even bigger reasons Tim didn't want this story broadcast around the country. Eight of them.

Moe and I sat in the room in silence trying to absorb what we had just learned as Lieutenant Schuler took Tim back to his cell. Eventually, I leaned toward him.

"Moe, that was almost unbelievable! He just answered the questions that Dismore, Joost, Trella and the rest of us have been trying to figure out for twenty-five years!"

"What a monster!" Moe said back to me.

Soon we heard the door locks and Lieutenant Schuler's keys jingle as he made his way back.

"So I am assuming he confessed to her murder?" he asked.

"Yes, he did. He gave us a complete confession. He killed Deborah Sheppard and confessed to some rapes in Pennsylvania from years ago. I will be contacting authorities there and letting them know."

"Is there anything we need to do here? I mean, we will have to isolate him for his own protection. Since his victim was black and he is white, we might have problems with some of the black inmates seeking retaliation. They will see this on the news," Lieutenant Schuler said.

"You'll have some time. It won't hit the media for a about a week or so. I will be meeting with the state's attorney as soon as I get the tape transcribed. I will get a murder warrant and I'll need to come back and serve it on Tim. I will be back in touch with you."

Once back at the station, we went into Moe's office. Several detectives gathered to hear our news. It was somber as we explained what Tim had told us. Soon, Chief Ledbetter stopped in to hear the story. He congratulated us. Later he shook my hand and congratulated me once more. It was a good feeling. That night, I finally got a good night's sleep.

The next day I set out to unravel the web of mysteries Deborah's murder had left in so many minds—starting with a call to Bernie. I didn't want to tell him about his daughter's final moments over the phone, but he was six hours away and I knew he needed to know. I closed my office door and spent forty-five minutes telling him how his daughter died at the hands of Tim Krajcir. As a father, I couldn't imagine what it was like for him to hear it. I expected him to be more emotional. Perhaps he had played out the scenario hundreds of times in his head through the years and this just helped him fill in the blanks. Bernie said he would bring his wife with him for Tim's court appearance in a few weeks. I couldn't wait to meet them and shake Bernie's hand.

I spent the rest of the day compiling reports for the prosecutor. Once the paperwork was finished, I reached out to Deborah's friends, most of whom I only knew by their names and the details they had provided to investigators through the years. I started with Curt Reichert.

"Curt, I just wanted to let you know that we've made an arrest in the Deborah Sheppard murder."

"Really? Who did it?"

"It was no one you guys knew. An older white guy named Tim Krajcir. He confessed and we have his DNA."

Curt fell silent.

"Are you still there?" I asked hesitantly. After a moment, I could tell he was crying.

"Yes. All these years I was afraid my roommate Murray did it. He has called me a few times over the years, but because I thought he did it, I never returned his calls. We were best friends. Lieutenant Echols, this may sound strange, but do you have his phone number?" Curt asked.

"Yes."

"I really want to call Murray and apologize. We have a lot of catching up to do."

I gave him the phone number and was surprised by his emotional reaction to the news. I'm sure he felt guilty for not believing in his friend's innocence. I was glad I could help the two of them reconnect, at least, I hoped.

I wasn't sure how Murray would react to my call, since he once was questioned as a suspect, but he seemed glad to hear from me.

"I am very pleased to hear that. You know, those guys really put me through hell."

"Yes, I know. I have read about that in the reports. On behalf of the Carbondale Police Department, let me apologize. But also understand the detectives did not know who killed Deborah. They were just doing their jobs."

"I am glad it is over and the person who did it has been caught. Thanks for taking the time to find me and let me know."

I also reached out to Randy Dickerson, who had found Deborah's body just as their relationship had begun to rekindle.

"Lieutenant Echols, not a day goes by that I don't think of her," Randy told me. "Thanks for letting me know."

I could tell he wanted to reflect about how all that he had experienced so many years ago had just ended. Next I reached out to Deborah's good friend Jo Goodson, hoping she could also put me in touch with some of Deborah's other friends.

"Lieutenant Echols, this is great news. I am so happy to hear this. You know, I talked to Deb that evening. She called me when she was leaving the Recreation Center. That was the last time we spoke. You know, her murder is why I left SIU. I will call her parents tonight. Thank you."

"Jo, I can't find a phone number for Deborah's good friend Cathy Johnson. Do you know where she might be?"

"Oh, lieutenant, Cathy was killed in a car wreck many years ago."

"I am sorry to hear that. Thanks anyhow."

It was sad to hear that one of Deborah's close friends had also died violently. Her roommate, Anthony, also was dead. And yet, so many unanswered questions were still surfacing for so many people.

But there was one case I couldn't tie up. And I couldn't get it out of my mind. Why wouldn't Tim confess to Sarah's rape? It fit his modus operandi, or MO, as they say. His abrupt denial was typical of the guilty. He had no reason to worry about more charges. The statute of limitations had run out on the case. So why not confess? More importantly, I thought, if he was holding onto this, what else could he be hiding?

9

Redemption

About a week after Tim's confession, I picked up arrest warrant 07-CF-471 from the Jackson County State's Attorney Mike Wepsiec's office. In the charges, Mike alleged that Tim had strangled Deborah with intent to kill her; strangled her knowing that his actions would kill her; strangled her knowing that his actions created a strong possibility of death or great bodily harm; strangled her during the commission of a forcible felony. I wanted to personally serve Tim with the warrant and make it another opportunity to build rapport with him. I knew he had more to hide. I just didn't know what yet.

When I got to Big Muddy to make the arrest, Lieutenant Schuler took me to the conference room where Moe and I had interviewed Tim the week before. After about an hour of waiting, I began to worry about Tim's whereabouts. *What if Tim had succumbed to the pressure and done something stupid, like hurt himself?* I wondered. I was relieved when I heard the shuffle of chains and the buzzing of door locks. Looking up, I saw Lieutenant Schuler had removed Tim's shackles so Tim could sit across from me. I showed Tim a copy of the warrant and explained it. He had few questions about the warrant. He knew how it worked.

"Hey…uh…there's something I need to correct from our conversation last week. I didn't have vaginal sex with Deborah. It was just oral."

I wondered how he could get confused on that point, seeing how his recall up to that point had been so sharp. I wondered how many other suspects later voluntarily corrected their murder confessions. His recollection fit the evidence we had from the crime scene perfectly and explained why examiners didn't find any semen on the vaginal swabs. The slip up added to my already growing suspicion about Tim's refusal to admit to Sarah's rape. *There has to be more.*

"I appreciate that information, Tim."

I didn't push him to talk about anything else, because I had not read him his Miranda rights and nothing was being recorded. But this time he wasn't as guarded. He kept the conversation going.

"So how do you think life might change for me when this story hits the news?"

"Well, it's hard to say. I really don't know. I don't know if DOC will allow you to stay at Big Muddy when you get convicted."

"I hope they do. I really like it here. This is where all the sexually dangerous inmates are kept. Well, I've been to just about every joint in this state. Guess it doesn't matter."

"Didn't you play baseball at the Menard Correctional Center?"

"Yeah. I had some pretty good years playing for the Menard Cubs."

"What do you think of the Cardinals this season?"

"Well, they're not doing as well as last year."

It was odd talking to Tim as if we were buddies. I could tell, though, that it was making him feel more at ease with me. I asked if I could snap a couple pictures of him with plans to give one to the media when we had our press conference. He put his elbows on the table, leaned forward a bit and stared at my digital camera. His face was stoic.

"Well, all right, Tim. That'll do it. I'm gonna get going. You take care."

"You too."

I called the station from my car so we could send a press release announcing to the world that after twenty-five years Carbondale Police had arrested a suspect in Deborah's murder. The release was vague. We wanted to reveal Tim's name at a press conference the next day. I talked to Bernie again and told him to be prepared if reporters called. A week earlier I had asked him to send me a picture of his daughter to use when we held the press conference. He went to his staircase, the same stairs where Deborah's sisters had listened to police tell their father about Deborah's murder all those years ago, took down an eleven-by-fourteen inch black and white portrait of Deborah and mailed it to me, picture frame and all. I took it home to see if my computer program could erase some of the damage that years of sunlight had done to the photograph. It looked almost new when I was done, but I needed a frame for the new copy. I took my wife's photo out of a gold and black picture frame that stood on our bedroom dresser.

By evening, the story led the television news. Reporters talked about the history of Deborah's case. They promised to bring the identity of the killer to the public the next day. It seemed the spotlight Tim so desperately wanted dimmed had instead begun to glare.

I tried to go to bed, but couldn't fall asleep. I was too excited. Investigators dream of resolving a murder mystery; this was my second! I said a little prayer, thanking God for His guidance in helping me—and all of those who worked on the sister cases—resolve them both. After intermittent sleep, I finally gave up. I left for work about two hours earlier than normal. My wife was concerned about my lack of sleep, but after twenty-five years of marriage, she knew how I was feeling and that I needed to get to the station and begin this day for which I had been waiting so long.

Once I got to my desk my cell phone rang. I didn't recognize the number. It was a Missouri area code.

"Hello?"

"Lieutenant Echols?"

"Yes?"

"This is Detective Jim Smith with the Cape Girardeau Police Department. How are you this morning?"

"Fine," I replied.

"I called Detective Banks and he gave me your cell number. I hope you don't mind."

"Of course not. I'm surprised he answered your call this early in the morning, he avoids mine," I said jokingly of Kevin Banks, who was one of my detectives with whom Jim had worked an unrelated case.

"I wanted to ask you about your suspect in the 1982 murder. Detective Banks said you could tell me all about him. What can you tell me?"

"His name is Timothy Wayne Krajcir. He is incarcerated in the Illinois Big Muddy Correctional Center. He is originally from Pennsylvania. He has been in jail or prison since January 1983."

"Does he have any Cape Girardeau connections? I am looking into several old murder cases here."

"So far I haven't noticed anything in his background that puts him in Cape, but I am still learning about him."

"We had three women murdered in 1977 and then two more in 1982, the same year as the Sheppard murder, and then they stopped."

"I'm guessing one of those cases is Sheila Cole's unsolved murder? I am familiar with it. As I recall, she was the girl abducted from a discount store and then found shot to death in the rest area near McClure. Maybe your guy is in prison or dead."

"I hope not. I want to arrest him. Well, I know you have a big day ahead of you. Congratulations."

"Thanks and good luck with your cases as well."

Sheila Cole's case was really the first cold case I had ever heard about. As a young boy, I often drove to Cape Girardeau, Missouri, with my mother to visit relatives. Every time we went she pointed to a rest stop that was on our way. "You know, a young college girl was found murdered there. Such a shame." Even when she wasn't with me, my mother's words echoed in my mind every time I passed the desolate rest stop along Illinois Route 3. Sheila's car was found at a discount store's parking lot in Cape Girardeau. Investigators suspected she had been kidnapped and later killed at the rest stop.

At my desk I saw the morning newspaper. The front page headline of the *Southern Illinoisan* declared: "Arrest made in 25-year-old murder case." The story was fairly short. We hadn't released any details. The reporter used a few quotes from an interview with me several weeks earlier about some of our other unsolved murders. I wondered if she would be upset now knowing I had been on the verge of solving Deborah's murder and hadn't mentioned it. But at that time, I couldn't say a word. She would have to understand.

After a brief visit to the courthouse, I returned to the police department. When I got back, the chief asked me to review his statement for the press. It was a well-done historical account of the investigation, giving credit to many.

Before long, it was time to read it to the media. A few television trucks were parked at city hall when I got there about thirty minutes early. Cameras and reporters were waiting inside. Most of them were familiar faces. I walked to a table in the corner of the room and placed Deborah's portrait there. The chief and state's attorney arrived. I stood to the left of the chief and Mike Wepsiec stood to his right. Mayor Brad Cole greeted the media and then the chief read his statement. Chief Ledbetter went through the history of Deborah's case and thanked several agencies and individuals, including the crime lab experts and me. It was his statement about Bernie, though, that meant the most to me. The chief and I had discussed how to address some of the problems that happened early on in the investigation. We agreed the best way to handle it was directly and honestly. The chief told the press:

> We owe a debt of gratitude to Bernie Sheppard and the entire Sheppard family for helping us with this case. Twenty-five years ago, Mr. Sheppard set us on the right track for this investigation. He said, "I want her murderer arrested, convicted and jailed. I don't care how much effort, money, time or heartache it takes to do it." It is truly unfortunate that we had to wait for technology to catch up in order to solve this crime. It is unfortunate that the Sheppard family has to now, again, relive their daughter and sister's death, but the end result here is Deborah Sheppard's murderer has been arrested.

Mike then read a statement, explaining how his involvement in the case dated to 1996, when Moe and Lynn Trella brought him Deborah's case file for a fresh look. He explained how the laws in effect in 1982 would apply to Deborah's murder. If the case went to trial, Tim could be sentenced to life in prison if a jury found him guilty. If the case didn't go to trial, Tim could get no fewer than twenty years but not more than forty. Reporters probed the chief and the state's attorney for more details after they read their statements. Then it was my turn. I stepped up to the mountain of microphones at the lectern. As I did, I saw my wife and daughter Morgan standing at the back of the room. Stacie and Suzanne were there, too. Monica Joost, one of the original detectives in Deborah's case, stood quietly behind the media, along with many current investigators. I knew Taylor Scott was watching the press conference live on the Internet at the DNA lab in Springfield.

"Lieutenant Echols, what can you tell us about the Sheppard family?" a reporter asked.

"Well, Deborah's parents, Bernie and Hazel, are very pleased with this arrest, but it's been hard for them after all these years to have their daughter's murder brought up again."

"Lieutenant Echols, what does it feel like to resolve two major cold cases?" another asked.

To give credit where it was due, I replied, "This was not just something I did. There were many people involved who helped resolve these cases."

After answering a few more questions I stepped back from the microphones to end the press conference. A few reporters sought me out for a few individual comments. I gave them the photo I took of Tim when I arrested him as well as copies of Deborah's picture. Later, media organizations that couldn't make it to the press conference called. I wondered how the story would come out in the media.

I was looking forward to decompressing with my family after such a big day. Sheila picked me up from work. We went to supper and to watch my daughter perform as the drum major for her high school band at a football game. My break from the day's events didn't last long. Jackson County Coroner Dr. Thomas Kupferer called me after the game. We had worked cases together through the years.

"I just saw you on the news talking about the arrest of Tim Krajcir."

"Yeah, guilty as charged."

"You know, many years ago I was friends with Tim. We worked together on the Jackson County Ambulance Service. Matter of fact, he was at my wedding and even danced with my new bride. We were all very close back then. I've gotta tell you, Paul, I'm shocked."

"Well, I can tell you, you're not alone in that. I talked to Dottie about it, too. She pretty much said the same thing as you did, that Tim was a good friend."

"Well, congratulations anyhow. What a trip."

That night, all the local television news channels carried the press conference as their lead story. My family and I watched the reports. That night sleep finally came easy. I took my time walking to our rural mailbox in the morning to get my newspaper. A photo of the chief was on the front page. I was in the background, behind his shoulder, and I was fine with that. The headline read: "Cold Case No Longer: Suspect Named in 1982 Murder."

The *Chicago Tribune* carried the story on its front page: "Justice delayed, perhaps not denied." Bernie called to tell me he had done some interviews with television stations in Chicago. He was in high spirits and had done a good job weathering the media blitz. I watched on the Internet one of the interviews he did. It was the first time I had seen his face besides the old newspaper clips. It was neat to put a face with the voice that I had talked with for four months. He had aged gracefully. The publicity and phone calls continued into the next week. Most of it focused on me. It was getting to be a bit much. The chief said that the *St. Louis Post-Dispatch* wanted to do a story on me. That was the breaking point.

"I told them the Sheppard case is not about Lieutenant Echols; it is about all the investigators who worked the case," he said.

He was right. I knew I was getting too much media attention. I gave credit to the others involved in solving the case during every interview, but the stories focused on me. And with Tim's impending arraignment on September 6, 2007, there was no sign of the attention slowing.

I wanted to personally handle Tim's intake at our jail when he arrived for his arraignment. I saw it as another chance to build more rapport with him. Corrections guards made sure to provide extra security for Tim when he arrived. I watched from the doorway of our county jail as a convoy of vehicles pulled into the parking lot with Tim in tow. Even though we weren't expecting Bernie to be there, you never know how far a father might go to avenge his daughter's death. And you never know if Tim might try to escape again. A guard walked Tim in through a sally port and toward me. Shackles dangled from his wrists and ankles. He seemed nervous when we got to the processing counter, as if he was in a foreign land unsure of where to go. I guess that's what happens when you haven't been away from prison in almost twenty years.

"How was your trip?"

"Oh, it was okay. I recognized a few things. This is new," he said, looking at the walls surrounding us.

"Well, not anymore, but it was. Do you realize that you are standing on the site of the old Jackson County Ambulance facility?"

"I knew it was in this area, but I did not realize it was right here."

"Yes, they tore it down in 1988 to make room for the new Jackson County Sheriff's Department and jail."

"That would have been the same year I came back to Illinois from Pennsylvania."

"When I spoke to Dottie Miles, well, you knew her as Dottie Wilson, she said that you worked on a crew with her and another woman. She said you guys were assigned in Murphysboro at the facility that was located here. She said you guys even slept in the same room when not responding to calls."

"I knew them both well. Those were the good days."

To keep the small talk going, I told Tim a retired prison guard who had heard about his arrest called to tell me Tim was the best basketball player he had ever seen and an outstanding baseball player. The flattery seemed to put him at ease.

"Basketball was my first love. But I was pretty good at baseball too. Sports always came easy to me."

"Did you play sports in high school?"

"No, I was already twisted back then!"

"The same retired guard told me you worked in the commissary with him when some cigarettes turned up missing. He said he was suspended because of the incident and it was you who figured out what had happened and got him out of a jam. He was quite beholding to you."

"I remember that," Tim said, as the ends of his handlebar mustache rose with his smile. "He might have lost his job if I hadn't figured out that another inmate was taking them."

I finished taking his fingerprints and filling out his paperwork. He posed for a mug shot. It was time for Tim to make his first public appearance as a killer. I walked into the tiny courtroom and sat at the prosecutor's table. The guards brought Tim in. Several reporters and onlookers filled the dozen or so seats for observers to get their first peek at Deborah's killer.

"All rise," the bailiff said. "Court is now in session."

Jackson County Associate Judge Dan Kimmel walked in. He addressed some administrative issues regarding Tim's charges and asked if he needed a public defender.

"Yes, sir," Tim said.

Judge Kimmel granted his request and set Tim's preliminary hearing for September 28, 2007. With that, Tim's first court appearance was over. The prison's security team, including Lieutenant Schuler, took Tim out of the room. Jackson County Public Defender Patricia Gross followed Tim to meet her new client for the first time. A few reporters cornered me before I left. I made some simple comments and headed to my unmarked squad car. Just then, the contingent of vehicles drove past, on their way to return Tim to Big Muddy. Tim nodded at me. I nodded back, wondering what it was like to look out a window, seeing sidewalks you knew you could never walk upon again.

I called Bernie to update him about Tim's next court date.

"We are going to be there this time."

"Well, we'll certainly have to plan on spending some time together," I said, hoping he couldn't sense the concern in my voice. I still worried that Bernie might try to hurt Tim.

"You know, we've driven by the Carbondale exit on Interstate 57 a few times over the years, but we haven't been back there since the inquest. Just seeing the word *Carbondale* on the sign brings back a flood of memories of Deborah. Hazel and I just ignored the sign and never spoke about it, but I knew she was thinking the same thing."

In their minds, Carbondale was synonymous with murder and sadness. I could never change that, but I wanted to make sure their return trip was as pleasant as possible, even though they were coming to see Deborah's killer. I made sure Bernie's reservations were at one of Carbondale's better hotels, the same one where the Schumake family had stayed. I also set up lunch with SIU's Vice Chancellor for Student Affairs, Dr. Larry Dietz, and planned for them to meet Chief Ledbetter as well as Suzanne and Stacie at the crime lab.

Preparations for Tim's upcoming hearing also continued. Investigations Secretary Lauren Rader worked feverishly for a week transcribing eighty pages of conversation between me, Moe and Tim. I spent many hours reviewing the transcripts, trying to fill in words Lauren couldn't understand. Tim's missing teeth made his words sometimes hard to understand. While reviewing them, I found the conversation about Sarah's rape. *Why was he denying it?* I thought. *He had to be hiding something. I wonder if he ever chatted with his cell mates.* I called Lieutenant Schuler to find out.

"I think Tim might have more secrets. Do you know if Tim shared a cell with anyone over the years?"

"Oh, yeah, there have been several."

"Do you think you can seek out those inmates and ask them if Tim ever talked about other crimes he committed?"

"Absolutely," Lieutenant Schuler agreed.

A few days later, he called me back.

"Hey, Paul, this is Schuler," he began. "You were right. There is more."

"What did they have to say?"

"Tim told one guy that he never hunted in his backyard and went to Cairo and Paducah to hunt. He told another guy that he did something in Pennsylvania that could get him the death penalty."

"Is that right?"

"Yes. I'm going to interview some more guys in the next few days. I'll get back to you as soon as I hear anything else."

"That's great. Thanks, Lieutenant Schuler. We'll be in touch, I'm sure."

I immediately turned to my computer to write an e-mail describing Tim's MO to send to police in Paducah and Cairo. Even though there was no mention of Cape Girardeau in Lieutenant Schuler's interviews, it was still geographically close enough to Tim's hunting grounds and I wanted to be safe. I included Cape Girardeau Lieutenant Tracy Lemonds in on the e-mail.

I am Paul Echols, Carbondale Police Investigations Commander. You might have seen on the news where we recently made an arrest in a rape/murder from 1982. As we have continued our investigation into the background of the suspect Timothy Krajcir (pronounced Kry-cher) we have learned he might have been driving down to Paducah and committing some rapes during those years. It is not impossible he might have committed a homicide if you have any unresolved during that time. I am providing a time line and his information.

As you will see, he was in and out of prison, so that will help you with your search. You can search his name on the Internet and read the stories in the news about him related to our case. He was a deviate power rapist and rarely raped women vaginally. He was more into oral sex on himself by the victim and vise-versa. In many cases he chose women who had small children and threatened to harm the children if they did not do what he demanded. He also at times wore a bandanna and was known in the Allentown, PA, area as the "Bandanna Rapist." He sometimes just touched the victim's body as he masturbated and frequently masturbated publicly. He was usually armed with a small gun. He also seemed to favor black women as victims. Part of his MO was to go to shopping centers and follow women home. I wanted to provide this info to you so you can look back at your old cases and see if you have any he might have committed. He would have been out of prison from 1976 to 1979 and then 1981 to about July 1982 when he left to return to PA where he was involved in a string of rapes and maybe one murder. Let me know if you receive this information and if you need more on him. I have a current photo and one from twenty-five years ago. Krajcir is currently incarcerated in the IL Big Muddy Correctional Center. I am available if you have any questions.
Timothy W. Krajcir
M/W DOB 11/28/1944
IL DOC #C96201
SID #IL08941720

Within hours, Tracy was the first to bite. He described a 1982 rape case about a mother who was assaulted in her home while her young daughter was there. The victim described the attacker as having a handgun, wearing a blue bandanna and demanding oral sex. The attacker threatened the woman's daughter to make the women cooperate. Tracy ended his e-mail by saying he or Detective Jim Smith would call me the following day.

Oh, yes, Jim Smith, I remembered. *He called me the morning of Deborah's press conference.* I read the e-mail again. The words "blue bandanna" perked my interest, as did the fact that the victim was a black female. While intrigued, I couldn't follow up immediately. Tim's preliminary hearing was the next day and the Sheppards were arriving in a few hours. I also had a criminal justice class to teach at the Shawnee Community College campus in Anna, about a half hour south of Carbondale. I passed the Union County Hospital on my way there, a place where Tim had worked in the 1970s with the prison's ambulance service. It seemed everywhere I turned something reminded me of Tim.

Bernie had told me he would call my cell phone when he arrived in Carbondale. I told my students I might have to take his call during class, which would violate one of the rules I had laid down to them. They kidded with me and gave me some grief. Class was almost over when my phone rang. It was late, so Bernie and I decided to meet for coffee in the morning at the hotel. On the way home, I thought about Tracy's e-mail. I couldn't wait to learn more, but I would have to.

This was one case I didn't have to review the night before the hearing. I knew it by heart. Sleep was once again elusive though. I gave up and got ready for work early. I put on my suit and tied my tie. Not only was I going to meet the Sheppards, but also I might be testifying at the preliminary hearing should Tim decide not to waive it. I wanted to look good.

I was at my desk by 7 A.M. preparing documents Moe would need to manage the detectives' daily meeting. I left him a note saying I was going to meet Bernie for coffee and then head to the hearing. *Coffee with Bernie Sheppard.* It sounded strange. Only four months ago, I didn't even know if he was alive. He was easy to find among the people milling about the hotel lobby. He was by himself sipping coffee and reading a newspaper.

"Mr. Sheppard?" I approached him.

He looked up from his newspaper.

"I'm Paul Echols."

He smiled, stood up and reached for my hand. He was a little taller than I thought, in good shape and dressed in a mint green shirt and gold patterned tie. I could see Deborah's face in her father's. She had had the same wide round brown eyes as him. Through the years, his hair had turned white, while I had lost much of mine. He sported a closely cropped goatee, which matched the color of his hair. He lightly embraced me.

"It sure is good to finally meet you."

"Bernie, it is good to finally meet you too."

I grabbed a small cup of coffee, trying not to spill it and embarrass myself. We sat and chatted about his trip and if he had found things comfortable. I laughed when he asked how long it would take to get to the courthouse, which was about ten miles away. It was typical of someone who had spent most of his life driving in the traffic jam capital of Chicago. Deborah's sister Nicole and her husband soon joined us. They were dressed professionally and seemed to be the perfect couple. Nicole's smooth, almost perfect skin and her red lipstick made her just as beautiful as Deborah had been. Hazel came down from the room and sat on a couch near the door. Bernie brought me to her. She was a very beautiful lady too. Deborah's captivating smile came from her mother, as did her petite model-worthy figure. But it was obvious Hazel was having a difficult time dealing with all that was going on. During the past few weeks, Hazel had seemed cold to me when I called. She and I had never had a conversation. The Sheppards piled into a rented mini-van to follow my unmarked car to the courthouse. On the way, Lieutenant Schuler called. His security detail escorting Tim was only about ten minutes away.

The hearing was in the same small courtroom in the jail where Judge Kimmel had arraigned Tim a few weeks earlier. When we pulled up, a few television trucks were parked outside. Reporters were standing around. We exited our cars and the family passed through metal detectors. *Whew*, I sighed. *Bernie must have left his gun at home.*

"Is he here?" Bernie asked me of Tim.

"Yes, he's in the building."

Hazel walked away from us, sat down and pulled out a book to read. She had decided she couldn't lay eyes on the evil man who had taken her daughter's life. I told one of the bailiffs to watch over her and I brought the rest of the family into a small interview room. Mike sat behind a desk across from Bernie and began to tell them about his role as state's attorney and how he was going to handle the case.

"You guys will hate me before all this is over," Mike declared. "Everyone does."

I was a bit surprised by Mike's approach, but I knew he was a good state's attorney who had tried dozens of murderers. The Sheppards had puzzled looks on their faces. Mike told them there would be delays and other things they would not understand about the process.

"I will seek your advice as we negotiate a sentence, but I will ultimately have the final say," Mike said to Bernie.

"Mr. Wepsiec, I want to make it clear here. I want the man to get the maximum sentence allowed by law. As I understand it from Paul, that would be life in prison."

"Mr. Sheppard, can I ask you a question?"

"Yes."

"Do you believe in God?"

Okay, Mike. Where are you going with this? I asked myself.

"Yes, sir, I do."

"Well, then you understand then that Mr. Krajcir will receive his maximum sentence after he is dead."

"Yes, sir, I understand that, but I am not so worried about what God does with him. I am concerned about the here and now."

The two then exchanged a few Bible verses to make their points about the afterlife. Moe walked in and shot me a look of confusion. Soon, a bailiff came to the door and told Mike that the judge was ready. I was glad the time had come.

I walked toward the prosecutor's table and sat next to Bernie. Nicole and her husband sat on his other side. Reporters filled the rest of the seats along with a few police officers. Moe stood near the doorway. Tim was wearing his blue prison uniform with leg irons and belly chains when armed guards brought him into the room. He talked quietly for a bit with his attorney. Bernie's eyes were glued on Tim. Only the prosecutor's table stood between them. I kept one hand near Bernie, just in case he tried to lunge toward Tim. Tim never looked at Bernie.

"Is the state ready to proceed, Mr. Wepsiec?" asked Circuit Judge Ron Eckiss.

"Yes, your honor, the state is ready."

"Ms. Gross, is the defense ready?"

"Your honor, I have discussed the purpose of the preliminary hearing with Mr. Krajcir and he is willing to waive his preliminary hearing and the formal reading of the charges."

The judge asked Tim a few other administrative questions to make sure he understood his rights. He answered respectfully, just as he had done with Judge Kimmel a few weeks earlier. He pled not guilty, as most criminals do to buy more time for their attorneys to negotiate deals with prosecutors who usually want to avoid trials. In this case, it made the most sense. Our evidence was solid, but most of the original investigators had passed away or had long since moved on. A jury could sentence Tim to life in prison, but there was the risk of an appeal and something could always go wrong at trial. I figured Patricia knew the evidence was good and would be willing to make a deal. The judge scheduled the trial for December 10, 2007. In minutes, the hearing was over.

Several reporters converged on Bernie as we left the courtroom. He answered their questions with ease. I was impressed with how he handled it.

"Because of what this man did, we will never know what Deborah could have contributed to this world. I will never have any grandchildren from Deborah and her sisters will never have any nieces or nephews from her. We will never know what could have been."

It dawned on me that Bernie had never said Tim's name. It was his way of showing disrespect. Hazel was still sitting to the side with tears in her eyes. It was time to get them out of there and off to the events I had scheduled for them to make them feel like the honored guests they were in our town. They followed me to the station to meet the department's top brass. Bernie, Nicole, her husband and I talked and took pictures together while Hazel stayed in the van to read. I brought them to Chief Ledbetter's office. Bernie asked Nicole to bring Hazel in. It was obvious that she was avoiding anyone associated with Deborah's death. It wasn't my place to ask why.

"I want to thank you and the Carbondale Police Department for finally bringing justice in Deborah's case," Bernie told the chief.

"Well, sir, we'd like to thank you for your persistent efforts in the early days of the investigation."

The chief had once again handled it correctly. Then I walked with the family to the crime lab, where Director Steve Klingaman greeted us. We sat at the same table where Suzanne and I had talked about Deborah's case during the taping of the *Cold Case Files* show. Now, a year and a half later, I was sitting there with the Sheppards discussing the resolution of the case. Stacie joined us. Suzanne was out of town. Bernie thanked Steve and Stacie for their work and asked that they thank all who were involved in examining the evidence through the years.

Afterward, we met Dr. Dietz at the SIU Student Center for lunch. My wife and son joined us. Everyone enjoyed themselves, just as I had hoped. When it was time to say our good-byes, Hazel unexpectedly hugged me.

"I'm sorry for not talking to you and avoiding you. It's just…it's just been so tough to relive all of this again. I can't thank you enough for all that you've done. I promise I will talk to you the next time you call to talk to Bernie."

"You're very welcome, Mrs. Sheppard, and no offense taken. I can't imagine what this must be like for you."

Bernie shook my hand.

"I want to formally invite you and your family to our home in Olympia Fields for Thanksgiving dinner. We always have a large gathering of family and a large meal. We would be honored to have you and your family at our table."

"Bernie, I'm flattered. Let me talk to my wife and I'll get back to you."

Meeting the Sheppard family was one of the highlights of my career. In murder cases, there is a feeling that is hard to describe when you bring justice to a family. It is the one small piece of salvation a family can get, because they know their loved one is never coming back. I thought of how fast things had progressed since my phone call to Bernie just months before. I would never have imagined this case would have come together as fast as it did. All I could think about on the way home was how it might have been the first of many court dates for Tim should the leads from Lieutenant Schuler and Cape Girardeau pan out.

10

Suspicion Spreads

With all of the leads developing in Tim's case, weekends were becoming my only time to jump back into my father role. My wife and I followed our daughter and the marching band to Sparta, Illinois, where they competed against several other high school bands. Her high school band had the reputation of being one of the best in the state. In Sparta, they lived up to their reputation and won several awards. To make it even more special, my daughter won the Drum Major Award. While they were celebrating the victory, my nineteen-year-old son decided to jump out of a perfectly good airplane. My wife and I had tried to discourage him from doing it, but he was dead set on it. But as my mother always said, "You have to let them live their lives." I was only able to enjoy the rest of my day after he called to report a safe landing. All of the extracurricular activities briefly took my mind away from the excitement that was building across the river in Cape Girardeau.

Lieutenant Tracy Lemonds and I settled on a Wednesday to meet and discuss Tim and his department's cold cases. Detective Jim Smith, Captain Roger Fields and Police Chief Carl Kinnison as well as Illinois State Police Lieutenant Steve Shields were expected to be there. Sheila Cole was murdered in Illinois, so the investigation had been a joint effort among the Cape Girardeau Police, Alexander County Sheriff's Department and Illinois State Police. They asked me to bring copies of my video interviews so they could get their first look at Tim, as well as a set of Tim's finger and palm prints. I told Calvin of the upcoming meeting. The deputy chief seemed excited about the possibilities too. Everything seemed to be falling into place.

Then my phone rang.

"Chief Ledbetter has denied your request to go to the meeting in Cape Girardeau," Calvin said.

"Why?" I asked, unable to hide my annoyed tone.

"He doesn't want you to miss his command staff meeting Wednesday. You'll have to wait until Thursday to go."

I could feel my blood pressure begin to rise. I felt it would be a fairly routine weekly meeting. Calvin could've easily covered for me. But the chief wanted me there to update everyone on several active murder investigations. There was no changing it. Tracy was frustrated too, after having coordinated everyone's schedules to meet. He said I should still come Thursday.

I couldn't get out of the station fast enough that morning to take off to Cape Girardeau. I drove west to Illinois Route 3 and then south, paralleling the Mississippi River for the forty-five minute ride. Several farmers were working in their fields harvesting the fall crops against the backdrop of the changing colors of the Shawnee National Forest that lined the horizon to the east. I crossed the Mississippi River on the Bill Emerson Memorial Bridge, a modern four-lane, four-year-old cable-stayed bridge. As I had done hundreds of times, I looked down at the beautiful river town overlooking the mighty Mississippi River about 100 miles south of St. Louis. Like Carbondale, it too is a college town. About 10,000 students attend Southeast Missouri State University. About 37,000 people call Cape Girardeau home. It is considerably older than Carbondale, with pockets of beautiful Victorian architecture scattered in some areas. Jean Baptiste de Girardot founded the town as a trading post along the river in 1733. The city also is known as "The City of Roses," because a nine-mile stretch of highway that ran through town was once lined with rose bushes.

I knew the town well. I was born and raised in Ullin, only about a half hour east of Cape. Some of my earliest childhood memories include Christmas shopping with my family at the town plaza. Somehow, my three sisters and I were able to buy gifts for one another with the five dollars our dad gave us. He sat in the car as my mother shopped with us. Most of the time we ended up at the dime store to find our gifts. Along with all the fond moments I shared with my father there, the town also harbored my last memory of him. He passed away in Cape Girardeau's Southeast Missouri Hospital in November 1972. It was the last time I saw him. My sister later became a nurse at the same hospital and raised her daughter in Cape. My niece also became a nurse and worked in the obstetrics unit there. I met the love of my life in Cape one fall night while barhopping with friends. When my wife and I started dating, we spent every weekend in Cape as our relationship grew. So many important milestones in my life took place there.

My reminiscing ended as I pulled up to the white brick and mirrored glass building that the Cape Girardeau Police Department has called home since 1975. Once inside, I followed Tracy to his chief's office. Just past a large conference table, my former SIU classmate, now police chief, Carl Kinnison was sitting in a black high-back chair behind his wooden desk. We shook hands. It was always great to see Carl. I had often seen him on television acting as his department's public information officer through the years. He really didn't look too much different than he did when we shared a criminal justice class at SIU.

"Paul, thanks for coming over. Tracy and Jim have been keeping me updated on the information about this Krajcir guy. This sounds very interesting."

Two more men walked into the chief's office. Carl introduced us.

"Paul, let me introduce you to Detective Jim Smith. He is our cold case investigator."

"Detective Smith, nice to finally meet you," I said.

"Good to finally meet you too, lieutenant."

I appreciated the respect he showed by acknowledging my rank, but it was apparent Jim was my senior. He was a tall, medium complexioned man with distinctive snow white hair and dark almond-shaped eyes. His handshake was firm. His expression was serious. He was dressed in a neatly pressed button-down white shirt and a red tie, looking much younger than his age.

In 1992, Jim got the position he had coveted for years and became a detective. He noticed several three-ring binders that were falling apart on a shelf in the copy room. One day he began looking through them. Inside, he found the cases of five unsolved murders. Jim was not in town at the time of the murders, so he tapped veteran Lieutenant John Brown, who had spent much of his career pursuing the killer or killers.

"If you want to read the case files go ahead," Brown told him. "If you solve them, it'd be the greatest thing to ever happen in the history of the Cape Girardeau Police Department."

For the next several years, Jim took the reports home to read them on his own time, just as I had done with the unsolved Carbondale cases. After Lieutenant Brown retired, Jim became the department's unofficial cold case detective. He reorganized the three-ring binders and they became part of the environment around his desk.

We had much in common and it was good to finally meet him. I wanted him to be comfortable with me, so I asked him to forgo the rank.

"Just call me Paul."

Carl then introduced me to the other man, who was in uniform. I immediately noticed the white shirt, black tie and two gold bars on each collar reserved only for police commanders.

"Paul, this is Captain Roger Fields. He is in charge of our investigations division."

"Captain, nice to meet you."

"The honor is all mine," he said smiling.

I sat on the window side of the conference table with Jim and Carl. Roger and Tracy sat across from us. The office was nice, but somewhat small, making the conversation feel a bit more intimate and intense. Carl started it off.

"Paul, after reviewing what you sent to us describing Tim Krajcir, it appears he could be the person who raped a young woman here in January 1982. We have looked through our records and as far as we know we have never had any contact with him. What can you tell us about Tim Krajcir?"

I outlined what I knew about Tim and provided some details from his confession about how he killed Deborah. When I asked a few questions about the rape Carl had mentioned, everyone deferred to Jim. It was obvious he knew the case the best, so I directed my questions to him.

"How did you find this case so fast?"

"This case was associated many years ago with the murders of Margie Call and Mildred Wallace, two of the cold cases I have been investigating."

In 2003, after the Southeast Missouri Crime Laboratory received a grant to test old cases for DNA, Jim helped submit some of the evidence from the murders. This included a rape kit taken from the body of Marjorie "Margie" Call, several pieces of fabric cut from her bedding, a cigarette butt found outside the crime scene, a leather shoelace used to bind and likely strangle Margie, some of her clothing and some hairs found on her body that were not hers. Unfortunately, no DNA was found in her case and only partial profiles were obtained from another—not enough to enter into the CODIS database. Jim asked the lab to consider processing an unknown pubic hair found on Margie's neck for DNA, but the crime lab deferred testing the hair, saying it was unlikely to yield a full profile. This frustrated Jim, to say the least. But he too was at the lab's mercy. In March 2007, Jim was officially assigned as a cold case detective and resubmitted several items from both cases. This time, the lab developed a full DNA profile in Mildred's case and a partial profile in Margie's case. Still, no matches were made among several suspects he submitted and no match was found in CODIS.

Jim explained that he also had been investigating three other murders that had occurred in 1977. They included the Sheila Cole case, with which I was familiar, and Mary and Brenda Parsh, a mother and daughter. While it was looking like Tim may have been involved in the rape of a woman named Holly Jones, no one really wanted to consider him as a serious suspect in the five murders—at least not yet. Jim had found Holly's rape report tucked into Mildred Wallace's murder file. Once again, Jim explained.

"Holly's case was placed into the file just because it happened around the same time frame. No physical evidence has ever been linked between Holly's case and the murders. The only evidence we've ever had that seemed to link any of the cases was the make and caliber of the gun used to murder Mary and Brenda Parsh and Sheila Cole. Margie Call was not shot; she was strangled with a leather shoelace. Mildred Wallace was shot, but the FBI said she was shot with a different gun. The four victims who were shot were all shot in the head."

Jim had my attention. I was impressed by his recall of exact dates and details. He knew these cases as well as I had gotten to know Deborah's.

"What kind of gun did the FBI think was used to kill the women?"

Jim looked through some folders he brought to the meeting, all meticulously organized. There was no shuffling of the paperwork. He knew right where to find it.

"Here's what they said in the Cole case. It was a .38 special lead bullet, which was fired from the barrel of a weapon rifled with eight lands and groves, right twist. The FBI said the gun might be a revolver. The FBI said the bullets did not bear sufficient individual microscopic marks of value for identification purposes. So they couldn't say with certainty if the same gun was used to kill the Parshes, but they said it likely was."

I remembered that when John Kluge arrested Tim for sexual abuse of his landlord's daughters, he had searched his trailer and seized two guns. I wanted to check what types of guns were in Kluge's report before getting anyone's ears up for what could be a false alarm.

"Thanks, Jim. We can talk more after you guys watch the video," I said.

Roger put in the DVD of Tim's confession and suddenly, bigger than life on the chief's television screen was Tim in his blue prison uniform. Tim's soft voice filled the room. Jim slid me a three-ring binder containing Holly Jones's rape report. At the same time, I handed him Tim's finger and palm prints. The others watched the interview intently as I dove into the report.

The report detailed that Holly Jones kept her mopping bucket under a leaky drain in her kitchen. Her ten-year-old daughter was watching television in the front room when Holly opened her back door to throw the water out. A man then pushed her back into her kitchen. The thirty-four-year-old screamed as the stranger pushed his way in, closed the door and grabbed her.

"Don't look at me," the man's soft yet intimidating voice told her.

She turned away but could see that he had dark hair and something covering his face. She could smell a hint of cigarette smoke on him. She told detectives: "He was kind of dark complected, not olive skin, but kinda dark complected, kinda ruddy skin looking. Mighta been the cold, ruddy looking or something and that is all I remember right then. His voice was kinda soft. It wasn't a feminine voice, but it wasn't like a husky or deep voice. It was a soft voice."

As I was reading, Tim's voice echoed throughout the conference room where we had gathered to watch his confession to Deborah's murder. *She described his voice to a T*, I thought. Holly's daughter heard her mother's scream and ran into the kitchen. He ordered both of them to the living room floor and warned them to be quiet.

"I've been watching you. I know you're not married and there's no man living here," he told Holly.

Eventually, he took both of them upstairs, where he made them lie on a bed and covered them with a bedspread. Holly told detectives:

He kinda laid on the bed, like this, and then he pulled off his pants…At first he's telling me don't look at me, don't try to see him or anything. That's when he said, take off your clothes and make it a good show. Then at first I was trying to talk to him and I told him I was a Jehovah's Witness. I just could not do some of the things he's asking and he said, you do it and you won't get hurt. You give me any trouble and you and the kid get it and everything else. I took off my clothes.

He ordered Holly to perform oral sex on him as her daughter lay next to her with her head still covered by the bedspread. Holly resisted, telling him it was against her religion and she didn't know how to do it. So he provided step-by-step instructions as she tried to please him.

And he wanted me to start in with a blow job again and then he made me lay on the bed for a while and he was you know, using his tongue and everything on me and then got up off the bed and he sat down and he said, "Why don't you just stick your finger up my ass." I said, "What?" And he said, "Take your finger and stick it up my ass." I took my finger, you know, and stuck my fingers up there and then he started wanting a blow job again.

Holly tried to get her attacker to take her to another bedroom away from her daughter so she would not have to listen to the assault. She also wanted to try to defend herself: "I kept trying to get him to the other room. First of all, because I have a hammer under my bed and I wanted to see if he was real relaxed and at that point both of his hands was free, so he didn't have the gun."

But her attempts to get him out of the room and away from her daughter failed. At one point, the man told Holly that her daughter should join in. He promised not to rape her, he just wanted to see her naked. Holly was able to keep him distracted. At one point, she pretended to get sick, so he allowed Holly to use the bathroom and take some medicine from her purse. She continued to look for weapons but never found anything she felt confident to use. As soon as the suspect climaxed, the assault ended. He let Holly put on her housecoat before tying her and her daughter up and warning them not to move for about fifteen minutes or call the police. As soon as she felt the man was out of her house, Holly called her brother. Then she called the police.

I tried to imagine the terror Holly must have endured in those moments. I couldn't help but think how courageous she was to do what she needed to survive, protect her daughter and provide such detail to police. I was also pretty convinced that Tim was her attacker. The MO was very similar to Sarah's rape, which he had denied. It also fit some of the things Tim had done in the past that he had confessed to Moe and me.

"So what do you think about that rape case?" Jim asked after the video of Tim's interview ended.

"I think it could be him. But what about Missouri's statute of limitations? In Illinois, a case like this couldn't be prosecuted."

"Our prosecutor tells us we are good. By 1982, in Missouri there was no statute of limitation for the crime of rape," Carl said.

"Are you guys still holding any evidence in this case?"

"Yes. We should have Holly's coat and a few other things that were collected as evidence. It appears he ejaculated on her coat and that is in our evidence room. We plan on sending that to the lab over the next few days," Jim said.

"Okay, well, gentlemen, my plan is to continue to dig deeper into interviews with Tim's cell mates. I'll let Jim know if I find out anything new."

"I'd like to interview Tim. Would you be willing to go with me?" Jim asked.

"Of course."

"I'd really like to go at him with a DNA match, so we'll hold off until the Missouri crime lab can get a look at the evidence," Jim said.

With that, we shook hands and it was time for me to head back to Carbondale. As I turned north on Illinois Route 3, I noticed the rest area where Sheila Cole had been murdered. I thought of how senseless her murder had been and of all the times my late mother reminded everyone of the "poor young girl" who was murdered there. She never knew Sheila, but it looked like her son might be getting to know her case a lot better. I also thought about the gun Jim described. I couldn't wait to see what kind of gun Kluge took from Tim's trailer in February 1979. *Could it be the same gun used in the three Cape murders?* I wondered. But I still needed to confirm Tim had even been to Cape Girardeau. I wondered if his work with the ambulance service ever brought him there. It was time to visit Dottie again.

"Hey, Dottie, how's it going?" I started the conversation as I entered her office.

"Fine. How's Tim? Have you seen him lately?"

"I saw him last week. He's doing fine. Dottie, can we talk in confidence for a moment?"

"Of course. Just a moment; let me shut my office door. What's up?"

"Dottie, when Tim worked for the Jackson County Ambulance Service, would he have gone to Cape Girardeau very often?"

"Oh, I don't really know how often, but we did transports to both the Southeast Missouri and St. Francis hospitals. So yes, we went there. Why?"

"It's still too soon to say, but there is a chance that Tim is responsible for some crimes down there."

"You're kidding."

"No, I'm afraid I'm not. It's still too early to know so please don't say anything."

"I won't. You know, I remember something else. Back in those days you could only buy a certain beer west of the Mississippi. Tim really liked that special beer. So I know we made trips down there to get it."

"Any particular place?"

"No, not that I can recall. Tim went by himself sometimes. In fact, on a few occasions we went across the Mississippi River in a boat from Grand Tower. I had an uncle who owned a bar on the other side of the river. We bought the beer from him."

"Damn, you guys wanted that beer awful bad!"

"Well, we were young and, in some ways, stupid back then. Don't know now when I last saw a can of that beer."

We both laughed at the dedication to obtain the beer. It had been almost three decades since they made their beer runs. The beer had lost its notoriety since it was now available on both sides of the Mississippi River. I told her I would try to stop in soon and talk a bit further about Tim, but with everything that was going on, it would be sometime in the future.

As soon as I got back to my office, I pulled the search warrant that Kluge did on Tim's trailer on February 21, 1979. Ten items were listed. I did not have to read far; the gun Holly described was listed first: "One (1) Revolver, .38 blued, 5 shot Model 1382 with a 2" barrel, undercover." John also had recovered another gun, a small silver .25 caliber semiautomatic.

Damn! I thought. *Did John seize the gun that killed the three women in Cape?* It was the same kind of gun for which the FBI had told them to look. *Better yet, have we stored the gun Cape Girardeau has spent thirty years looking for in our evidence room?* I knew from my days working and supervising the evidence room that our department generally wouldn't have kept the gun for more than a year. It was likely destroyed, because Tim couldn't have ever claimed the gun, because he was a convicted felon. It was a long shot, but I had to look. The evidence technician searched for it but found no record of the gun. The archived evidence sheets were gone too. But I had to know if the gun Kluge seized was even in the same ballpark as the one investigators believed was used in the murders. I sent an e-mail to a good friend of mine who was a firearms expert. He said the undercover revolver Kluge recovered would have been a gun with a barrel that had eight lands and grooves that would have spun the bullet to the right when it was fired. This was consistent to what Cape police had been seeking. It was what I feared. It appeared our department may have found the gun used in the murders of Mary and Brenda Parsh and Sheila Cole. The find was intriguing, but that type of gun was too common to be a definite link.

I dug deeper to understand the timing of when Tim acquired the gun. In the reports that Joe Kocevar had sent me from Pennsylvania was a note that Kluge had made about how both guns he had seized had been purchased by a woman named Betsy. Kluge had interviewed her in March 1979. She was a nurse at the Carbondale Hospital and was friends with Tim. She bought the .38 revolver for Tim a year earlier per his request. She said Tim was very particular about the type of gun he wanted, claiming that he was planning a trip to Pennsylvania and wanted it for protection and to hunt. The word "hunt" jumped off the page at me. *No one hunts with a .38 caliber handgun unless they are hunting people*, I thought. Betsy also said Tim gave her the money to buy the gun and that she had bought the .25 automatic gun for Tim from another ambulance worker in Williamson County and gave it to Tim as a birthday gift. I had to talk to her.

"Tim was a nice guy with a sweet disposition," she said.

"Well, it appears there were two Tims. The other Tim was a murderer."

She couldn't believe what I was telling her. She remembered buying the guns for Tim, because he said he couldn't buy the guns for himself. She didn't know why and she didn't ask. She said she thought she had bought the gun in 1978, the year before Tim was arrested. I drove to the gun shop where Betsy said she had bought it. The manager said the records were long gone. If she bought the gun, it couldn't have been used in Cape Girardeau. But I couldn't be sure.

I kept Jim and Tracy informed of my search for what became of the murder weapon as well as another lead that was developing. The Paducah Police Department in Kentucky had responded to my e-mail regarding Tim's MO. Investigative Assistant Malinda Elrod said they had been searching through their old rape and murder cases and found a murder in June of 1981 that was consistent with the information she read in my e-mail.

"There are notes in the case file where investigators commented that it was similar to the Call and Wallace murders in Cape Girardeau," she said.

"Really? In what ways?"

"The victim was a seventy-four-year-old white female who was raped and murdered. I'll send you the report so you can read it. We're currently reassessing evidence to determine if there is any DNA to compare against Tim Krajcir. I'll be in touch to let you know what we find."

"Great and thanks for following up on this. We'll be in touch, I'm sure."

I reviewed the case. And, as Malinda had noted, there were some similarities to the Call and Wallace murders. The victim was an older lady who lived alone. The intruder broke in through the back of the house and raped and strangled her.

I was more interested to see what the evidence from Holly's rape case might yield once the Missouri State Police Crime Laboratory had a look at it. Jim asked me to put together a photo lineup including a photograph of Tim from the time period to see if Holly could identify Tim after all these years. With all the time that had passed and the fact that her rapist had covered his face, it was a long shot, but they felt they had nothing to lose. Jim struggled, as do most investigators, with taking the photos to Holly and reopening a wound that time had perhaps begun to heal. At least he wasn't going into the interview with Holly as a stranger. They had worked together years ago. She agreed to meet Jim at the police department to view the lineup. Unfortunately, Holly couldn't pick Tim from the photos.

"Jim, that's too bad. Maybe the crime lab will find semen on some of the evidence so you can get a DNA profile. Speaking of that, didn't you say in 2003 you had some evidence in your 1982 murders of Margie Call and Mildred Wallace?"

"Yes, but we did not have much luck then. Since then, I have resubmitted some evidence and we now have a partial profile in the Call case and a full profile in the Wallace case. But none of our suspects matched and nothing matched in the national database. What are your thoughts on comparing Tim's DNA?"

"Technically, he has been compared if your lab person ran your full profile through CODIS. But you're right; we need to compare him directly."

"Maybe your DNA person in Illinois can talk to my person in Missouri."

"Better yet, can you fax your lab reports on Call and Wallace to me?"

"Sure, they are on the way."

It was very discouraging that the unknown profile from Mildred's crime scene had not matched Tim's profile in the national database. Still, I wanted to see the codes with my own eyes. There were several items processed for DNA in that case, including blood found at the bottom of a window where investigators believed the attacker cut himself while breaking in. Also, there was a box of bandages on the bathroom counter that was thought to have blood on it. Experts also processed a leather bootlace used to bind Mildred's hands as well as fingernail scrapings from each of her hands. And last, a stain from Mildred's right thigh was collected. Jim had collected and compared DNA standards from fifteen suspects developed through the years against the partial DNA profile. All had been eliminated. I could tell investigators had been very busy, just like we had been with Deborah's case. It amazed me how many suspects had been considered in both Deborah's and Mildred's cases.

The DNA report from the Missouri State Highway Patrol Crime Laboratory was quite different from the Illinois State Police Crime Laboratory reports, which I was accustomed to reading. The DNA codes weren't on the report as commonly found on the Illinois reports. Jim told me to call DNA expert Stacey Bollinger in Jefferson City, Missouri, because she had worked the cases. I didn't know why I felt the need to see the codes, but I did that in the investigation of Susan Schumake's case and identified the murder suspect, who was not in the national database. I just had that gut feeling. I wasn't sure how my call would be received but I made it anyway.

"Hello, Stacey, my name is Paul Echols," I introduced myself when she answered the phone. "I am a lieutenant with the Carbondale Illinois Police Department. I am working with the Cape Girardeau Police Department on some of their cold murder cases and an old rape case."

"Yes, the Southeast Missouri crime lab called and told me about the old rape case and about a suspect you guys arrested in a 1982 murder case in Illinois. What can I do for you?"

"Jim sent me the DNA reports you wrote in the DNA analysis in the Mildred Wallace case. I was looking for the DNA codes you developed. In Illinois, they are part of the report, but it appears you don't include them with the Missouri reports?"

"No, we don't put those on our reports."

"Can you send me those codes? I want to compare them to Tim Krajcir's profile that I have."

There was dead silence. I was about to see if she had hung up on me when she finally responded. Her tone had changed to slightly condescending.

"Isn't your guy in CODIS?"

"Yes."

"Well…it can't be him. I searched CODIS and there were no matches. Sorry I couldn't be of any help to you. Bye."

I put the phone back in the cradle and sat back with a blank look, thankful my door was shut and no one could see me. It was quite apparent that Stacey didn't want to discuss the case. I started to rethink whether Tim really could be our guy. The DNA profile was almost certain to have originated from the suspect. Cape police speculated that the same suspect had killed all five women, but they could never be sure. Almost five years had lapsed between the other two murders. *Maybe Tim was responsible for at least some of them?* I thought. *Tim had been out of prison during each murder, but could it just be a coincidence?* As I sat there thinking, I realized my conversation with Stacey had been solely on Mildred's case, because it had the full profile. I had forgotten to ask about Margie Call's case, about which Jim said the lab developed a partial profile. I hated to call again. It had only been about a minute since she hung up on me.

"Hello?" she answered.

"Stacey, this is Lieutenant Echols again. I am sorry to bother you, but I forgot to ask you about the Marjorie Call murder. Jim said you guys were able to get a partial profile in her case which was not enough to search through CODIS. Can you send me that partial profile?"

Once again there were a few seconds of silence.

"Do you have your guy's profile?"

"Yes."

"Well, just send it to me and I will look."

She might as well have told me to quit bothering her. To make it even worse, I didn't have a paper copy of Tim's DNA profile. All I had was a digital photograph of the computer screen that I took at the crime lab on the day I received the DNA hit in Deborah's case. *Oh boy, how do I explain this to her?*

"Stacey, I have Tim Krajcir's DNA codes, but I don't have them on a report."

"What do you mean?"

"Well, I have not received the report from the lab yet. But I do have a photograph of the computer screen showing his DNA codes. It does not show Tim's name."

"You have what?" she asked, confused.

"Well, the printer was not working the day we received the DNA hit on Tim, so I had a camera with me and I took a picture of the computer screen that showed the hit. I can e-mail it."

There was that silence again.

"Just send me the picture."

Then she reluctantly gave me her e-mail address and said good-bye. I felt so odd about the conversation. All I could do was hope she would look at the profiles. I was at her mercy. Stacey, a criminalist for the Missouri crime lab, had never received a DNA profile in a picture before. Her current responsibility was working homicide cases and training new DNA experts. She began her career with the Missouri Highway Patrol Criminal Records Division in 1998 after graduating with her bachelor of science degree in biology from Central Missouri State University. Her first job was entering fingerprint cards. She was later promoted to the position of laboratory technician, which brought her to prisons and to probation and parole offices to collect blood samples from those convicted of violent and sexual offenses to be entered into CODIS.

A couple years later, she became a criminalist and began to work DNA cases. She had worked with the evidence from Mildred and Margie's crime scenes, but because the evidence was old and had not been preserved very well, she struck out in finding a full DNA profile for CODIS. She thought, and hoped, she would never see those cases again. Old evidence is difficult to work with and is rarely successful. She felt it was a waste of her time to look at something she had already done.

Reluctantly, she printed the picture of the computer screen with Tim's DNA profile and sat down to compare it against the partial profile from the Call case that wasn't strong enough to enter into CODIS. Stacey had looked at the profiles so many times that she knew there were some similarities between them right off the bat. Then she compared the profile against the full profile from the Wallace case that she had run through CODIS. She was floored. She went through the codes three or four times. Ten of the thirteen genetic markers were consistent. But she didn't want to make any rash decisions or place any bias on the profiles, so she showed them to some of her fellow analysts. All of them agreed that it appeared Tim was the killer. It was time to tell Jim. She had mixed feelings about the find. She felt a little relief because she might now be done with the case. She also felt a little guilt, which is best told in her words: "If it hadn't been for Lieutenant Echols' persistence, we would have never done the comparison and established additional information for the investigators."

It was almost the end of the day and Jim was preparing to leave his office when his phone rang. He hesitated on answering, debating on whether to let the call go to his voicemail and deal with it the next day. Instead, he picked up.

"Detective Smith, this is Stacey Bolinger with the Missouri State Highway Patrol Crime Lab. I've compared the profile from the Wallace case to Tim Krajcir's profile that Lieutenant Echols sent and I must tell you that I'm rather excited about it."

"Well, just how excited are you?"

"I'm pretty excited. I think the DNA from the Wallace crime scene is that of Tim or that of a sibling."

"Well, he has two half brothers, so he doesn't have a full-blooded sibling."

"I'll need to do more testing, but it looks like Tim Krajcir is your guy. I need a buccal swab directly from him before I can be more certain. See if you can get one to me. I'll call you back in a couple days."

After hanging up the phone, Jim sat back in his chair and looked around. Some of the other detectives were still in the office, totally oblivious to the significance of the phone call. Many things ran through Jim's mind. With that one simple call, Mildred Wallace's killer had been identified. The unknown coward who had raped and then shot her in the head now had a face and a name: Tim Krajcir. A tear came into Jim's eye. He felt a deep sense of utter disbelief that this could really be happening. The moment he had waited so long for had finally arrived. He quickly shook off the emotion and walked into Captain Roger Fields' office to tell him the news. Roger was speechless. The two went to their chief's office and delivered the news to Carl. Jim didn't stick around to see his chief's reaction. He went back to his desk and called me. I was looking up a report in records when I saw Jim's phone number on my cell phone.

"Paul, Jim Smith. Do you have a minute?"

"Sure, what's up?"

"I just got off the phone with Stacey. Krajcir seems to be our man in the Wallace case. She said there's a strong probability that the blood found on Ms. Wallace's bathroom window belongs to Tim. She said she matched ten of thirteen loci. She needs a buccal swab for further tests to confirm it."

It was one of those times when I wanted just to yell out with joy. While Stacey had been careful with her words, I just knew it was a match. Lab experts are good at hiding their true emotions or committing when there is still some work to be done. They're trained in black and white. Even though she knew statistically that Tim killed Mildred, she couldn't commit until final testing was done.

Later I consulted with my friends at the Illinois State Police Crime Laboratory to understand why Stacey didn't get a match when she entered the genetic codes from the Wallace case into CODIS earlier that year. They told me that when Stacey entered her genetic codes into the CODIS through her Missouri entry point, the computer was set for high sensitivity to keep the number of close matches to a minimum. But with that setting, only a perfect match would have come up. The three markers that did not match Tim's genetic profile were likely due to an interpretation issue, routinely encountered when evidence is degraded over time or when there is a mixed stain. I suspected there was more to this issue, but all I could do at that moment was wish I was with Jim to share a high five or at least a good firm handshake. His hard work and the work of many others before him was finally paying off. It was my honor to share this moment with them.

"Jim, this is great! I took two buccal swabs when I swabbed Krajcir in the Sheppard case, so I have an extra. I'll get the state's attorney's permission to give it to you."

Experts generally need only one swab to establish a DNA standard, but the sterile swabs are packaged in pairs, so we always use both. I hung up the phone. My excitement paled in comparison to what was going on across the river. For the first time in thirty years, there was a break in the murders that had haunted the Cape Girardeau community for decades. Finally, evidence had linked a suspect to one of the murders. Still, a lot of work was ahead before we could tell the world. In the back of everyone's mind was the question: Did Tim kill all of them?

11

It's Official

Mike Wepsiec didn't hesitate to give me permission to give Tim's second buccal swab to Stacey in the Missouri crime laboratory. I walked to the crime lab and met with Suzanne Kidd to get the swab that contained Tim's genetic profile. She was excited to hear that Tim might be connected to some of Cape's cases. After all, her work in finding the DNA on Deborah's shirt had played a significant part in this. I asked her to call Stacey at the Missouri crime lab and discuss the tentative DNA match. Later, after speaking with Stacey, Suzanne called to tell me that it was her opinion the DNA would match once some technical issues were ironed out. I also called Stacey to let her know I was bringing the buccal swab to Jim. This time, Stacey was excited to hear from me, unlike the previous two times. She said she would test everything once she received the buccal swab and let us know if Tim definitely was our guy.

Jim met me in the lobby of his department when I arrived with Tim's sample. As always, we shook hands. Each time I was amazed at how big and strong his hands felt. On our way toward his office, he stopped and directed me into a small sound-proof room used for polygraph examinations. Looking around, I was amused by the shag carpeting lining the walls to help soundproof the room.

He leaned toward me. "Paul, I want to talk to you."

Taking a deep breath, Jim looked me in the eye and exhaled. "I want your opinion. Do you really think this Krajcir guy is responsible for Mildred Wallace's murder?"

"Yes, I'm convinced," I told him. "I spoke with Stacey again yesterday. I also had Suzanne Kidd, the DNA expert of the Illinois State Police lab call and talk to her. Stacey won't totally commit, but Suzanne tells me this looks very good. From a statistical standpoint, it is highly unlikely to be anybody else."

He nodded. It was exactly what Jim wanted to hear. His voice rose.

"I want to go out in the hallway and run up and down yelling this news. But I know I can't. We have to wait until Stacey gets her tests done. I've experienced a lot of frustration trying to pursue these cases. Your detectives are very lucky to have you as their lieutenant."

"Thanks, Jim. That's quite a compliment."

Afterward, we went to his office where Jim signed my evidence receipt and I turned over the manila envelope sealed with red evidence tape. As I left, Jim was preparing to send the file to Stacey. When I got back to my office, I got busy catching up on unrelated cases and administrative paperwork. Tim was certainly on my mind, but my other duties did not stop; they had to get done. Just before I left for the day to teach at Shawnee College, Records Clerk Rhonda Gaugh called me.

"Paul, there's a Lieutenant Schuler at my desk to see you. He said you'd know what it's about."

"Thanks, Rhonda, I'll be right down."

I was surprised Lieutenant Schuler was at our station. He had never been here before. It must be about Tim Krajcir. I heard his booming voice echo in our stairwell as I approached the door.

"Hey, Paul, I had to bring some evidence to the Illinois State Police crime lab, so I thought I would drop by and see you."

"Come on up, lieutenant."

I shut my office door so we wouldn't be interrupted. He was carrying some paperwork. I hoped it was for me.

"I was going to fax these to you, but since I was coming to Carbondale, I thought I'd just deliver them personally. I've interviewed a few more of Tim's old cell mates. I think there're some things here that you'll find interesting."

Schuler gave me several pages of his handwritten reports. I wanted to read them, but unfortunately it was getting late and I had to drive to Anna, Illinois, to meet the schedule for the criminal law class I taught. I'd have to wait until I got home to read the accounts. I told him about the possibility that Tim was connected with other cases and the DNA match in Mildred's murder. He was excited.

"Paul, are you okay with my advising the warden about this?"

"Sure, I know you need to keep him in the loop. Just tell him we have a lot of work to do yet before Tim can be charged, so I can't risk the danger of Tim finding out about this. We should have something firm back from the Missouri DNA lab in a few weeks and then we'll want to come talk to Tim. We'll want to ambush him."

"Oh, that won't be a problem. No one else inside the facility will know about it. I still have a few more interviews to do with Tim's cell mates, so I'm sure we will be talking."

I escorted Lieutenant Schuler back downstairs. We shook hands. Like Jim and me, the lieutenant was getting caught up in all that was unfolding. Having someone like him inside of the prison to help us was a huge asset. We were very lucky. I finished up a few last minute things at my desk and quickly put Schuler's reports in a folder. Then I headed out the door for class. It would be an early dismissal for my students tonight and they would have no idea why.

When I finally got home, I devoured a quick supper and settled into my recliner to read Schuler's reports. The inmates said Tim never confessed to any murders and kept specific details to himself. But he didn't keep everything a secret. One inmate revealed that Tim once told him Tim could never let himself be paroled, because he was too dangerous and would no doubt hurt people again. Tim also told the inmate that if he ever got tired of being in an Illinois prison, he would confess to some serious crimes he did in Pennsylvania and they would come get him. Tim told the cell mate that he preferred to rape black women over white women. This was consistent with the attack on a young black female in Pennsylvania and with Deborah Sheppard's murder. It was also consistent with the attack on Holly Jones, but the cell mate said Tim never mentioned anything about crimes in Kentucky or Missouri. Though Tim bragged about certain facts of his crimes, he never gave any one of his cell mates enough information to jam him up.

As I began to read a second inmate's interview, two words jumped off the page at me: *Jehovah's Witness*. Tim told a cell mate he had raped a "Jehovah's Witness." *Damn! That fits,* I realized. Holly had told her attacker she couldn't do some of the sexual things he wanted, because she was a Jehovah's Witness! There were too many things lining up for it to be just a coincidence. My eyes opened even wider when the inmate reported that Tim said it was the second time he had raped the woman. I didn't recall Jim telling me Holly had been raped twice, nor did I remember seeing it in the report. I wanted to check the report again, but it was too late to call Jim or so I thought. Unbeknownst to me, he was having trouble sleeping, too.

Once again, I got in to work about an hour early. As I was parking my truck, my cell phone rang. It was 7:14 A.M. and the caller was someone from the Cape Girardeau Police Department.

"Hello?" I answered.

"I didn't wake you, did I?" asked Jim's now familiar voice.

"No, I'm just arriving at work."

"Well, I have been up for a while. I can't stop thinking about Krajcir. I'm having trouble sleeping."

"Well, I can relate—why do you think I am almost an hour early coming to work? I can't remember the last time I slept well! Can you fax me the preliminary report in Holly's rape case, the part I read yesterday? There's something I need to look at and then I will get back to you."

"No problem, man. I'll get that to you within the next few minutes. I wanted you to know we took Tim's finger and palm prints to David Warren, the latent print examiner, at the lab. Tracy and Dave were part of the team who processed the 1982 Call and Wallace homicides."

"Did he lift the palm print from Ms. Wallace's window?"

"No, Curt Casteel was the guy who lifted the print, but Dave was there. In fact, Chief Kinnison was there that day."

"Well, I hope he makes the print. Krajcir will be screwed."

"Yes, he will. I'll fax that report to you now," he said and we hung up.

As I prepared for my daily briefing with detectives, I went downstairs to get Jim's fax. Scanning it quickly, I found the sentence I was looking for: "Then at first I was trying to talk to him and I told him I was a Jehovah's Witness. I just could not do some of the things he's asking and he said, you do it and you won't get hurt." I read the rest of the report but never saw anything about this being a second rape. I had to go to an investigations meeting before I could call Jim back. This was going to get his attention.

As soon as I was free I dialed his number. "Hey, Jim. Got a second?"

"Yesssss I do." Jim's passion for the cases and connecting the dots was contagious.

"Are you sitting down?"

"Uh, yes I am."

"Last evening Schuler stopped by. He brought me a couple more reports of his interviews with some of Tim's cell mates. I took them home last night and reviewed them. Tim was careful not to give anyone specific details of his crimes, but there was something that jumped out at me and that is why I needed your report. One of the inmates said Tim admitted he raped a Jehovah's Witness."

I waited for Jim to absorb what I said. Of course, he had read the reports so many times he immediately recognized the importance of the information.

"Incredible!"

"Jim, it gets better. He said it was the second rape. The inmate said Tim admitted this was the second time he had raped Holly. Do you know of any other rapes she reported?"

"No, I don't recall that being in the report. I'll call her and ask. I'll let you know what I find out."

As soon as I hung up I reached out to Illinois State Police Investigator Tom Parks, who was the assigned investigator in Sheila Cole's murder. Because she had been murdered in Illinois, his agency held the evidence in the case. He said he was in the process of collecting the remaining evidence and resubmitting it to the crime lab. They were having trouble finding Sheila's underwear, but he promised to keep looking. That afternoon, my cell phone rang. It was Jim.

"Are you sitting down?"

It was Jim's turn to surprise me. "Well, yes I am."

"I called Holly and asked her if she had been raped before. She immediately broke into tears. She said she couldn't talk on the phone, so she came in and met with me. Holly said she was the victim of another rape several years before. She said she and her daughter were walking to her car in a discount store's parking lot when a man with a gun jumped into her car, pushing her over and placing her daughter in the backseat of the car."

"That's unbelievable!"

Of course Jim and I both knew the significance of the location. It was the same parking lot where Sheila Cole had been abducted.

"Jim, did she say what year?"

"Well, she said her daughter was five years old at the time, but she does not recall the month. She knew the weather was still warm."

Holly's daughter was ten years old when Holly was raped the second time.

"Jim, that's incredible. That puts Tim at the same parking lot in 1977."

"Yessss it does. She was an emotional mess as she recalled the first incident. Her attacker told her daughter to lie down in the backseat and he covered her head with something while he drove around Cape forcing Holly to perform oral sex on him. She said he made her keep her head down all the time, so she doesn't know where they drove. She said he told her he would not rape her, but eventually he made her climb on top of him and raped her vaginally. Then he brought them back to the parking lot, gave her twenty dollars and left."

"He paid her twenty dollars?"

"That's what she said."

"When she was assaulted in 1982, did she recognize that her attacker was the same person who raped her five years earlier?"

"Not at first. But after a while, she kind of figured he was the same guy. But she never told anyone. She said her daughter is now grown and has moved away from Cape Girardeau. She said she doesn't want her daughter to know."

Even though I had never met either one, I couldn't help but feel empathy for Holly and her daughter. As I spoke to Jim, it was apparent he too had been through an emotional experience interviewing Holly. We were getting closer to our destination. We had now bridged the five-year gap linking Tim to the earlier crimes. But there were still lots of questions. *How did Tim find Holly five years later?* She said she had moved during those five years, so it was unlikely he followed her home after the first rape. *Why didn't she report the rape so police would have known there was a problem around that parking lot back then?* Of course it was easy to second guess Holly. But rape is such a personal crime. Victims often don't report it for so many reasons.

I briefed my bosses about the new information and met with Stacie and Suzanne at the crime lab. They couldn't believe where this trail was going. Just as I prepared to leave my office, my phone rang. It was Chief Carl Kinnison.

"Hey, Paul. Jim told me about the developments today in Holly's case. I'm amazed at what he told me. I wanted to call and thank you for your help. It's sounding more and more like Tim Krajcir is the guy for whom we have been looking for the past thirty years. I must admit, sleeping is getting even more difficult."

I laughed. Jim and I weren't the only ones finding it hard to sleep.

"Thanks, Carl. I'm enjoying working with Jim. We'll plan an interview with Tim as soon as we hear back from the Missouri crime lab and after the Illinois lab gets a chance to rework the Sheila Cole evidence."

So much was coming together so quickly, I needed to organize all of the leads we were chasing. Over the weekend, using the basic police reports Jim provided, I put together a time line and spreadsheet outlining all the cases in which Tim had been convicted, those that he had confessed to and those in which he was now a suspect. Next to each case, I included Tim's MO, time of occurrence, point of entry, suspect description and weapon used. I was amazed at how many descriptions matched. I color coded each case by highlighting confirmed cases in red and indicating possible links to Tim in yellow. Jim was out sick the day I sent the spreadsheet to him and Tracy. About an hour later, Tracy called to tell me he had discovered an error on the document.

"What did I get wrong?" I asked.

"Well, you color coded the Wallace case as yellow. You need to change that to red. A few minutes ago, David Warren called advising he had just officially matched the unknown palm print lifted from Ms. Wallace's window to the inked palm prints you provided for Krajcir!"

"That's great, Tracy! It's all coming together. That ought to make Jim feel better!"

I talked to Jim the next day. He still was not feeling very well but said there was so much going on he couldn't stand to be away.

"I've been looking through the Wallace case. There are some other reports attached to it I think you should look at."

Jim faxed me Cape Girardeau Investigations Sergeant John Brown's one-page report. In it he described a phone call he had with Williamson County Sheriff's Detective Phil Richey the day after Mildred Wallace's body was found. Phil was a member of the Williamson County Major Case Squad. I had met both men at their respective departments while I was working other cases years before. In the document, Richey said he saw news reports about the Wallace murder, which happened on a Sunday evening, and wanted to compare notes. Richey was investigating three rapes in Williamson County, Illinois, involving three older women who had been attacked on Sunday nights. Richey said the rapist had been described as a young white male, armed with a small caliber pistol. The suspect bound several of his victims, including their husbands in two cases, with leather-like shoelaces and stole cash from the victims as he fled.

Jim also faxed me copies of the Williamson County cases. The first occurred in Marion, Illinois, in March 1982. The victim was a sixty-five-year-old widow who lived alone. She had just returned from church and was accosted by the intruder inside her house. He forced the victim to perform oral sex on him. The second case occurred in Johnston City, Illinois, in April of that same year. The victim was a sixty-three-year-old woman who was home with her sixty-nine-year-old husband when the suspect walked into their home through an open back door. The suspect tied up the elderly man, robbed the couple and then fondled the woman while masturbating. After ejaculating into her hands, he left the house. The third case again was in Marion, two months later in June. This was just two weeks before the murder of Mildred Wallace. The victim was a seventy-year-old woman who was sitting on her back porch with her seventy-two-year-old husband. When the couple went inside their house, the suspect was there waiting for them. The suspect raped the woman, made her remove her dentures and forced her to perform oral sex on him. Richey told Brown that during the last rape, the suspect had stolen a .38 caliber revolver and a box of copper-jacketed ammunition. Brown noted that the stolen gun was the same class and caliber of the gun used to kill Mildred Wallace. The copper-jacketed ammunition also was the same. The detectives realized the similarities were significant but neither had a suspect in mind. I plugged the details into my growing spreadsheet. Everything continued to fit Tim's MO perfectly.

Jim and I discussed the cases and agreed it was a good time to meet with the Illinois State Police and the Marion Police Department. Gathered at the Carbondale Police Department, Jim and I explained the most recent developments. The other investigators were quite amazed. Marion Detective Jeff McCoskey said he would see if there was any other evidence in their cases. Illinois State Police Investigator Tom Parks said he still couldn't find Sheila Cole's underwear in their evidence vault. He said it had tested negative for semen years ago, but he found other articles of her clothing and would take them to the lab for analysis. Jim shared the crime scene photos from the Parsh, Cole, Call and Wallace cases with the group. For the first time I saw the faces that fit the names of the victims we had been discussing. It brought to life the terror of what the victims must have experienced. Assuming Tim was responsible for them, he had been a monster. My thoughts turned to Deborah. Like Deborah, Margie Call had been strangled. The others had been shot in the head.

After lunch I took Jim on a tour of Tim's Carbondale haunts. I drove him to the south Graham address where Tim had climbed through Deborah's window to kill her. We discussed how Deborah's murder, the one in his "backyard", was beginning to unravel all of his secrets. We drove to my old neighborhood and I showed Jim the little trailer where my wife and I lived for five years and pointed to the trailer at the other end of the block where Tim had lived when he molested his landlord's adolescent daughters. For our last stop, I drove Jim to the trailer where Tim had lived when he killed Mildred Wallace and Deborah Sheppard.

After the tour, Jim came back to my office. I called Joe Kocevar to introduce him on speakerphone to Jim. The two talked for a while about the similarities in the Cape cases to the murder during the same year of a school teacher. Joe had worked on that case for a large part of his career and was now a retired investigator of the Lehigh County District Attorney's Office in Pennsylvania. Joe also was looking into a case that seemed similar to Tim's MO. Joe was highly interested in our upcoming interview with Tim, hoping that if Tim began to confess, he would confess to his case too. Joe believed the comment Tim had made to his cell mate about doing something in Pennsylvania that would get him the death penalty linked him to the murder of the school teacher. Joe told us he was working to have some of the evidence in his case tested for DNA. We told Joe we would keep him updated and would consult with him before our interview with Tim.

As promised, Lieutenant Schuler called me after spending time with a couple more former cell mates of Tim's.

"Paul, I have several more things for you."

My heart quickened. "What do you have?"

"I interviewed two more past cell mates. Tim told the first guy that he followed an older white female with silver/gray hair from a grocery parking lot to her home in Paducah and raped her. The inmate said Tim was not specific to when this occurred. Most of the other stuff is the same as he told the other inmates I have already interviewed. The second inmate had the most information of all of them. He said Tim told him several things, but none very specific. For example, he said Tim told him he liked to lick his victims before doing anything to them. He also said Tim said one time he went partying with a woman at a rest stop and it was raining. The cell mate said he thought it was some type of an expressway rest stop, but he could not be sure.

"Tim also told the man that, one time, he tied up a husband and raped the man's wife in front of him. He said Tim said a couple times he gave the victims money. Also, Paul, this inmate said Tim talked about his strategy. He said Tim mentioned he followed his victims home for a couple weeks to get familiar with their habits and to determine if there were men in the houses. He said Tim described his stalking as "hunting for prey." He went to grocery stores and mall parking lots to stalk his victims. He said Tim told him he always carried a gun. And, finally, he said Tim never told him about killing anyone, just rapes."

"Well, you're right. That's a lot of things to follow up on. Several cases come to mind."

"I'll fax you my reports now, so you can have them. You can read the inmate's statements for yourself."

"Thanks, lieutenant, I'll be getting back to you."

We were assembling so many bits and pieces. It was like a big puzzle. The pieces kept coming in and a brutal picture was starting to develop. Tying up the old man and woman could've been either the Johnston City or Marion case. Licking the victims was not something I had heard, but I didn't doubt he did that. Tim was a deviate rapist. Traditional sex was not something that got him excited: He had to take it to extremes to get sexually aroused. The comments about stalking and hunting his prey sounded just how a wildlife or game hunter would talk. Except Southern Illinois, Southeast Missouri and Western Kentucky were Tim's hunting grounds and women were his prey. The comment that really caught my attention was the one about "partying at a rest stop." Offenders sometimes used the term *partying* to refer to a sexual assault. It fit with the rape and murder of Sheila Cole. Time to call Jim again.

"Hey, Jim, one more question. Do you know if it was raining the night Sheila Cole was murdered?"

"Let me take a quick look at the crime scene photos, I have them right here. The wipers are in the middle of Sheila's windshield, so it must've been raining when she parked to go into the discount store. There's a puddle behind her car on the parking lot. So it does appear it was raining when she parked her car at the store."

"Are you sitting down again?"

"Yes."

"Lieutenant Schuler sent me two more interviews with Krajcir's cell mates. Tim told one of them that he partied with a girl at a rest area when it was raining."

"Damn, once again that fits. We have to get this interview right. We may not get a second chance."

I heard my voice harden. "We'll be ready."

"I think it's time to call and brief our prosecutor so he will know what's coming. You know, a conviction in the Wallace case could earn Tim the death penalty."

"Having the death penalty on the table is a huge bargaining chip to get his confession."

I thought of the moral dilemma I was in. I had the chance to push for the death penalty, just like Bernie had wanted us to do in Deborah's murder. Now I was willing to bargain it away for the sake of a full confession. Sooner or later, I would have to tell Bernie and hope he would understand. It all hinged on whether Cape Girardeau Prosecuting Attorney Morley Swingle would give us the authority to use the death penalty to negotiate a confession from Tim if we got the chance.

A few days later, Jim sent an e-mail describing his meeting with Morley and Morley's reluctance to forgo the death penalty. Jim was hopeful that Morley would be willing to negotiate once Krajcir was charged and that Krajcir would eventually confess to all. Jim, like others, wanted the other victims' families to have the opportunity to know the truth.

Soon the trail to Tim's secrets heated up again when my friend Stacie Speith of the Illinois crime lab called.

"I don't know if I told you I was going, but I'm out here in San Francisco at the FBI CODIS Conference. I just learned something I think you'll find interesting."

"What's up?"

"The director of the Illinois CODIS is here with me. He was just notified by his office that a short time ago they got another hit on Tim Krajcir."

"Who got a hit on him?"

"I don't know what agency, but it's in Pennsylvania on an old murder case."

Immediately I thought of Joe Kocevar and the cases he had been working in Pennsylvania. But I didn't think they had worked up a DNA profile yet in those cases. Maybe things had progressed quicker than I thought.

"Well, he told one of his cell mates several months ago that he did something in Pennsylvania that would get him the death penalty. I know a guy who is working on those cases. I guess they finally got lucky."

"I don't have details. In fact, that agency doesn't even know yet. They won't know for a few days. When I find out, I'll let you know."

"Hey," I said to Stacie, "see if the Illinois CODIS people working on the case will provide my name and phone number to the agency who got the hit. Ask them to call me when they are notified."

"Okay, I will pass along your information. Hey, one more thing. After you get through this case you need to come to the CODIS Conference and tell your story. I listened to a few today and it sounds like what you're working on will be even better!"

"I'd like that. I guess we'll have to see how this all turns out."

I hung up and, once again, sat back in my chair in amazement. This whole thing was so wild I had to call Jim. We had quit asking each other if we were sitting down when he called me or I called him. By this time, we just automatically found the nearest chair.

"I just got a call from my Stacie," I said, qualifying which Stacie I was talking about, because the DNA expert in Missouri was also named Stacey. "She's out in San Francisco attending the FBI CODIS Conference. She said Pennsylvania just got a DNA hit on Tim."

"Another match?"

"Yes. I don't have details yet, but in a few days I expect we'll know."

"Well, I have not heard anything back from my Stacey. Getting the DNA buccal swab from the SEMO crime lab to Jefferson City took longer than I thought. If I had known it was going to take them this long to get it to Stacey, I would have driven it up there myself! But I hope to hear something soon."

"Okay. Well, I need to call Joe Kocevar to see if the hit is one of his cases and if not, I need to find out whose case it is."

Joe was quite surprised to hear from me. He said the hit was not one of his cases but suspected it might be one from the Reading, Pennsylvania, area. He knew investigators there were working on an old case and had found semen on a bedspread, but he did not know the details. He said he would get back to me if he found out any information. A few days later, my desk phone rang. It was the call from Pennsylvania for which I had been waiting.

"Lieutenant Echols?" The voice asked over the phone line.

"Yes?"

"Sir, my name is Corporal William Moyer. I'm a criminal investigator with Troop L of the Pennsylvania State Police. I had a DNA hit in an old rape and murder case out here and was told to contact you for further information regarding the suspect in this case: Tim Krajcir."

"Yes, I've been expecting your call. Tim Krajcir lived here in the late seventies and early eighties. I made a DNA match on him in a 1982 murder here. Physical evidence has since linked him to a 1982 murder in Cape Girardeau, Missouri. I'm working with their detective, Jim Smith, on these cases. It's beginning to look like Tim may be responsible for even more crimes, including other murders. He told a cell mate some time back that he had committed a crime in your state that would get him the death penalty," I explained. "I guess he was telling the truth."

"Yes, he raped and strangled a fifty-one-year-old widow named Myrtle Rupp on April 16, 1979, in a small town called Temple. I reopened this case back in May of 2006. I resubmitted some evidence earlier this year, which was found to have Tim Krajcir's DNA on it. Do you think he will talk to me if I come out there?"

"I don't know. Detective Smith and I are preparing to talk to him about their cases when we get the lab report back in his case. We hope to do that within the next couple weeks. I'll have a better sense if he will talk after that."

Moyer and I talked for quite a while about Tim. He told me a call from Myrtle's nephew prompted him to reopen the case. He sent me copies of his reports. The information was sadly familiar. On his way to work the morning of April 17, 1979, Myrtle's neighbor, Ryan Groves, noticed her front door was open. It seemed odd to him, especially when he noticed it was still open when he returned from work that afternoon. He knew Myrtle's home had been burglarized the week before, so he and his wife walked to their fifty-one-year-old neighbor's house to check on her. Her front door was unlocked and a radio was playing in the living room. Groves yelled her name. There was no answer. They checked her bedroom and found her body. She was lying facedown, nude on her bed with her hands and feet bound with her drapery cords. She had been raped, beaten over her head and strangled with her drapery cords. The couple ran back to their home and called the police. Muhlenberg Township Police Department detectives responded and began the investigation with help from the Pennsylvania State Police.

Myrtle lived in a quaint two-story split level brick home on a corner lot on the north end of the quiet unincorporated town of Temple, Pennsylvania. Murders in the little town were quite rare, although while Myrtle's husband was alive, the couple had been burglarized twice. They had no children, so Myrtle dedicated most of her life to her career as a registered nurse. She had worked her way up to a supervisory position with the local hospital and was known as a strict, no-nonsense supervisor and a very hard worker.

Myrtle's mother and sister were the last to see her alive, two days before her murder at an Easter church service. Investigators noted that she had parked her car in the basement level garage on the north end of her home and made her way to the main level before being attacked. Investigators looked at the burglary from the previous week, unsure if it was related to her murder. The burglar had broken in through the front door, cut her phone line, drank a soda and ate some brownies while inside. Myrtle had also reported some money had been taken and that the burglar had apparently lain on her bed, messing it up.

There had been suspects along the way, including the neighbor who reported her death and other men who had visited or attempted to court Myrtle. All had cooperated with the investigation, taking and passing polygraph tests and providing blood and hair standards. Many investigators had worked hard trying to find Myrtle's killer but had been unsuccessful.

I added Myrtle's murder to my growing spreadsheet of murders I was certain Tim had committed. This now meant we had evidence linking Tim to three homicides. He had officially become a serial killer. Jim and I planned to meet at his police department that afternoon, so I gave him the details in person. He closed his eyes and shook his head in disbelief.

"Paul, I'm even more convinced he murdered all of these women here in Cape."

"It sure looks like it. Now, we just have to prove it."

"I just wonder how many other cases are out there. My God, he was only out for five years; think how many he would have murdered if he had been free all these years."

"Who knows? Thankfully, he wasn't."

"You said the Rupp murder occurred in April 1979?"

"Yes, between Sunday, April 15 and Tuesday, April 17, 1979. She was last seen on April 15 and her body was found on the afternoon of April 17."

"That's a very strange coincidence. I have been thinking about another murder. It is not a Cape case, but it's only about eight miles south of Cape on Interstate 55. The young girl's name was Cheryl Ann Scherer. She was working at a gas station there and just disappeared. That happened on April 17, 1979. In the 1980s, investigators went down south and interviewed serial killers Ottis Toole and Henry Lee Lucas thinking they might've abducted her, but Scherer's murder is still unsolved. We need to look at the dates to see if Tim had time to get back to this area to have abducted her. If he gets to talking with us, maybe we can ask him about that one."

"That's a long haul from Temple, Pennsylvania, to Scott City, Missouri, but not impossible, especially if he killed her on that Sunday night. For whatever reason, he liked Sunday nights. I don't think there's anything that would surprise me after all we've found."

"I hope we can nail him," Jim exclaimed. "I just want to see justice done for these families and give them a little peace of mind. Closure will never happen, but they might find some peace in knowing what happened to their loved ones. This thing is absolutely consuming me and I know you know what I mean. You've been a great help to me and I look forward to interviewing Krajcir with you."

"Thanks, Jim," I replied, equally as anxious as he was. "It won't be long now."

12

Terror in the City of Roses

It was time for another meeting to update everyone. This time, Carl, Tracy and Roger joined us for a meeting at the Cape Girardeau Police Department as well as FBI Agent Brian Ritter and his boss, Tom Blades Jr.

Brian asked if there was anything the FBI could do to assist in the case. Jim and I felt we had things under control, but because so many jurisdictions were now getting involved, we thought the FBI might be a good partner. Brian also offered to check their databases for any references to Tim Krajcir. We all agreed we should wait for the DNA results from the Wallace case before we interviewed Tim again. I knew Stacey was being very careful with her analysis of the DNA at the Missouri lab. She was dealing with very old and degraded evidence and I understood that complicated things. We didn't want to pressure her; she knew everyone was waiting for her final report.

When it arrived in early November, the report confirmed our theory. The DNA from the blood found on the bathroom window where Tim broke into Ms. Wallace's home was consistent with Tim's DNA profile. Stacey agreed to test the unknown pubic hair found on Mrs. Call's neck that Jim had wanted tested years ago. But Jim and I wouldn't have to wait for those results. We now had the DNA we needed to confront Tim about the Wallace case.

Brian came through on his promise of the FBI's help. He found a file when the Williamson County Major Case Squad requested Tim's inked fingerprints, along with many others, to be compared against the unknown latent fingerprints recovered from the 1978 murder scene of Virginia Witte, a fifty-one-year-old wife and mother whose husband found her nearly disemboweled on their bed in Marion, Illinois. *That's the same age Myrtle Rupp was when she was murdered,* I thought. My next thought was that maybe Tim was moonlighting as an ambulance driver in Williamson County that day and maybe had been on a crew that took the body from the scene. I wanted to know for sure. I learned that my good friend, the late Illinois State Police Lieutenant Richard

"Dick" Evans, who had helped investigate Sheila Cole's murder, also was instrumental in Virginia's case. It was just another example of how many investigators had gone to their graves never knowing who killed these women. It was frustrating and sad not to be able to talk to them about the cases. I tried calling another of Dick's fellow investigators who had also investigated the Witte murder, Sergeant Les "Boomer" Snyder. He was a retired Marion Police detective with whom I had worked through the years.

"Hey, Boomer, how's retirement?"

"It's good. I recommend it," he replied. "Why are you calling me? Do you need me to solve a case for you?"

I chuckled. "Well, maybe I can solve one for you. What do you remember about the Virginia Witte case?"

"We theorized that a serial killer by the name of Anthony Joe Larette Jr. killed her. Missouri executed him back in 1995. He murdered over a dozen women and raped even more in several states. He finally got caught after killing a girl in St. Charles, Missouri. Dick Evans and I went to a prison in Missouri and interviewed him before he was put to death. So what's up?"

"Did he confess to killing Virginia?"

"Well, sort of. He played games with us. He invited us to talk to him so he could confess to her murder. When we got into the room with him, he told us that he didn't feel like talking about Virginia Witte's murder that day. He told us that when he felt like talking about it, he would call us back to the prison. We never talked to him again. He was a mean son of a bitch. So do you think someone else did it?"

"I don't know yet. Did you see the news a few months ago, when I arrested a guy named Tim Krajcir for a 1982 Carbondale murder?"

"I saw that you solved a case for Carbondale."

"Does the name Krajcir mean anything to you?"

"No."

"Well, his name showed up on a FBI file where you guys had his fingerprints compared against those lifted at the Witte crime scene."

"Really? We compared a lot of people in that case before we connected Larette to her death. It was a brutal murder. When the Williamson County Major Case Squad dissolved, the case went back to the Marion Police Department. So they have the report. You'll have to look there to find out why we had his prints compared."

"Thanks, Boomer. Keep enjoying that retirement."

"Thanks, Paul. If there's something else I can do for you, give me a call."

Detective Tina Morrow took my call at the Marion Police Department. She invited me over to review the case. She'd only been an investigator for a few years and had seen Virginia Witte's name on some old files but didn't know much about the case. She rounded up several folders and the crime scene pictures for me to look over. The murder was, in some ways, similar to what seemed to be a pattern of Tim's but different in its level of violence.

David Sr. and Virginia Witte were originally from St. Louis. Virginia, known as "Ginny" to all of her friends, went to Webster College and was working toward a nursing degree when she decided to forgo her career and be a full-time wife and mom. David, a World War II veteran and graduate of St. Louis University, worked for an automobile maker for many years. His job required them to move a few times. Along the way, the couple raised two sons.

David loved his wife dearly and often teased her by calling her "Elizabethan" because of her proper ways and habits. She always had perfect posture. Always looked good. Never cursed. And never seemed to have a bad thought. She painted and made other crafts when time permitted.

At one point, David's career brought him to Marion, Illinois, where he worked for a car dealership. David's career moved the family again to St. Joseph, Missouri. It was the last move before he retired. The couple decided to move back to Marion for their retirement. They still had friends there and liked the area. They settled on the southeast side of Marion and their first granddaughter was born. Ginny had decided her grandchildren would call her "Grand-Gin."

In May 1978, David and Virginia drove their conversion van west to visit family and to babysit for a few days. Virginia loved her granddaughter dearly and wanted to spend time with her. David and Virginia enjoyed their trip, but David cut himself while cooking. He needed stitches to repair his finger, so the couple returned home later than they had expected. The next day, David went to lunch with his old boss and some other friends. While he was gone, Virginia went grocery shopping.

About an hour later, David came home. He noticed the garage door was open and the kitchen door was insecure. He saw the grocery bags sitting on the counter. He knew this was very uncharacteristic of his very prim and proper wife.

"Ginny?"

There was no answer. When he walked into the bedroom, he found his wife naked, lying on her back across their bed. A knife was buried in her chest. Only its handle was visible. She had been sexually assaulted, strangled and stabbed multiple times. Her abdomen had been sliced open, exposing her organs. It was a horrific scene.

David was in shock. He called for help as best he could. The crime scene was even more brutal than the other murders we believed Tim had done. One of the biggest differences was that it happened during the day. Tim's MO up to that point suggested he preferred to terrorize his victims in the evening.

During the investigation, Virginia Witte's neighbor told police that she saw someone circling the neighborhood around the time of the murder whom she didn't recognize. Investigators put together a composite of the possible suspect and released it to the media. Three days after the murder, Parole Officer John "Jack" Jones called the Major Case Squad and told them that the composite looked remarkably like a guy on his parole list—Timothy Wayne Krajcir. I looked at the suspect description and composite included in the report. The witness described the suspect as "a white male, thirty to forty years old, very, very neat dark hair, heavy and muscular build." The composite depicted the suspect with a full head of dark hair and plastic frame glasses. Tim was completely bald on the top of his head and didn't wear glasses. I didn't think the overall composite looked like Tim, but the shape of the face and eyes were similar. I tried to find Jack Jones to see why he had thought the suspect was Tim, but he had moved and I couldn't locate him. Someday I hope to tell him just how right he was.

Another witness told police that she noticed a second car, silver, parked in Virginia's driveway about the time of the murder. There were several homes located in the fairly affluent area. *If this was Tim, he was being very bold,* I noted.

I read that another friend of mine from the past, Illinois State Police Special Agent Gary Ashman, had been assigned to assist the Williamson County Major Case Squad. Gary had helped investigate the Sheila Cole case too. Based upon the information provided by Jack Jones, Gary surveyed the little trailer where Tim lived in Carbondale. Gary watched Tim walk from his car to his trailer. Gary also learned that Tim was off duty from his job as an ambulance driver the day Virginia was murdered. Williamson County investigators later contacted the North Chicago Police Department and received detailed information about the rapes Tim committed there.

While much of the information from witnesses seemed to point to Tim, it wasn't enough for investigators to see Tim as a serious suspect. They didn't interview him about the crime. His fingerprints, along with many others, didn't render an identification. The case went cold. I couldn't wait to fill Jim in.

"Jim, get this: investigators put together a composite of the suspect's face in the Witte murder and sent it out to the media. A few days later, a parole agent contacted the police. He said the composite looked an awful lot like one of his parolees. Jim, guess what the parolee's name was?"

"Tim Krajcir!"

"Yep, you guessed it: Tim Krajcir."

"So do you think he did it?"

"Well, I can't be sure, but it sounds similar. Larette never confessed to it. Missouri executed him, just like Morley wants to do to Tim. The information and reports I received from a retired Marion detective reveal Larette killed and raped many women during the 1970s until he was arrested in August 1980 in Topeka, Kansas. His crimes were in Kansas, Arkansas, Florida, Illinois, Missouri and Texas. It looks like the murder of eighteen-year-old Mary Michelle Flemming in St. Charles, Missouri, finally got him."

"I've heard of him. I'll have to look through our Missouri records for him. I guess we have another case to discuss with Tim, don't we?"

"Yes, we do. It's going to be a very long interview. If we can get Morley to give us the death penalty as a bargaining chip, I think he'll tell us everything."

We had to make sure we approached Tim just right. I had to make sure my wife, who knew what was going on, didn't let it slip to her mother, whose sister had been close friends with Margie Call. I knew some reporters were following the Sheppard case closely and if they saw me at the Cape Police Department with some frequency, it would stir some curiosity. We had to keep everything covert for now. Our interview with Tim had to be an ambush.

I drove to Cape Girardeau to meet with Jim, Carl, Tracy and Roger to strategize for the big day. I wondered if the desk sergeant had a clue about why I was there so frequently. We met in Carl's office again and sat around the large conference table. We watched excerpts of the video from Tim's confession to Deborah's case. We agreed we had to be soft-handed in our approach to Tim to gain his cooperation. I suggested we not introduce Jim as a Cape Girardeau detective until later in the interview, so Tim wouldn't immediately guess what was coming his way. Everyone agreed.

On the same day as our meeting, Tim was back in Jackson County for a pretrial conference in Deborah's case with his public defender. Tim's court date was set for December 10, 2007. Mike Wepsiec told me he expected Tim would plead guilty and that they had agreed on a forty-year sentence. Originally, I had hoped Mike would pursue a life sentence, but now that I knew other cases were looming, I was okay with the plea agreement. Tim had already told corrections officials that he planned to stay in prison for the rest of his life. Now, the forty-year sentence would take that decision out of his hands. Plus, those forty years would surely pale in comparison to the sentences he would be facing in the cases we now had on him.

I wanted Bernie and Hazel to know it was their daughter's case that led us possibly to clear up all of these other old cases and gave him a call. Bernie felt quite satisfied when he realized that a murder conviction in Missouri would make Tim eligible for the death penalty. I decided not to discuss the chance that it could be a bargaining chip that I was willing to fight for in order to get a confession. I figured we'd talk about it if it happened. At least Bernie knew Tim would never be free again.

After our strategic meeting, Jim offered to take me on a tour of the three murder scenes in town where four women lost their lives. It was a unique opportunity to have Jim act as my tour guide. I could tell this was just one of many times Jim had driven past the sites. With each stop, Jim told me more about the women whom he had come to know from their case files, just as I had come to know Deborah.

Our first stop on the tour was once home to Floyd and Mary Parsh. The home had been virtually unchanged through the years. To my surprise, I was familiar with the area. My niece and her family had once lived directly across the street from the former Parsh residence. I had visited my niece a couple times through the years, not realizing the horror that had taken place in that quaint little wooden-framed one-story home on the opposite side of the road. It was now painted baby blue with white trim. A carport was on the north side.

"Well, I think somebody might be living there, but it looks like no one's home right now. Want to take a closer look?" Jim asked.

"Sure."

Jim and I walked to the back of the home and examined the window that the killer had broken and pushed to an almost ninety degree angle, making it difficult for neighbors to realize it was broken. The window now looked perfectly normal. The lighting on that side of the home was minimal, allowing Tim to come and go under the cover of darkness. It felt strange to walk exactly where Tim had walked so many years ago.

As we walked through the carport, my mind flashed to the crime scene photos. I envisioned Mary Parsh's car parked there. I thought of that moment in time when Mary and her daughter Brenda got out of their car, happy and carefree, making their way into the house, unaware that a rapist and killer lurked inside. I looked at the door and envisioned the keys still dangling from the deadbolt that Mary assumed had kept her home safe while she was gone. Mary was so excited to see the younger of her two daughters that night. Floyd's job had brought the family to the town from St. Louis.

It was a happy time, but both sisters were concerned about their father, who had suffered a heart attack and had been in the hospital for about two weeks. He was doing better, but doctors wanted to implant a pacemaker, which meant he wouldn't be out of the hospital in time to drive his wife to her fortieth high school class reunion in Alton, Illinois. Since her sister, Karen, was pregnant and coping with morning sickness, Brenda, who was at that point a fashion buyer in Wisconsin, volunteered to take a plane to St. Louis and catch a connecting flight to Cape Girardeau on her way back from a buying trip to New York. It was a decision that may have saved her sister's and her unborn nephew's lives.

The stress of Floyd's hospitalization had been tough, making Brenda's impending visit and the weekend they planned to share together that much more special. After work, Mary drove to the hospital to visit her husband as she had every evening. She watched the clock, thinking about Brenda's flight. At 8:45 P.M., she kissed her husband good-bye and drove to the Cape Girardeau Regional Airport. Her daughter's flight was on time, arriving at 9:25 P.M. The excited mother greeted her daughter and the two headed home after gathering Brenda's two suitcases.

By 10:20 P.M. that night, Floyd wondered why his daughter hadn't called him. He called home from his hospital bed. Several rings later, he finally heard his daughter's voice.

"Hi, how are you?" he asked.

"Fine, Daddy."

"Let me talk to your mother."

"She's in the bathroom. Daddy, I'm really tired. I've flown from New York then down here and I'm tired. I'd like to go to bed."

"Okay, bye," Floyd said, confused by his daughter's abruptness.

"Bye, Daddy."

Click. He later told police, "Brenda did not sound like her chipper self. She didn't inquire about my health and seemed to be in a hurry to get off the phone." The call disturbed Floyd to the point where he didn't sleep well that night. He knew the two would be gone the following day to the class reunion, so he wasn't surprised when no one called Saturday. But when Brenda, whom he called Sissy, didn't come to see him or call on Sunday, he became concerned. He eventually called his older daughter Karen.

"I talked to Bren Friday night. She sounded funny. They should have been back by now."

"Don't worry, Dad," his older daughter tried to reassure him. "Just get some rest and I'll try to get hold of them."

The call made Karen even more nervous. Earlier, her uncle, who lived in Alton, Illinois, had called to tell her that neither Brenda nor her mother had been at the reunion. He called their hotel after the reunion and learned they had never arrived. She didn't tell her father about her uncle's phone call, to keep him from worrying. She called her mother's house late Sunday evening. There was no answer. She called Brenda's apartment in Wisconsin, because she was supposed to fly back there Sunday afternoon, but there was no answer. She called the airline and learned her sister never boarded her plane. She called the Illinois and Missouri State Police to see if they had been involved in an accident, but they had not. She barely slept that night. When the next morning arrived, she called her mother's house once more. Again there was no answer. She called her parent's neighbor, Doris, who lived across the street from the Parshes. She told Karen that Mary's car had been parked under the carport all weekend. Nothing seemed amiss, but she agreed to knock on the door to check, just in case.

As Doris walked closer to the door, she noticed Saturday's newspaper was still on the stairs. The headline was about the arrest of a serial killer named David Berkowitz, also known as the "Son of Sam." It was one of those stories from New York City that seemed would never happen in a small, safe community like Cape Girardeau. As the citizens of the big city were finally beginning to breathe a sigh of relief, terror was about to come to Cape Girardeau for generations to come.

"Hello?" Doris asked as she knocked on the door, noticing Mary's keys were dangling from the lock. "Mary? Brenda? Mary, you have left your keys in the door."

The door was not locked. It pushed right open. It had been a hot summer weekend. She stepped inside and was overwhelmed by a foul odor.

"Mary, what's that smell?" she innocently yelled, expecting an explanation.

Once she got to the doorway of the Parshes' bedroom, she saw what she thought were Mary and Brenda laying side-by-side on the bed. They were covered with a bedspread. She slowly pulled the cover back, revealing the naked and decomposing bodies. Their hands were tied behind their backs with electrical cords cut from appliances. Both had been shot once in the head. Mary had been struck in the face during the attack, knocking a tooth loose. Doris almost fainted at the sight. She grabbed the wall to hold herself up. She stumbled out of the house and ran to call the police.

Cape Girardeau Police dispatchers recorded the time of Doris' call at 7:14 A.M. *Wow, the three numbers that had routinely brought me luck served as the start of a serial killer's terror in Cape Girardeau,* I thought. Doris called Karen and told her that she and her husband had to come to Cape immediately. She was shaken but refused to tell Karen what had happened. Karen pleaded with Doris to tell her what was wrong. Finally, Doris reluctantly told Karen that her mother and sister were dead. The shock was unbearable. Karen's husband took the phone and spoke with Doris, who was still in a state of shock herself. She again refused to provide details. She told the sister's husband only that they needed to get to Cape Girardeau as soon as possible. Karen's mind raced during the drive, speculating as to what had killed her mother and sister. A gas leak, perhaps? She never considered that they had been murdered. She didn't call her father. She didn't want him to find out before she arrived so she could tell him in the presence of his doctor. She worried the news could send his heart into shock. The drive from St. Louis to Cape was the longest two hours in Karen's life.

Like many older people in those years, Floyd enjoyed passing the time listening to his radio instead of watching television. While waiting to hear from his wife, he listened to his morning programs and heard the news that would break his heart forever: "Cape Girardeau Police are on the scene of a double homicide on Koch Street this morning. This is a breaking news story and we will bring you more later in this newscast," the broadcaster said.

Karen found her father sitting on the side of his bed, crying. Karen was furious that the news had reached him before she could. She never spoke to the media because of it. One day after the bodies were found, news of Elvis Presley's death bumped the story from the front pages of most of the newspapers.

Floyd couldn't handle attending his wife and daughter's funeral. Karen did it all by herself. Karen's doctor gave her a drug to reduce her anxieties during the visitation. She took one and felt as if she were in a fog the entire evening. She threw away the other pills, shocked by the side effects. Her mother and sister were buried on Karen's grandmothers' birthday, August 17, robbing her of yet another once happy memory of how both her grandmothers had been born on the same day. Karen hoped that the reward being offered would shake something loose in the investigation. But nothing did.

Once Floyd was released from the hospital, Karen and her husband tried to find a place where he could rehabilitate close to his doctors. Along with his heart problems, Floyd had rheumatoid arthritis and had relied on his wife of thirty-six years to do just about everything for him. But every facility was full. They settled on a simple care facility across the street from the Cape Girardeau Police station. Crime scene tape still clung to the front door of the house when Karen and her husband went there to get some of Floyd's belongings. Karen said a prayer, asking God for the strength to handle what she was about to see on the other side of the door. She felt a warm sensation come over her and moved quickly through the house to get what she needed. It would be a strange coincidence that her dad's new living quarters were next to the house where Sheila Cole, who would soon be murdered, lived with two classmates.

The temporary apartment turned out to be a dump for Floyd, so he only stayed there a few weeks. He decided to return to the home where half of his family had been murdered. He closed the door to the bedroom where their bodies had been found and never opened it for the four years he lived there. No one was allowed inside the room. In late 1981, Floyd's health began to fail. Karen gave birth to her third baby that February and sneaked the infant into her father's hospital room. He died days later at the age of sixty-four from internal bleeding.

After his death, Karen opened the door to the room her father had forbidden anyone from entering. Everything had been left just as it was the day the bodies were removed. Blood still covered the bedpost and floor. Karen had to clean up the crime scene. She believed that her father never wanted her to deal with it, but the time had come when someone had to. For the same reasons, she was glad he never had to deal with it.

Floyd was buried along with his wife and daughter at the Upper Alton Cemetery. Floyd had not wanted them buried in Cape Girardeau. Jim and I speculated that the stress of it all never let Floyd's heart and mind fully heal. We felt as though Tim had essentially taken Karen's parents and sister away from her.

"I don't know how she made it," I said as we stared at the home.

"All these years never knowing who did this to her family," Jim added.

"Unreal."

The crime also had left deep scars for the Parshes' neighbor Doris. After she found the bodies, she drew the blinds on her house so she wouldn't have to look at the Parsh home across the street. They pretty much stayed that way for the next thirty years. It was almost as if she had mentally blocked the home from her sight, so if she ever did need to look in the house's direction, she didn't even see it there. She wouldn't even walk on that side of the street.

Jim and I drove only two blocks south to reach Margie Call's house. Jim pointed out the beige single-story brick ranch-style home with a carport on its west side. Margie and her husband built the house on Brink Street. We drove to the back of the house, into a church parking lot that had been built since the murder.

"That window there is the point of entry," Jim said as he pointed to a bathroom window above an air conditioning unit. "Margie lived there by herself. Her husband worked for the post office. He died of a heart attack about three years before the murder."

We could tell someone was living there and we didn't feel like explaining why we wanted a closer look at the backyard. A new white fence had recently been built, shielding the backyard from intruders. I wondered if the current owners built the fence knowing the crime that had unfolded there.

Margie Call was fifty-eight years old when she was killed, the same age as my mother. I couldn't help but think of her when learning of Margie's case. Margie was the mother of two grown sons. Both of them lived out of town and had started families of their own. Margie kept busy with church, extended family and working for forty years at the local dime store in the town plaza with my wife's aunt. After all those years, she was well-known in town, well-liked and very dependable. She greeted most customers by their first names.

Margie left work at 5:05 P.M. the evening before she was killed, coming home briefly before leaving to have supper with friends. She left dinner at 9:30 P.M. and drove home, parking her car under her attached carport. When she didn't show up for work the next day and didn't answer a phone call from her coworkers, they knew something must be wrong. They called Margie's brother, Albert Bertling, who worked in town. He went to check on his sister. When he arrived, he found the door to her house from the carport was unlocked.

"Margie?" he yelled.

There was no response. He made his way through the house until he stopped in horror at the doorway to her bedroom. He found his sister's nude body lying facedown across her bed. She had been gagged and strangled. Her hands were bound behind her. Only her black boots remained on her body. The killer left leather shoelaces apparently used to strangle and bind Margie floating in her toilet. He had also either cut or bitten off her left nipple after he killed her. Margie's brother went to the phone in the kitchen to call police. Officers Brad Moore and Sam Minor soon arrived, finding Albert outside and distraught. They went inside and checked Margie's pulse but found none. They radioed back to the department about what they had found.

It had been five years since the last mysterious homicide claimed the life of an innocent woman in town. Citizens of Cape Girardeau were just beginning to relax and believe the terror of the murders had subsided. Mrs. Call's murder rekindled the fear among residents. And again, no one felt safe. The thought that someone could get away with murder in a neighborhood where one could almost hear one's neighbor sneeze terrorized the community—as did the thought that someone could abduct a girl from a well-lit, bustling retail parking lot. Tim had single-handedly changed the way of life in Cape Girardeau. Police advised women to avoid traveling and shopping by themselves. The sales of guns in the area escalated. Neighbors locked doors behind them anytime they entered or left their homes. Husbands doing yard work found themselves stranded outside of their homes, because their wives had locked the doors behind them. Shades were drawn. Fences were built. And suspicion and speculation brewed in nearly every corner of the community. Investigators theorized all of the murders were related but could never be sure. They seemed so different on the surface. But what tied most of them together was the MO of a man lurking in the shadows of his victims' homes.

Some residents refused to let fear paralyze them. Among them was Mildred Wallace. At sixty-five she was an elegant, respected businesswoman and neighborhood activist. She had dedicated much of her life to caring for her mother. Mildred never married, had no children and, according to her family, never even had a boyfriend. After her mother passed away, she had plenty of time to get involved in her community. She was a member of the business and professional women's club, a member of the board of directors for the local vocational technical institute and a founding member of the choral group the "Cape Choraliers." After her neighbor Mrs. Call was murdered, Ms. Wallace set out to see what she could do to restore a sense of security to her community. She scheduled a meeting to discuss the formation of a neighborhood watch program in her neighborhood along with a crime prevention workshop to begin that fall.

Jim and I drove seven blocks north and almost seven blocks east of Mrs. Call's house to William Street, where he pointed to Ms. Wallace's house. I had driven by the home hundreds of times, not realizing its horrific history. Like the others, the home hadn't changed much from the time of the murder, although someone had painted a light gray color over the white Ms. Wallace preferred. Its location intrigued me. The little wooden-framed home was along one of the city's major thoroughfares and sandwiched between two other houses. I thought how bold Tim had been breaking into the home, given the close proximity of the other homes as well as the well-lit public street. I remembered seeing Ms. Wallace's light blue car sitting neatly under her carport in the crime scene pictures. Jim and I parked our car and walked behind the home to get a closer look at the bathroom window on the west side of the house where Tim had broken in. In my mind, I envisioned a much younger Tim as he slithered through the broken window, cutting himself as he slipped through the shards of glass.

"That's the window where we got Tim's palm print," Jim said as he pointed to the bedroom window on the north side of the structure. "I'm betting that's the first window Krajcir looked through after he followed her home the first time. They found a half gallon of orange juice sitting on her kitchen counter, so they think she must have come home from the grocery store, realized she forgot the juice and went back to buy it. They believed the killer broke into her home through the bathroom window and waited for her in her bedroom."

Reminiscent of Margie Call's murder, it was Mildred Wallace's employer who first realized something was wrong. Mildred was the office manager and long-time employee for a major cement company in town along the Mississippi River. She was religiously prompt for work, always at her desk by 7 A.M. Like Margie, her dependable nature set an example for her office. When she was an hour late on Monday morning, June 21, 1982, and had not called in sick, coworkers knew something was terribly wrong. They tried calling her. There was no answer. They called her sister, Bernice Mercer, to ask if she knew where Mildred might be. Her sister had been at her own home all day Sunday, visiting with Mildred and her daughter, who had come in from out of town. Bernice said Mildred left for home at about 10 P.M. She tried to call her sister, but received no answer. So Bernice and her daughter drove to Mildred's house to check on her.

There was no answer after they knocked on her door, even though Mildred's car was in the driveway. They broke the window on the locked storm door and Bernice used her key to open the kitchen door. The two called out for Mildred, but once again there was no response. As they walked into the bedroom, they found Mildred lying face up and nude from the waist down on her bed inside her home. Her hands were bound behind her. She had been raped and shot once in the head. The single .38 caliber bullet had come to rest under her night stand. Her head hung slightly over the edge of her bed. Blood ran down the side of her comforter and pooled below her on the carpet. The killer had also cut the cord to her kitchen phone. The two ran to a neighbor's house to call police, but no one was home. They rushed back to Bernice's home to use a different phone. Police now believed a serial killer was living among them. Community pressure to find him was intense. The town hoped newly-hired Chief Ray Johnson would bring a new set of eyes to the cases and that they would be solved under his leadership. Margie had been murdered just weeks before his arrival. Now he was dealing with the second high-profile case of the year.

Our last stop was the parking lot of the old discount store where Sheila Cole had been abducted on November 16, 1977. Sheila was a twenty-one-year-old college coed who was studying zoology and living with two of her fellow coeds in an apartment across the street from the Cape Girardeau Police Department. She told them the night she disappeared that she had to pick up some pictures. She never returned. At about 7:40 A.M. the next morning, the Alexander County Illinois Sheriff's Department received a call that a passerby had found a body in the bathroom of the roadside rest area along Illinois Route 3, south of McClure, Illinois. The first deputy on the scene was my wife's cousin, Kenneth Calvert Jr. He found Sheila fully clothed, with her hands tucked in the pockets of her yellow jacket. She had been shot once in the back of the head and once in the face. Her purse was found in the trash can outside, which helped police identify her. Her car was found in the discount store's parking lot. Puddles from the previous night's rainfall pooled around her tires. The driver's side door was unlocked. The keys were in the ignition. A store bag was inside her trunk. Among the pictures she picked up that night was a portrait of herself that she planned to give her parents for Christmas.

Her brother was an over-the-road trucker listening to his radio on his way home to St. Louis from Chicago when he heard that a SEMO student had been murdered in Cape Girardeau. He learned it was his sister when he got home that evening. Sheila also left behind a sister as well as her parents, Naomi and Harold. The family lived in St. Louis, Missouri. When she wasn't at school, Sheila worked at a fast-food restaurant in Shrewsbury, Missouri, a small municipality just outside the city limits of St. Louis. Her mother was a nurse at a nearby hospital. Her dad was a car salesman and later became the general manager of a used automobile business in St. Louis. Their daughter's murder consumed them. Her father retired. Her mother bonded with former *St. Louis Post-Dispatch* reporter Jo Mannies, who wrote the first stories of her daughter's murder. The grieving mother called Jo regularly, sometimes weekly, for about three years. As Naomi was nearing the end of her battle with cancer, Sheila's father drove to Cape Girardeau and begged then Police Chief Henry Gerecke to tell him something, anything about his daughter's case that he could tell his dying wife. Gerecke had nothing to offer. The encounter haunted the chief for decades.

Sheila's brother watched his father's health also decline and he died two years after his wife. Her brother blamed the stress of his sister's unsolved murder for his parents' deaths. The brother had been the last member of his family to see Sheila alive. He had delivered a load of salt to McClure, Illinois, about two weeks before she was found shot to death. He had stopped by his sister's apartment before heading home to check on her and make sure she had money. On his way there, he passed the rest stop where later she was killed.

Investigators interviewed Sheila's college boyfriend. Her roommates told them the relationship was in trouble but had no reason to suspect he had killed her.

Even though the store had since moved, I remembered it. I had shopped there many times, before and after Sheila's murder. Before we had even met, my wife had shopped at that store during the same time period, even at night. I wondered if Tim had ever watched her walk across the parking lot. A friend of mine who works in the Jackson County State's Attorney's Office told me she too had shopped by herself at the store the same evening Sheila was abducted. It could've been any woman that night, but Tim picked Sheila Cole. It was also the place where Tim had abducted Holly and her daughter earlier that same year and ordered Holly to drive around town as he sexually assaulted her.

We concluded the somber tour and I headed back to Carbondale. On the way back, I once again approached the rest area. I pulled my unmarked police car into the same parking lot, wondering if Tim had parked his car in that very spot. The restrooms no longer existed. They had been removed shortly after the murder, but I knew exactly where they had once stood and I walked to the spot. At this last scene, I took a moment to say a prayer in memory of all five women and for what Jim and I were about to do. Jim had just taken me on an emotional journey through time and murder. It was time to confront the man responsible for it.

13

"It Wasn't Me"

Most of the night before our big interview with Tim I lay in bed staring at the ceiling. I shut the alarm off well before it rang. *Maybe after this I will be able to sleep better,* I thought, getting up to dress. I doubted Jim Smith slept any better. I didn't know how he could. The hunt for the person responsible for the senseless brutal murders of five women could end that day if our plan worked. We had been preparing for weeks to confront Tim with the evidence we had gathered in the crimes he committed in the quiet little river town of Cape Girardeau and who knows where else. Now the day had come.

With everything going on, I had almost forgotten it was my birthday—the birthday I had dreaded. I turned forty-eight years old that day, which was the same age my father was when he died. I now realized just how young he was when cancer took his life. I was grateful to have so many more things on my mind that day. I hopped into my truck with my usual non-healthy breakfast of a soda and a breakfast bar in hand. It was déjà vu. I felt just like I did the morning Moe and I were about to confront Tim about Deborah's murder. That had only been a couple months ago, but it seemed much longer. Suddenly my thoughts were interrupted by a very bad sound. Click…click…click…click…click. It snapped me back to reality. My battery was dead. *Damn.* I realized I had left the dome light on after returning home late the night before. I used cables to jumpstart my truck's battery and a few minutes later I heard the roar of the engine and finally I was on my way.

My mind soon returned to thoughts of the day ahead and the events of the past three months. It had been incredible. The resolution of Deborah's murder by itself had been phenomenal and now, after teaming up with Jim, we might resolve at least five more murders and several rapes from multiple jurisdictions including my own. I felt strongly that Tim Krajcir had raped Sarah in February 1979. His strategy to deny it had backfired. It had caused me to push harder to understand. And now I understood. He was hoping the confession in the Sheppard case would quickly go away and he could return to the prison life to which he had grown accustomed. He didn't want exposure from that case to attract the attention of other law enforcement agencies. Tim was smart, but his roll of the dice in confessing to Deborah's case had turned up snake eyes.

Jim and I were sure Tim was responsible for the murder of Myrtle Rupp in Pennsylvania, but we decided not to confront him with that case unless he started confessing to everything. I wasn't so sure about the rape and murder of a seventy-four-year-old woman in Paducah, Kentucky. That case had some similarities to Tim's MO, but other things didn't fit. I still planned on asking him about it, if we got to that point. I was confident he had done something in Paducah but just did not know what. Investigators there were still searching their old cases for something that matched Tim's MO. Tim held most of the answers, but his DNA was doing most of the talking. But we didn't have DNA in each case. The evidence was old and degraded and, in the Sheila Cole case, some items had been lost. That made dealing with evidence in these cases sometimes frustrating. Jim and I knew it would take some maneuvering to get Tim's cooperation.

I pulled my truck into the parking lot of the Carbondale Police Department at 7:35 A.M. As I walked toward the front of the building, I noticed Jim's maroon unmarked police car already there. We had agreed to leave at 8 A.M., but Jim was like me. He liked to be early and plan for the unexpected. Jim was waiting for me in the lobby.

"Good morning, Jim. Did you sleep here last night?" I jokingly greeted him.

"No, but I might as well have, considering how much sleep I got."

Murder cases are the worst for sleep—especially cold cases. The crime scene photos never stop popping into one's mind. The faces of all five women kept coming into mine. Jim had them engrained in his memory too. He may not have gotten much sleep, but he looked sharp as always.

"You ready to do this?"

"Ready as I'll ever be."

I left Moe a note and we loaded up my unmarked police car. Jim brought multiple three-ring binders containing reports from the Cape cases. He also brought boxes of crime scene photos. I brought my mini-DVD video recorder, several blank mini-DVDs and a short tripod. Tim would be familiar with it, because I had used it to record his confession to Deborah's murder. On our ride to Big Muddy Jim and I made small talk about family and life in general, trying to relax a bit before we arrived at the prison. Less than an hour later, we were there. We removed our guns and secured them in the car's trunk along with Jim's pager and my cell phone. As we walked from the parking lot to the main gate, I sensed the eyes of the guards in the towers watching us. Even as a cop, prisons are intimidating. We were walking into a building unarmed, knowing on the other side of the fences were likely a few violent guys we had helped put there.

Lieutenant Schuler quickly arrived at the front gate to greet us. Each time I came to the prison to meet with Tim, those with me and any equipment I brought had to be approved up the line. Lieutenant Schuler always made sure everything we needed was in order before we even got there. He was very efficient and saved us from the frustration of the red tape. He escorted us into the familiar room where Moe and I had interviewed Tim about Deborah's case. I set up the recording equipment. We waited. Within minutes, Tim was standing before us.

"Hey, Tim," I said, keeping my tone as friendly as I could make it.

"Hi," Tim said.

"The other detective couldn't come with me. This is Detective Smith and we just want to talk to you about a couple of things. Is there anything I can get you? They have some coffee over there," I said.

"Yeah. I'll take a cup."

"Black or how do you want it?" Jim asked.

"Black is fine."

Jim went over to the coffee pot in the corner of the room and poured some for Tim in a cup while I read Tim his Miranda rights. I wanted to get his mind off of his right to an attorney quickly.

"Okay, so how are things going for you?"

"Well, I'm still in segregation."

"Are you? Well, I don't...you know I don't know anything about prisons. I've never worked in a prison. I would think sooner or later that that would end, but I just don't know. I think one of the things that was their concern, and I don't know if they've told you this, was in regards to the Sheppard case, since the victim was black, they were a little concerned for your safety with some of the black male inmates here. Now that was part of it."

"Yeah, I sort of figured that."

I had to get his mind away from how his life changed for the worse in the wake of his confession to Deborah's murder. I changed the topic to the one positive thing his confession to her murder did bring: a field trip. Just the day before he had been to Carbondale for a pretrial conference with his public defender.

"It was a rainy day yesterday, wasn't it? You didn't have a good chance to see the leaves."

Karen and Brenda Parsh with their mother Mary, just a few months before Brenda and Mary were murdered. They were Tim Krajcir's first two murder victims.

The back of the Parsh home where Tim forced entry into the window on the right and waited for Mary Parsh to come home.

Sheila Ellen Cole at the foot of the St. Louis Gateway Arch. This picture was in the package of photos Sheila had just purchased the night she was murdered.

Sheila's body was found in a rest area bathroom along Illinois Route 3 just a few miles from Cape Girardeau. She was Tim's third murder victim.

Virginia Witte and her first grandchild. Virginia became Tim Krajcir's fourth murder victim.

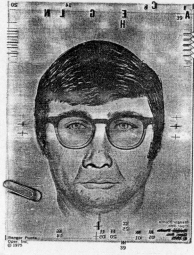

A composite of the suspect as described by Virginia Witte's neighbor.

Joyce Tharp, just a few months before she became Tim Krajcir's fifth murder victim.

Joyce Tharp's apartment in Paducah, Kentucky. Tim broke through her kitchen window, took her from her bed and drove her to Carbondale where he sexually assaulted and strangled her.

Myrtle Rupp allowed Tim Krajcir into her house after he pretended to be a police detective. She became his sixth murder victim.

Tim burglarized Myrtle Rupp's home in Temple, Pennsylvania, a week before he raped and murdered her.

Marjorie Call, a loving grandmother, mother and aunt, was raped and murdered by Tim Krajcir. She was his seventh victim.

Marjorie Call's home, where Tim broke in through the bathroom window and waited for her to come home.

As a child, one of Deborah Sheppard's favorite gifts was the bicycle her father Bernie gave her.

Deborah Sheppard and Paul Echols graduated from high school on the same day. She was victim number eight.

Meeting Bernie Sheppard was one of the highlights of Paul's career.

Deborah's beauty came from her mother Hazel (left), a model in her younger days.

Grover Thompson's mugshot. He was arrested by the Mount Vernon, Illinois, Police Department for stabbing Ida White.

Mildred Wallace asked Tim if he was the same person who killed Majorie Call. He told her no and proceeded to rape and kill her. She was his ninth and last murder victim.

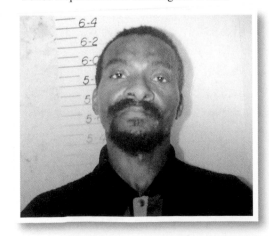

Grover Thompson was wrongfully convicted of a crime that Tim Krajcir later admitted he committed. Grover died in prison three years after this photo was taken.

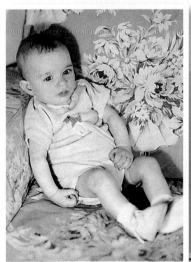

Timothy Wayne McBride, later changed to Krajcir, was born in West Mahoney, Pennsylvania.

As a young teenager, Tim's relationship with his stepfather was troubled. At about the same time, Tim began window peeping and committing other petty crimes.

At age seventeen, Tim Krajcir joined the Navy and was sent to the Naval Station in Great Lakes, Illinois. He committed his first rapes in that area.

Tim Krajcir at the Vienna Correctional Center. His uncle took this photo during a visit with him.

Tim and his mother Fern. Tim had been paroled only a few months earlier after serving thirteen years of a forty-year sentence for raping two women near Chicago.

Tim attended Southern Illinois University and obtained his bachelor's degree in the Administration of Justice Program.

Just twelve hours after killing Brenda and Mary Parsh, Tim served as a groomsman in a friend's wedding.

Echols took this picture of Tim while serving him the arrest warrant for the murder of Deborah Sheppard.

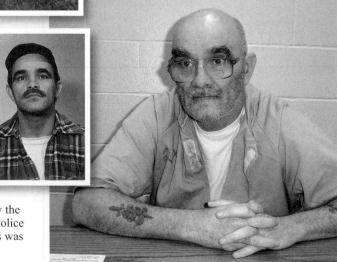

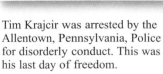

Tim Krajcir was arrested by the Allentown, Pennsylvania, Police for disorderly conduct. This was his last day of freedom.

A rare picture of Paul Echols and his father. He died when Paul was twelve.

Hired by the Carbondale Police Department, Paul married Sheila and moved to North Springer Street, the same block where Tim had lived and committed many of his crimes.

When he graduated from the FBI National Academy, Paul's wife and children flew out to celebrate with him. His experiences at the FBI Academy gave him the confidence to investigate Deborah Sheppard's cold case.

Illinois Department of Corrections Lieutenant Harold Schuler was a tremendous help during the investigation of Tim Krajcir.

Paul watched with excitement as a DNA match in Deborah Sheppard's murder occurred.

Illinois State Police DNA Expert Suzanne Kidd posed with Paul after the press conference announcing the arrest of Tim Krajcir for Deborah's murder.

During the press conference in Cape Girardeau, Missouri, police displayed the photos of the five women murdered there by Tim.

After the press conference, Carbondale Chief Bob Ledbetter, Echols, Cape Girardeau Detective Jim Smith and Cape Girardeau Police Chief Carl Kinnison posed for a photo.

The team of Carbondale Police detectives, from left: Sergeant Mike Osifcin, Aaron Baril, Brian Gleason, Eric Ruhe, Jeff Gill, Kevin Banks, Brooke Hammel, Angelo Aldrigetti and Echols.

Cape Girardeau, Missouri, Detective Jim Smith and Echols were honored by the Cape Girardeau City Council for their efforts in resolving the five Cape murders.

Photo courtesy of the *St. Louis Post Dispatch.*

"I enjoyed the ride," he said dryly.

"The reason I'm here: there're a couple of old cases that we've looked into and we believe it's you. And I'm trying to bring closure to these cases too. They're sexual assault cases. I know last time when we talked, you seemed willing to bring closure to some of these old cases. And we've done a lot of forensic testing. There's a lot of forensic testing that's pending. Some of them we will never mess with, because if indeed you acknowledge that it's you then that's all I'm going to do. I just want to give closure to that. So if you don't mind, I'll just run through some of the cases that I believe you were involved with.

"Some of them were…two of them were in Marion, Illinois. One was in Johnston City, Illinois. One of them was…March 1982, it was…an older lady who lived by herself. The suspect entered through the window with a gun, had the face covered. She had come home from church. She'd put her car in the garage and she was, well, the person was hiding in the bedroom. Came out and tied her hands. And then there was oral sex involved. And again, I'm just trying to bring closure to…this lady is still alive. There're two out of three who are still alive. And this lady immediately, within the next few weeks, moved out of that house. She could never live there again after what happened. I talked to a guy who knows her personally yesterday and this is still a big deal with her. I would like to be able to tell her that the person who did this has some remorse; he's sorry for it and just bring an end to that. Can you do that for me?"

I thought it would be good to start by making sure Tim understood that the statute of limitations had expired and he could not be charged. Then I planned to move into the Cape cases, but Tim would have none of it. He knew if he did, it might cause the dominos to fall. But he didn't know that the dominos were already tumbling out of control.

"Nah," Tim said, shaking his head no.

"You can't do that for me?"

"I very seldom went over to Marion."

"Okay. The other cases. Do you know where Johnston City is?"

"Yeah."

"Just north of Marion. The same scenario: it was an older man and his wife. The suspect came through the back door. Armed with a gun. Tied the older man's hands and feet and put him on the floor and tied the lady's hands. Led her into the bathroom or bedroom. Brought her back and actually put her on the floor. There was not a rape in that case, although the suspect did masturbate onto her hands."

"Nah," Tim said, again shaking his head no.

"I'm here shooting straight with you. I've treated you, you know, well."

"Yeah, you have."

"I just want to bring closure to these cases. The old man in that case is dead, but the woman is still alive. And that's all I want to be able to do, is before…you know we're talking up in age now, I mean, what's left? I mean just to clear that up with her while she's alive. She probably has no more than a few more years left."

I ran through the scenarios of the cases again with Tim.

"I've talked to Marion PD, to Johnston City PD. There is evidence in this; I don't have any intention ever to have that evidence tested unless…if you continue to say it's not you then, yeah, that's what I'll have to do. I really don't want to do that. So that's where I'm at with these two cases. So just think about that for a minute. And I had talked to you about a Carbondale case, which was on North Almond Street. Remember, you said no…"

"Yes. I remember that because an officer, I think Carbondale PD, came to me and was talking to me about that."

"Did they come and interview you in that case? I don't show that with the report." *I wish I had the damn report.* It had long since been thrown away.

"A young guy. That's when they had that big snowstorm. It was about eighteen inches of snow in one day."

"You're right," I said, marveling at how his memory was impeccable. *I bet his memory of that day is so clear, because he remembers walking in the snow to Sarah's house.*

"Were you snowed in somewhere?"

"Yeah, out at the Carbondale Mobile Home Park."

As long as he was talking about something, I was going to keep him on it. I told him about how I was working at a gas station to work my way through college and remembered how they shut the interstate down during the storm.

"You know, the reason I came to you to talk about these is, once again, the Tim to whom I'm talking is not the same Tim who was having these issues back in those days. I know you talked about the fact that this was something you could not control. But the fact that you have controlled it by staying in prison and not going to the counseling and by that you have essentially sentenced yourself to stay in prison for the rest of your life. I don't know whether that will ever change, but trying to get to the bottom of these situations and get the truth from you, I think it also opens you up to be able to start your programming again at some point if you choose to do so. Now you told me before that one of the reasons you could not go to the program was because you couldn't be open and honest with everybody."

"Uh huh."

"And there're a couple of things here with your being open and honest and helping me clear up these cases. Then it may allow you, should you choose to ever do so, go back to the programming and seek some of the professional help that they offer. And you should. You should. Because you've done it halfway. You've actually went part of the way here by staying in prison. And while nobody can respect what you did back in those days and the things with which you were involved, I think there is, you know, a sense of respect on your choices that you've made since then. You've saved a lot of people heartache because of that."

Tim nodded in agreement with my words. So I continued.

"Because had you stayed out and about, I'm afraid you're right. You probably couldn't have controlled it. And other people might have gotten hurt. But the fact that you recognized that and were willing to do what you could, what was within your control, that's admirable. And I think that's a good thing. And you're getting older. These women here in these cases are…well, very old. And I don't know what else is left to do. I mean, there's no investigation left to do here. It's just simply clear them up so I can tell these ladies."

"Sorry, but like I say, the only time I went to Marion was in 1980. Somebody… I had to take somebody over to the hospital. But one time I was gonna go over there and they had the tornado. Well, I'm glad…my girl called me and then I went out there instead though. Other than that, I don't think I've been to Marion…no more than four or five times."

"May of 1982. That would have been the tornado. It was around Memorial Day."

"Yeah, it was. About two o'clock," he responded. Again, he was right on.

"Yep, I remember. I was working midnight shift and sleeping when all that took place…Well, you know, I don't know what else I can say. I…I have lots of reasons to believe it's you. Everything fits. I look back at the Sheppard case. I know what was involved there. You know, you talked to me and told me some of the things about that. I've looked at the Pennsylvania cases that they had on you back in '82 and it all fits. I'm just trying to bring some closure to these two old ladies and I know you can respect that."

"I can understand that…Nah, I didn't do them."

"I'm also trying to play on the fact that, last time I was here, you admitted that if there's something you could do, you would want to do it. You don't have a whole lot of years left either, probably. How old are you now?"

"I'll be sixty-three this month."

"Tim, did you say it wasn't you in those cases? Do you remember anything about those cases? See any news at the time?" Jim asked.

"I didn't hear anything. Usually I'd be at work at that time. I was working night shift then. And about the only thing I watched on TV was sports."

I changed the topic once more, pretending to tell Jim for the first time about Tim's athletic prowess inside the prison walls.

"Basketball was my favorite sport," Jim said. "I've played a lot of basketball. I'm sixty-one and you said you're sixty-two?"

"Yeah."

"I'm pretty close."

"Although, unlike you and me, he's kept his hair," I said of Jim.

Tim smiled. Jim and I chuckled. It was time to punch up the pressure on Tim.

"Well, I'm gonna move on. Jim is here with the Cape Girardeau Police Department. Cape Girardeau has some cases on you. And I'm not gonna make any bones about it. They've actually done some work with some of the forensic things that needed to be done as well as photo lineups. So he has a case that he needs to discuss with you."

Tim continued to look calm, cool and collected, but with the mention of those simple words, *Cape Girardeau*, I imagined Tim's pulse got faster and his blood pressure a bit higher. His past was now coming back to revisit him. I wondered what he was thinking at that very moment.

"Tim, in my case, I'm gonna talk to you about what occurred January 9, 1982," Jim said. "It was a black lady and her daughter. Nice looking black lady. She lived out on the west side of town. Do you remember where the fairgrounds were located in Cape Girardeau?"

"Nah."

Jim summarized the second sexual assault on Holly to Tim.

"She's also picked you out of a photo lineup. She was also a Jehovah's Witness, which should ring a bell with you."

"Nah," Tim said, shaking his head no.

"Well, once again, I know the Tim that was involved with these cases is totally different from the guy I've kind of got to know in these interviews. So I guess the question is: Does the Tim today have the responsibility for acknowledging what that evil part of you did back in those years?"

Jim told Tim that Holly was once his coworker. He described how emotional Holly had been in discussing the assaults on her with him. He made up a story about how her daughter refused to return to Cape Girardeau to visit her mother, because it was too painful. We felt if Tim had any real remorse, maybe this would nudge him toward talking. As Jim and I had planned, we wanted to ease in with the rape crimes first.

"There's no doubt in her mind that it was you," Jim said.

"Nah. Didn't do it."

It was time to change gears again. I wanted to see if we could get him to admit to being in Cape Girardeau at all and during several key time frames.

"Did you ever go to Cape?"

"Occasionally. My girl's best friend went to school down there. And once a month we'd drive her down there."

"Who was the girl you were going with at the time?"

Tim told us his girlfriend's full name. I jotted it in my notebook, planning to track her down later. He said she was from Carbondale as was her friend, who was going to the same school where Sheila Cole had been a student.

"What year would that have been? I mean, you're pretty sharp. You have a pretty good recall."

"Well, Cape was '79, '80. Right in there somewhere. I'm not sure."

How convenient: his impeccable memory suddenly became foggy.

"So you were over there every week or so? Is that what you're saying?" Jim asked.

"No, I'm talking probably not no more than five or six times."

Again, it was time to turn up the pressure and let Tim know that we had a lot more information about him than he might think.

"I understand that you like a special beer and occasionally went to Cape to get it."

"One time. Went down to Cape one time."

I told him I had spoken with Dottie.

"She sure had a lot of good things to say about you. I mean she found that, like everybody with whom I've talked, she was pretty amazed that you were involved in some of the things that you were. It's like there are two Tims."

"Yeah, I agree to that."

"And I guess, like you said, when you got one of these impulses to go out and do something, that was the other Tim."

"Yeah, rationality went out the window...I've been twisted since I was a little kid. Can't blame it on nothing else. The first six or seven years of my life I was left alone too much. And it twisted me. It just got worse when I grew up I guess."

"Do you have brothers?" Jim asked.

"Two half brothers. One of them almost went the same way I did, but I told my mom to get him a psychiatrist. He joined the Army and he turned out pretty good...All three of us had problems."

"You know, you're probably the smartest guy I've ever talked with or interviewed on these sides of the walls and it's interesting to talk to you. One of the big things is the fact that you seem to have figured yourself out. I mean, I know you've been through a lot of psychological testing and interviews and you've talked with psychologists and tried to figure out what's gone on, but the interesting fact is, I don't know if they ever figured it out, but it seems like you have pretty much self-diagnosed yourself. Is that fair to say?"

"Yeah, that's fair."

"And obviously I keep coming back to the fact that in that self-diagnosis you have been able to remove yourself from society. I don't know anybody who's ever been able to do that. Most people will deny they have a problem and keep working their way out, whether it's just spending the time that they've been sentenced. I don't know that much about people who have been deemed sexually dangerous offenders. You're around them a lot and I'm sure there are some who have come in and actually went out. I don't know if you've seen very many come back. Have you ever seen some of the guys come back after they've went back out?"

"Some."

"I think you even said this: that if you went back out there would be a chance that you might hurt somebody again."

"No, I knew."

"You know, I think that reflects so much, but what do we do with the old stuff? What do we do with the things that happened when you were out? I mean, do we just leave them alone and leave them linger until the people die? Or do we try to make something good out of something that was so bad? What can you reap out of all this and do good out of it? I mean there's no doubt that the victim and her daughter were somebody whom you raped. There's no doubt. Can you bring closure to that for her?"

"No. I told you most of the stuff that I did. I mean, there's a lot of little incident things that I, you know, there was no, uh…you know, like all that exposure that I did and stuff like that. But other than that, I told you mostly everything."

"I know we're talking, I guess, to two Tims," Jim said, "and it's a little bit difficult for me to understand that at some time…I know you've tried to put the other Tim behind you for many years and I understand that part of it, I think. You know, I'm not gonna sit here and try to pretend I know what makes you tick. This is my first time ever to talk with you and I never knew you before, obviously, and it's hard for me to understand this. You know, you say that there was another person and it's somebody from years ago. And I appreciate that. But in forgiving yourself for what you may or may not have done years ago…"

"Well, I have never done that."

"You've never forgiven yourself?" Jim asked.

"No."

"Well, maybe a way that you could get to that point is by giving people like this woman an opportunity to know about you and forgive you for what happened. You know that can be done," Jim said.

"Does it matter what I said about how Mrs. Sheppard forgave you? Does that mean anything to you at all?" I asked.

"It's nice, but..."

"Well, it's huge on the other end. I mean, it really is, because not only does that resonate through us in law enforcement, but also it also resonates with the rest of her family...It's a tragic event that will carry through the generations, the same way with this. I mean, the situation with their case, with the rape that took place, you know, the little girl was ten years old. And thankfully you didn't rape her," I said.

Tim nodded in agreement.

"You know I sit with you here today and I know you denied Deborah's murder the first day, but I also saw the relief in you on the second day. That you finally felt like you got it off your chest. And that's kind of where we're at with this. I don't know how you feel when you acknowledge something like that. But I know the other end of it and I know what it does for the families. And that's why we're here. I've got lots of current cases. I don't have to dig back into these, but I see an opportunity here and I see a guy who has expressed some desire to help these families bring closure to this. What's left? That's the only thing left that you can do and that's where we're at."

"You can't be locked up any more than forever, you know. Forever's forever. Part of that was on your own doings. You wanted that," Jim added.

"You wanted that because you knew you had to. And then again, that's commendable. Help this lady and her daughter."

"I can't do it. It wasn't me. Someone that might have resembled me maybe, but it wasn't me."

It was time for us to try another angle.

"Explain this to me: what does that mean when they talk about DOC counseling. Is it a counseling session?"

"Pretty much, yeah."

"Is that where you actually discuss some of the things that occurred in the past?"

"Yes."

"So that's why you have to be honest to actually go into those?"

"If you're not honest, there ain't no sense in going. And then you just…fooling yourself."

"Do you foresee yourself ever going to those?"

"Yeah, I thought I would probably get back into it."

"Okay, well I don't think you're going to be able to until you come clean on this one."

"Ain't me."

"Well," Jim said, "we're in the process of doing DNA testing on that case and like Paul just said, she's convinced. And I'm convinced. He's convinced. It's got to be you, Tim…You know, you said you've been twisted for a long time and you thought it had happened when you were a very young child. About being left alone, were you sexually abused? Physically abused?"

"No, it was all emotional."

"How young would you have been when you were left by yourself?" I asked.

"From about year one to six."

"Where were your brothers at the time?" Jim asked.

"Well, one is three years younger and the other is ten years younger. And, like, uh, when I was four years old, I can remember pushing my younger brother off the porch and broke his leg."

"Ouch," I said.

"When I was five years old I went into somebody's house and trashed it. I think at eight years old I was on probation for stealing a bicycle. And when I was fourteen I started burglarizing and voyeurizing. Anything if I could get immediate gratification."

"Well, that's certainly erratic behavior, but, you know…I grew up on a farm with three brothers and we fought all the time. And I can never remember my father saying a kind word to me—" Jim said.

"Yeah, but you had a father," Tim interrupted.

"Well, I had a father; yes I did."

"I had no father. And my mother was never there. And a child that young, you have to have something from a female or a father, some kind of, you know, attention. If you don't, you just go twisted…"

"Become a wild dog," Jim said.

"Yeah, it happens. It happened to me. It was unfortunate. That's the way it goes I guess."

"But at that time you didn't realize it necessarily. I mean, as old as you are you look back and…and it sounds like you've gotten better control over everything. You have a better understanding of what you did and I don't think you'll ever know why you did it. Is that fair to say?" I asked.

"Probably. Probably. Unless, I just, uh…somehow getting back at a mom that was never there or something. I don't know."

We turned conversation to more small talk about Tim's past. I didn't want to lose him. I asked him about his girlfriend to distract him temporarily, hoping to place him in Cape Girardeau during the time frames we needed to tie him to the cases.

"I never went down there that much. When we went to, uh, when I was at the ambulance service, went down there a few times," Tim said.

"Now, you know, one of the things you told me is talking about all the lies that you told through the years to protect yourself and of course you did that with the Sheppard case as well. Then you told me that it was time to quit lying. And I still don't feel like you're coming, well, I know you're not being truthful with me now."

"How did you make that decision?" Jim asked.

"Which one?" Tim asked.

"On denying and then the next day deciding that you were gonna come forth with the truth?"

"I think a lot of it, I just wanted to get it off my mind, I think. I'd…I'd figured at one time or another some of this was going to catch up with me. I think I told Mr. Echols that I had planned as my health started to fail, later on in years, I was gonna go to a full disclosure. And then, they, you know, came and seen me and that sort of changed everything."

"And the other thing I don't understand, why wait? You know, I don't mean to put religion on this thing, I don't consider myself an overly religious person, but I do believe in God and do believe that we all have to stand before Him and be judged. I don't know if you believe that or not, but I do. And also I think that if we ask forgiveness from our heart we can be forgiven. I don't know if you believe that. I believe that…"

"Well, I'm not religious so…"

"I understand," Jim said.

Again, it was time to increase the pressure. Jim told Tim that Holly Jones had been assaulted by the same attacker twice. He described the first attack, which began with her abduction from the discount store parking lot.

"She said both times it was you. And we believe her. And there's evidence that's probably going to show that. You need us to bring you that evidence?" I asked.

"No, it wasn't me," Tim said.

"We're going to have to do that again, because DNA, as you found out, I mean with all this new science and technology, that's what's catching up to you. And it's catching up. I'm not telling you everything here, because I wanted you to do this on your own," I said.

"I think Paul hit the nail on the head: you're not gonna talk about anything unless we have something scientifically to lay in front of you, right? We can get that cleared up now, I assume?" Jim asked.

"Well, I've talked about everything I've done. And I think I'm just gonna stop…stop talking period."

I was afraid we were going to lose him before we got to confront him with the DNA evidence in the Wallace case. It was obvious he had mounted his defense and it was going to be tough to break through it. It was time to bring in the big guns.

"Well, let us run one more for you, which he does have the DNA. Let him tell you about that one."

Midway through his description of Mildred Wallace I passed Jim a note reminding him to show Tim the pictures of the outside of her house if he denied it. I knew that would help in the prosecution if this landed in court, especially if he just happened to later recall that he did know her. He got Tim to deny knowing Mildred, ever being in her house or breaking into anyone's home along the street where Mildred lived. Once again it was about getting the denial so he would have to explain to a jury how his DNA was found in her home if he claimed he never knew her. If he did later try to explain his DNA away, saying he and Mildred had somehow met that evening and had a sexual encounter, Mildred's reputation would have easily trumped that. She was not promiscuous. Her family believed she was still a virgin. Then Jim showed Tim pictures of Mildred's house. Again he denied ever being there or seeing it. Jim handed Tim a copy of the DNA report matching his genetic profile to evidence found in her house.

"Any questions?" Jim asked.

"Nah," Tim said, shaking his head no.

Jim then handed him a copy of the report showing Tim's palm print matched a palm print lifted from Mildred's back window.

"What went wrong in that case? What did she do?" I asked.

"I don't want to talk about it," he insisted.

The "I don't want to talk about it" line was a big breakthrough in our opinions. He had passed the point of denial and now acknowledged that he was responsible and just chose not to talk about it. We had to keep pressing him, but we had to be careful. With some suspects, this is where one really puts on the pressure. But not with Tim.

"Do you want to know what's gonna happen?" Jim asked.

"It doesn't matter."

Again, Tim teetered on ending our interview by saying he didn't want to talk about it, so it was time to change the subject once more and gather more information we needed to rule out the possibility that one of his brothers could have been an accomplice. He said they never came to Cape Girardeau with him.

"Do you have any questions, Tim, about what's gonna happen with this case?" Jim asked.

"I have no idea."

"Well, I can tell you that we have a meeting tomorrow with our prosecutor. And it is a capital case. Are you aware of that?" Jim said as Tim nodded in agreement. "So I'll be back over, I assume, to see you in the next few days to serve your warrant to you. And I can't, I can't make any deals with you or anything like that. I'm not even going to profess that I can even begin to do that, but I can certainly relay something from you to our prosecutor. Now, he's...it's a death penalty case. And it will be filed as such. And my recommendation...I know if I were in your position I would want to think about some way that I could negotiate my way out of that. It's your decision."

"I think I'm done talking and I'll take whatever comes...Like I said, I've been twisted since I was a little kid and now it is just catching up with me."

"For me, it looks like the best thing would be to accept what you just said, 'it is just catching up with me', meet the issue head-on and try to negotiate your best deal or whatever, you know," Jim said.

"Well, maybe if I had a life, you know. But I don't have any life. I haven't had a life for twenty years. This is no life. I'm ready to give up this life tomorrow. I mean I don't want to spend another thirty years in here. I mean...why should I look forward to tomorrow? Why do I want to wake up tomorrow? I mean, I'm doing this these last two years trying to fight that kind of depression."

"I know it's a sad situation," Jim said.

"So...it's all in here. If I die tomorrow, I don't care."

"You've done a lot of bad things on Earth. There's no doubt about that. A lot of bad things to a lot of different people and you've also hurt yourself in return. But now, when it's all meeting you head-on, it may be an opportunity for you to stand up and admit to that. Admit to yourself that you've done all those bad things and try to give yourself some peace too."

"I've already made peace with myself. I'm just waiting for death."

"Are you sure about that?" Jim asked.

"Yes."

"Then why can't you share some of that with some of these victims?" I asked.

"No…no…I'm done talking now. I'm not gonna talk about any of that stuff anymore. Whatever happens, happens, but if I die tomorrow, I don't care."

"So you don't care about the families that are living…" Jim asked.

"Don't care about anything, pretty much."

It was time for us to really press him.

"Tim, it doesn't stop with that case either. It just keeps going. There're other cases. And there're a lot of people hurting out there and you're the only one who can bring closure and help them through that. I mean, once again, what's left? What's left with your life?"

"After this, I'm…I'm…I'm not gonna have any life, so…"

"So you knew one day it would all catch up with you?"

"I thought so."

"What was it that caused you to click?"

"If I knew those answers, it would have never happened."

I told Jim to summarize the other cases to which we had connected Tim. He ran through the Parsh murder. Tim listened with no reaction to Jim's words. Then Jim described the disappearance of Cheryl Ann Scherer, who vanished along with $450 in cash from the register from a gas station where she worked in Scott City when she was nineteen years old. His eyebrows furrowed at Jim's description of the case.

"So you're not interested in any type of cooperation? Talking about other cases and trying to negotiate anything?" Jim asked.

"I don't have…a death wish, but I don't have a life either."

"If you had some assurance that you could negotiate yourself out of the death penalty, what would you think about that?" Jim asked.

"I would think about it. That's all I'm gonna say. But I don't think that's gonna happen though."

I told Tim that Cape Girardeau's prosecuting attorney was waiting for Jim's phone call to see how Tim reacted to the evidence we showed him.

"Let Jim go make a phone call, if that's what you want to do. If you're not interested in that, then we'll stop. But if you'd like to hear at least what the prosecutor has to say, let Jim make the phone call."

"I'll hear what he's got to say."

An hour and a half in, we finally had reached a breaking point with Tim. I had begun to fear we were losing the only bargaining chip we had with him—his own mortality—as he continued to say his life was not worth living. But finally he had shown us a glimmer of hope that he might care enough to see another day. Jim left to call Morley. Tim took a bathroom break. I went to get him some water.

Jim found me and said it was apparent from the first few minutes of his conversation that Morley wasn't budging on the death penalty issue. We were so frustrated, knowing how close Tim was to telling us everything in his closet if we could just dangle a life sentence in front of him. We knew Morley's opinion, but we had hoped that if we got in this position he might give us the green light to move forward. It made no sense to argue this until we knew for sure whether it would matter to Tim. Even though Morley didn't appear to be in a bargaining mood, Jim and I decided it would be best to keep the news from Tim and try to convince Morley in person. A half hour later, we went back into the interview room with Tim and lied, telling him we couldn't reach Morley.

"There's nothing we can provide you at this time. Obviously, we'll be willing to convey anything on your behalf if you choose to do that. So it's kind of left up to you at this point if you'd like to talk about this and we'd like to see you bring closure to these."

"Yeah…I…I need…I need some time just…"

"Need some time to think?"

"Yeah."

"We've thrown a lot of things at you for you to consider and it is our understanding, though, that once we are to get a hold of the prosecutor that you might be willing to discuss these cases. The cases we've talked about?"

"I…I…I got to think about everything."

"Okay. Were there any of these cases that we mentioned that should be just totally excluded?"

This was a trick question. If he ruled out something, he would have to rule in something.

"Yeah."

"Which one?"

He hesitated for a second.

"I ain't going there either."

Damn. Almost had him.

"Try to give me at least a couple of days to think this thing through."

"Okay. Well, that'll give us time to talk to the district attorney and we almost need to know kind of what you want as we approach him. So can you put that in your words?"

"I thought…I'm gonna…At this point in time…"

"Got your head spinning, huh?"

"Yeah."

I turned off all of the recording devices. Tim just watched us gather our things. Then he said something that took me by surprise.

"Hey, that Paducah case you asked me about," he said.

"Yeah, about the seventy-four-year-old lady," I replied.

"That ain't me," he said.

"Okay, well, thanks for letting us know. We'll get back to you," I nodded.

Of all the cases we had asked Tim about that day that was the only one he denied. It reinforced that we were on track with the others. Two hours after our meeting began, Jim and I walked out. We were so close, but it was clearer than ever that we needed Morley to agree to waive the death penalty if we were truly ever to learn all of Tim's secrets.

14

Negotiating Death

As Jim and I drove away, we talked about how we wished we could've gotten a full confession. Morley's decision about seeking the death penalty had blocked that and we weren't happy. But we also understood that he and others felt differently about this brutal serial killer's sentence. We hoped that maybe we had said enough to get Tim to call us back, just like he did the day after my first interview with him in the Sheppard case. If not, then we needed to convince Morley to change his mind. That was not going to be easy.

The next day, I got a message from Lieutenant Schuler on my voicemail. He had called late the day before. My heart raced as I waited to hear him say that Tim wanted us to come back so he could confess, but the message went in a different direction.

"Hey, Paul, this is Schuler. Tim called me to his cell after you and Jim left yesterday. He wanted me to tell you guys he doesn't want to talk to you again until he gets an attorney. Sorry."

Damn, I thought. *We missed our best opportunity. We pushed him too far.* I had been afraid of that. Jim and I had discussed how far to push him. We had known it was a gamble but a gamble we had to take. I called Jim immediately.

"He told Schuler he's not going to talk to us again until he gets an attorney."

The line was silent on Jim's side. I heard him take a deep breath followed by an expletive. We both grew even more upset at Morley for not giving us the latitude we felt we needed to get Tim to admit the real scope of his crimes. Jim told me Carl also was upset with Morley. We now had to focus on trying to change Morley's mind. There was no chance of a death penalty in Illinois. In 2003, Illinois Governor George Ryan, who was serving time in a federal prison himself, had commuted the death sentences of 167 Illinois death row inmates. Then he placed a moratorium on death sentences while a commission studied the situation. Unlike Illinois, Missouri was still carrying out death warrants. And Morley knew that.

I found myself in an awful quandary. I was pushing hard to save Tim's life to get a full confession, knowing he deserved to die. In a way, I felt as if I was betraying Bernie Sheppard, Deborah's father, who would be willing to personally place the needle in Tim's arm if given the chance. But I also thought about the practical side of pushing for the death penalty. Tim was about to turn sixty-three years old. *Was it really possible to go through a trial, convict him, get a judge to give him the death penalty and then wait out his automatic appeals and put him to death before he died a natural death?* To me, it didn't seem likely. It was frustrating, but there was nothing I could do.

All we could do was move ahead with nailing Tim for the other cases as best we could. I started with a call to Suzanne at the crime lab to ask if we could give half our buccal swab obtained from Tim in the Sheppard case to Pennsylvania investigators.

"I'll have to check on that, but I've got some good news."

"Oh, really?" I said.

"I've been working on the evidence in the Sheila Cole murder. I found traces of semen in the crotch of her blue jeans."

I felt better. This was good news. No one had been able to find evidence of sexual assault, even on Sheila Cole's undergarments, which were now missing. Tom Parks had submitted her blue jeans and a few other items for analysis in the absence of her underwear.

"It's a very small stain, so we shouldn't get our hopes up just yet," Suzanne warned.

Once again, I called Jim. We were talking and e-mailing so frequently that we almost needed to keep a phone line open between us all the time. He was pleased at the news and reminded me that we were still waiting on DNA results from Holly's rape kit and the pubic hair recovered from Margie Call. Still, we weren't ready to give up on persuading Morley to forgo the death penalty. I was trading just about as many e-mails with Carl. He told me he had even considered bringing coffee and a box of doughnuts to Morley's house unannounced on a Saturday, thinking maybe catching Morley away from the office where the two men could sit comfortably and talk openly without interruption might help. But Morley was out of town.

Other states, too, had to decide how to handle the death penalty in their cases. I told Pennsylvania State Police Corporal Bill Moyer that if he could waive the death penalty there, Tim would likely confess to Myrtle Rupp's murder. Bill was facing his own dilemma. In Berks County, where Myrtle Rupp was murdered, the local district attorney had just lost the election and was a lame duck. He was fine with giving Tim a pass on the death penalty for his confession, but by the time the case got to court, the new DA would be in place. Bill would have to wait to talk with the incoming DA, who could see the case as an opportunity to prove himself. He also asked me to get a court order for Tim's DNA, rather than using a portion of our sample from the Sheppard case.

Shortly after our conversation, another Pennsylvania area code popped up on my caller ID. It was Joe Kocevar and he had an unusual proposal. Tim's cousin Donna had reached out to him, hoping he would ask me to deliver a letter from her to the Sheppard family. He passed my phone number to her. She struck me as a kind, soft-hearted woman who felt sympathy for Tim. Like many of Tim's friends whom I had interviewed, his cousin found Tim to be charismatic and enjoyed his letters and occasional phone calls. She had been Tim's advocate for many years, sending him sports magazines and money for the commissary, even though many in his family had turned their backs on him. She kept her contact with Tim a secret from her own mother.

It was strange to talk to a member of Tim's family after having been so involved with the Sheppards. Donna never claimed he was innocent nor harbored any anger toward me for bringing him down. Talking to me about the case was perhaps the only thing she could do to convince herself that the gentle soul she knew could be capable of such violence.

She described Tim's mother as a beautiful, funny, friendly person who loved to party and to laugh and who never turned her back on Tim. She went to Illinois with his stepfather to be at Tim's trial when he was convicted of the first rapes. Whenever Tim came home from prison, he was welcome at his mother's home. She acknowledged that Tim's family moved a lot, but said her uncle had to go wherever work took him. She said Tim was right in saying that his mother may not have been as affectionate and loving to her kids as they all would have liked but said that things were different back then and lots of parents didn't tell their kids how much they loved them all the time. Showing Tim affection would have been hard with all the trouble that Tim got into when he was young. At that time, therapy was not as accepted as it is now. She said Tim's mother could be stubborn, obstinate and argumentative just like her father, Tim's mother's brother. They butted heads, but Tim's mother was loyal to Donna's family even when her parents divorced. She said neither Tim's mother nor stepfather were monsters and did not try to raise a monster; they just tried to live life to the best of their ability.

"You can send me your letter to the Sheppards, but I'm telling you right now, I don't think it's going to be well received. But I promise you that I will get it to them," I told Tim's cousin.

When the note arrived, I read it to make sure it was written in the same good-hearted tone that Donna had promised. She offered to send the Sheppards a bouquet of flowers every year on Deborah's birthday if they would allow her to do so. Donna didn't know about the other cases yet. *Boy, you're going to go bankrupt with a promise like that,* I thought. *There are at least eight more birthdays you'll need to remember!* The Sheppards never responded to the letter.

Meanwhile, Morley was beefing up his arsenal against Tim.

"He told me everything was looking good and he was quite pleased with the DNA evidence Stacey was putting together against Tim. He says he wants to meet to discuss everything with us," Jim told me.

"Well, at least we'll have another chance to argue our point."

Carl wasn't giving up either. He wanted to wait until we learned whether the DNA on Sheila Cole's jeans belonged to Tim before planning a press conference. Carl grew up in Cape. He had lived through the murders in 1977 and worked the other two in 1982. He felt just as Jim and I did that if he could announce a resolution to all the murders, not just one, it would provide relief to the victims' families and the entire community. Carl had spent fifteen years as the Cape Girardeau Police Department's public information officer and he realized this press conference was very important. He enlisted the help of Marine Lieutenant Colonel Jim Vance, a media affairs instructor at the FBI Academy in Quantico, Virginia. Vance was the media advisor during the Washington, D.C., area sniper shootings in 2002. It was still up in the air whether the press conference would be discussing one murder or more.

As Carl prepared to tell the world about the man who killed these women, he thought of those who had worked the cases through the years. Old cops savor their successes, but they never forget the cases they could not resolve. Carl wanted these dedicated men to hear the news from him. He called retired Cape Girardeau Police Officer John Brown and former chiefs Howard "Butch" Boyd Jr., Steve Strong, retired colonel Henry Gerecke and Ray Johnson. Brown and Strong had personally poured countless hours into resolving the cases and Brown warned Jim that solving the cases would be the biggest deal in the town's history. Gerecke served as chief during the Parsh murders and had hired Carl. Carl had the same respect for Gerecke as I had for retired Carbondale chief Ed Hogan, who had hired me. He told Carl he hadn't thought he would live long enough to see the cases resolved. Johnson, who replaced Gerecke in 1982, was only about a week away from taking the reins when the body of Margie Call was found. Like Chief Gerecke, he retired with frustration, because no arrests had been made. When the retired officers heard Tim's name, each searched their memories, trying to connect the name to the hundreds of leads they had pursued. None recognized the name. The news was exciting for them. It was particularly emotional for Boyd. Like everyone else, he had taken the cases personally. A flood of memories came back to each man. It had been a long time coming.

Before long, it was time for our meeting with Morley. Jim was waiting for me in the lobby at the Cape Girardeau Police Department when I arrived. Brian Ritter and another FBI agent from Marion, Illinois, Marty Williams, were already there. Morley arrived shortly afterward. Carl introduced us. I had seen Morley on television several times through the years but had never met him. It was time to talk. There was a lot riding on this meeting.

Jim and I described our interview with Tim and why we believed he'd confess to everything if we could dangle death in front of him. Carl concurred and told Morley how important it was to the families and the community to finally put all of the cases to rest at one time. Our arguments fell on deaf ears. Morley wouldn't budge. He bragged about his success in achieving the death penalty in other cases and how one man had already been executed. He was convincing. Not only did he want Tim to get the death penalty, but also he knew he could do it. We moved forward, trying to salvage the meeting. If Morley wasn't going to reconsider, then there was nothing else to talk to Tim about. We turned to the timing of Tim's arrest for the murder of Mildred Wallace and his guilty plea in Deborah's case.

Morley said he'd use Tim's guilty plea in Deborah's murder as an aggravating factor as he sought the death penalty for Tim. Indirectly, Deborah's murder could still get Tim the death penalty. *That will please Bernie,* I reminded myself. For a moment I forgot about the Cape cases and thought of Deborah's dead body lying on her bedroom floor. It seemed to me right for Tim to die for what he did to her. I volunteered to call Mike Wepsiec so he and Morley could talk about the timing of the charges. Morley agreed to charge Tim after he pled guilty on December 10, 2007. It would be a crucial day for Tim as well as the city and the family members who had waited so many years for that moment.

After our meeting with Morley, Jim and I went back to his office. We felt a bit down. Though Tim's upcoming arrest for Mildred's murder was meaningful, not obtaining a full confession in all the other crimes we worked so hard to get him to admit and wanted him to pay for was difficult to accept. In trying to regroup, I reminded Jim of how important this arrest would be. He had worked very hard to get to that point and I wanted him to relish it. The motivational speech was as much for me as it was for Jim. By the time I had to leave, we were both more upbeat and beginning to think about the positive side of all of this.

"We've still got a lot of evidence in various stages of analysis and we might still be able to build other cases against Tim, even without confessions," I said.

"Yeah, I guess you're right. You know, I read a book about a serial killer, Gary Ridgeway, the Green River killer. He killed forty-eight women during the 1980s and 1990s in the Seattle, Washington, area. In order to clear all forty-eight cases, the prosecutor led the effort to spare Ridgeway the death penalty for his cooperation in showing police where to find several of the victims. It's very similar to what we're arguing; only in that case, the prosecutor took the lead to make the deal."

Jim decided to mark the parts pertaining to the plea agreement that spared the life of one of the most notorious serial killers in history and give the book to Morley. We didn't know if he'd read them or if they'd make any difference. I admired Jim for trying the unorthodox move. I grabbed a sandwich and headed to Carbondale. I hadn't been back to my desk very long when my phone rang. It was Tim's attorney, Jackson County Public Defender Patricia Gross.

"Hey, Paul, I received an interesting letter from Tim Krajcir today."

"Oh, really? What's up with Tim?"

"He said you and a detective from Cape Girardeau had been to see him last week about some murders in Missouri. He was asking me if I thought he should confess to them. Can you enlighten me on what this is all about?"

I had known Patricia for many years. She had questioned me on the witness stand many times and always treated me professionally as I did her. I wondered if she could help steer him to confess. I concluded my summary of the cases and evidence we had against him with a gentle suggestion.

"Cape Girardeau County District Attorney Morley Swingle is planning to seek the death penalty against Tim. Tim should confess to avoid the death penalty."

"That's incredible! You know I can't legally advise him on crimes that occurred in other states. I'll be going to the prison soon to meet with him. I'll suggest he confess to avoid the death penalty if the evidence against him is that strong."

"So do you think he's still going to plead guilty in Deborah's case?"

"I haven't heard otherwise from him, but he's going to make that final decision when I meet with him next week. Thanks for this new information, Paul. We'll be in touch."

Immediately I called Jim.

"I just got off the phone with Tim's public defender. She said she'd advise him to confess to avoid the death penalty."

"I'll tell Morley about it. He's here right now on an unrelated issue."

A few minutes later Jim called back.

"I think everything we've told him has changed his mind on the death penalty. He told me and Carl that if all of the families of the Cape murder victims agree to forgo the death penalty for Tim's full and detailed confession in each case, he'll waive the death penalty. He wants us to arrange a meeting with each family."

"That's great, Jim! If I can do anything to help, let me know."

Morley was making, in my opinion, a smart move. *Maybe he did read the Gary*

Ridgeway book Jim gave him, I thought. Doing it this way, he placed the burden on the families who were the most affected. He had been very firm with Carl and Jim about how the agreement had to be unanimous or he would not do it. Assuming they all agreed, the next hurdle would be how to get back into Tim's mind. But the meetings with the families had to come first.

Through the years, Jim had been in touch with the families periodically, letting them know he was the lead detective in the cases. Jim and Carl tried to arrange individual meetings with them on the same day. They didn't give out specific details to those they reached and on the messages they left but told them they needed to talk to them about a break in their cases.

The first family representative contacted for a meeting was Teresa Haubold, who was considered Mildred Wallace's next of kin and arguably the lynchpin among the families that we needed to be on board. After all, Mildred's case was made. It was the only one in which we had definitive DNA and fingerprint evidence. Teresa could've decided that justice for Mildred was more important than a confession and she was the only one who had the power to make that call at that time. And she wasn't even a blood relative of Mildred's, whose parents and siblings had since passed away.

Mildred, who grew up on a cotton farm, moved to Oran, Missouri, when her father bought a store there. She remained there until a cement company in Cape Girardeau hired her and she moved to Cape. Teresa's aunt married Mildred's brother, Bill. Teresa's father also had grown up with Mildred in Vanduser, Missouri. Mildred struck the much younger Teresa as a beautiful, tall and poised woman when Teresa saw Mildred during visits with her uncle Bill. He was never the same after Mildred's murder. When Bill was dying from Leukemia, he told Teresa that his greatest regret in life was not knowing what happened to his sister. After he died, Teresa inherited a rolltop desk from her uncle. He kept a framed picture of a Mildred on top of it. While clearing out the drawers to the desk, she found newspaper clippings detailing Mildred's death. Teresa and her father became the only members of Mildred's family left for investigators to contact.

Teresa also knew the Parshes and Margie Call. They were neighbors. She grew up only three houses from the Parshes and only two blocks from Margie Call. She remembered how Margie often stopped by and complimented her father about his award-winning garden. She went to high school with Brenda and Karen. She remembered when the girls moved to Cape from St. Louis and how quickly Karen made friends and was picked as a cheerleader for the basketball team.

The neighborhood where Teresa and the Parsh girls grew up was a quiet peaceful place, where children played freely and doors were never locked. Everyone trusted their neighbors. But in August 1977, the Parsh murders shattered that sense of security. Teresa's mother grew paranoid when she was alone at home. With each murder, it became almost unbearable to be an older person and live by yourself in Cape Girardeau. Through her mother, Teresa had heard rumors for years about possible suspects in the neighborhood.

The invitation to come to the Cape Girardeau Police Department rekindled Teresa's interest, but it was hard for her to believe that, after all these years, something substantial had suddenly surfaced. It was the first time she had ever been asked to come to the station. She had never been there, so her husband went with her. She didn't expect much.

Carl greeted Teresa and her husband when they got to his office. Teresa noticed two thick folders sitting on the wood conference table where they took their seats. Carl began telling them about the DNA match in Mildred's murder and the firm belief that Tim was responsible for all of the Cape murders. Carl gently slid a mug shot of Tim Krajcir in front of Teresa that was taken of him around the time of the murders. Then he pulled a copy of the most recent picture I had taken of him during his confession to Deborah's murder. Teresa began to cry as she realized that after twenty-five years it was finally over. For the first time there was a name and a face to the monster that had murdered Mildred. Teresa remembered seeing Tim's picture on the news a few months before when I arrested him for Deborah's murder.

"Jim Smith and Paul Echols tried to get Tim to confess to all of this but were unsuccessful. They believe that if he could be spared the death penalty, he might confess to Mildred's case along with the others. But Mr. Swingle is waiting to hear from you and the rest of the families on how to proceed. He's ready to seek the death penalty on Mildred's case alone."

Thirty years after the Cape murders began, Teresa, a kind and gentle lady, a loving mother and grandmother, who now worked for the Cape Girardeau Public School System, had just been cast into a historical role that would change dozens of lives. She had to decide if Tim Krajcir, the killer and rapist who had eluded authorities for three decades, should live or die. Her thoughts turned to the other families. She knew justice was now imminent in Mildred's case and she thought of what she could do to help others find that same justice.

"You are the first of four families we are talking to about this. If we get a unanimous decision, Mr. Swingle said he will be willing to offer Tim a deal," Carl told her.

Teresa didn't balk.

"Yes," she said. "I want to help the other families feel just as I am feeling and get the answers they need."

"I'm going to ask you not to discuss what is happening with anyone," Carl said.

"We still have a lot to do in this case and can't risk it getting out to the public just yet."

Teresa's first trip to the police department had been a memorable one. She left in shock. She thought of her uncle Bill and how she wished he could've lived long enough to learn who killed his sister. Once she got home, she prayed that success would come to me and Jim, a ritual she continued for days.

The Cole and Call families agreed to meet at the Cape Girardeau Police station on the day after Thanksgiving. Karen Parsh said she had other commitments and couldn't make the meeting. So Carl told her about Tim over the phone. She, like Teresa, didn't think the police would have anything too substantial to tell her in her mother and sister's case. News of a pending arrest ripped everything open again. Then, after giving her some insight into the man who had torn her family apart, Carl asked if she would be willing to spare his life in exchange for a confession. As much as Karen would have liked to see Tim die, her faith would not allow her to say it. She agreed to the deal. Carl promised to pass the information on to Morley and told her he would be back in touch.

Sheila Cole's brother and sister drove from the St. Louis area to meet with Jim, Carl and Morley in Carl's office. Sheila's sister showed Jim a photo of Sheila standing in front of the Gateway Arch, saying it was sealed among the photos Sheila picked up from the store the night she was murdered. Once again, Carl explained how the investigation had led us to Tim. Jim provided a bit of background about Tim and told them about our interview with him the week before. Morley explained his plan.

"Now, there's always a chance that enough evidence could be gathered to try Tim for Sheila's murder, but we're not there yet," he said. "Would you be willing to waive the death penalty for a full confession? Another positive thing to consider is that there would be no trial."

The siblings talked briefly and agreed to Morley's proposal. It was a decision they thought their parents would want them to make. They wanted the man responsible for robbing them of their kid sister to suffer the rest of his life in prison.

Later that same day, Margie's side of the family along with the Calls showed up in the lobby en masse. After Margie's murder, Margie's side of the family became surrogate parents to Margie's sons Don and Gary. The close knit family wouldn't allow Don and his wife to do this alone. About thirty cousins, aunts and uncles were there to stand beside him to hear his mother's killer named. His brother Gary, who had been an outstanding athlete and great coach, had died the year before. Carl's office couldn't hold that many people, so he moved the meeting to the department's upstairs classroom. Don said there would've been many more had twenty-five years not taken its toll on the family. Many had driven from other states, all thinking this could be the big break for which they had hoped. Carl, Jim and Morley again explained the intricate pieces that had led us to Tim. They, too, saw for the first time a photo of Tim and learned how I had arrested him for Deborah's murder. After hearing the facts, Morley invited the family to ask questions. Some asked about the evidence. Some asked how they could be so sure this was the right killer. Don asked if Tim had picked the victims because they were all office workers who lived alone and their first names began with "M" (Mary, Margie and Mildred).

"The truth is, we won't know until Tim confesses," Jim said.

Morley then reviewed the legal issues and explained the decision the family had to make. Don polled the group of relatives in the room and quickly called a few aunts and uncles who were unable to make the trip. Everyone agreed. Tim's life should be spared in exchange for the truth. Don realized the irony in the decision. Tim had killed a member of this family and now the same group had just voted to spare his life. Don hoped that someday Tim would appreciate what they did for him, considering what he had forever taken from them. It was a decision that he knew his mother, father and grandparents would have wanted.

Carl called to give me an update. It had been an emotional day.

"They all agreed to negotiate the death penalty," he said. "Morley wants to prepare a letter over the weekend for Tim, outlining the specifics of the deal. Jim will bring it over to you. Can you give it to Tim's attorney in the Sheppard case?"

"Sure, I'll do whatever it takes to get the letter to Tim."

Jim brought the letter Morley had hammered out over the weekend. Before we left my office, I read it. He outlined six conditions that Tim would have to meet to avoid the death penalty, including a polygraph, a guilty plea to each case, ten to twenty-page written statements on each case and a warning that if Tim lied to me or Jim the agreement would be off and he would seek the death penalty against him for the murder of Mildred Wallace. I must admit, I was impressed by Morley's letter. He was extremely thorough. If anything, I was a bit concerned that he was too thorough. But after having to fight to get him to give us this opportunity, it was worth a try. Morley didn't have the legal authority to negotiate any sentences for the cases I had against Tim in Illinois. Since the statute of limitations had expired, there could not be any charges. I figured if Tim went along with this, I'd do the best I could to piggyback onto the deal.

Jim and I jumped into the car and headed to the Jackson County Courthouse in Murphysboro to meet with Mike Wepsiec. I wanted him to read the letter to make sure there wasn't anything that might jeopardize the plea agreement in Deborah's case. He didn't see any conflicts, so we walked across the street to deliver the letter to Tim's attorney. She agreed to deliver it to Tim later that week. I figured that if we could just get the letter to Tim, we might be able to get our foot in the door.

It appeared another district attorney was coming on board with our strategy. Bill Moyer called to schedule an interview with Tim about Myrtle Rupp's murder and wanted me to be there. Apparently the new DA with whom he was dealing saw the value in a full confession too. I had his search warrant ready to get Tim's DNA and updated him on where things stood with the Cape cases. I also told him about Tim's intent to plead guilty to Deborah's murder the day before he planned to interview Tim.

So far, Bill had managed to keep the case under wraps from the local media. I, on the other hand, got a phone call from a television reporter. She knew me well and had covered many cases I had worked. She said she got a tip that Carbondale police were working with Cape Girardeau police on their five old murder cases and that an arrest was pending. I trusted her, she was very professional, but knew that I couldn't make any comments. I promised to call her back. I immediately called Carl and told him about it. Carl, too, had just received a call from a newspaper reporter who had the same information. We suspected that someone from one of the families had called the press. We were at a critical point in our investigation and couldn't afford for the story to break. Carl and I promised the reporters a story if they would hold off on running it for a few days. The strategy worked. Not a word about Tim or our investigation was uttered to the public. We breathed a sigh of relief. The relationships we had developed with the media had paid off. Otherwise, Tim could have found out just how much, or how little, we had on him before his attorney Patricia Gross got the chance to deliver Morley's letter.

News had spread to Tim's family as well. His cousin Donna called me to say Tim had told her about the visit Jim and I had with him.

"Please be honest with me. Do you really think Tim has killed other women?"

"I know that he has killed at least two more women and as many as six more."

I could hear her sobs through the phone as it all sank in. Even though she had not seen her cousin in twenty-five years, she still loved him.

"Thank you for being so honest with me. So what's going to happen to Tim?"

I decided that she might have some influence with Tim. So I took a chance.

"Well, there's the possibility of the death penalty, unless he cooperates. He's likely going to be receiving a letter tomorrow offering a waiver on the death penalty in exchange for his cooperation and confession in his crimes."

"Would it help if I wrote him a letter, telling him to tell all?"

"It might."

"Okay, I'm going to write one immediately and mail it with overnight delivery," she said, as if she had discovered a new sense of purpose.

I found out she made good on her promise the next day when I called to give

Lieutenant Schuler a heads up about Patricia's upcoming visit and Morley's letter.

"You know, Tim got another letter, but I haven't given it to him yet. It was from a female cousin of his," he said.

"Yeah, I talked to her yesterday about all of this. Apparently Tim called to tell her about our most recent visit with him. She agreed to do what she could to convince him to cooperate. Can you make sure Tim gets the letter as soon as possible? I'd really like him to get it before he meets with Patricia today."

"Sure. I'll personally deliver it to him as soon as we hang up."

Once again, Lieutenant Schuler had come through for us. I couldn't just sit at my desk, waiting for Patricia's call. I drove to the Marion FBI office to pick up some documents they had found on Tim. On my way back, my cell phone rang. It was Patricia. I held my breath waiting to hear his reaction to the letter.

"Tim is going to plead guilty on December 10 to Deborah's murder. He's accepted the forty years Mike has offered."

I couldn't wait any longer.

"Patricia, what did he say about the letter? Did he read it?"

"I was going to tell you about that. The guard wouldn't let me give him the letter. They said I'd have to mail it to him."

"You're kidding, right?"

"No, I'm not. I still have it with me."

"How far are you away from the Big Muddy prison?"

"I left about ten minutes ago. I can turn around."

"Yes, please turn around and head back. I'll make a quick call and get back with you."

Damn! If we mailed the letter it could be weeks before he got it. The prison screens all mail to inmates and it's not always a priority. I called my lifeline, Lieutenant Schuler.

"Tim Krajcir's public defender just met with him at the prison. She's carrying the letter we talked about. She said the guard wouldn't let her give it to him and that she'd have to mail it."

"Where is she right now?"

"She's on her way back to the prison to hopefully meet with you."

"I'll meet her at the main gate and escort her back in and see that he gets the letter today."

"Lieutenant, you are my hero! Thanks so much."

"Glad I could help."

I called Patricia back and told her to meet Lieutenant Schuler at the gate. About fifteen minutes later, she called to say she personally gave the letter to Tim.

"Did he say anything about it?"

"He didn't read the letter while I was there. I don't know what he's planning to do. I did tell him he should wait until he's charged and gets an attorney in Missouri before doing anything."

That didn't surprise me. She was doing her job. I thanked her and called Lieutenant Schuler to thank him again.

"No problem, Paul. I was going to call you anyhow. As I was walking Tim back to his cell, he was quite talkative. He told me about the plea agreement in the Sheppard murder. Tim is happy to get that done."

"Yes, that's what I understand. I'm very happy to hear that too. I hated to see the Sheppard family go through a trial and relive Deborah's murder all over again."

"Paul, I told him I was aware that you have been working very hard to get him a deal with Cape Girardeau authorities. He said, 'Echols is a good guy. I know he's trying to help. I have a decision to make.' We talked a bit more and he really feels you are in his corner."

"I guess we'll see what he has to say after he reads the letter."

It was strange to hear that Tim felt that way about me. The truth was I was trying to help the victims' families. I was trying to do whatever it took to get him to confess. I thought about how I could best take advantage of my rapport with Tim and decided it might be time to take a big risk. I believed I could convince Tim into confessing if I had him one-on-one, off-the-record, no lawyers, no other cops, no recording devices and no threats to use what he said to me against him in court. He had spoken to his attorney as he had wanted. Plus, Tim had nothing but time. Why would he make the first move to contact us? *Maybe he has some concerns about the conditions of Morley's letter. Maybe I could alleviate those concerns.* I knew Lieutenant Schuler would feel Tim out for me about the idea. I didn't think Morley needed to know about an off-the-record conversation. In the worst-case scenario, the court would throw out Tim's confession and Morley would seek the death penalty against Tim. But I wasn't willing to take the risk without Carl and Jim's blessing.

15

Serial Secrets Unraveled

I sent Carl an e-mail explaining that I wanted to try to meet with Tim alone. I expected he would tell me to wait and let Tim contact us. But by now I felt I knew Tim very well. I thought if we could prod him just a little, I could take advantage of the rapport I had built with him. I was afraid time would only erode that trust. A phone call that Lieutenant Schuler intercepted in which Tim talked to his half brother added more urgency. Tim made several statements reminding his brother where to scatter his ashes if he died. We worried that Tim might be considering suicide. Lieutenant Schuler stepped up the watch on him. We didn't want to see all of Tim's secrets go to the grave with him. Time was important. We needed to do something, fast.

Carl responded quickly to my e-mail. As my surrogate police chief, he saw the value in my meeting with Tim one-on-one as well but struggled over whether to involve Morley, as I had. We both didn't want to give the district attorney the impression that we were trying to circumvent him, but Carl didn't see the harm in my meeting with Tim either. Ultimately, he gave me the green light to move forward.

Jim, like me, wanted Tim to talk. We hoped this nudge would work. Jim told me he would be at his desk all day so just to call. I was, of course, in early. So was Jim. Neither of us was on the official clock yet. After my morning investigation meeting, I came back to my desk and called Lieutenant Schuler. I was quite pleased to hear his distinctive deep voice.

"I'm calling to ask you a favor."

"What can I do for you?"

"I need you to ask Tim if he wants me to come there and discuss Morley's changes, I will. Tell him I won't ask him any questions about any cases, there won't be a Miranda warning and I won't record anything or take notes. It'll just be me and him, talking completely off-the-record."

"I can do that. I'll go talk to him in a few minutes and let you know what he says."

I called Jim again. He picked up the phone on the first ring. We were both on pins and needles. As the morning passed, I noticed just how slow my watch seemed to be running. By lunchtime, there was no word from Schuler. I was beginning to think Tim had decided to take his chances with being charged. I couldn't stand it any longer, so I called Lieutenant Schuler.

"I was just checking in with you to see if you had met with Tim."

"Paul, I'm sorry. Right after I spoke with you we had a big fight at the prison and I've been dealing with that. I'll try to go talk to him soon, I promise."

I was glad to hear he hadn't talked to Tim yet. That rejuvenated my confidence that the plan had not failed, at least, not yet. I went for my lunch hour run with Heather. We were about a mile into it when my cell phone rang.

"Hey, Paul, it's Schuler. I just met with Tim. I told him exactly what you asked me to. He wants you to come up and talk to him. I'll get the paperwork started to get you clearance now."

I went back to my office to call Jim. I promised Jim that if Tim wanted to confess, I would wait for him. These were Cape cases and he would be the lead interviewer. Jim said he'd be waiting for my call. I gathered my equipment and headed to Big Muddy. I stopped in DuQuoin, Illinois, to buy some mini-DVDs for my camcorder. I wanted to make sure I was ready if this was going to be a long night.

Arriving at the prison at 2:30 P.M., I left everything in my car, hoping to be back out to get the stuff. Lieutenant Schuler escorted me to the conference room. Once again I heard the sounds of chains moving in my direction. Tim emerged through the door, wearing a tan one-piece jumpsuit. There was no smile or grin. He was unshaven and looked pretty haggard. After Lieutenant Schuler took off the chains, Tim shook my hand. Schuler offered him a cup of coffee. We both took a seat across the wooden conference table from each other.

"How are you doing?" I asked.

"Oh, okay I guess," he lied.

To make him relax a little I brought up general things, like how it was getting colder outside and sports. Tim was extremely knowledgeable about sports. He followed the SIU Saluki basketball team in particular and we talked about how their season was going. Soon, I felt the time had come to steer our conversation toward the real reason I was there.

"Tim, Schuler said you wanted me to come here and discuss the letter you received from the Cape Girardeau district attorney. I want you to know that I'm here just to answer your questions. I'm not here to interview or interrogate you. I'm purposely not providing you a Miranda warning, so things you say to me can't be used against you in court. And, as you can see, I'm not recording this in any way. This is just a conversation between you and me. Are you okay with that?"

"Yes, I'm okay with that. I did ask Schuler for you to come up. I've read the prosecutor's letter and I'm okay with most of it, but he wants me to write out ten to twenty pages about each of these crimes. I don't think I can do that. Some of these cases were spontaneous. I didn't plan for them, so I can't write about planning and preparation. There isn't that much to write."

With that statement, I realized Tim had just confessed to killing the five women in Cape. His concern wasn't that he was suspected of things he didn't do, he was concerned about how many pages he could write about them. Of course, all of this was off-the-record, but it was still important. I couldn't believe the number of pages was Tim's biggest concern, one that might have even jeopardized his decision to confess. But I guess when you're dealing with a contract to essentially spare your life, you look for the devil in the details.

"Tim, I believe Morley is looking for honesty and thoroughness. I don't think he's looking for a particular page count. He threw that number out there, assuming it would take that many pages. As long as you are being honest and providing details that only the killer would know, then you will have complied."

"Well, I'm just not sure what I need to do."

"Do you remember when we first met and I told you I had a DNA match on you in the Sheppard case? And then you said, 'I knew this was going to catch up to me one of these days.' Well, the science is catching up with you. As you know, there's a DNA match and a palm print match in one of the Cape cases. I had not told you this, but there is a DNA match on you in a Pennsylvania murder and there are other cases out there where the DNA is being analyzed. I just had a 1976 case where we used a new technique called mini-STR DNA profiling. We matched a suspect in that case from the victim's fingernail scrapings. The science is getting better all the time.

"If you decide it's worth the risk to wait, each day you run the risk of having more DNA matches made against you. At some point, a prosecutor is going to decide he doesn't need you to confess and isn't going to offer you a deal. I'm telling you right now, it hasn't been easy getting the Cape Girardeau DA to make this deal. He's been very vocal with me and Jim; he feels very strongly that you ought to get the death penalty. If he gets a few more DNA matches against you, I doubt he's going to be interested in making any deals with you. He's been successful in seeking the death penalty in his cases and one man has already been put to death. Here's the way I see it. You are sixty-three years old. You've recognized you're dangerous. You've purposely kept yourself in prison as a sexually dangerous person by not attending counseling. I can continue to argue for you to avoid the death penalty because of that. But, in return, you must do your part. You know you'll never be out of prison. You have to help us bring closure to these cases. You have to confess what you've done and plead guilty so the families don't have to relive these murders in a courtroom. That's all that you can do. What you did is done. It's your decision to make, but I suggest you don't take too long. There are several DNA experts out there as we speak trying to find you under their microscopes. We expect new lab reports any day."

My comments were not entirely a bluff. I knew the lab reports in the Call and Cole cases were near completion. But I also knew there was no evidence in the Parsh murders and in the 1977 rape of Holly. Plus, a lot of valuable time and resources were being spent trying to tie these cases to Tim and it was all a moot point. He was never going to get out of jail. The time and resources were needed in other open cases.

"I've been thinking about disclosing for a while now, but just could never bring myself to doing it. When you got me on the Sheppard case, I hoped it would stop then and I would have more time to think about it, but now these other cases are closing in on me."

"Well, if you want to do this deal, you need to accept it before Morley calls and takes it back. I can't guarantee you it'll be here tomorrow."

But I was using Morley's determination as a talking point that seemed to be convincing Tim to confess.

"I don't have a death wish. This is really no life, but it's the only thing I have left. Okay, let's do it."

"Okay. I need to go get Schuler. It's near suppertime. Go back to your cell so I can get Jim up here and by the time you eat supper, we'll sit down and take your confession."

"Okay."

"Hey, Tim, I have one quick question for you before we break. What's your number? You don't have to give me details, but I am curious."

"Nine."

I quickly did the math in my mind. I knew of seven murders for sure by then. I know the look on my face revealed my confusion. Tim voluntarily offered a few details on one.

"Remember in November when you asked me about the seventy-four-year-old lady from Paducah and I told you I didn't do that one?"

"Yes, I remember. It was at the end of our interview and we had turned off the recorder."

"Well, I didn't do that one, but I did another one down there. It was a young black gal. I took her from her apartment at night and brought her to Carbondale. I killed her at a trailer I was staying in and then took her back to Paducah and dumped her body behind a church at night."

"Okay, I'll have to get with them to figure out what case that was. Do you remember what year?"

"It was when I was out on bond, so it would have been 1979."

"If I get them to waive the death penalty on that case in Paducah will you talk to them?"

"Yes, but only if they give me a waiver."

I summoned Lieutenant Schuler and told him what Tim had agreed to do. He took Tim back to his cell and I called Jim. As luck would have it, his line was busy. So I called Carl.

"Carl, this is Echols. I tried to call Jim, but his phone is busy. I need to get him up to Big Muddy as soon as possible. Krajcir is ready to confess."

"Well, I'm surprised. I guess it worked."

"Yes. We sat and talked for a couple hours and he's now ready."

Carl quickly made his way down the hallway with his cell phone and handed it to Jim.

"What's going on?" Jim asked.

"Do you have gas in your car?"

"Yes, of course. I just filled it up."

"Then get your ass on up here. Time is a wasting and Tim wants to talk."

"I'll be on my way."

Jim loaded about ten large three-ring binders containing the case files along with a folder full of crime scene pictures into his trunk. He jumped into his maroon car and drove east across the Mississippi River Bridge into Illinois, much like Tim had done so many times. He carried with him the hopes and dreams of so many police officers and investigators who had tried and failed to do what he was doing at that very moment.

I called my boss Calvin to let him know I was going to be gone a while, because Tim wanted to talk. Lieutenant Schuler escorted me back to the front gate so I could get my recording devices from my car. I was glad I had stopped and picked up the extra mini-DVDs for my camera. I checked my cell phone for missed calls and messages. I had a text from Carl wishing me good luck and asking for an update later when I had a chance.

I couldn't help but wonder what Carl was doing as chief of a department that was about to finally resolve the most notorious crimes in his city's history. Some months earlier, I had looked at the Cape Girardeau Police Department Web site and one of the first things that popped up was a story about the five murders and a plea for citizens to call with information. *Soon the Web site will need to be updated!* I thought excitedly. Carl told me he was keeping City Manager Doug Leslie informed on the investigations but had not yet told Mayor Jay Knudtson. A public safety tax had been passed a few years before, which helped allow Jim to become their first full-time cold case investigator. *Mayor Knudtson has some shocking news coming his way tomorrow if all goes right.* It was going to be a long night, but I was so psyched, it did not matter. I figured Carl would be sitting with his cell phone in his hand tonight. I hoped Jim would make it to the prison without meeting the radar gun of an Illinois State Trooper.

Lieutenant Schuler made some phone calls to make sure he too could stay for the duration. It was important that he be available to help us move Tim around for water and bathroom breaks. I was trying to anticipate everything so we would not be interrupted. I set up the camcorder and arranged the seats. Jim would sit directly across from Tim and I would sit slightly to Jim's right side taking notes and manning the camcorder. I knew Jim was bringing his reports and photos.

Jim arrived at the front gate at about 5:45 P.M. Lieutenant Schuler helped him carry everything. When Jim walked into the interview room, his smile was a mile wide. He unloaded the reports and boxes of pictures onto the table.

"So our guy is ready to talk, is he?"

"Yes, we spent about two hours discussing what he should do. He had some questions about what Morley wants. His biggest concern is that he can't write ten to twenty pages on each murder. He said some of these things just happened and he didn't think he could write that much. I told him Morley isn't as interested in the number of pages as he is in details. I told him to honestly provide as much as he could remember. At the end, I asked him what he believed the number of murders was. He told me nine. He also confessed to a murder in Paducah but wants a deal before officially confessing. It's not the seventy-four-year-old lady either."

"Nine, huh? We thought he did one in Paducah. I guess we'll find out about that one later and the others now."

We talked about strategy and how Jim would be the lead interviewer and I would only jump in when he finished his questions. I told Jim we'd make sure we received a confession in all the Cape cases first, but if all was going well we would flow directly into the Illinois rapes and maybe even Virginia Witte's murder. I promised to contact Paducah police and see what deal I could arrange. I didn't want him going into detail until we were on-the-record.

"Well, I'm ready," Jim said.

"I am too. Lieutenant Schuler, can you go get Tim for us?" I asked.

The time to end decades of mystery had come. Tim emerged through the door.

"We've got coffee over there," Schuler said.

"I've already poured him a cup," I answered.

"I'm gonna get him a root beer. I've got one in my refrigerator."

"Is that what you'd prefer first? If so, I'll put your coffee back," I told Tim.

"I've already had about three cups of coffee. I'm gonna have a buzz here in a little bit."

Schuler offered to get the root beer for Tim.

"You can wait a while if you want. I'm gonna be here a while."

"Well, just get comfortable. That's the most important part."

I read him his Miranda rights. Jim read him Morley's letter, as required by Morley.

"Have any questions, Tim, about anything?" Jim asked.

"Well, I was telling Mr. Echols this afternoon…he said it was like fifteen or twenty pages on each thing. I mean that's impossible. These things were, some of them were spur-of-the-moment, where it was like twenty minutes."

"That's just an estimate on his part…All we want is the truth. If we can put it in a shorter form, well, so be it," Jim assured him.

He signed a copy of the letter, acknowledging that he understood its parameters. Then we looked at him and he looked back at us. The formalities were over.

"Any particular place you want to begin Tim?" Jim asked.

"Let's begin where it started, when I first raped Holly."

"Now, you remember that to be 1977?" Jim asked.

"I know I'd been out eight or nine months and I had a relationship with this one gal I knew. At the time we broke up, it was at that point that I made…probably the most stupidest thing in my life, which was to go out and rape again. So that night or a couple of days in there somewhere, I drove down. I didn't want to do nothing around Carbondale. I was living there."

"Was your girlfriend from Carbondale or Missouri?" Jim asked.

"She was a married girl that I had met."

"In Illinois?" Jim asked as Tim nodded yes.

"Anyway, I was in a depressing type of mood, which usually triggers me to go out and do something. I drove to Cape Girardeau…I went to the…discount store right there…I think it was a partially rainy night. I said to myself, 'The first good-looking gal that comes up there by herself I'm going to assault.' I was parked in the parking lot, just waiting."

"Do you recall how you were dressed?" Jim asked.

"Probably a baseball hat, dungarees and a shirt…I think I had a knife. She was the first one that pulled up…She had her daughter with her."

"Could you describe this lady for me, please?" Jim asked.

"She was a young black woman. Pretty attractive from what I could see. Like I say, it was dark and I got out of my car and she was opening the door and I went and threatened her with a knife. At first, we got into her car. I didn't want to do anything there, so we got in my car. And I was threatening her all the time with violence if she didn't do what I said. We just drove around. I don't know where I was going."

"Where did the little girl sit?" Jim asked.

"I think she was laying down in the backseat."

"Do you recall how old she was?" Jim asked.

"Probably four or five, something like that. She was kind of small. I don't think she really knew what was going on, but…so I drove to this dark area…I know it was raining. I told her to take her clothes off and she says, 'Rather than have intercourse with you would you let me do you orally?' After a while I told her to stop and I was going to have intercourse with her…Got in the position for intercourse, but we never…I…I never did have intercourse with her. I stopped and got up. I think she put her clothes back on and I took her back. She got in her car and I took off."

"Did you take anything from her?" Jim asked.

"Before I left I tried to bribe her. I gave her some money. It was like a twenty dollar bill or something like that. I was gonna give her more, but I didn't have it. And I think I apologized to her even. That was the first time I had done anything since I'd been released. And…I don't think I felt too good about it. I remember I did give her the money and then she said something…I think it was a sarcastic remark…and I took off after that."

"Do you recall how long you'd been in Cape Girardeau that night before you picked her up?" Jim asked.

"I'd say no more than a half hour or forty-five minutes."

"How did you happen to pick the discount store parking lot?" Jim asked.

"Well, I just figured a lot of women would go there."

"How many times do you think you'd been to Cape prior to that, for anything?" Jim asked.

"Probably no more than four or five times. And those were all trips to either Southeast or St. Francis," Tim said of the hospitals in Cape Girardeau.

"What's the next thing you remember?" Jim asked.

"Do you want me to finish up with her or…Because that was in '77 and the other rape occurred in '82."

"How do you recall that?" Jim asked.

"Well, it was almost the same…same thing how it started. I drove to a mall, the new one across from St. Francis…I drove there and was going to find a victim like I did the first time. And I seen her come out. I didn't know her. I didn't really even, when the whole thing was going on, I didn't know it was her."

"She came out of a store at the mall?" Jim asked.

"With her daughter again, but much bigger…I didn't even recognize her when I followed her home to the house. I thought she looked familiar, but I didn't know for sure. Anyway, I seen her come out and got in the car. She had a different car this time. I remember that. So I didn't, you know, put two and two together. I followed her home and I had no idea where that was…I parked about a block away…And I went to the back porch and it was…I know it was real cold that night. I was about half frozen and getting ready to leave…And I keep looking in the back door. She was doing something with a mop bucket and a mop. I think she wanted to shake out the mop or something. She opened the door. That's how I got in."

"How long had you been standing there?" Jim asked.

"I'd say a good thirty minutes…I went on in and her daughter was in another room somewhere in the house. I think this time I had like a .25 automatic. I'm not sure."

"Was it the same gun that was later taken from you in Pennsylvania? The same one that was used in the Sheppard murder?" I asked.

"Yeah, I think so."

"Anyway, she said something like, 'You scared me to death.' I think she recognized me, but I still wasn't thinking this is the same woman that I had raped before… I might have had a handkerchief over my face. I'm not sure. I used to do that a lot."

"What color would it have been?" Jim asked.

"Probably blue or something…I think at that time, her daughter come running up there and said something and she tried to calm her daughter down. I don't think I said anything to her daughter and I took her…up them steps. I told her to take her clothes off. She put her daughter on the bed. I think she covered her up with a blanket or something. Told her to just lay there and be quiet with her face to the wall so she didn't have to watch. I'm sure I threatened her…I never threatened the child. Other than, you know, I might've told the mother you know, do what I say or somebody will get hurt…Most of the time, if I threatened, I didn't have to hurt them, because they would do what I wanted. That's why I would threaten them and try and scare them.

"Anyway, she came over by the bed. I was sitting on the bed and she disrobed. I started fondling her then I told her to get down. We had oral sex…She did on me…And then I…I…I had intercourse with her. It's unreal, because at the time I was having intercourse with her, she told me she was a Jehovah's Witness and she would try and save me. It was kind of strange."

"Had you ever been to that apartment before?"

"No."

"Did you know she wasn't married?"

"No."

"Did you know where she worked?"

"No."

"Do you recall telling her that you knew she had recently moved there from down the street?" Jim asked.

"Yes…I remember that."

"Did you know that?" Jim asked.

"Yeah…I think that must've been the second time I followed her. I followed her once before and she went to this house in that same area, up a couple blocks, right across from there I think there was a center…I don't know if it was a Christian Center or what it was…I was gonna attack her that night but for some reason I didn't…I think she had just gone grocery shopping or something like that."

"Did you know at that time that she was the same woman you had raped in 1977?" Jim asked.

"No…It was by chance that I followed her that second time…Like I say, I wasn't looking for her. I didn't know she was living in that particular spot. Just by chance she came walking out, you know…It's weird how I would…she would be the one to come walking out of there, you know? After we had intercourse, I tied them up. She said don't…don't tie it tight or something like that. I can't remember if I used shoestrings or…"

"Can we jump back? The shoestrings: did you bring those with you or were they something there at the apartment?" Jim asked.

"I think I brought them with me. I think they were rawhide."

Ah ha, I thought. *Same thing he used to tie up Margie Call.*

"What about the little girl? Did you touch her in any way that night?" Jim asked.

"I think when I was tying her up…And when I got up to leave, I think I touched her on her butt. That was all. I didn't really molest her or nothing."

"How long do you think you were in her residence that night?" Jim asked.

"I don't think it was no more than thirty or forty minutes."

"Which way do you want to go from here?" Jim asked.

"Sometime after that rape, I burglarized a home in Carbondale about a block from where I was living. And I think it was an insurance salesman's house or something. I'm not sure. And that's when I made the biggest mistake of my life. He had a gun in there. It was a .38 police special with a box of ammunition…Taking that gun was like a rush of adrenaline. You know, all powerful feeling, which is part of the rape thing, you know. It's power and control."

"Sure," I lied.

"How can you not be more powerful than when you had that gun, you know? God, I wish I had never picked that gun up."

"Do you remember how you broke into that house?" I asked.

"I think it was a basement window on the side of the house. I think they were on vacation. There was nobody there…I fired the gun in the house…I wanted to see if it was working, I guess. And I put it between two mattresses in one of the bedrooms and fired it."

"Obviously it worked?" I asked.

"Yeah…And I took it with me. Eventually that led to the mother and daughter one. I don't know their names…It was August, maybe, I'm not sure."

"What was going on that made you think it was August?" I asked.

"One of my friends was getting married."

"He worked for the ambulance service?" I asked.

"Yeah. I think it was a Friday night even, if I'm not mistaken. They was having a party that Friday night and I had to make my mind up if I was gonna be going to Cape…I didn't know that the daughter was gonna be there."

"Mary is the mother…Brenda is the daughter," Jim said.

"What led me to that home was one night, I went to Cape. I was out looking around and parked in that neighborhood and—"

"How did you happen to pick that neighborhood?" Jim interrupted.

"It was kind of dark. Wasn't well lit. I'd went Peeping Tommin', you know, looking in windows and stuff like that and I noticed that she was living, as far as I could tell, by herself. Later I think I found out that her—"

"How did you make that determination that she was living by herself?" Jim asked.

"Well, there was no…well, I didn't see no man in the house."

"But you'd only been there one time?" Jim asked.

"Yeah."

"That night?" Jim asked.

"Yeah…I was walking around looking and I think I looked in the bedroom window…And I seen her…It was kind of a small house…No garage. She had a big long car. I can't remember what it was…Anyway, I looked in the window. Like, I didn't, I didn't see anybody or anything…I decided to wait a week and then come back and assault her."

"On that night you were there, peeping through the window, did you see the lady?" Jim asked.

"Yes…and when I went back the second time…nobody was home. Maybe even the first time she might not have been home or was around there and might've come home…I know the second time she wasn't home. I broke a back window. It was a window that didn't go up and down, you had to crank it. And it came this way," Tim said as he motioned toward his chest. "That's how I entered…crawled in. I smashed the window and opened it…I think I put my coat against it and hit it with a rock or something…Once I got inside, there was glass there. I think I tried to hide it and…just…just…just waiting for her to come home. I think maybe… maybe thirty minutes or less. She…she came home. She had her daughter with her. So I didn't know that was gonna…gonna happen. But I was already in the house… They both came in. I waited a few minutes and they went to a room on the side of the house. It must've been the master…"

"Where were you when they came in the front door?" Jim asked.

"I think I was in the master bedroom…The one that I crawled into…And, uh, they came in and I think they were talking. Went to this room where there were two bunk beds and that's where, uh, I accosted them. Brought them out of there and I think they was both kneeled down…I had that .38 with me that I got in that… I stole in the burglary and, uh…I had them kneel down there in front…to threaten them, uh, do what I say or, you know, I'm gonna have to hurt somebody. That's… that was my usual thing. When I first accosted them, I think…the mother hollered that she was real scared and the daughter tried to calm her down. I…I…I, like I said, I took them out and they go down by the couch I think or something…Made them both undress. I ask them for oral sex and they both undressed, both sit down on the bed and I didn't do anything with the mother that night…I think I caressed her a few times whenever I…when I laid her on the bed, but I didn't have any…sex with her at all or oral or intercourse or nothing."

"Did they follow instructions or did you at anytime have to…" Jim asked.

"No, they were scared. They were going along…along with it."

"Did you ever strike either one of them in any way?" Jim asked.

"No. Uh…I was…I…think…I did a little oral sex on the young, the younger woman. What did you say her name was?"

"Brenda," I answered.

"Okay, I did not have intercourse with her. And I don't think I ejaculated either. I'd…I had…I had a climax, but it was like a dry climax. I don't think there was any semen."

"Did you at any time bind either of them?" Jim asked.

"To be truthful, it's like fifty-fifty. I remember maybe tying them up, but I'm not 100 percent sure of it. I think I did…"

"Maybe I can jog your memory a little bit. Do you ever recall anywhere where you would have happened to cut an electrical cord?" Jim asked.

"Yes…I might've tied them up with a lamp cord…I remember that because it put a hole in my knife I think I had…Sort of shocked there."

"Quite a spark, huh?" Jim asked.

"Yeah…The same thing happened in another rape that I did, but I can't remember for sure. That wasn't in Cape Girardeau; it was in Pennsylvania."

"How do you recall having them tied up?" Jim asked.

"I think I had them laying on their stomachs and then I covered them up…I think the daughter was on the right hand side of the bed and the mother on the left side of the bed…No particular reason. I would like to say something here."

"Sure," Jim said.

"It's directly related to what happens after, uh, 1963. They sent me to Menard Psychiatric Center. At that time I was eighteen. Probably the worst place anybody could send any youngster. Cause at the time, it was filled with the criminally insane. Every kind of sexual deviate that you can imagine. A couple of guys off of death row who were, like, crazy. I'm talking about the whole population was that kind of mix. Criminally insane. And I'm not…I don't mean normal people, I mean they were criminally insane. And it was probably the worst two years of my life, the first two years I was there. Anyway, they kept me there for about five years. When I left there I was full of rage and anger. It was unbelievable. Uh, the first couple of years was full of humiliations. If it wouldn't have been for sports coming in at the time, only thing that kept me sane all of these years.

"Anyway, while there, I would talk to some of the guys in the yard. Do you remember a guy named Kenneth Rogers? He's up in Dixon Psychiatric for killing his wife and another young girl in Carbondale and somebody else…Me and him were friends. He was there for, I think for assault and battery at that time. He hadn't killed his wife or anybody. And I remember when we would sit there and talk about different things. I was a youngster, very impressionable. And one of the things that really stuck on my mind, he said, 'Tim, if you ever do anything, don't leave no witnesses.' And for some reason, that just stuck in my brain."

"I know exactly whom you are talking about," I said.

Kenneth was an artist and a good one at that. People paid hundreds of dollars for his paintings. He was hired by a bookstore when he paroled to Carbondale in 1969. Life was good for a while. But on November 25, 1969, Kenneth abducted fourteen-year-old Lisa Levering as she was leaving the Carbondale Teen Center. Her body was found six days later near Chatauqua Lake. My former boss, Lieutenant Larry Hill, who was just a patrol officer in those days, helped carry Lisa's small frozen body from the woods near Lake Chautauqua, west of Carbondale. She had been sexually assaulted, manually strangled and her jeans were tied around her neck. Two other girls whom Rogers tried to pick up that night had provided valuable clues that led to him, but it was too late for Lisa. Larry never forgot Lisa and the man who took the little girl's life. It was strange that Kenneth had had such an influence over Tim. It was even stranger that the two, at different times in their lives, came to Carbondale, drawn by the university, to stalk and kill. Kenneth had practiced what he preached and Tim had followed his sermon.

Although Larry had seen a lot in his career, the heinousness of Lisa's murder was marked in his memory. One month after Lisa's murder, Kenneth killed his wife of three months. Right after killing her, he murdered his wife's friend, after she arrived to bring his wife a Christmas present. Kenneth went back to prison in December 1969, where he spent the rest of his life.

"And then when I decided to step across the line again in '77 and go back to doing those things, that was it in my head. But I hadn't done anything like that, because I didn't have the weapons to do it. I didn't know if I could do it. Anyway, when I tied the two ladies up—"

"So let me ask you a question about what you just said. Is that…are you saying that's the first time, 1977, that you committed a murder?" Jim interrupted.

"Yes. Anyway, I got them tied up. At that point, I…I shot the young girl in the back of the head. I shot the mother in the back of the head…At that time, I…went to a room like a den or something and found a fold wallet with sixty or seventy dollars in it. I took it."

"From a desk drawer?" Jim asked.

"Yeah, a desk drawer from the den. I went back into the bedroom and the mother was still alive. She was crying next to her daughter, so I fired another shot. And I left."

"Did you ever really sexually assault or do anything at all physical with the mother that night?" Jim asked.

"Well, when I was…with intercourse with her daughter on the bed…She was laying right next to me and I may have run my hands over her, but that was it. I didn't have intercourse or oral sex or any of those with her."

"What would've been the reason that you would have the mother undress?" Jim asked.

"Well, I think it was initially to assault both of them…Usually I had that first climax and that would take care of the need…and I'd split. There was no reason to shoot them. I mean, I don't think they had a good look at my face or anything. But I had that shit in my head."

"Was your face covered?" Jim asked.

"I know it was when I first went in there with the blue bandanna."

"Did they threaten you that they would call the police?"

"No, they was too scared I think to…I forgot something…like right in the middle of all of this, when I was, the daughter was giving me oral sex or something if I'm not mistaken, the phone rang. And I think it was her father who was in a hospital on the phone and she talked to her father and I listened in for like two or three minutes. And then she hung up. And I went back to doing what we were doing."

"How long do you think you'd been in the house when the phone rang?" Jim asked.

"Twenty to twenty-five minutes maybe."

"Was there any conversation between you and either of the two? Do you remember them talking to you? Anything that was said? Obviously, I would think that they were begging you not to do things, but…" I said.

"Actually, I don't believe they said very much."

"Were you aware that her husband was in the hospital?" Jim asked.

"No, I think…I learned that later. Either from the phone call, yeah, I think from the phone call. Some kind of surgery or something."

"Do you recall what Brenda may have said to her father?" Jim asked.

"Oh, man. I would say that I probably did threaten them not to say anything out of line. I think she said something like, 'I love you, Daddy' or 'I'll see you tomorrow.'"

"I don't know if we covered this or not…where you said you got the gun, but what happened to it after that night?" Jim asked.

"Well, I kept it. I think I used it one more time."

"Do you recall where you parked your car?"

"Maybe two blocks down that way somewhere."

"How did you exit the house?" Jim asked.

"Front door. Oh and I remember something else. Evidently when she…she came home, she left all her keys in the door. I remember when I was shutting the door I heard all the keys jangle. The door was open."

"One of those ladies evidently had a broken tooth and maybe a bruise to her face. Do you recall striking either one of them by any chance?" Jim asked.

"No, did not. I don't think I ever hit any of my victims. I mean, I didn't torture them. I didn't beat them or none of that. Just used a threat with the gun to make them do what I wanted."

I found Tim's use of the word "torture" and the fact that he didn't find what he did to these women as such to be unbelievable.

"Did you tell them that they were gonna die?" Jim asked.

"No. Probably up until the time I shot them, I didn't know if I could, if I would."

"Had she not died, would you have left thinking you had already killed her?" I asked.

"Yes."

"How long from start to finish, from the time you went in the house or let's say the time when they arrived that you confronted them, until you left out the front door?" I asked.

"I'd say less than an hour."

"Did you follow the news on TV?" I asked.

"Not a whole lot of it. I think I remember seeing it once or twice…I do remember hearing something about it on the news, you know, how terrible the crime was…After I do these things, no, I didn't take no newspaper clippings or none of that stuff."

Jim passed pictures of the Parsh residence to Tim. He picked out the front door to the house, identified the back bedroom where he went in. He saw a picture of a cut electrical cord to a television set, but said he didn't remember cutting it. He didn't remember dumping the purses that night when he saw a picture of coins on the couch cushion but didn't deny it either. He identified Brenda from a picture.

"You know, some of these, I'm not sure of some of the stuff, but the best I recollect…I know I was coming to Cape pretty regularly after some of this stuff 'cause…If I wanted to do something, Cape was one of my first choices before I'd go somewhere else."

"Why would that be?" Jim asked.

"A long ways from home. I think I found an area up near where the post office was that was real dark, where I could act out and I remember going down this gravel road. There's an older black woman lived there with her family of girls. And one night I was looking in the window. The Peeping Tom thing. And then one night I sexually assaulted her…She was sleeping when I went in. I woke her up, made her perform oral sex. She was fighting me a little bit. I grabbed her and threw her on the floor…Then she started cooperating."

Well, this was a new one, I realized.

"There's another part in that same area that I burglarized, I think, later on too. That was '82. Two young black girls were living there. And I was going to assault them but never did."

"Were they at home when you did the burglary?" I asked.

"I think one of them was…She was in the bedroom. And I came in and I was walking around the apartment and I heard her. She started screaming like crazy and I took off out the door. Never did assault her."

"So this was about the same time as the sexual assault on the older black lady?" I asked.

"Yeah. Anyway, speaking of that black lady…I don't think they had a phone there or anything. A sweet old lady. She was so embarrassed that she never told nobody or called the police. I don't know if she did or not…I don't know if it was four or five or three months later, I went back to that same place at about nine o'clock in the evening and…and…broke in again and there was a teenager in there, I think. A girl, with her mom and some kids. And I took the teenage girl in the back room. Made her undress. She performed oral sex and I split. Didn't hurt nobody."

"Well, if there were multiple people in there, how did you secure the others?" I asked.

"Well, they were in the front room. It was in the back room…I just told everybody to stay right there…In the front room, I think there was three or four children. And I think a grandmother, the older lady was holding the baby."

"When you secured them, do you remember how you did that? Whether you had them sit, lie or whatever?" Jim asked.

"I think they were all sitting on the couch and the grandma was sitting on the floor, by…by…a window I think. I didn't hurt nobody and left. Other than the sexual assault…I was looking in the window and I heard her say she was gonna run up to the store and get something and come back. So I waited until she came back and like a minute after she went in the door, I went in the door…Do you want anything more on that one?"

"All total, how many forcible rapes do you think you committed in Cape Girardeau?" Jim asked.

"Oh, there really weren't that many…I burglarized that one little house there with the two young black girls. But never did anything to either one of them. Though I was going to go again. I went back to the basement apartment where the two black girls were, knocked on the door and pretended to be a police officer. Showed her… I think I had a fake badge or something…You can buy them anywhere…Anyway, she let me in and I had planned to assault her, but she was a pretty smart gal. As I was getting ready to pull a gun and accost her, she had got up and ran out the door, went upstairs and got her girl from upstairs to come down with her and I said a few words and then I got out of there as quick as I could get out of there…She was lucky, too, you know, that I didn't do anything there."

"Any other residence on the street you described as being a gravel street?" Jim asked.

"There was another incident. I think this was in '82. It was on the other side of Cape. Wasn't near the post office. There was three black women in a little house… A week prior, maybe two weeks prior, I had been to a grocery store I think and followed her home. She was a young black woman by herself and looked like an easy victim…Seen she was a single mom with a couple of children and I didn't do anything that night. And I think I came back a week or two later and I looked in and she wasn't there. There was two other women in there. And usually something like that would…I wouldn't even…I'd split. But this night I think…I'm pretty sure I was armed. And, uh…I'd say it was a little house. In the back there was a little screened-in porch. The door was locked. I couldn't get in the door. So I think I cut the screen on the back of the porch with my knife and crawled in the back porch. Went in through the kitchen. They were in the front room and I think it was in the summertime, 'cause I remember the door, the front door was open. So they was letting the fresh air come in…Before I went in, I…I…was in the back of the house. This other woman came home. So that made three of them in there…

"Another thing I was doing, I don't think I've mentioned this, but while I was locked up I used to imagine sexual fantasies. And I decided when I got out that I would do whatever I fantasized about. If I could, two or three women or whatever. Anyway, I think that's why I went in. I went into the front room. There was three of them sitting on the couch. They were talking and I think they were drinking or something. They had some kind of whiskey there or something. Anyway, there's a chair over here and a couch over here. She took the kids, I think there's two or three of them and put them in a side room, closed the door so they wouldn't see anything. Told them to be quiet and behave themselves. And I had the three girls on the couch, had them take their clothes off. I sat there and I was masturbating while they were taking their clothes off. And the woman who lived there, she came over and I asked her to do it, oral sex. She did 'til I reached climax and the other two I caressed a couple of times, but didn't have no sexual relations with either one of them…I think I also asked them if they had any money. They said no and I left. I didn't hang around."

"Why don't we take a break? Bathroom break and everything else?" I asked.

Everyone agreed. We had been talking for two hours and Jim and I were losing feeling in our writing hands as we had been feverishly taking notes. I turned off the recording and summoned Lieutenant Schuler. He took Tim to the restroom.

"Wow!" Jim said.

"I'd say. This is overwhelming and we're not done yet. Hey, your chief wanted me to call him and let him know how things were going. Do you want me to do that?"

"You go ahead. I need to find the restroom myself."

I walked into an adjoining room where there was a desk and phone.

"Hey, Paul, how's it going?" Carl asked after answering my phone call.

"We just took our first break. Everything is going just as planned. Tim is giving us step-by-step details of the murders and rapes. He started out at the beginning with Holly's rape in 1977. He has talked about some rapes in Cape that we weren't aware of and then he talked about the Parsh murders. I guess the most horrific thing he has told us so far was that after shooting Mary and Brenda, he walked out of the room to steal money from their purses. He said he apparently missed Mary and he heard her crying. So he went back in and shot her again. This time he killed her. If she had not cried, he wouldn't have known and gone back in."

"You're kidding me. That's terrible. Is there anything you guys need me to do?"

"No, Lieutenant Schuler is taking good care of us. It's going to take a long time to go through so many cases, but we want to discuss them all tonight. We'll stay as long as it takes."

"Okay. Tell Jim I'll get him first thing in the morning so he can brief me."

Fifteen minutes later, it was time to resume.

16

The Confession Continues

Istarted to record again and reminded Tim that he had confessed to using the gun he used to kill the Parshes one more time.

"I think it was a college girl. Young girl that was found on the other side of the river."

"Where did you happen to see her?" Jim asked.

"The same place I had seen Holly the first time...Exact same scenario, except I took her to my home in Carbondale where I assaulted her."

"In whose vehicle?" Jim asked.

"Mine...I think it was still the blue car...I know when I accosted her it was still sort of light outside, so it was early in the evening. She had parked next to a pretty big truck that had blocked the view from the store. I came around and got her out of the car, put her in my car to go to Carbondale. I was living in the trailer. I took her in the bedroom."

"Did you have to tie her hands or anything?" Jim asked.

"No, I had her lay on the front seat with her head in my lap. I just told her to be quiet and I won't hurt her. I took her out of the car, went in my place and I had her disrobe. Fondled her a little bit. Made her perform oral sex. That was all we did. Didn't have intercourse."

"Did you ejaculate?" Jim asked.

"Yes. It was oral sex."

"In her mouth? Or could it have gone somewhere else, like on her clothing?" Jim asked, knowing we were in the process of testing semen found on Sheila's jeans.

"I don't think it was on her clothing. I think she took it in her mouth. All of it. That was all we did. She got dressed. I told her that I was gonna take her home. We drove back down towards Cape, stopped there at that rest stop. I had to go to the bathroom. She came in there with me and I went to the bathroom. She asked if she could go too...I took her in there. Shot her one time, I think. I might've shot her twice, I'm not sure."

"Do you know where you shot her? What part of her body?" Jim asked.

"I think I shot her in the head. Again, it was dark in there...As I left, I think I took her purse and put it in the garbage disposal thing and just went back home."

"Are you sure you took your car to Carbondale?" I asked.

"I took my car. I left hers in the parking lot. It think it was blue maybe or gray?"

"Do you know if she had anything with her from the store?" Jim asked.

"I think she had a bag of something...I think she left it in the car."

"How long had you been in the parking lot when she came out?" Jim asked.

"I think it was pretty quick. I don't think I was there very long."

"As you recall, how many times do you think you'd been there prior to that?" Jim asked.

"I think seven or eight times, maybe...She was a young girl. I think she had dark brown hair. She was fairly attractive."

"You mentioned earlier that she was a college student. Did she tell you that?" Jim asked.

"Yeah, I believe she did. She said she was living with two roommates."

"Had you already planned to take her back to Carbondale?" Jim asked.

"That was probably spur-of-the-moment."

"Why would you risk taking her all the way back to Carbondale?" Jim asked.

"When I was in that mode, I didn't think."

"When did you decide to kill her?" Jim asked.

"Probably not 'til I was...got close to Cape. I mean, it wasn't premeditated. It...It was like I said, I had that thing in my head about, you know, no witnesses. And I...I was still in that mode. I was in that mode for a couple of years before it finally started to wear out on me."

"Had she done anything that would've irritated you that night?" Jim asked.

"No. No."

Jim showed Tim a photo of the restroom and of Sheila's car. He recognized both. My mind kept flashing to whether the semen Suzanne was analyzing from Sheila's pants could have come from someone else, given Tim's relative certainty that he didn't leave anything behind.

"Tim, when you took her to Carbondale, now, there was a period of time that you had a roommate...So obviously that wasn't a concern—of a roommate coming in at that point?"

"Yeah, even then it was stupid on my part, because any one of my friends could've come over. And how could I explain what was going on, you know? It's just one of those things that you do without thinking."

"After you shot her, did you, when you left the rest area, did you go back to Carbondale or did you go back to Cape?" I asked.

"I drove over the bridge and chucked the gun," Tim said.

"You threw the gun in the Mississippi River?" I asked.

"Yes."

"You actually got out of your vehicle?" I asked.

"Yeah, chucked it…I gave it a pretty good chuck, sixty…seventy feet."

"The next incident?" Jim asked.

"I think the next one was the lady down…down the road from where the mother and daughter were. Straight down the road."

"Can you describe the lady for me?" Jim asked.

"Late forties, maybe early fifties. Think she wore glasses. Not sure, again, I initially saw her…maybe a week or so before. I think it was a Wednesday night…I followed her home. Seen that she lived alone. Went and looked in the window, you know, at the back of the house…It was around nine or nine thirty when she got back to her house. So I waited about a week and went to the house…I went through a bedroom or bathroom window, I think. Broke it. I think there was two bathrooms. There was a bathroom here and a real small bathroom here and the bedroom here," Tim said as he sketched the floor plan of Margie Call's house.

"Went in there and waited until she came home…I think the lights were on. She would be home in like twenty or thirty minutes…She come in and she went… went to the back bedroom and I was in the living room. I come out of the living room. She was coming back down this way like she didn't see me. She was going for her bathroom and then…then she seen the window was broken, she…she was like running towards the front of the house so I accosted her. I took her into the bedroom…And still pretty much the same thing. Made her disrobe."

"I don't know if I asked you what year," Jim said.

"1982, I think…She was scared and she went along with the program. And again, I had her perform oral sex…I don't think we had intercourse…I remember when I was at the supermarket I wanted to get a better look at her…And I was in the store. I might've even went in there and bought some of those rawhide shoestrings…Yeah, I remember she had a payment book or something in her purse…I go home and about a week later I made the sexual assault."

"Had you ever been inside before?" Jim asked.

"No…After I took her in the bathroom, the regular bathroom, I was fondling her in there and then I took her back into the main bedroom…because the window was broken, it was cold in there…I think I tied her up and I…I strangled her, I think."

"Was she cooperative?" Jim asked.

"Yes."

"Do you recall trying to flush anything?" Jim asked.

"No."

"Were there any injuries to her body?" Jim asked.

"Um…not that I'm aware of, no."

"Like, would you have bitten her anywhere that you recall?" Jim asked.

"Okay, I was gonna take a souvenir if I'm not mistaken. And I…I…I cut one of her nipples…with a knife…I think it was the left one. I'm not positive."

"And did you, in fact, take it with you?" Jim asked.

"No, I think I might've flushed it."

"Did you take anything else from her home?" Jim asked.

"I think she had a bunch of, uh, church envelopes or something. I think I emptied those."

"Why did you decide to kill her?" Jim asked.

"I'd say at the time, I…I had never planned to kill any of them, but…I don't know why some of them I…I…killed and then some of them I didn't. I don't… what the trigger was."

"Did you remove her nipple before she died or afterward?" Jim asked.

"It was after."

"Would you happen to recall if she was wearing any type of boots when she performed the sexual act on you?" Jim asked.

"I couldn't say for sure."

Jim showed Tim a picture of the back of Margie's house.

"I think the reason I went in that window there was 'cause I could stand on this thing here," he said.

"The air conditioning unit?" Jim asked.

"Yeah. And she did have boots on."

"Do you recall, all together, how long you were in the residence that night?" Jim asked.

"Probably from when I went in initially 'til I left, maybe an hour. Hour and five minutes. Usually when the woman would come home, I mean it would be real quick and I'd be gone."

"Did you happen to see a rose anywhere in the house that night?" Jim asked.

"A rose? I can't remember it."

A single white rose had been found in one of Margie's guest bedrooms. Investigators wondered if the killer had done it as some type of symbol. It now appeared to be a coincidence.

"What's the next incident that you recall, Tim?" Jim asked.

"Well, I think the only other one that happened in Cape is the Wallace case."

"Do you know her name?" Jim asked.

"You told it to me…I didn't know her. Again, it was the same MO. I followed her home from a supermarket."

"How long before you actually committed the assault on her?" Jim asked.

"That was the same night…I think it was a Sunday night. I was real frantic. Usually on a Sunday night I would never go out…I was looking in a bathroom window after she'd pulled in and went into the house…And she put her coat back on and left…She went somewhere and when she left, that's when I…I decided, well, here's an opportunity to go in the house. So that's…that's what I did. I smashed her window. And I remember I cut myself…My left hand was a little cut. It bled just a tiny bit and I got a bandage out of her bathroom, put it on, stopped the bleeding and waited 'til she came home…Maybe ten, fifteen minutes…It was almost like she went out to get a newspaper or something. I'm not exactly sure. Anyway, I was waiting in the room down at the end of the hall and she went into the bedroom, started taking her…coat off and then I came down the hallway and accosted her in her bedroom. I made her take her clothes off. I had a…had a gun and I threatened her with a gun."

"Where did you get that gun?"

"From a burglary in Marion."

Investigators had always suspected that the gun taken from the rape in which Tim forced his way in on an elderly couple in Marion was used to kill Mildred and it seemed he had confirmed it.

"Would it be from one of the cases that I mentioned earlier?" I asked.

"Yes. I need to take a break. Got to take a whiz."

Now three hours into the confession, it was apparent that Jim and I were going to have a lot of work to research all of the cases Tim was bringing up. About ten minutes later, Lieutenant Schuler brought him back and we settled in for some more discussion.

"Did you again go in that store when she entered?" Jim asked.

"No, I was sitting in the parking lot waiting…Seen her come out."

"Can you describe her?" Jim asked.

"She was about five foot ten. I remember her hair was kind of short…I wasn't real close…I didn't realize she was that old…She looked a lot younger…I accosted her in the bedroom…I don't…there was a lot of oral sex…I think I was masturbating…I think I did try and have intercourse with her, but…she didn't give me the impression that she was that old…I mean she was a younger looking woman…So, anyway, doing intercourse with her for a while, then I pulled out. And I wanted her to do oral sex to finish it. She did and I laid on the bed…Anyway, she was laying on the bed. I pulled out, maybe I did tie her up…I think I went on and looked around the apartment. I looked for money…Any valuables. Went back in the room. I walked real softly in there and then shot her one time and left."

"Where did you shoot her? In what part of her body?" Jim asked.

"I think it was in the head…She was laying on the edge of the bed."

"How long were you in that residence?" Jim asked.

"I'd say thirty-five, forty minutes max."

"Do you recall looking in any other window besides the bathroom window at the residence?" Jim asked, fishing for how investigators lifted his palm print from the other window.

"I think I wanted to see if there was an easier entrance than the bathroom… It's possible I might've done something like that."

"Do you recall anything she may have said to you? Or anything you may have said to her specifically?" Jim asked.

"I remember she asked me if I was the guy who killed a woman across town, the one we were just talking about. Evidently she was fearful of an attack. And she had something in her kitchen to block the door. I noticed that when I went in there. She had the door blocked, like, so nobody could come in."

"When she asked you if you were the same man who killed Mrs. Call, what did you tell her?" I asked.

"I think I denied it."

Jim showed Tim a picture of Mildred's house.

"This window over here, I do remember putting a towel in the window…so there won't be any cold air going through there or she wouldn't notice it right away."

He learned that from when Margie Call began running from her broken window, I thought.

"What was the reason for shooting her?" Jim asked.

"There wasn't any reason…I mean, she didn't fight me. She went along with the program…I…I…I didn't have any reason hardly to kill any of these women… Just that mind-set. That was in my head then."

"Were you alone this night?" Jim asked.

"Oh, always, always alone. But I…I think there might've been more to it than that…you know, I thought about why do I…why do I sometimes kill them and sometimes, I don't…And a lot of the women I killed resembled my mother. You know, age-wise and body build."

"Did these ladies resemble your mother?" Jim asked.

"I think they did a little…little bit. I'm just wondering maybe if that wasn't in the back of my mind or…uh…the rage and the age of my mom as I was growing up."

This was making no sense to me. Deborah certainly didn't look like his mother. Neither did Sheila Cole or Brenda Parsh. And none of them looked alike. I couldn't help but believe some psychiatrist had put that in his mind through the years. It didn't make sense.

"What year was your mother born?" Jim asked.

"Oh, she died in, uh, '80…'88. And I think she was sixty-four or sixty-five. So she had me when she was, like, sixteen."

"That would've…put her exactly the same age as Mrs. Call," I noted, thinking my mother was that same age as well.

"Did you ever get to see her when you were inside?" Jim asked.

"I seen her once or twice…She was starting to show her age real bad, because she had congestive heart failure and diabetes and all the problems that go along with that. When she was younger she was a real attractive woman. And as she got older I don't think she was. I had this fetish for women who had nice-looking butts. You know, I think that comes from the time when I was about six or seven years old and I walked in on my mom and she was dressing. And I remember she hollered and screamed at me…And I remember it set off kind of weird things to me and I was embarrassed and I got flushed and it got really encrusted in my mind, you know."

"Had you been sexually assaulted prior to that?" Jim asked.

"No, I've never been sexually assaulted."

Jim jumped back into clearing up some details about Mildred Wallace's murder, including how Tim parked on the busy thoroughfare and walked out her front door in plain sight.

"Now the only type of sexual act that was performed was oral sex on you?" Jim asked.

"No, I said initially I had intercourse with her…She was…was real dry and said it was hurting her so I stopped and then she did the oral sex."

"You did ejaculate?" Jim asked.

"Yes."

"In her mouth?" Jim asked.

"Yes…I remember seeing a typewriter."

Jim showed him a picture of Mildred's typewriter. He nodded.

"Can you think of anything else concerning this incident? After you shot Mrs. Wallace that night, what did you do with that gun?"

"Chucked it when I was going back to Carbondale somewhere on…the east side on Route 3 in the woods. I'd say, uh, man, five, ten miles up the road I stopped. There was just a little turn off in this one place where there are railroad tracks. And when I… I drove down there, maybe thirty, forty, fifty feet, got out of the car…and chucked it."

"Just a couple of things, Tim. We keep talking about these shoestrings. Now, earlier you had started telling the story that you'd went into the supermarket and purchased some. Would that have happened with Ms. Wallace? Would you have gone into the store to purchase the boot laces or…"

"I don't think I did that night…I think I would do it whenever I planned to do a crime."

"Did you buy the same kind each time?"

"I tried to get the rawhide because they were, like, stronger."

"Okay, in regards to guns…Again there're no charges coming out of these. These are just to clean up these cases. That would've been June 6, 1982. There was a robbery and a rape of the lady…Her husband also lived there. And that's where this report says the gun comes from. Is that correct?"

"Correct."

"This was a situation where it looks like it was on a Sunday night, probably around 9 P.M. They had actually been sitting out on the back porch of their house. They were inside. I think the lady was lying on the couch. Her husband was in the bedroom. Does that sound familiar?" I asked.

"Yes…I think he was laying outside the bedroom. I think I did tie them up and cover them up with a sheet."

As Tim and I spoke, I heard something to my left where Jim was sitting and I noticed Tim's facial expression change. His bushy eyebrows rose and his handlebar mustache did as well as he cracked a smile. I looked over my left shoulder and realized what had happened. As Jim relaxed while I was asking questions, he had leaned back in his chair too far and tipped backwards. Fortunately, he was close enough that the wall prevented him from falling all the way down. Jim's feet were dangling off the floor preventing him from tipping himself back to the table. I reached over and tipped his chair back to the table.

"Thank you," Jim said. It was a bit of comic relief that we needed while discussing such horrendous things.

Tim admitted to all the cases I had come to talk to him about. He told me that there were three sexual assaults in Mount Vernon, about forty-five miles north of Marion.

"The first one was…I followed a black woman home. There is a discount store when you first go into the town and she lived behind the store, maybe a couple of miles behind there in an apartment complex. And she was like twenty-three or twenty-four. Her mother was there at the time. And there was a little girl there at the time…The mother and grandbaby were sitting on the couch…They left the door open. I guess that she was taking something in from the car and hadn't closed the door yet and I just went in right behind her. I think I was carrying a .25 automatic and threatened them with that. Took her in the bathroom and made her perform oral sex. Didn't do nothing to the mom. Mom and the little girl stayed out in the living room…And there was another one in Mount Vernon…A gal about fifty, fifty-one, real good-looking woman I'd seen at the mall."

"White? Black?" I asked.

"White. And she lived right behind Mount Vernon Hospital, I think, I followed her home. Come back a couple weeks later…went in through the screen door. Tickled the screen door a little bit and it popped open. She was by herself…When I saw her she was in the sewing room. Where I accosted her…I took her in the living room first…And I had intercourse with her. And then the oral sex. Took her in the bedroom, wrapped her in a blanket, tied her up then I left."

"And the third one?" I asked.

"Come straight into Mount Vernon near the post office. You know, facing the apartment right across the street from the post office. There was an old woman that lived there. Fifty, fifty-one or something like that. Maybe older…White. Crawled in through a basement window…I didn't have to break it. Accosted her in the bathroom…Couldn't stop her screaming. I had a knife…Kept on telling her to be quiet and she kept on screaming and screaming. And I…I…I just stabbed her once or twice with a knife. And I made myself stop and I ran and jumped out the window and ran away. She didn't die. She was hurt pretty good, but she pulled through. I remember reading that somewhere or seeing that somewhere. That's all I did…I think."

"Now, I'm trying to be fair with you. We…we talked about something in Paducah, which I'm going to research and get back to you on that one. That was our agreement, but the one in Marion, that's a different one, correct?" I asked.

"Yes…about the same everything…Strangled her. Stabbed her…There was intercourse and oral sex. It was an afternoon assault. Back in '77 and '78, I just went a little crazy."

"Yeah…think a little further on how she was killed. Because I think there's more than a strangle with that one," I said.

"Yeah. I…I…I cut her with a knife, too…It was more like a cut on her stomach than it was a stab I guess."

"Is it possible that it was still left in her chest?" I asked.

"I don't think so."

"Do you know where you got that knife?" Jim asked.

"I got it out of her kitchen."

"To back up just a little bit on that one, when you say it's the same scenario, did you see her at a shopping mall, in a grocery store somewhere?" I asked.

"Yes…I think it was a mini-mall right off of Route 13."

"Had you seen her before?" I asked.

"No…That was when I was just, uh, I was lucky I didn't get caught that time… I parked where she parked her car and went inside the house…I think she was a couple minutes ahead of me and I pulled up and parked right next to the car and then…"

"And did you knock on the door or how did that take place?" I asked.

"I think I knocked on the door. And I had, like, a package in my hand, like I was delivering a package…And she opened the door and I went in. There was a little dog there…It looked like an English bulldog or something…I threatened her with a knife."

"So you had a knife of your own as well, is that what you mean?" I asked.

"Yeah."

"Now, if you strangled her, why did you cut her stomach?" I asked.

"She…she wouldn't die. For some reason, she kept on trying to breathe even when I was strangling her. I just…go nuts."

"What did you do in the bathroom?" I asked, knowing that the report mentioned that a bandages box was found on Virginia's bathroom counter along with some of her blood.

"I remember she got the knife out of my hand, but I didn't want to yank it out of her hand cause I was afraid I'd cut her."

"She had hold of the blade?" I asked, thinking how strange it was for Tim to care if she cut her hand, seeing as he sliced her open just a few minutes after that.

"Yeah. And then she gave me my knife back and I took her in the bedroom."

"Do you recall cleaning up afterward, 'cause I would've thought there would be a lot of blood there," I said.

"Like one slice and I felt her die. And felt the air leave her body or whatever it was and I thought she was dead and I was gone."

"Anything else?" I asked.

"I imagine you want to talk about that one in Pennsylvania?"

I had already asked Pennsylvania authorities if we could take his confession to Myrtle Rupp's murder to get it on record. I was told not to. They wanted to do it. I guess I couldn't blame them, but it was also a bit dangerous not to accept a confession when it's offered. It was the first time in my career that I had to tell a murder suspect not to tell me what happened. After years of trying to get suspects to tell what happened, this one went against the grain. I told him I'd accompany the Pennsylvania investigators who would come to take his confession.

"There's just one more thing I want to go through…I will be in contact with Kentucky officials and see what I can work out about that one. I think you said 1979."

"Yes…Black female, probably in her early twenties."

"And based upon what you said, you actually brought her to Carbondale and then took her back?" I asked.

"Yes."

"She would have died there in Paducah?" I asked.

"No, I killed her in Carbondale…took her back the next night. I left her…I think near a park somewhere."

"Okay, so you…you were living in the trailer park at that time?" I asked, realizing that this was now an Illinois case that I had the authority to question him about.

"Yes, sir."

"And how did she die?"

"I strangled her."

"It was a home in Paducah where she was taken from?" I asked.

"It looked like one of those housing projects."

"Did you have a gun at the time?" I asked.

"No…Knife."

"And you brought her over to Illinois. Brought her to your house. Or your trailer. A…sexual assault? Vaginal? Oral?" I asked.

"Oral."

"When you took her back, was she clothed?"

"No, she was in the nude."

"You said you strangled her. She was in your trailer for the rest of the day? And then it was under the darkness, so you took her back?"

"Yes. I'm gonna have to go to the bathroom. I gotta take another pee."

"Okay. We'll go ahead and stop right now."

Four hours in, we were done. We both shook Tim's hand and thanked him for his cooperation. I guess one might ask, "How do you shake a man's hand after he has just confessed to raping and murdering so many with those same hands?" Law enforcement is a strange career. Strange in the sense that you do things you never thought you'd ever do. Being able to disconnect your personal emotions, at least for the moment, is tough, but necessary. The whole point was to gain Tim's cooperation and get a detailed confession to his crimes. I learned many years ago that you don't reveal your horror and disgust to the person whose cooperation you're enlisting. Telling Tim at the end of the interview that he was the scum of the earth would've likely ended any future conversations with him.

Lieutenant Schuler took Tim back to his cell so he could begin writing the confessions Morley wanted. We told him we would be back in a few days to pick them up. When Lieutenant Schuler joined us, we all sat and talked for a little while about the ghastly multitude of crimes to which Tim had confessed in Cape and other jurisdictions. I told Lieutenant Schuler that I would be in touch and he escorted Jim and I back to the front gate. Exhausted and hungry, I suggested we drive to Marion and find a restaurant along the interstate. So Jim followed me south.

Only one restaurant was open just before midnight. It really didn't matter. Though we were sort of hungry, the agitation evoked by what we'd experienced had left us almost numb. The restaurant was empty for the most part. Several Illinois State Trooper squad cars were in the parking lot. Jim and I were in plain clothes and our guns were covered, so when we walked in the officers just looked up, nodded and went back to talking. The group of six or eight officers appeared to have been working a traffic detail somewhere. Weary, I smiled. I too had wanted to be a trooper once upon a time.

After Jim and I ordered our food, we began to tally up the horrifying crimes to which Tim had confessed. The young group of troopers were loudly talking with one another about how successful their night had been writing citations. Jim and I looked at each other knowingly.

17

Closure Comes to the City of Roses and Beyond

Word spread fast around the police station about Tim's confession. Several officers and detectives stopped by my office to hear the details and to congratulate me. I briefed Mike Wepsiec, Chief Ledbetter and Calvin about the interview along with Stacie and Suzanne at the crime lab. Stacie's reaction was quite animated and filled with responses like "No way!" and "Get out of here!"

The week also brought with it a flurry of phone calls to seal up the loose ends Tim had left. I told Malinda at the Paducah Police Department about the murder Tim said he did in the area. She said she needed to research the case and get back to me. Marion Detective Tina Morrow was shocked to learn Tim had confessed to murdering Virginia Witte as well as two open rapes from 1982. She, too, wanted to interview Tim about the cases. Pennsylvania State Police Corporal Bill Moyer planned to interview Tim about Myrtle Rupp's murder the day after Tim's final court appearance in Deborah's case. He wanted me to accompany him. I agreed. I also reached out to the Mount Vernon Police Department, since Tim had provided details of a woman he stabbed in their area and two rapes. Detective Roger Hayse took the call but didn't remember the crimes. He said he'd check the files.

Jim's work didn't stop either. He found out that the DNA in Margie Call's case and Holly's rape kit both came back to Tim. The hair recovered from Margie Call's neck yielded a ratio of one in 4.5 quadrillion. It doesn't get much better than that. The statistical odds in Sheila Cole's case didn't turn out to be as high. Suzanne Kidd said the DNA profile she found in the crotch of Sheila's blue jeans was likely Tim's, but further testing could say it with more certainty. With Tim's confession and the other DNA matches, though, we didn't need it.

I also dug into our files to find out about the burglary to which Tim had confessed and found a logbook entry in which Officer Leon Hamlin took a burglary report at the address. The suspect stole a .38 special revolver. I found a Crime Information Bulletin from then Cape Girardeau Corporal John Brown glued to a page in another logbook. It was a confidential synopsis of the Parsh murders and included the type of gun used in the crime, a .38 special. They didn't know it then, but the gun they were looking for was described in a burglary case just one logbook away. I showed Moe what I had found. He recognized the burglary victim as a relative of Don Strom, who later became Carbondale's Police Chief. As a detective, Don helped investigate Deborah's murder. I called Don, now police chief at Washington University in St. Louis, Missouri.

"Hey, I need to tell you something. I told you a few weeks ago about the investigation into Tim Krajcir, the one you and Kluge interviewed in the Schumake murder."

"Tim is the guy who killed Deborah Sheppard, right?"

"Yes. Well, last night he confessed to eight more murders, five of them in Cape Girardeau."

He was surprised and said he remembered only the Cape murders.

"Well, this gets a bit closer to home to you. Do you remember when your relative was burglarized in July 1977?"

"Yes. I had been on vacation with them down to the Lake of the Ozarks and we found his home burglarized when we came back to Carbondale. If I remember correctly, the suspect took a gun he found in the house and shot it into a mattress in one of the bedrooms. They had experienced problems with someone peeping into their windows."

"Well, it was Tim Krajcir who stole the gun and had been peeping into the windows. He was living in the trailer just a few houses south of your relative. It gets worse. He used the gun he stole to kill three of five women in Cape."

"That's incredible! Was the gun ever recovered?"

"No. He told me and Cape Detective Jim Smith last night that he threw it off the south side of the old Mississippi River Bridge. I figure it's in the silt under the new bridge they built. We probably drive across it every time we go to Cape."

"Thanks for letting me know. Good job!"

I also wanted to let Larry Hill know about Tim's connection to Kenneth Rogers.

"When Jim and I asked him why he killed some and not others, guess what he said?"

"What did he tell you?"

"Kenneth Rogers."

"Kenneth Rogers, the one who killed little Lisa Levering?"

"Yep, he was in prison with Kenneth and was friends with him."

"If he hung around with that guy, no wonder Krajcir was so evil."

"He said that Kenneth told him one time when they were comparing crimes, 'Tim, you never leave a witness.' He said those words sometimes came into his head and he killed to prevent the victim from being a witness. I wouldn't have known who Kenneth was if it wasn't for your stories. I checked and found Kenneth Paul Rogers died in prison in 2003."

One call that stuck with me in those days following Tim's confession came from Don Call. He called while I was at home one evening to thank me for my efforts in helping resolve his mother's murder. Don had played basketball for Southeast Missouri University and he had known my cousin, who had also played basketball. Don said when he lived in Chester, Illinois, he coached a basketball team that played an inmate team from the Menard Correctional Center. He and I both wondered if his team had played against Tim's team. I told Don of Tim's upcoming court appearance for Deborah's murder. He vowed to be there.

Bernie, Deborah's father, however, would not. He told me he didn't see the point of making the long trip to watch Tim plead guilty and go back to prison. I was disappointed that he wouldn't be there but understood how upset Bernie felt that Tim wouldn't be put to death for the other murders. We talked at length about why I did what I did. He didn't like it, but he understood. Deborah's mother Hazel talked to me too. She thanked me and told me she had been praying for me.

District Attorney Morley planned a press conference to start four hours after Tim was scheduled to plead guilty to Deborah's murder December 10, 2007. Carl invited me and told me I'd be sitting at a table at the front of the room with him and Jim, facing the media. I asked if Carl could include my chief at the table and he agreed. I wanted to make sure Bob was there. We did not always see eye-to-eye on everything, but he had promoted me to the position, which gave me the ability to accomplish what I did.

The day and the details were planned to the minute. Tim was to make his plea in Jackson County Court at 8 A.M. in Deborah's murder. At precisely 8:30 A.M., the Cape Girardeau Police Department and the Carbondale Police Department would simultaneously send out press releases announcing a press conference at 2 P.M. at the Osage Center in Cape Girardeau to announce an arrest in five cold Cape murder cases. Simultaneous to that, television reporter Kathy Sweeney would tell viewers about the press conference and outline each of the five murders without revealing Tim's name until after the press conference. Newspapers would post similar stories on their Web sites.

The weekend before the big day brought some much needed relaxation and family time. My wife and I went to do some Christmas shopping. She chose our favorite spot, Cape Girardeau. The City of Roses held many good memories for us.

During the past few months, I realized the little river town also held some horrific memories for others. I wondered if I would ever get Tim off my mind. Everywhere I went, I thought about how Tim had traveled the same locations. Unintentionally, our route included the old discount store parking lot where Tim had stalked. We drove by Mildred Wallace's home and then we drove past the rest stop where Tim had killed Sheila Cole on our way home. In just a few short hours, everyone would know the truth.

I traded several e-mails with Carl while I was shopping. He was still trying to get everything lined up for the big day. All was going well. It was likely to be the biggest day in my career, which I thought I had already experienced twice before with the arrests and press conferences in the Schumake and Sheppard murders. But this one would be different.

Getting up that morning was, once again, not a problem. The rainy day set the somber tone. Lieutenant Schuler and his Illinois Department of Corrections Security Team brought Tim up the courthouse steps on the south side of the building. I watched as Tim tripped and almost fell onto the steps. His chains dangled around him. There were several onlookers, some who didn't have a clue about what was going on. They were there to pay traffic tickets or plead to other crimes. The team escorted Tim off the elevator and onto the second level of the courthouse to the courtroom where his trial was to begin. Everyone stepped out of the way so the team could pass. Just then, Don Call happened to be holding the door to the courtroom open. *Of all the people in the courthouse,* I thought, *Don is the one who's holding the door so his mother's killer can walk into the courtroom.* Don introduced himself and his wife to me as we stood waiting for the judge to make his way into the courtroom.

"You know," Don reflected, "it was at that moment when Tim Krajcir passed by that I realized the man I had envisioned in my dreams was now old and just a shell of a man. It was like a burden had been lifted off my chest. I no longer hate the man. I actually feel sorry for him."

A few minutes later Judge W. Charles Grace called the court to order. Mike Wepsiec and Patricia Gross sat at their respective tables. The hearing was quick and to the point. There was no testimony. Patricia told the judge about the plea agreement. Judge Grace accepted and asked Tim to stand.

"How do you plead, Mr. Krajcir?"

"Guilty, your honor," he replied in his soft, raspy voice.

As expected, the judge accepted his plea and the state's suggestion of a forty-year sentence. Twenty-five years and eight months after he slithered through Deborah's bedroom window and sexually assaulted and murdered her, it was over. Lieutenant

Schuler and his officers whisked Tim out of the courtroom, down the elevator and into the transportation van to return to Big Muddy. I walked outside the courtroom and was immediately inundated by the press. *They are going to get tired of seeing me before this day is over,* I mused. After making a few comments to the reporters, I went back upstairs to see Judge Grace to have him sign the court order for Bill Moyer to get Tim's DNA when he arrived the next day. I had gotten to know Judge Grace very well through the years and considered him a friend. When he wasn't wearing the robe, I called him Chuck. He grew up and went to high school in the Carbondale area, so he was familiar with many of the cases I had worked through the years. He read the probable cause statement I had prepared and was surprised, realizing this was related to another murder committed by the man whom he had just sentenced to forty years. Then I told him about the new charges from Missouri on Tim and the other two murders. He looked stunned and shook his head in disbelief. Chuck had seen a lot in his criminal justice career, but this was something new.

I jumped into my car to head toward my office.

The parking lot at the Osage Community Center in Cape Girardeau was already filling when Chief Bob Ledbetter and I arrived about a half hour before showtime. Several television trucks were near the front of the building. I had no idea what to expect. I knew it would be much bigger than any press conference I had ever attended. Bob and I walked inside and followed the signs directing everyone to the room for the press conference. Jim met us at the entrance. We shook hands. We didn't need to say anything to each other; we both knew what the other was thinking and feeling. Jim looked calm, cool and collected and that's how I felt. He had dreamt of this day and it was here. Carl and Tracy stood next to him. We all shook hands.

"Well, buddy, we did it, didn't we?"

"Yes, we did."

I walked into the crowded room, recognizing I had been there before. In October 2003, my niece had her wedding reception there. This was the same niece who had lived across from the Parsh house, many years after the murder. The media was in a frenzy assembling up lights, positioning cameras and setting up microphones. I saw several reporters I knew. Some acted surprised to see me and Bob there. They would soon understand the Carbondale connection.

A lectern drowning in a pile of microphones was in the middle of two long tables. Cards bearing our names sat on the table in front of where we were to sit. Just off to the side was another table that served as a memorial to the five victims. Black iron stands held five large mounted portraits with name plates and a single white rose in front of each photo. From left to right, in the order in which their lives were taken, were Brenda Parsh, Mary Parsh, Sheila Cole, Margie Call and Mildred Wallace. Each photo was taken at a time of joy and happiness in their lives. A basket of pink carnations and white daises rested in the middle of the table, just behind Sheila's photo. It was very touching. It even brought a tear to my eye. I now knew how they lived, as told by family members, and how they died, as told by the man who took their lives.

My quiet moment at the table was quick as the room kept filling and there were more introductions to make and more hands to shake. My sister, my wife Sheila and my son arrived at about the same. I introduced them to Carl and Jim. Carl then introduced me to Mayor Jay Knudtson. He shook my hand and told me how appreciative he and the City of Cape Girardeau were of my help. Next, I met the whole Call clan. Don introduced me to his daughter and several other relatives. Along the way, I met so many people, I lost track of who they were.

Soon we took our seats. The room grew amazingly quiet. Carl was seated just to the left of the lectern. Jim was to his left and I was next to Jim. Bob was next to me. I thought it was cool to have both detectives flanked by their respective chiefs. Morley sat on the other side of the lectern. To his right was Illinois State Police Lieutenant Steve Shields, next to Steve was Diane Higgins of the Missouri State Highway Patrol Crime Lab and then FBI Agent Thomas Blades Jr. Seated behind the Mayor was Cape City Manager Doug Leslie. I looked out at the large crowd, including current and former police officers, victims' family members and town residents, eager to learn the identity of the man who had terrorized their community all those years ago.

"Good afternoon, ladies and gentleman. My name is Jay Knudtson. I have the privilege of being Mayor of Cape Girardeau. We called this meeting today to make an announcement that I am certain will be filled with mixed emotions. While the announcement is clearly an example of superb detective work and reflects teamwork of the highest level, teamwork between many of our friends, friends in Carbondale, Lieutenant Echols, of whom we will hear how critical a role he played in his department, and our own Morley Swingle, representing Cape Girardeau County, and the terrific prosecutor he is and the role he played. But it is also a reflection of a lot of hurt and a lot of pain, pain that family and friends have had to endure. I think it is important as we spend this time together that those families and friends know Cape Girardeau went through this with you back then and we stand with you today. We stand with you with heavy hearts. This is a defining moment in Cape Girardeau's history and a defining moment in the history of our beloved police department also. At this time, it is my pleasure to introduce you to the leader of our team: City Manager Doug Leslie."

The city manager spoke for a few minutes about how the recently approved public safety tax paid for the creation of the cold case team, specifically Jim's role as a cold case detective. He acknowledged the investigators, both past and present, who worked on the case. He recognized Jim, Carl and myself for our work. Then he called Carl to the microphone.

Carl read a chronological account of what had led to Tim's arrest. He discussed the joint investigation between Cape Girardeau and Carbondale and the interview with Tim that eventually led to the deal to avoid the death penalty. Carl recognized everyone sitting at the head table. He introduced everyone to his right and then those to his left.

"Detective Jim Smith is our cold case investigator who has had a passion for investigating these crimes for many years. Fortunately, we were able to assign him to that full-time back in March and I believe it played a critical role in the successful resolution of these cases."

Carl then looked at me and smiled.

"I've kind of adopted the lieutenant from the Carbondale Police Department and I thank you, chief, very much for that," he said, as he looked toward Bob. "Lieutenant Echols was primarily responsible for the arrest of Krajcir in the Carbondale, Illinois, murder in 1982. He has developed a strong relationship and rapport with Mr. Krajcir and we took advantage of that and they very, very willingly assisted us in that investigation. Without them making their case on Krajcir, we probably would not be here today."

Carl also thanked Lieutenant Schuler and the Illinois Department of Corrections and the Illinois State Police Crime Laboratory.

"While this is some of the best news the Cape Girardeau Police Department will ever be in the position to deliver, it's tempered with a degree of sadness and sorrow. While we have brought one person to justice for these vicious crimes, there can truly never really be justice. Our hearts, our thoughts and our prayers go out to these victims and our hope is that, at least, we have been able to bring some degree of closure."

Carl had nailed it. He then introduced Morley.

"This is a historic day in the history of crime and punishment in Cape Girardeau," Morley said. "Those of us who have lived here more than twenty years remember when these crimes happened and remember when Cape Girardeau... was a scary place to be. Nowadays, it's hard to think back to what it was like in the times when we were having women murdered in their homes. So it's historic today that these crimes have been solved after all these years."

Morley's words were brief and to the point. He then asked the family members to stand. Much of the audience stood. Morley also spoke of the number of family members who had passed away since the killing spree took place. He commended Carl and his predecessors who had never forgotten and continued to work the cold cases.

"I want to extend a tremendous debt of thanks to Jim Smith for being the ferocious determined investigator he is, because he was able to bring this case to closure."

Morley then looked my way and continued.

"And to Paul Echols. We would not be standing here today if it hadn't been for the hard work that he did. So many, many police officers, many more than can be named, deserve credit for this case being solved. These two in particular are the ones who were filling the shoes at the time the big break occurred."

One of the Call family members stood up and began clapping. Next thing I knew, the whole room was standing and clapping, including our chiefs. Jim and I just sat there for a few moments, not really sure what to do. The standing ovation was overwhelming. I patted Jim on the back thinking how emotional this roller coaster ride had been for us. As everyone sat down again, I thought, *Oh man, I hope Moe doesn't hear about that. He'll give me some shit tomorrow.* But it was being broadcast live and there were so many cameras and newspaper reporters, I guessed I'd just have to suck it up and take it.

Morley began to take questions. Some asked Morley about the death penalty and some asked about the evidence. He told the audience about the meetings that took place with the families during the Thanksgiving week and how Tim's life was spared by the very people whose loved ones he had raped and killed.

Carl pointed to former Police Chief Henry Gerecke. He was now in his eighties but looked good. Chief Gerecke pointed out his former detectives, John Brown and Howard "Butch" Boyd. What Jim and I had done could never have been possible without their efforts.

Chief Gerecke then said, "I was proud of my men, but from time to time, I had to give them a kick in the ass to keep them going." The audience erupted in laughter.

As the press conference drew to a close, the audience was invited to ask questions. Carl fielded a few as did Morley. Former Chief Boyd had a question.

"Hey, Carl, can I ask you a question?"

"Wait, do you have a media tag?" Carl said jokingly, again sending the audience into laughter. It was apparent that the crowd was starting to loosen up. The burdens carried by so many for so many years were being lifted.

"Why was this guy coming to Cape?" Boyd asked. Carl answered by going through how Tim arrived in Carbondale and was hired by the ambulance service, which brought him to the town on occasion for patient transfers.

After a few more questions, Carl ended the press conference, thanking everyone for coming. Carl had mentioned that Tim had committed three other murders, but we would not be discussing them. Afterward, it became a flurry of activity as the reporters all staked out those they wanted to interview. I made my way toward Henry Gerecke, who was being interviewed by Kathy Sweeney, a Cape Girardeau television reporter.

"Let me tell you something, young lady…Sheila Cole's father and mother are both dead. Mary Cole, Sheila's mother was dying of cancer. One day, it was a Saturday, I was in the police station parking lot. The father said to me, 'Chief Gerecke, can you tell me anything that I can tell Mary, because she is dying.' How would you like to be in that position? I couldn't tell him anything. I felt bad, very bad."

"But now you know it wasn't a failure, maybe justice delayed, but no failure," Kathy told him. "Because of what your men did back then, these guys were able to break this case wide open. Does that give you some sense of satisfaction?"

"Yes, it does. I promised myself I would not get emotional about it, but I do feel it," Henry said as the tears he fought back returned to his eyes.

After meeting with many reporters and family members, it was time to leave. As I was preparing to get into my car, Captain Roger Fields chased me down. He handed me one of the white roses that had lain in front of one of the victims' pictures. He told me to keep it as a memento of the day. In a sense, it felt like one of the victims had handed the rose to me to say thank you.

On the way back to Carbondale, my phone began to ring with kudos from family and friends. I had several voicemail messages at my desk, but I decided to wait to listen to them. It was time to switch back to the father role and head to my daughter's Christmas concert.

18

Final Moments

I was sitting in my usual seat when Moe walked into our daily investigators meeting and, just as I had predicted, he began kidding me.

"Echols, a standing ovation? You're killing me man!"

I would've done the same thing to him. Trading jabs had become a way of life. We knew just how far to take it. It was a cop thing. The other detectives began to laugh. I just shrugged my shoulders and smiled. While the jab was in jest, they had just congratulated me in their own way.

When I got back to my office, my voicemail box was full. News of one of the nation's most heinous serial killers had spread fast. Many agencies around the country wanted to see if Tim could be responsible for their crimes. Tim was still at Big Muddy, where I planned to meet Corporal Bill Moyer and Trooper James Cuttitta of the Pennsylvania State Police. The two had driven in to take Tim's confession in Myrtle Rupp's murder.

Lieutenant Schuler greeted us at the front gate and escorted us to the conference room that was getting familiar to me. I set up my camcorder to record the interview. I introduced Tim to Bill and James when Lieutenant Schuler brought him in. They shook hands and then Bill began.

"I understand a lot of things have been happening with you in the last few months. We're here to talk about Myrtle Rupp's murder in Pennsylvania," Bill explained.

"I already told Mr. Echols that I would make a full disclosure, so there won't be a problem," Tim said.

Bill read Tim his Miranda rights and explained how they got a CODIS hit off of semen found at the scene of Myrtle Rupp's murder. It was time to hear what Tim had to say for himself.

"Okay...what can you tell me about this case?" Bill asked.

"I did it...Went to the front door...broke a window...I was gonna assault her that night, in the evening and, um, she wasn't home. I was waiting for her to come home. I heard her pull into the garage, but someone was with her. I got scared and I took off. Didn't do anything that night. What I did, about a week later, I came back in the afternoon, pretending to be a police officer with one of those nickel badges that you can buy anywhere and, um, she let me in and I assaulted her after she let me in."

"When you say assaulted her, how did you assault her?"

"Uh, vaginally then orally…and, uh, I had a knife, no other weapons than that…stayed there maybe twenty-five, thirty minutes and after I was done assaulting her sexually…I can't remember if I tied her up or not…then I strangled her."

"Did you use any bindings on her?"

"Might have tied her hands up. I'm not…again, it's thirty years ago."

"Okay, if I told you that drapery cord was used, does that sound familiar?"

"Yeah, probably. I think something like that…"

"Okay, when you had vaginal intercourse, did you leave your semen inside her. "

"No. I don't think so…As a matter of fact, there was no oral sex either…just vaginal. And after I was done with that, I think I masturbated. Finished it by masturbating…"

"Okay…she was alive and then, after, uh, you pulled out, then you masturbated and where did your semen go?"

"Um…either on the carpet or on the bed…I'm not sure…"

"Now, you told me that you had entered her house twice…When was the first time you came in contact, saw her and knew that she lived in that residence?"

"Well, let's see, in early '59 or '60 we lived in that area…My family and I lived over in Muhlenberg Township. When I was about fourteen, fifteen and sixteen, I was already a voyeur, I was already looking in windows and stuff like that and, um, I would go in the areas around there, I go out to that area too. I left the trailer park one afternoon…I was just driving around. I was looking for a victim. That evening, I circled that area, because I've been there when I was a youngster and that's how I came across her…I was looking in the window."

"Okay, did you go into her bedroom at all the first time you were in there?"

"Yes. Laid on her bed for a while. Just waited. This was evening…It was dark…"

"Did you do anything with the telephone lines while you were in there?"

"I had a habit of cutting the telephone lines while I was in their homes…I was on bail, out on bail for indecent liberties with a minor…And I had to turn myself back in, in September, to go back to prison."

"So, then you returned to her residence about a week later. Tell me what happened then."

"That's when I pretended I was a police officer, flashed a badge at her and told her that I was investigating her burglary and she let me in and that was when I…"

"So…when did you produce the knife?"

"I'll say about five minutes after I was in there I just had her clothes off and she was in the hands and knees position on the bed and I just had intercourse with her from behind…no anal intercourse."

"Okay…and so she complied with you?"

"Yes."

"Why did you kill her?"

"There was no reason to. She did not give me a reason, other than the fact that I did not want any witnesses."

"Tim, you said you went back to ask her about her burglary?" James said.

"Yes," Tim said, his eyes shifting toward James.

"How did you know that she reported that to the police?" he asked.

"Well, I didn't. It was just an assumption."

"Prior to your entering her house that first time when the burglary was committed, were you watching her?"

"I think I did go back one time."

"You did not enter that night?"

"No…She was home and everything was locked."

"Do you remember anything she said during this assault? Did she ask you why you were doing this? Who you were?" I asked.

"Nah, not really."

"When you strangled her, where you on top of her holding her down or behind her?"

"I think I was behind her."

"There was some, um, she was assaulted—someone hit her in the head," Bill said.

"I don't remember hitting her, if I hit her, I…"

"Maybe during the struggle; did she struggle hard or did she comply completely?"

"No, she did not struggle."

Again, Tim denied striking his victim, just as he had denied hitting Mary Parsh. It seemed like such a minor detail to deny. I couldn't understand it.

"You just knew her as a face that you peeped in through her window. Was her husband still alive when you were peeping? Did you know that?"

"I don't know. I can't remember hitting her, though. I just never did that with most of my victims. I never had to. Usually I would just go into the house, give them a real good scare. And they would do whatever I wanted...Couldn't it have been an old bruise or something?"

"Well, maybe that could be something we can look into...Is the memory vivid from the assault?"

"No, not really, but I would remember if I had hit her."

"You remember her bedroom...and the house and where it was located; and you remember Myrtle, right?"

"Yeah, I would remember if I hit her or not and I just don't remember that I hit her. I know it's not a big thing but..."

Bill's prosecutor also wanted Tim to make a handwritten confession. We gave him about thirty minutes to write his three-page statement summarizing what we had just talked about during the past hour. Then it was time for more questions.

"Tim, I know that you have been very cooperative in this case; there're more cases out there in Pennsylvania that I believe you are involved in...There are certainly at least two they believe you did, okay? We need closure on them...The crime scene matches your profile to a 'T.'"

"They've talked to me about them several times and it just wasn't me. I mean... I told them to take my DNA, blood, lie detector; I took the lie detector test and it's not me...I'm not going to say something I did not do...It was not me. This is it."

"Do you think that your brother could've done this?"

"No...no way..."

"Tim and I talked about the conversation he had with his brother..." I interjected, realizing that Bill was wondering whether Tim's bizarre conversation with his brother was actually code for disposing of another body in that area.

"That was in case I decided to do something to myself or had a heart attack or whatever. He was going to come out and get me and cremate me and throw my ashes over the valley that's there, that's all," Tim added.

"Did you like that area?" Bill continued.

"Yeah, that was the only place that I ever lived when I was a kid, that it was a wonderful area and wonderful people. That's all that was; aren't no bodies up there."

"So the statements you made to other inmates, that when you got close to death, this was the body that you were going to give the police and disclosure that you had committed this crime, that Myrtle—" Bill said.

"Yes, sir."

"And why were you going to do that?"

"Well, I was going to disclose all of it. I've been debating the last, probably the last five or six years, the positive of disclosure and the negative of disclosure. I had not made up my mind, but I was waiting until I got a little older."

After a few more denials of the other rapes Bill questioned Tim about, he went into another confession.

"When I was telling you about them rapes in Mountain View, I remembered about one more I did not tell you about, but the victim wasn't hurt," Tim said, pointing to me.

"Good, good. Go ahead and tell us about it," I said.

"I think on the northwest side of Allentown, there was a young girl about eighteen, nineteen. She lived in a corner house and she had a small apartment attached to this big house and she lived by herself; and I was just out cruising, like I do sometimes…Went through a bedroom window. She had like a little filter for air in the window and the window was open…And I went in, I had…this was in, I guess this was '81 or '82…She was by herself when I went in there with a .25 automatic. I made her perform oral sex in the bedroom. I think I tied her up and then I left. Didn't hurt her, not physically anyway…I just remember she had this big shoe rack on the wall…I went out the back door…She was real pretty, I think she was blonde or dirty blonde; she was sitting on the couch watching TV when I went in… I'd say around 9 P.M., probably 9:30 P.M., maybe."

I took notes, planning to contact the other agency. Bill continued his prodding.

"Let me ask you this: when you killed Myrtle, how did you feel?" Bill said.

"With me it's…pretty much nothing. I mean that's a terrible thing to say, I know, but I guess that at that time there was something in me that didn't care for other people. I never learned how to care for other people, respect other people; I never learned that as I was growing up…We never spent enough time in a place to learn about the people that were living around us to develop a respect for them and I don't even think that I learned that up to the last fifteen, twenty years…because I've been living with the same group of people for all this time. And for a long period of time, you learn to care more and respect them and I just…I think that part of me, when I was growing up, just got left out and I just didn't care about other people. I wanted what I wanted when I wanted it."

"Was this for sexual gratification?"

"Yes. It was like a power trip, I guess."

"So, it was control? That's why they were restrained?"

"Pretty much power control, yes."

"Why would you leave them; were you displaying them on the bed after you left? Was there a reason why you left them lying like they were?"

"Uh, nothing in particular, I don't think."

"Was there a reason that their heads were facedown on the beds when you

left them there? Or did it matter, because I know some victims were face up with…
Was there really a reason other than you committed your crime and you wanted to
flee and not be detected. Is that basically the case or…"

"No, I don't think there was a reason."

"Why didn't you have a weapon in some of these?"

"Well, probably some of them were like just spur-of-the–moment, you know.
Even though I did not get caught, they weren't…some of these things were not
planned out."

"What was your preference? What were your likes?" James asked.

"Uh, just a woman that was alone, a black female with a young child. Like I
told Mr. Echols over here, an easy victim. I imagine that a lot of them didn't even
tell. Sometimes I would give them money."

"Let me ask you this, Tim. Obviously I haven't been privy to all of Lieutenant
Echols' interviews with, uh, Missouri and his, but I did get transcripts of the conversation and obviously I was not in the room to see your reactions to a lot of the
questions and stuff, but correct me if I'm wrong, it seems to me, you seem more
upset about this Myrtle Rupp case than some of these other victims. Is that true or
because it seems to bother you a little bit more, is there some type of relationship
with her, with the family that, um…" Bill said.

"No, um, just that, let's see, how can I say this? Like I say, I have learned a lot
about myself the past fifteen, twenty years. One of the things that they teach us
over there in that SDP program is trying to put yourself in the victim's place, try
and feel her pain and keep doing this, you know, as a block from doing it again. I've
tried to do that; I haven't been real successful, but I'm trying to do that."

"Have you felt Myrtle's pain?"

"Not any more than the others. All of them are pretty nasty cold-blooded
stuff."

It was time to end the interview. Lieutenant Schuler came in with sandwiches
for all of us. So we sat with Tim as we ate our lunches. Sitting there having lunch
with him, I was struck by how perfectly normal he seemed. He was so much different
than most of the criminals I had met through the years. He was very intelligent and
just uncanny.

After we finished eating, Bill and James headed back to Pennsylvania. I told
Bill I'd make copies of the interview for them. Bill said he'd provide their district
attorney with a report and charges would be forthcoming. We said our good-byes
and I turned to Tim.

"Are you okay with my calling Marion Detective Tina Morrow and having her
come up here to take your confession to the Virginia Witte murder?"

"Sure. Might as well."

"Now, Tim, she is a woman. Is that going to be a problem for you?"

"No, it's fine."

I called Tina and she agreed to come up. While waiting on her, Tim and I discussed the Cape charges.

"You know, I remembered a robbery that I did in Cape that I forgot to mention to you and Jim," he said.

"Well, that's okay. I'll ask you about it when we are almost finished with the
interview for Tina's case so we can get it recorded. Jim will likely be up here tomorrow to serve the arrest warrants on you," I said.

"Are you coming with him?"

"No, I've got some mandatory training tomorrow."

"Do you or Jim have any old sports magazines that I could have?"

"I'll see what I can do."

Since his arrest in the Sheppard case, Tim was fairly isolated and spent much
of his time in his cell with very little to do. I knew we needed to do what we could
within reason to keep his cooperation. Still, a large part of me struggled with even
granting that little a request.

Lieutenant Schuler soon brought Tina into the room and I introduced her to
Tim. They shook hands. Tina had discussed Tim's confession with Williamson
County State's Attorney Charles Garnatti. Like his counterpart in Jackson County,
he was willing to negotiate a sentence with Tim for his confession and plea. Again,
Tim waived his right to an attorney and signed the paperwork without blinking.

"Why don't you tell us...in your words what happened," I said, prompting
him to reveal his encounter with Virginia Witte.

"Yeah, she was shopping. I was over...uh...right off of Route 13 there by
where they have the mall. And I initially spotted her car there. And just followed
her home...I think she had a station wagon."

"Okay, what were you driving, sir?" Tina asked.

"Silver...uh...well, I followed her home. And, uh...she pulled in the driveway
and went in the house. And I pulled in behind her. And, uh...I had, uh...a box I
was carrying. Like, you know, a package or something. I knocked on the door. She
came to the door. And once she opened the door, I stepped in real quick and, uh...
I remember there was dog there next to her. Some kind of, uh...British bulldog or
a boxer or something. And then I accosted her, uh...knife. A knife. And, uh...took
her into her a...I think I went into the bathroom first. I'm not sure. Had her...yeah,
I went in the bathroom first. We stopped. We were talking. I don't remember what

I said, but, uh…I remember she grabbed the knife and I didn't yank on it. I let her take it out of my hand. Uh…and we talked a couple minutes. I can't remember the conversation, but I got the knife back.

"Took her into the bedroom. Told her to disrobe. Uh…had intercourse. Then we had, uh…oral sex. Uh…I think at that time I took her into another room. Across the hall. Yeah, I think I'd…a bedroom and, uh…that's where I, uh…strangled her. Uh…strangled for a good four or five minutes and she had…you know, she…she…she wouldn't stop breathing. And I went in the kitchen. Got a knife and…tried to stab her a couple of times and it…it wouldn't penetrate, so I think I ended up slicing her along her…her stomach. And…at that time I…I…I felt her cease, uh…breathing. And I knew she was dead. Uh…I got dressed and took off and left…I don't figure I was there no more than twenty to twenty-five minutes, I don't think. I was lucky her husband didn't come walking in on us."

"Do you remember about what time of day this took place?" Tina asked.

"I think it was early afternoon. About one thirty, two. Somewhere in there."

"Okay. Do you remember seeing anybody along the way there or were you following her vehicle?"

"I seen, uh…there was a couple people outside doing various chores, I think."

"Okay. Did she struggle with you at all? Was it—"

"No, not really. Other than just grabbing the knife there."

"Do you remember how you ended up with the knife back?"

"I know I…I just reached over and grabbed it and took it…She gave it back to me."

"Did…did you cut yourself or she cut herself during that?"

"I didn't cut myself. I…I don't remember her cutting…cutting herself. I think it would've been her left hand if she had cut herself. I…I don't recall it. I remember when I was there, uh…I think a train went by too."

Wow, I realized. *I remember seeing the train tracks behind her house.*

"Okay. And from there you went into another room?"

"A bedroom on the right side I believe…That's where we had a…intercourse and oral sex. And after that I took her into the room."

"Would you be able to draw a basic floor plan of what you remember? To help explain that?" I interjected.

Tim drew the floor plan to Virginia's house exactly as investigators had noted it in the report. His recall of his surroundings was amazing.

"Okay. The box that you appeared to be delivering—that was something you just had in your car?" I asked.

"Yeah."

"Did you take that back with you?"

"Yeah. Um…I think I did."

"Now, in our earlier interview, you had mentioned something about her maybe standing up on the…was it the toilet?"

"Yeah, up on the toilet, yeah. Yeah. I think I was gonna ask her to disrobe right there. And…and then she, that's when she grabbed the knife. Right…I think right about that time."

"Did…did she try to swipe at you with the knife at all?"

"No. I think she was just too scared."

"Did she struggle with you? Try to scratch you or anything at all as you can recall?"

"I believe she was struggling a bit, yes."

"Do you remember trying to clean up the blood or anything?" I asked.

"No. I think as soon as I realized she was, uh…gone I…I took off."

"Did you have to clean up your hands? I mean, this would've been a fairly bloody scene."

"I don't think I did. Because I would've just stepped away from her. I don't think I got any blood on me. I don't know."

"You said that you strangled her four or five minutes on the bed and she just lay back on the bed. When did you realize that that wasn't going to—" Tina said.

"She was uh…not, like, choking. She was making some kind of reflexes with her…with her head. That indicated to me that she was still alive…That's when I went, uh…tried to stab her with the knife. It wouldn't penetrate, so I went and got a…a larger knife in the kitchen. Came back in and tried to stab her with that and that wouldn't penetrate either and then I tried to slash her one time and that cut her open."

"When you cut her abdomen, I mean you…exactly how did you do that? How big of a wound?" I asked.

"Well, I went like this, I think," Tim said, mimicking a slashing from side-to-side. "It…it split her open pretty good. I'd say at least seven or eight inches long."

"Okay. Was it the kitchen knife that you used to slice the abdomen?"

"I…I…I don't know what I did with that. To tell you the truth, I can't remember. I don't know if I left it laying there on the floor or I took it back to the kitchen or…"

"I'm gonna show you a picture. We talked about this in our previous interview and I told you that…I asked if you left the knife in her. You didn't remember doing that," I said, handing Tim a picture of Virginia's crime scene. He looked at it in disbelief.

"Is that a knife in her?" he asked.

"That's the knife that's in her, yes," I said.

"Um. I don't remember that."

"Okay. Here also you'll notice that she's got a rag in her hand."

"Um, she must've cut her hand on that knife…No. That's a horrible looking picture."

"Yeah, it is. There's…up by her head, there's a bloody shirt or I don't know if you remember what that was. Detective Morrow, do you know what that was?"

"It is a shirt. And there was towel on the other side," she said.

"Do you recall that?" I asked.

"No."

"Now, on this brown chair here, there was a knife that was left on the chair. There was, uh…the knife that was, uh…in….left in the body. And then there was a knife on the chair. That's why I asked you if there could've possibly been more than two knives," Tina said.

"Okay, the picture that depicts the knife still in the chest—you don't remember that at all?" I asked.

"I don't know if it was in the…the moment or what I…I think…maybe I did that after, I don't know. I don't remember it. Uh, I don't know if I'm blocking it out or…but I…I…I honestly don't remember stabbing her with that knife, where it was sticking up."

"Is there any doubt in your mind that you did this?"

"No, I did it…I remember doing it."

I continued to show him pictures of the inside of Virginia's home, hoping to jog his memory some more.

"There's a…looks like a cabinet door open underneath, like maybe that's where the rag came from or something. Is it possible when she was in the bathroom and there was a little fight over the knife, she cut herself and grabbed a rag then?" I asked, showing him a picture of her kitchen sink, which was a distinctive dark color that he said he didn't remember seeing.

"Could be. Could be…Yeah. At that time I was probably trying to get the hell out, because I don't think I ever did anything during the daylight and it was just quick…quick…quick…quick and I just can't remember that clearly…I think somebody spotted the…or asked somebody about my car. And I guess they never followed up on it. I guess I was…probably should've got caught right away."

"How do you remember that?"

"Uh…somebody called me. I…I don't know if it was from the car dealership or something where I bought the car. Somebody said, 'Hey, the FBI was here asking about a guy that had silver cars or new cars' and...so I was sort of expecting a visit from the FBI, but they never..."

"Nobody ever questioned you about that case?" I asked, unable to hide my bewilderment.

"No."

"Did you ever see a composite that they did? An image of what somebody... somebody saw?" I asked.

"I think I...I think I seen a composite, yeah, it was...it didn't look nothing like me though. I don't think...I'm sure I had a baseball hat on and they didn't even see that. So I..."

"Do you remember this composite?" I asked, handing him a copy of it.

"Yeah...that...that could've been it. I think I was wearing a pair of sunglasses."

"Would this have been something like your car? A two-door?" I asked, showing him a picture of that make and model of car.

"Yeah...yeah. It was a real sharp looking little car. All silver with rally wheels."

"If you saw her actually go in, you must've driven by at least once and then come back. Is that what happened? If you didn't pull in immediately behind her. Unless you kind of went real slow down the street. How did that work?"

"I think she was like a minute ahead of me. And she turned in. I think I might've slowed down a little bit. And then, when I turned in that direction, I didn't see her, so I figured she was already in and I just went in right behind her...I think I did knock and she came to the door, 'cause I had, like, a package thing I was telling you about. And I don't think she seen that and...I raised it up, yeah, I got a package for you. And she opened the door to...in I went."

"We're gonna shift gears here for just a minute," I announced. "We're gonna talk about Cape Girardeau's case. Earlier today, as we were talking, you had a recollection about an incident in Cape which involved a male. What was that?"

"A...a man and woman. I was out walking around looking, you know, looking in windows like I did. And I seen this woman in there. And a man. So I put a bandanna on, the screen door in the back of the house was open and I went in and I ended up just robbing them and leaving. For some reason I didn't go through with that sexual type thing. I tied the husband up on the floor...I don't think I tied her up. Anyway I...I took the money out of his wallet. I think like sixty or seventy dollars. And initially, I was thinking sexual assault, but I...I didn't and I ended up just leaving. I didn't hurt nobody, physically...It was a white man and woman. Older couple...The man was kind of slow and slender. The gal was a sort of well built. A little heavy...I'd say they were middle fifties...I think it was a warm time of the year, because they had the screen door open...I was thinking about it the other night when I remembered it and that…I didn't even think of it until about…I'd say it was three, four days ago, it just popped in my mind. I was trying to, uh…trying to think of all the different rapes I had…I think I initially said like around thirty. And I was trying to count them. And ended up, like, about, somewhere in fifteen to twenty right in there somewhere. And that's when I thought about this one here…Initially he…he started walking towards the door, he was gonna walk outside and holler for help."

"Armed with what?" I asked.

"I think I brought that .25 automatic I had. And then he came back in and laid down. And I think I had her lay across his shoulders. Not 100 percent positive of that, but that's the way I did it with that…That one other time. In Johnston City and, uh…tied them up. Took the money and then…for some reason, I don't know if I just wasn't in…in the sexual thing at that time or what, but, uh…then I left."

"Was there anything else in Carbondale that you remembered?"

"None I could think of…I…I didn't want to do anything around Carbondale. I must've really got frantic when I did."

Tina and I went on to question Tim about some other unsolved cold cases in and around the area, including the rape and strangling of an eleven-year-old girl as well as another girl who was thrown from a bridge. Tim denied both.

"What was the youngest age sexual assault victim?" I asked.

"As far as I know, eighteen…nineteen…The only time I ever got involved with a young girl was at, uh…when I got busted for that in '79."

"The landlord's daughter?"

"Yeah…You know I…I…and I tried to stop that before it got started, but I wasn't strong enough. They just kept on coming back. They weren't young innocent girls."

"How long did you have a relationship with her?"

"I'd say close to a year…It was all consensual. And I must've told her twenty times to stay away. That it was wrong. I even told her it was wrong. We…we…we needed to stop, but I…I wasn't strong enough to make her stay away. It ended up…I think she kept a diary or something and her mother found it and that's how it ended."

We ended our interview and with that, Tim had now confessed to eight of the nine murder cases. The confession in the Paducah case would have to wait until the Paducah police were ready to take it.

A television reporter broke the story about Virginia's murderer, catching the Marion Police Department off guard. Tina told me that her chief, Gene Goolsby, had decided to rush a press conference. Bob and I stood off to the side as Tina and Chief Goolsby read their press release and answered questions. Tina held a photo of Virginia for the media to see. It was the first time that the Witte case had been back in the news in almost thirty years. The chief and Tina were nervous, but they did fine. I was asked to answer some general questions about Tim Krajcir, so I stepped up to the microphones. It seemed a bit strange, a Carbondale lieutenant answering questions at a Marion press conference. Chief Goolsby thanked everyone for attending. I slipped away, eager to return to my office.

Forensic Files also came by to interview me about the Susan Schumake case. It was fitting to be talking about the case during the height of the media storm around Tim. After all, Susan's case inspired me to continue my efforts toward resolving Deborah's. The show *48 Hours* contacted me about doing an episode on Tim. We planned a meeting with Carl, Jim and some of the family members. I invited Bob to go with me.

A lot was going on in Tim's life too. Lieutenant Schuler called to update me.

"Tim has been transferred to the Illinois Department of Corrections Tamms Supermax Prison," he said. "This is where the worst of the worst are kept."

"Why did they transfer him?"

"Because of the crimes associated with him now. The administration decided that Big Muddy no longer fit Tim's status. Tim probably won't stay at Tamms, but until the Cape Girardeau cases are done, he'll be housed there."

Tamms is about forty-five minutes south of Carbondale just off old Illinois Route 127 and about five miles from my hometown of Ullin.

"I sure am going to miss your help, lieutenant," I said. "Thank you once again for everything you have done to help me and Jim."

"Oh, I really haven't done that much, Paul. You know, for the first time in my life I have feared for the safety of my wife and daughters. Always before, if my wife wanted to go shopping, I stayed at home or at least stayed in the car. I read Tim's confessions. I know all about his crimes. I have seen a lot of crazy things in my career, but this has bothered me more than anything else I have been associated with. I must admit, Tim and his crimes have caused me to become paranoid. I know it will pass with time, but for now I don't let my wife go shopping or to the grocery store alone. And I'm after my daughters to be careful. Tim's crimes have changed my life."

"You're not the only one who has told me that," I replied. "I've felt the same way about my wife and daughter. I've wondered if Tim ever saw my wife in the days before we were married. She shopped by herself at the Cape Girardeau mall. I wonder how close she came to becoming a victim. Thankfully, he'll never be outside the prison walls again, but of course I, too, worry how many other Tim Krajcirs there are out there."

19

Hunting in the Bluegrass State

Jim and I had provided Paducah officials with what we'd learned from Tim about another horrific crime, the abduction and murder of Joyce Tharp. Now they had matched her file to our revelations. It was mid-December and I was driving south from Marion on Interstate 57 to meet them and interview Tim again. I passed the interchange with Interstate 24. As I drove on I thought, *This was the route Tim took when he drove to Paducah to "hunt" in the Bluegrass State.* I thought of the horror Joyce must have experienced.

Joyce, a beautiful, petite twenty-nine-year-old African-American woman, was born and raised in Fulton, Kentucky. She was smart, athletic and a good student with many friends who loved to be around her. When Tim abducted Joyce and took her to Carbondale, it was a place with which she was very familiar. She had lived there while attending and working at Southern Illinois University. During her college years, Joyce gave birth to a daughter, Debbie, whom she loved dearly. Joyce's mother took care of the little girl while Joyce finished her bachelor's degree. After graduation, Joyce returned to Paducah and worked other jobs until she could find the job she wanted. Then she settled down in the town as her child grew and went to elementary school.

Egbert Tharp had been at his sister's apartment in the Forest Hills area of Paducah until about 11:30 P.M. on March 22, 1979. He and another one of Joyce's brothers left to go out with friends. His sister chose to go to bed. When he returned at 1:30 A.M., the kitchen lights were on and the window was missing, as was his sister. He called his aunt, who then called the police at 8 A.M. One neighbor told police that around 1:30 A.M., she heard someone go up the steps inside Joyce's apartment and, a few seconds later, there was a scream. The neighbor said she then heard two people come back down the steps, but never saw or heard anything after that. When Joyce did not show up for work, her coworkers knew something was wrong. Debbie was ten years old when her great-aunt called her grandmother to tell her that Joyce was missing. The child knew something was wrong, but her grandmother did not want her to worry and sent her to school.

At around noon on Saturday, April 23, a deliveryman pulled in behind the Park Avenue Church to deliver flowers. As he got out of his van, he noticed a shadow wedged in the corner where the brick exterior wall of the church met the exterior wall of the foyer. When he looked closer, he realized the shadow was the body of a woman lying with her left cheek against the wall of the church. With the exception of curlers in her hair and a watch on her wrist, she was naked. Based on the way she had been propped up, investigators could tell that the body had been in a state of rigor mortis before she was dumped there. An autopsy revealed that she had been strangled with a ligature and likely a garrote. She also had been struck on the right side of her head and the pathologist found a superficial laceration to her right nipple.

The news was devastating for Joyce's daughter, but her grandparents, while grieving themselves, consoled her and helped her through the tragedy. They never let her forget her mother and she continued to prosper under their loving care. Joyce's murder was as much a mystery to the family as it was to the police. Joyce had had no enemies. No one could conceive of a single person who would harm her, but they did not know Tim Krajcir. It was strange to think Tim had traveled the hour to Paducah in order to get away from his home base and unknowingly picked a fellow SIU alumnus as his victim.

I met the group of Kentucky officials near my hometown of Ullin, just off Interstate 57, next to a gas station where I had worked in junior college. Assistant Police Chief Danny Carroll, Investigative Assistant Malinda Elrod and McCracken County Sheriff's Detective Tom Emery made the trip. I led them through Ullin, down the same streets where I rode bicycles as a young boy, and continued west to the Tamms Supermax Prison. It was my first trip into the 500-cell prison since I had toured the place just before it opened. The prison was the site of the state's last execution in 1999. It was home to many evil people. Now, Tim had joined them.

I hoped we would find another helpful guard at Tamms as we had found in Lieutenant Schuler. Thankfully, we were left in good hands when Lieutenant Randy Clark met us at the front gate and led us to an interview room. Lieutenant Clark told us that they did not put Tim in a regular cell, because Tim had been a model inmate. They put him in the infirmary because of lack of a better place to hold him. Eventually, I heard the familiar sounds of chains dragging across the concrete floor followed by the echo of heavy doors slamming shut. Tim was wearing a green jumpsuit with yellow trim.

"These mine?" Tim asked the guard as he looked at eyeglasses on the table.

Tim's glasses had been taken from him because they had wire in the frames, which was unacceptable at Tamms. A new pair of black plastic-framed glasses had been ordered for him. Tim was glad to get them. He said he had been unable to see very well since being brought to Tamms.

"Yes, they are. You can put those on," I said.

I introduced Tim to Danny. Then he read a letter from the commonwealth attorney in Kentucky's McCracken County, Tim Call, agreeing to waive the death penalty in exchange for a full confession to the murder of Joyce Tharp. Tim waived his right to an attorney.

"I think Tim could probably recite those to us by now," I quipped. "This came as a little of a surprise to me that they moved you down here. Maybe it didn't to you, I don't know."

"Uh…it came as little surprise."

"They treating you okay?"

"This place is crazy…I'm in a worse cell than I was up there. Got a mattress on the floor. Had to eat with my fingers so far. They don't even give you a spoon, a cup or nothing…Every time you come out of your cell you get strip searched. Every time…Handcuffs and feet cuffs…Hopefully I won't be, like…too much longer."

"Tim, the first thing I want to talk to you about has to do with a homicide that took place in 1979, in Paducah…You have been to Paducah before. Is that correct?" Danny asked.

"Um hum…I'd say no more than three or four times maybe. A couple times with the ambulance…Only twice that I was down there did I ever do anything…"

"Okay. Now some of these questions I'm gonna ask you, I'm sure you've answered before, but it…it will clarify for me what—"

"The longer you keep me out here, the longer I'm out of that cell."

Danny, Tim and I laughed.

"I'm trying to maintain a sense of humor down here, but these guys don't play."

"What ambulance service were you working for at that time?" Danny asked.

"Vienna Correctional Center…I was an inmate at the Correctional Center… And they had, uh…an emergency medical tech program…And I was in the first class. I was working outside the institution."

"Okay, so when you were released…talk about the times you were in Paducah after that. Beginning with the first time you were there after you were released."

"Uh, shoot…I probably didn't even go to Paducah probably 'til…'79. I…I didn't go to Paducah very often. Hardly ever…I think the only reason I went there to Paducah that time was 'cause I was out on bond and just wanted to, uh…get far away."

"Okay. Did you go to Paducah specifically to commit a crime or…?"

"Well, I was cruising. Looking…Like I said, it was only two incidents…I'm not sure which was first, to tell you the truth; it was a long time ago. One was, uh… an older woman. This fits my MO. Uh…I was at a…I think it was a little department store parking lot. Followed her home. No idea where, to be truthful with you…Her house was right across from a…a…Laundromat…"

"Let's go back to that one…if you don't care. The interview that you had with Paul last time, you…you talked about a black girl. Tell me about that incident."

"I was just out cruising, you know, and, uh…was in the neighborhood…Uh, parked my car…It was like one block of houses, almost like an apartment complex there…And, uh…just got out. Just looking in windows. And, uh…I seen her in the house. And I think there was, uh…two guys in there. When I was looking in the window, the two guys left the apartment and went somewhere…"

"Any particular reason that you went to this neighborhood?"

"Well, it was out of the…the flow. And it wasn't real dark either. It was, you know, a little dark area. You know, an area…you know, something like I would go looking for…Wouldn't be seen. I was in the back of the house. I come through the kitchen. The girl had retired…went to bed. And I walked away and was looking in other places. But I knew that the guys were gone, so I came back about, I think, maybe half hour, forty-five minutes, an hour later. Broke the window above the sink. Went in…crawled in over the sink. Went upstairs and the girl was, uh…sleeping in the bed. She had a blindfold on…on her…on…on…on her I remember…Like a… sleeping thing. For her eyes. Got her up out of the bed. I was gonna do something right then and there. For some reason I…I think I was thinking they…they might come home while I was there, so I had better get her out of there. I took her out to my car."

"Okay. Did she have any clothing on at that time?"

"I think she had a nightgown on or something."

"Okay. Any conversation? What happened when you first approached her?"

"Just told her to be quiet. She wouldn't get hurt. Do what I say. I don't know whether or not…I think I had a…I think I had a knife. I…I don't think I had anything else."

"What was her reaction when you first woke her up? Did she scream?"

"No, she was just scared. She said something, but I have no idea what it was."

"Okay, did you have…was there any struggle whatsoever or did she…"

"No…Pretty much cooperated."

"Okay. When she got out of bed, did she put any clothes…additional clothing items on?" Danny asked, trying to fathom how a woman wearing her nightgown could be forced into a man's car in a relatively well populated apartment complex without anyone noticing.

"No."

"Okay. Did you see anyone while you were walking her to the car?" Danny asked.

"No. It was probably one or two in the morning. I believe it took me a long time to get in there…Breaking the window and being quiet…Drove right back to Carbondale. To my, uh…trailer."

"Do you remember…how her hair was fixed or anything?

"I think she had some, uh…couple of curlers in her hair."

"Okay…you had her in your car…did you put her in the front seat with you?"

"Yeah…Front seat with me."

"Did you stop anywhere along the way?"

"No."

"What happened when she got to your trailer?"

"Just took her into the trailer and took her in the bedroom…She was cooperative…I told her to take her clothes off. She got in bed and, uh…she performed oral sex…That was pretty much it. We, uh…just that…it was just the one time. And I, uh…tied her up…Anyway after that, uh…I strangled her…I took her clothes and, uh…threw them in the trash."

"When you say you strangled her…how did you do that?" I asked.

"I think it was with my hands."

"Did you keep the sleeping mask on her during all this or did you take it off?" Danny asked.

"I'd say I took it off."

"And you're…and you're sure that there wasn't any vaginal intercourse or anal intercourse with her?"

"No…I believe she was menstruating at the time. I remember that."

"Okay. Uh…while you were strangling her, do you remember—"

"Well, she…she struggled a little bit, yeah."

"Why did you decide to go ahead and kill her?"

"I think it was just, uh…the same thing. I had ingrained in my brain about this witness idea. I didn't want no witnesses…You know how I probably got that didn't you? From '65 or '66 when I was talking to, uh…you know who."

I filled Danny in on Kenneth Paul Rogers and how he was Tim's inspiration to take his crimes to the next level.

"I see. Okay. Did you have it in your mind when you took her that you were going to kill her once it was over with?" Danny asked.

"No…I didn't know 'til I'd do it. Whether I was gonna kill them or not. Sometimes I would and sometimes I didn't. My rape victims were mostly black, but I never hurt them."

"Do you know…was it the next day when you strangled her or was it—"

"No, it was that night…It was probably quarter to five in the morning."

"So you strangled her immediately after she performed oral sex on you?" I asked.

"I'd say pretty…pretty quick. Yeah."

"And you had no roommates at that time?"

"Well, I was just…I was staying with a guy. It was his…his trailer…He was working at the ambulance service…He was nice enough to, uh…when I got out on, uh…bail, I had to find another place to live. And he let me stay there."

"Was he there that night?"

"I think he was working. He worked on an ambulance. We worked twenty-four hour shifts…I took the body that night and put it in the trunk of the car. Probably about five or five thirty in the morning. Just before dawn. Left her in the car that day and took her back that night."

"So did your roommate come home after his shift? The body was in the trunk?"

"I…don't think he did. I think he, uh…had to work a double. I think he called me that afternoon and said he wasn't coming back…"

"When you put her in the trunk of the car, was she…did you have her wrapped in anything?" Danny asked.

"No…She was naked. Nude…I left her behind a building. I think she was nude."

"Okay, so…you put her in the trunk of the car. And what did you do?"

"I stayed there at the trailer most of the day."

"Okay. And what time did you leave to come back to Paducah?"

"Probably close to dark."

"Tim…Their pathologist had reason to believe there was some injury to one of her nipples. Can you think real hard about how that might've happened?" I asked.

"I don't remember it. I honestly don't remember it."

"Do you remember what made you to decide to stop at this particular building?" Danny asked.

"I was just looking for a place, uh…to get rid of the body…I think it was behind the building…I think it was a brick building…I looked around and it was dark and I didn't see anybody, so I just took her out the trunk and put her over by the door and left her by some garbage cans over there in the back somewhere. Right by the door."

"Did you get any sleep at all that night? This happened or…I mean right after you strangled her…" Danny asked.

"I don't think I did."

"How did, and this might be a stupid question, how did you feel once she was dead?"

"I usually didn't even think about it, to be truthful…Those feelings just weren't there, uh…no sense denying it."

"How do you feel right now about it?" I asked.

"Uh, deeply regret all of that. Come a long way since then, but at that time I just…had no respect for anybody. Didn't know how to care for other people. A lot of that stuff I've learned over the last fifteen or twenty years. A little too late."

"I mean you're on the other end of that now, where you have learned that stuff. Was this a result of what had happened to you earlier on in your life, do you think?" Danny asked.

"Oh, without a doubt. I grew up with some parts missing. That's the way it goes."

"Once you dumped her, put her body there, did you go anywhere else that evening or did you just head straight back to Carbondale at that point?"

"I think I went straight back to Carbondale."

"So you…you said that you thought she was on her period. How…how do you remember that?" I asked.

"I remember seeing a…a…a white thing sticking out of her vagina."

"A tampon?"

"Right. Yeah. I'm almost a hundred percent sure I didn't have intercourse with her."

"When she performed oral sex on you, do you remember if you ejaculated?"

"If I did it was…was…was…was very…very little. I had problems that day. Just couldn't get it up. I think I'd been down there most of the day looking around. And doing that I would masturbate a lot when I was sitting in the car. And I think I just wore myself out that day and then couldn't do nothing that night."

"During the afternoon, you just parked somewhere?" Danny said.

"Wherever there was a lot of traffic…There was…it was like a double store. The department store was here and then there was another store right here. And a parking lot in the middle…I remember when I got out…I remember one time I got out of the car and followed a girl into the store to see what she looked like. Then went back to my car."

"When you took her out of the trunk…Where did you put her?" I asked.

"I think I leaned her against those cans…Yeah, cause I think rigor had already set in."

"Did you feel a…a rush out of this? Any other than the sexual act itself? What was the goal in all of this? What did you get out of all this that made it worthwhile?" Danny asked.

"Well…Usually I get the rush from the power trip. Power. Control. Making her do what I wanted her to do…But…you know, just nothing there that night."

"Ever any concern about getting caught? I mean, did that weigh on your mind heavily through those years or never really?"

"Only when I was doing it…Rationality goes out the window, you know. Like I told Paul, it's just like a crack addict, you know, you've got to have that fix and you don't care what you do to get it. That's pretty much how it was. I mean…and then five minutes after it was over you…you get wired up for the next time. It got ridiculous…She cooperated all the time. And I had no reason to kill her. I don't even think she had a look at my face."

Danny then showed Tim pictures of Joyce's apartment and the paper towel holder that had been put outside her broken window. Tim didn't seem certain on whether he put it out there.

"Okay. I'm gonna show you this photograph. Is that her?" Danny asked, showing Tim a picture of Joyce's body as it was found.

"I think so."

"Okay. Uh, Paul mentioned earlier about, uh…something to do with a breast and these are photos that were taken at the morgue at the hospital. And it was documented that there was a crescent-shaped cut around her nipple. Is it possible that you may have bitten her?"

"I don't remember doing it."

"It was noted that there was a ligature mark left about, I think, one and a half centimeters."

"Yeah, I may have done it with a…bandanna. That's…I used that before."

"Would you just roll that up and then would you use a…a…a garrote?" I asked trying to keep my voice emotionless.

"Yeah."

"What would you use as the garrote?"

"Um…some kind of hard object. A…knife maybe or…a folding knife or something."

"So then you would twist that from the back?"

"Yeah."

"There was also another injury documented on her, where she had a…a contusion behind her right ear. Do you remember striking her or…or anything like that?" Danny asked.

"No. Maybe she bumped it on something."

"How…how many times would you masturbate? Through orgasm?" I asked.

"I wouldn't…wouldn't get an orgasm."

"Did you ever get an orgasm?" Danny asked.

"Yeah, a lot of times. When…when I committed the rapes or whatever."

"Any particular reason you went to this apartment?" Danny asked.

"No."

"Just the first one that you came to?"

"Yeah, I looked into several apartments along that row there."

"Did you…after she's in your trunk, was there anything else? Did you fondle her after death or anything like that?" Danny asked.

"Uh uh," Tim said, shaking his head no.

I looked at Tim trying to keep my face expressionless. "Anything you would like me to…to relay to her family?"

"Just that I'm terribly sorry. Deeply regret it, but…"

"Okay. Well, I know that…her parents are dead now, so that's, I mean they went to their graves not really knowing what happened to their daughter. Which is sad, but that is something I will relay though."

"Okay. Uh…let me ask you one more question before we quit. Is there anything that a woman could do or could've done…that would've caused you to change your mind as far as killing them or would've allowed them to…to live?"

"I don't really know at this time. Like I say, most of the time I didn't know if I was gonna kill or not…It's hard to answer…There's so many times that I assaulted women that I…never harmed them. And…and…and then sometimes, boom. I don't know."

Malinda then joined us as the interview continued.

"Let's go back now and on…on the original one that you talked about, which was the older lady," Danny asked.

"Probably mid-fifties. She was pretty attractive. Followed her home from a department store. I had a gun. I remember I had a .38 and…so it had to be…it might be '78. Because I didn't have no gun in '79…It had never been used."

"This is the .38 purchased by your nurse friend?" I asked.

"I believe so. I remember when, uh…I went into the house. I knocked on the door. She opened the door. I'd seen her husband leave. That's why I was gonna try and go in. And, uh…what I didn't know, her son was still there in the house. And I'd say…I had…the gun. I tied him up. No. I didn't tie him up. I might've rolled him in a blanket or something. I can't remember for sure."

"How old was the son?" I asked.

"He was probably twenty."

"Where exactly was this house? What was it near?" Danny asked.

"I think there's a…a Laundromat…looked like a…a dry cleaning store or a store where you could pick up clothes, you know, that you had cleaned or something…And then right across…there's a road that goes up this way. A little hill. And then her house is right here. It was right off a main road. And there was an intersection there…I…I…ended up just fondling her. That's…that was the extent of that one. Followed her and masturbated. And, uh…left. I had intended to rape, but with her son and everything there, it…I couldn't do it that way…I remember I drove by there later on. Like maybe another time when I was…when I was in Paducah. And she was sitting right in the front yard. You know, maybe like she was looking for somebody that would pass by…She said something, uh…when it was going on, 'Do you know who I am?' Like she was somebody I should know. Like maybe she worked for a…like county government or something…like…like I should've known her. Like, 'What are you doing assaulting me; don't you know who I am?' type of lady…I was, uh…walking around behind a Laundromat. And I seen, looked like her husband come walking out of the apartment, like he was going bowling or something. He had a bowling ball in his hand…I think he walked. He didn't…he didn't drive, he walked. So I…I figured he's gonna be gone for a while."

"And you knocked on the door. Was it to pretend to deliver something this time?" I asked.

"Yeah."

"Did she let you in the door then?"

"Yeah. I think she initially thought I was coming to see her son or something. That's the impression I got."

"What happened from the point you went in the front door?" Danny asked.

"Pulled out the gun. I think it was in the main living room and, uh…I laid the guy down on the floor. The mother…I think I told the mother to get on top of him. Lay across his shoulders. And I think I…I…I, you know, I took the money. And then I took them into a…another room. And had him roll up in a blanket. And I fondled the woman. Masturbated. And then left…I think I ejaculated on…but I'm not sure if I put some on her or not. I may have…I…I fondled her from behind. Her, uh…rear end…I told her to take her clothes off…Her son was in the back of the room. Behind…maybe a couch or a bed or something like that."

"How did you roll him up so he couldn't get loose?" I asked.

"I don't think I rolled him very well. I think he could've got loose. I think he was trying to get loose. And I think that was one of the reasons I wanted to get out of there real quick."

Danny then questioned Tim about a cold case involving the murder of an eighty-one-year-old woman. He showed Tim pictures of the victim and several photos of the crime scene.

"No way. I mean most of the women I went after were attractive. She don't look very attractive laying like that…Sorry, but it's not me."

"Okay…That's one we sent to the lab and I think there was some DNA with this one, so we just don't have the results back yet."

"That's good. DNA brought me down. That will save me on that one."

"Okay. When you went in, where was the son? Was he in the main room also?"

"No, I think he was taking a nap in that back room…I think the mom hollered for him."

"Did he do anything to try to attack you or defend his mother?"

"No."

"How was her demeanor during all of this? Was she upset or was she—"

"She was trying to keep everybody calm. Cause she was afraid I might shoot somebody."

"It kind of made me think of the older man at Cape Girardeau, where he kept walking toward the door. I wondered if you would've shot him had he kept going to the door," I said.

"I don't think so. I'd have probably turned and ran."

"Is this the same item you would've had in Marion? Was it something that you kept in your car as a prop?"

"No, I think it was just a clipboard I had at the house and, uh…I didn't always use it."

"You said this time you did ejaculate?" Danny asked.

"I think I did…on the floor or against her butt. I'm not sure which though."

"Okay. How long were you in there you think? Total?"

"Probably twenty, twenty-five minutes maybe."

After Danny finished his questioning, Tim was taken out of the room for a bathroom break. We had been talking to him for two hours. I told Danny I would get him a copy of the video interview and transcript of the conversation as quick as possible.

Danny said he would provide his report and the transcript to the McCracken County commonwealth attorney for his consideration of charges. I told Danny that I'd be doing the same with the Jackson County state's attorney, because Joyce was murdered in Jackson County. The Paducah Police Department planned a press conference announcing Tim was the suspect in the abduction and murder of Joyce Tharp and that charges were forthcoming. We shook hands and he, Malinda and Tom left.

Lieutenant Clark brought Tim back into the room so I could interview him about some of the calls I had been getting from other agencies and some Carbondale cases. He denied the rape case from Carbondale, which involved a woman who had awoken to a man lying on top of her in the middle of the night in July 1981. He was wearing a brown bandanna.

"Okay. Everything else I have is just general questions. Just some follow-up. Now when you first came out of Vienna Correctional Center, you started taking some classes at SIU?"

"Yeah."

"Did…did you declare a major?"

"I think it was A.J. Uh…I don't know if I declared it right then, but uh…"

"But you did take administration of justice classes?"

"Yeah…A minor in psychology. Yeah, that's when I was trying to…figure myself out a little bit…Sure didn't work, did it?"

"Was there any intent of taking these classes to help you with any of the crimes you committed?"

"Oh, no…no…no. To help me stop them…I took courses like in child psychology and abnormal psychology…"

"Trying to understand why you were doing what you were doing and how to stop it?"

"Yeah."

"None with the intent of avoiding how to get caught by police?"

"No."

"Well, obviously that's something that some people have brought up that—"

"Oh, really?" Tim said as a smile crept across his face.

"Were you going to SIU in law enforcement classes to avoid getting caught? To use that as…as a tool to avoid leaving evidence and things like that…"

"No."

"So that wasn't part of it?"

"No."

"When you were at Vienna Correctional Center…you went on ambulance runs?"

"Yeah. The guys that went out on the runs were sort of the real trusted guys... I went all over Southern Illinois playing ball. All the tournaments."

"That was on the Vienna Correctional Softball Team?"

"Uh huh...And then you know, when I...wasn't on the ball team, I was playing basketball. Played in the arena at SIU."

"Who did you play?"

"I think we played a...SIU freshman team at that time."

"Did you win?"

"No, they killed us...We...we couldn't...we weren't used to the depth perception in that building...And all our shots were air balls."

"So, at some point, you did work in the PADCO Hospital in Cairo?"

"I think I only worked there for about...six months or so. And then they moved me up to Anna. I worked at Anna for like a...a...full year...You said, I wanted to ask you this, that you went on a tour at Vienna Correctional Center?"

"Yes, I did."

"Was it like a high school?"

"Probably would've been somewhere around 1972, '73, I'm guessing...I think it was more of a junior high class."

"I used to take the tours around there and afterwards sit down with them and talk."

"Yeah, I wasn't from Carbondale, though...I was from a little farther south. A little town called Ullin."

"Oh, I know where that's at."

"I know we had mentioned that, in Anna, there were times you worked in the ER when you were actually credited with saving some lives...Is that true?"

"I ran into a burning car one time. One time a car was overturned in the creek and I went in and got them out of there."

"Where was that at?"

"When I was at Union County. We worked out of the emergency room there...We were on the second floor of the hospital. That was a Vienna Group."

"Okay. Now, when you were working at the various nursing homes, were there any victims there?"

"Nah...I think you could check them and never a complaint on me."

"Is there anything else that's come up? Come to mind since last time we talked?"

"No, I think we went through the whole ball of wax. Talk to them guys from Pennsylvania lately?"

"Had an e-mail from one today," I said.

"Did they get the DNA back?"

"I'm sure if it had come back positive I would've heard."

We talked for about an hour. Once again, our conversation turned to baseball. He mentioned that there were pictures of his days on the Menard baseball team in his binder, his scrapbook. I asked Lieutenant Clark about the binder when he came to take Tim to his cell. He said they had stored it with some of Tim's other personal property that had come with him from Big Muddy. Tim signed a release allowing me to look at and copy the items in the scrapbook. Inside, I found the sports-related newspaper clippings he had mentioned, his transcripts from SIU and Shawnee College, his associate and bachelor degrees and several personal photos of Tim with friends and family. I made copies of it all before I made my way to Cape to meet with Jim.

Jim and I took a few minutes to catch up about the most recent interviews with Tim. I told him about the burglary of the older couple Tim had talked about during his confession to the Virginia Witte murder. We were both excited about some much needed time off we were getting for the holidays.

A few days after Christmas, my family and I met Jim, his then girlfriend and now wife and his son. We had dinner at a Cape restaurant and then we all climbed into my van to drive around town to look at Christmas lights. It was difficult for Jim and I to enjoy the holiday atmosphere. Just about everywhere we went we recognized an address or area where Tim had stalked and murdered. Jim and I talked quietly as the others said their good-byes.

"We need to go see Tim again soon to hammer out some fine points in his confession," I said, biting my lip.

"Yeah. Has Mount Vernon got back to you yet on that stabbing Tim said he did?"

I shook my head. "They said they can't find anything in their files to match it or any of the other rapes he talked about. Maybe Tim has the town mixed up?"

"He's been so dead on about the locations of his crimes so far, I doubt it."

"Yeah, me too."

20

Finding All the Pieces

I had been home for the holidays for a week but could not get my mind off Tim. Eagerly I returned to work, ready to uncover more of Tim's past. After my investigations meeting one day, I grabbed my video camera and headed to Tamms to meet Jim at the Supermax prison. Jim and I now had further questions about Sheila Cole's murder and we felt we needed to learn more about the stabbing and the rapes Tim said happened in Mount Vernon.

This was Jim's first trip inside Tamms and there was still an unsettling feeling as we passed through the heavy steel doors, knowing we were dependent on others to let us back out to freedom. Lieutenant Clark escorted us to the interview room. He was taking care of us like Lieutenant Schuler did, but we still missed seeing our friend. Soon we heard the unmistakable sounds of chains coming down the hall signaling Tim's arrival.

Tim appeared in his green jumpsuit with yellow trim. Once again, I gave him his glasses, because prison policies forbade him from taking them into his cell. He had grown a full beard. He was alert and seemed glad to see us. He said he was doing fine but was having a hard time sleeping, because he said it was quiet compared to the Big Muddy prison. As strange as that sounded, I could relate. I grew up just a few hundred feet from railroad tracks and had learned to sleep through the trains. When they weren't running, it made for a restless night. After he and Jim talked for a few minutes, I started the recorder and we began our interview.

"Tim, I want to start off by asking you about the girl you abducted from the discount store in Cape Girardeau. Her name was Sheila Cole...We're currently testing some of the evidence for DNA and the Illinois State Police Crime Laboratory has detected three male DNA profiles. One is likely you. Another may be a boyfriend. And then there's a third that we just don't know. You've disclosed everything that was required according to our understanding of the letter that was signed by Morley Swingle. And as far as we know, you've given us everything that you know. Our concern is: was there another person involved with that?"

"No, just me."

"Is there any chance that the guy with whom you once shared the trailer would have been involved with this?" I asked.

"No. I think if he had any ideas or suspicion of what I was doing he'd have kicked me out of the place."

"Well, the reason I asked you this is…he's gotten into some problems too. He was arrested a few years ago for indecent exposure. So it made me wonder if there was any chance that he might be involved in anything like that. Was there ever anyone with you when you committed any of these crimes?"

"No, I was always by myself."

"When you took her into the trailer in Carbondale, do you remember performing oral sex on her? The reason I ask that is the crime lab tells me that the DNA that they're getting might be more consistent with your saliva than with your semen," I said.

"I don't think so…but it has been a long time."

"They are still working on that. The profile they were getting does seem to be consistent with you, but it's on her jeans, so if she performed oral sex on you, I'm trying to explain how your DNA would get on her jeans."

"I don't know unless her clothes were lying close to the bed and she spit some of it out."

"Let's switch cases again. Mount Vernon. The woman you stabbed: was it directly across from the post office?"

"It was the bottom basement apartment. It was a house, which I think was split up into apartments. This woman had an apartment on the lower left-hand side of the building. I remember seeing somewhere that they arrested someone for that. And then turned him loose."

We tried to keep our faces expressionless. This was one of our biggest fears, that someone had been wrongly imprisoned for one of Tim's crimes. There had been so many suspects through the years on our cases alone, we worried that some suspect along the way might have ended up convicted but was really innocent.

"Oh, so you think they arrested somebody?" I continued.

"Yeah, I remember seeing that somewhere. Reading it or seeing it somewhere. They arrested somebody…I'm not positive, but I think he got turned loose."

"Well, that's something you didn't mention last time. I'll have to check in to that."

"Yeah, I was hiding in the shower when she walked in. I think she was just getting ready for bed and came in. I was in the shower. It was like one of those box showers. She came in to use the bathroom. And as soon as she sat down, I accosted her. She kept on screaming. Trying to scream and I had my hand over her mouth, trying to stop her from screaming. And that went on a couple of minutes like that. Just screaming, screaming. Wouldn't stop screaming. She was a pretty feisty old gal. And, uh…that's when…when I got the knife out. Told her to please stop…stop… stop. 'I'm not gonna hurt you. Stop. I'm not gonna hurt you. Stop.' She just kept on screaming. And, uh…I stabbed her. A couple of times around her stomach area. Or in the side. And then she stopped. You know, quiet. And I stopped. Took off."

"Okay, I will have to provide the additional information to Mount Vernon Police."

"Tim, has anything else come to mind from Cape? Like, oh, a house burglary or anything like that you happen to have thought of since we talked to you last?" Jim asked.

"No. Did you locate the one with the old man and old woman I robbed?"

"We did…The woman is still alive. She's eighty-eight years old. She's not living in Cape anymore, but she's still alive. And I have a copy of the report. They described you rather well. A white male. Very dark complexion. Twenty to thirty years old. Five-eight. One thirty. Slender build. Thick black hair, about your length. Thick eyebrows. Dark eyes. Wearing a blue shirt, blue jeans and a dark-colored handkerchief or bandanna over the lower part of his face. Soft-spoken and calm."

"That was me."

"How did you happen to locate that house? Do you remember?" Jim asked.

"Just cruising. You know, walking around a neighborhood looking for victims…"

"Speaking of cruising, you told us and some of the inmates to whom you'd talked through the years that you didn't hunt in your own backyard. You didn't want to do crimes around Carbondale, because people knew you and you feared you would be caught. But isn't it kind of ironic that that's the case that caught you?" I asked.

"Yeah. Went against my own rule. Like I said, rationality goes out the window. You get the need and the urge and you gotta do something."

"Did you say at one time you had a daughter?" Jim asked.

"Yeah. Her mother probably told her I was killed in a car wreck or something."

"I want to go back to the Parsh murder. You said the Parshes were your first time to really step over the line. The mother, daughter. How did you…how did you feel within yourself after that happened? Say the next few days or so?" Jim asked.

"I'll be honest with you, I didn't think about it at all. No, not much. It was just about, like, it was. Callous as it sounds it's the truth. That part of me just wasn't there to care about other people."

"Did you ever care about anybody?" Jim asked.

"Oh, yeah…the people I knew I could never hurt. All my victims were strangers. Complete strangers. And I never hurt anybody I knew and I have never hurt any children."

It had been an interesting follow-up interview. We had clarified a few things. The bombshell that Tim dropped that someone was arrested in the Mount Vernon case had our minds racing. I also had more details and a better description of the crime scene to give to Mount Vernon Detective Roger Hayse. I prayed that another man had not gone to prison for what Tim had done. I planned on calling Roger as soon as I got back to Carbondale to tell him everything. I had to find out about this crime now, whatever it took.

Jim and I left the prison together to go grab lunch. On the way we went by the Ullin Fire Station and Village Hall where my father had been the fire and police chief at the same time. We passed the baseball park that had been dedicated to my father, who had also been my baseball coach. My dad, the public servant, had made his mark on the little town in many ways during his short life. I was very proud to be his son.

Jim and I ended up at a little restaurant near Interstate 57, where several Illinois State Troopers were having lunch. It reminded us of the night we took Tim's confession. Only this time we knew several troopers. By now, news of Tim's arrest had spread and they were quick to congratulate us. There is no better compliment in law enforcement than receiving an accolade from one of your own.

After lunch I took Jim back to his car and drove to Carbondale. As soon as I got to my desk, I called Roger in Mount Vernon. I gave him all the details that Tim had provided about the stabbing in his town so they could find the case.

Another one of Tim's cases was moving forward. On January 4, 2008, McCracken County charged Tim with kidnapping and burglary in Joyce Tharp's case. I was hoping they could do what Missouri did in Sheila Cole's case and charge him with murder, even though she was killed in another state. I was learning about laws in different states. It seemed Missouri had some better laws in such cases than Illinois and Kentucky. I felt satisfaction that Tim could be charged with Sheila Cole's murder, because the crime had started in Missouri, even though she was killed in Illinois. He had also been charged in Holly's 1977 rape. Illinois had only recently changed the statute of limitations on sexual assaults. In 1977, rape suspects had to be charged within three years. I found that out in 1992 while working with a rape victim's mother from Pickneyville, Illinois. I helped her contact a local state representative and we were able to get the law changed to five years. It has since been extended to even more.

My opportunity to visit Joyce's crime scene came within days of the charges and just after a visit with Margie Call's family. Jim and I, along with our immediate families, had been invited to the family reunion for Margie's side of the family in Jackson, Missouri, just a few minutes north of Cape Girardeau. Those attending were many of the same family members who had been at the Cape Girardeau Police station the day after Thanksgiving to determine Tim's fate. It was emotional for everyone. Jim and I took turns addressing the family. At the end, they gave us a standing ovation.

After the event, Sheila and I drove to Paducah for a Vince Gill concert. We spent the night there. The next morning, I got up early to find the apartment where Joyce had lived and the church where her body was found. The apartment complex had not changed much in twenty-nine years. From the parking lot I could see the kitchen window. I imagined how Tim must have slipped through the broken window. I guessed that very few people knew of the terrible crime that had occurred there. Then I drove to the Park Avenue Baptist Church. From the front it appeared the building might have been vacant. I snapped a few pictures and drove toward the back to photograph where Tim had dumped Joyce's body. To my surprise, the parking lot was full. A person from the church must have thought I was lost and tried to wave me in. I thought about telling him what I was doing but just waved and kept going. I was afraid that I might have unintentionally alarmed the man and, if so, I would soon be seeing a Paducah Police car in my mirror. Fortunately, I didn't have to explain myself. I had now toured the crime scenes of all of Tim's murder victims except for Myrtle Rupp. I hoped someday to go to the place where her death had occurred too.

Afterward, I delivered my report and the transcripts of Tim's confession to Joyce's abduction, rape and murder to Mike. We talked about it for an hour and I wondered whether Mike would be charging Tim in Joyce's murder, since Tim killed her in Jackson County.

"The McCracken County Commonwealth Attorney will be charging Tim with kidnapping, but I'd like you to consider charging Tim with Joyce's murder since it occurred in Jackson County."

"Is anyone really expecting a prosecution in this case?" he asked.

"The Paducah Police Department hopes you will, but I haven't talked to her family."

"I don't see the need to prosecute Tim on this. He's already been charged in so many other cases. My office's efforts won't really benefit anyone."

"It would be good for the family to finally see justice and see Tim held accountable for Joyce's murder," I pressed.

While Mike did not say no, I could see he wasn't persuaded. His points were hard to argue. He was a busy man and I respected his opinions, not that we always agreed. I also knew more years on Tim's sentence were a moot point since he was going to die in prison anyhow.

Jim, too, was working hard to get more charges filed against Tim. It was about justice for the victims. And in Jim's case, he had at least five living victims with whom to follow up.

As Jim mentioned to Tim, he had some luck finding the robbery report involving the elderly couple. He sent me a copy. It happened in May 1982 at about 9:15 P.M., just as Elza Seabaugh was dozing in his living room recliner the night of his seventy-ninth birthday. His wife of forty years, Eunice, sat on the floor nearby, playing a gospel record loud so his failing ears could hear it. Suddenly, she had the feeling that they were not alone. She looked up and saw a man with a blue bandanna across his face. He was holding a gun. She screamed, waking her husband.

Tim ordered them to, "Be still and get on the floor" and demanded Elza's wallet. Elza started walking toward the suspect, threatening to cut his throat. He was trying to open his pocket knife inside his pocket and cut himself instead. But Tim didn't budge an inch and threatened, "I'll shoot somebody; I'll shoot somebody." Fearful that Tim might hurt her husband, Eunice pulled her husband by his belt and he fell backwards to the floor with her. Then Eunice took Elza's billfold from his pocket and threw it to Tim. He ordered them to put their heads down and not to look up for five minutes. He cut their phone line, looked around and left. "I don't want to hurt anyone, but I will," he warned them.

After a few minutes, Elza got up and grabbed his shotgun. Eunice went to a neighbor's to call the police. As I reviewed the report I thought, *This guy was lucky Tim didn't kill him.* The responding officer, Curt Casteel, later lifted Tim's palm print from Mildred Wallace's window. Elza told the officer that the suspect had taken $131 from his wallet.

Elza passed away in 1991. But Eunice was still alive when Jim called to tell her about Tim's confession to her case. She wept at the news and longed for her husband to hear it too. After the attack, Eunice said her husband was never the same. He was a very proud, old-fashioned type of man who could never get over the fact that another man had invaded his home. Tim had robbed him of much more than his money. He had taken his dignity. In an interview with the *St. Louis Post-Dispatch*, Eunice said that Elza reminded anyone who would listen that he could have taken that man had his wife just let him. The guilt and anger nearly tore the couple apart. Eunice slept in the back of the house and Elza slept at the front until they erected a six-foot fence around the perimeter of their home. They bought big dogs. Eunice told the newspaper that she rearranged everything in her home, from the furniture to the clothes in her closets, because she resented the man knowing where they kept things. She felt like a prisoner in her own home.

Eunice had since moved to Warrenton, Missouri, to live with her daughter. Later Eunice gave *St. Louis Post-Dispatch* reporter Christine Byers a Bible booklet to give to Tim in prison, saying, "I don't know if he's ever been exposed to God or not. If he hasn't, it won't be because I haven't tried."

Jim continued to search his department's files and found the triple sexual assault and the assaults of the mother and teenage daughter. They were exactly as Tim had described. Jim sent me copies of the reports.

What I read was almost unbelievable. *When does it stop?* I asked myself. A mother and daughter had been sexually assaulted by Tim at the same house almost a year and a half apart. Tim had been watching women come and go at a local grocery store not far from the Cape Girardeau Police Department when Kim Tyson, a very attractive, young African-American woman came out. Tim followed her to her home, not far from the Southeast Missouri University campus. A week or so later, on July 17, 1979, Tim came back at about 11:30 P.M. to find Kim and rape her. Tim was out on parole. Carbondale police had confiscated his guns, so he was unarmed. He found a garden rake in the front yard and walked into the house through an unlocked door. As luck would have it, the daughter was not at home. But her mother Monica was sleeping on the couch. She awoke to someone shaking her. When her eyes opened, a man was standing over her, holding the garden rake and wearing his trademark blue bandanna over the lower part of his face.

"Don't scream. I won't hurt you. I won't rob you. I was looking for your daughter, but you'll do. You can take it in the mouth or the butt," he told her.

Monica, five feet tall and weighing just under 100 pounds, tried to run for the door. The man easily grabbed her and threw her onto the floor. He pulled out his penis and pulled her head toward him. He also masturbated while holding onto her neck. Monica ran to the door to lock it after he left. She tried to call police, but her phone line had been cut. She ran into the bathroom and vomited in the toilet and screamed out her window. Her father-in-law came to her aid and called the police. When Officer Karen Sullinger arrived, Monica was crying uncontrollably and throwing up. She described Tim perfectly. Police investigated the case and questioned a few individuals, but it remained unresolved.

The story got worse as I read the next report. Only six months after an Illinois Department of Corrections Psychiatrist declared that Tim was ready to return to society, Tim again went to the same home. He was still looking for Kim. Once again, she wasn't there. The mother's other daughter, Cheryl, had just walked in from the store when Tim ran into the house behind her. Tim had hidden his face once again with the blue bandanna. Armed with a handgun and wearing latex gloves, Tim ordered Monica,

Cheryl and five children who were in the house onto the floor. As the children cried, Tim demanded money. Cheryl told him they didn't have any. Tim then kicked Cheryl's foot and ordered her to get up. He took her into the bedroom and told her to take off her clothes and began kissing her body.

"You are going to fuck me or give me a blow job. Hurry up and make up your mind. With all those babies, I bet you have a good pussy. Where's your sister?"

Tim then fondled the young woman and forced her head toward his penis. He ordered her to swallow his semen and not spill a single drop. After he climaxed, he told the daughter to put her clothes on and walked her back into the room where her mother and children were still huddled on the floor. Tim cut the phone line before he left.

Cheryl went to a neighbor's to call the police. Corporal Brad Moore arrived and began the investigation. Cheryl later assisted police in putting together a composite of the suspect, but it did not generate any substantial leads. Once again, investigators interviewed some known sex offenders, but no arrests were made. Tim had slipped in and out of Cape Girardeau again without being detected. Eleven days later, Tim came back and raped Holly Jones for the second time.

Cheryl told the *St. Louis Post-Dispatch* that the night of her mother's assault her mother asked her grandchildren to fetch her a cup of bleach, diluted it and gargled with it. The day after, Monica asked her son to take her home so she could clean her living room and never spoke of the attack again. Cheryl and her three children moved in with her mother shortly after the attack. The women never realized that they had been assaulted by the same person. Cheryl told the newspaper that she refused to use the family's silverware and plates after her assault, fearing that her attacker might have infected her with a disease. She refused to walk anywhere alone and tried to drown her fear and shame with alcohol. When Jim contacted Cheryl to tell her about the break in her case, they realized that Tim was also her mother's attacker. He couldn't be charged in Monica's crime because she had died of cancer in 1999. Cheryl visited her mother's grave shortly after her conversation with Jim to tell her their nightmare was over.

Cheryl also told Jim that she remembered how investigators thought the assault of three young women at the same time might be related to her attack. After an exhaustive search, Jim found the report and sent me a copy. Once again, I was amazed at Tim's boldness. This time, Tim was on the south side of Cape Girardeau on April 25 at about 9:20 P.M. The three women, Vivian, Jean and Anna, were sitting on Jean's living room floor sipping cocktails at the end of a long workweek. Their children were playing in the back of the house. Suddenly, the little ones filed into the room where their mothers were sitting. A man wearing a blue bandanna was behind them, holding a gun and wearing latex gloves. He had cut the screen on a door and walked onto the back porch and into the home. He ordered one of the women to put the children into a closet. He sat on a chair facing the couch and told the women to line up, take off their clothes, dance and bend over. During the next thirty minutes, he licked and kissed the women's buttocks and fondled them. He forced anal sex on one of them and then forced her to perform oral sex on him as he climaxed. The women cried, prayed and thought of ways to escape during the attack. Tim occasionally drank from their margarita glasses. Tim threatened to slap the children if the women did not do what he said. At one point during the assault, he asked the children if they were okay. The women told police that the suspect was intimidating and demanding and spoke to them in a calm and soft voice.

He told them not to move for five minutes. As soon as he left, the victims got dressed and embraced. They let the children out of the closet. Vivian drove home to call police, because Jean didn't have a phone. Sergeant Carl Eakins took the initial report. The victims viewed a photo lineup of students from the university, but they couldn't make any identifications.

In an interview with the *St. Louis Post-Dispatch*, Vivian said she had been married for only two months before the attack. She said the experience ruined her marriage and her life. She divorced her new husband just months after the attack and moved to another city. She said she tied a string to her doorknob to make sure no one had walked in before her and still sleeps with a bat under her bed.

Jean told the newspaper that she, too, grew paranoid. She pushed her couch against her door every night and still sleeps with a meat cleaver in her bed and a hammer underneath her bed. Learning that Tim was their attacker revived the memories that the women had worked hard to suppress. Anna declined an interview with the newspaper. Vivian said she was looking into installing burglar bars on her home in the wake of the news that she had come face-to-face with a serial killer. Jean said she had started pushing her couch back up against her door at night.

While meeting with Jim, the women determined that Tim must have first seen one of the women at the grocery store the week before the attack. Along with the news of Tim's confession to their case, Jim brought a note with him that had been intended for the women twenty-six years before. It was tucked in their file and authored by Pauline Brown, who was then a sixty-five-year-old widow from Marion, Illinois. She had been raped just a month earlier on March 28, 1982. The report did not explain how Pauline had learned of the triple assault. Jim guessed that she may have heard of the attack through the news and mailed the letter to the police department, hoping detectives would deliver it to the victims. They never got it. In January 2008, Marion Police told Pauline's family of Tim's confession to her rape, as well. The family was appreciative but told investigators that they'd rather not tell her because the ninety-year-old woman was in a nursing home and her health was failing. Jim read me the letter. It was touching and from the heart. He delivered it to the victims. Each accepted it with emotion and gratitude.

Tuesday Morning, Marion, IL.

Dear friends (thru having something in common)
I am writing this hoping the police will be kind enough to give this to you. Since I had the same tragic experience that you had, I thought perhaps knowing that, it might help you to cope with this problem. It happened to me on March 28th. I returned home from church and the intruder was in my home waiting for me. Since I am a widow I live by myself. I received so many cards and letters from my friends with words of encouragement and it helped so much. We don't understand why these things happen to people who are taking care of their own business and living a quiet life but only the good Lord can help us with this problem. Perhaps there is nothing that I can say that will take away the fear and the memory of what happened but knowing someone else has experienced the same thing and is fighting the same "battle" that you are might help a little. May God bless you and may your intruder be captured is my prayer."

Pauline Brown

I admired how this woman had reached out to comfort other women whom she didn't even know and whom she didn't know had been assaulted by the same man who attacked her. She had leaned on her faith to get her through the hell Tim had put her through and she wanted to give these women that same hope. Pauline had prayed that their "intruder" would be captured. Finally, her prayer had been answered.

The twists and turns of Tim's reign of terror were getting even stranger for me. I was having coffee and reading the morning paper when my sister called to tell me her boss, a prominent heart doctor, was Floyd Parsh's heart doctor when his wife and daughter were murdered.

"He remembers how distraught and devastated his patient was," my sister said. "When he learned you were my brother, he asked if he could send you some flowers."

"Thank him for me, but I really don't want any flowers. If he wants to send flowers, tell him to send them to the rest area where Sheila Cole was murdered. It's the only crime scene on public property."

The doctor did as I had requested. A heart-shaped wreath covered in pink roses with a pink ribbon hung at the rest area within days. A ribbon read, "In Remembrance of Sheila Cole."

I also found the girl whom Tim had considered his old girlfriend, Brooke Neal. Tim had pointed out several pictures of Brooke from the scrapbook that he let me copy. Brooke was a nurse, had since married and moved to another state. She said her friend told her about Tim and the stories in the news.

"I'm having a hard time dealing with the crimes that Tim committed. I'm kind of freaked out by them," Brooke told me.

"Yeah, I don't blame you there," I said.

Brooke said that she first met Tim at a bar in Murphysboro in 1977 or 1978 and that they dated until he went back to prison in the fall of 1979 for having the affair with the young girl. Brooke said that she didn't have even the slightest clue that he was committing violent crimes. I sent Brooke copies of the photos in Tim's scrapbook. She remembered them and said Tim loved the outdoors and enjoyed going to Crab Orchard and Campus Lakes. She said she remembered that Tim had dogs.

"He loved those dogs and treated them well," she recalled.

In 1979, Brooke went with Tim to Pennsylvania so she could meet his family. During the trip, they camped in the mountains. Brooke said she believed she had taken the photo of Tim during that trip sitting in a chaise lounge wearing a maroon and white T-shirt with "SIU" written across it. A red tent was behind him. I found the photo in his scrapbook.

"He was a good survivalist and told me that someday he would like to be a mountain man. He told me he had buried some camping gear high in the mountains so he could go up there if he wanted to get away from civilization," she said.

After Tim went back to prison in the fall of 1979, she visited him a few times at the Menard Correctional Center. She said her friend went with her sometimes. Eventually, though, their relationship faded.

"Brooke, did you know Tim has a rose tattoo with your name on his chest?" I asked.

"Oh, my God! No I did not know that, but Tim did have a lot of feelings for me. It just didn't work out. Can you get a message to him for me?"

"Yes, I can. You can e-mail it to me. Brooke, I need to ask you a very personal question."

"What?"

"What kind of sex life did you guys have?"

"I figured you were going to ask that. We only had sex one time that I can remember. He had a lot of difficulty and ultimately had to masturbate to reach a climax."

"I am sorry to ask you that, but I'm trying to figure out what some of his issues were that led him to do what he did."

Brooke sent me an e-mail to give to Tim reminiscing about the good times they had shared. It was apparent the two had been very good friends. She credited him for getting her involved in the medical field and becoming a nurse. She told him she now knew about the tattoo. She concluded by saying that she needed him to tell me everything he did and signed it, "Your Friend, Brooke." Like most of Tim's close friends, it was almost impossible for her to believe he was capable of such violence.

I also called Brooke's friend.

"They weren't a real hot and heavy couple; they were more like just good friends who hung out together," she said. "He was a nice guy. Whenever I was around him, he was courteous and kind."

I was about to end my interview with her when she sprung a question on me.

"Lieutenant Echols, do you remember the murder of Lisa Levering?"

"I wasn't on the department yet, but I'm familiar with the case."

"That was the one other time I was interviewed by police. I was a freshman in high school when Lisa was murdered. Her locker was next to mine and I knew her well. In November 1969, I was walking home with a friend and a guy tried to pick us up. We ran away from him and my friend told her parents. I guess a little while later he abducted, raped and murdered Lisa. When the police heard someone had tried to pick us up, they asked us to look at some pictures. We picked out the guy and they later arrested him. I doubt you ever heard of him, but his name was Kenneth Paul Rogers."

Damn! This is getting more and more weird, I thought. The man who told Tim to "Never leave any witnesses," whose advice he followed nine times, had attempted to abduct Brooke's friend. I wondered if Tim knew this woman helped put his friend back in prison for the rest of his life. I couldn't wait to tell Jim.

"Are you sitting down?" I said.

"Oh boy, what now?" he said.

We talked of how seemingly unreal all of the facts we had been finding about Tim's past were, but we were both still haunted by the ones we couldn't tie up. We were finding almost all the cases Tim had disclosed. I even found simple burglary reports in Carbondale that Tim had confessed to doing. I believed Roger Hayse was trying to find the case in Mount Vernon. I knew the stabbing had been reported, because Tim saw it on the news. I had no way to know if the rapes had been reported. It was time to try what some officers might view as unorthodox measures: time to get the media involved.

21

Another Victim

The idea of innocent people being convicted of horrific crimes Tim had committed continued to plague me. Now a new one surfaced. Could a black man have been convicted and gone to prison for a crime Tim committed? I had to be sure. In a few of the Cape cases, and in the North Chicago rape cases, Tim's skin was described as dark. Tim was bald on top of his head, but he sometimes wore a hat that left his black hair visible on the back and sides of his head. He had distinctive dark bushy eyebrows and dark eyes, was five feet ten inches and weighed 170 pounds. He covered his face most of the time. *Maybe someone could've thought he was black*, I thought. I needed to find out. The Mount Vernon Police hadn't found the case. I needed to find a different way to do it. Jim and Carl agreed with releasing the information to the media. Calvin was okay with it. Roger Hayse approved too.

My opportunity came when Tim arrived in mid-January at the Williamson County courthouse for his preliminary hearing in Virginia Witte's murder. Tim pled guilty and was sentenced to forty years. I was glad justice finally was done and quickly, because the case was holding up Tim's extradition to Missouri. When some reporters came by to interview me at the Carbondale police station after the hearing, I told them about the Mount Vernon cases.

On January 20, 2008, Bethany Krajelis, a reporter for the *Southern Illinoisan*, published a story about the two rapes and stabbing Tim had described. The next day, Cape Girardeau TV reporter Carly O'Keefe and her cameraman did a little research on their own. Carly called me from the Mount Vernon Library.

"You're not going to believe what I found," she said.

"Perhaps something on the stabbing."

"Yes, I did. I found newspaper accounts of the incident. It's exactly as Tim Krajcir described it."

Carly gave me copies of the clips she found. Police found Grover W. Thompson in the post office across the street from Ida White's apartment the night of September

7, 1981. An eyewitness said he had chased the suspect, a black man, out of the apartment and saved Ida, a seventy-three-year-old white woman. Grover had been convicted of attempted murder by a Jefferson County, Illinois, court on December 9, 1981, and sentenced to forty years. I couldn't tell whether Grover was still in prison based on the information I had.

Bethany's newspaper article generated a lead of sorts as well. Bruce Irish, a retired judge from Jefferson County, contacted me after he read the story. He had presided over the trial. In his opinion, either there was an error in the eyewitness testimony or Tim was screwing around with me.

At one point in my career, I knew several Mount Vernon Police officers. Richard Grimes and I had been hired and started our six weeks of police training at the Police Training Institute at the University of Illinois at Champaign at about the same time. At the very moment Ida White was being stabbed, Richard and I were driving back to training after a three-day weekend. When Richard passed away, I lost my personal contact with the department. So in my call to the chief of police, Chris Mendenhall, I introduced myself and told him what Carly had found. He seemed surprised and told me he would get back to me.

To me, it now was obvious. Grover had been wrongfully arrested and convicted. There was no way Tim could know the specific details of this crime without being the person who did it. There was no reason for him to make it up. I made a few comments to Carly on camera about what appeared to have been a wrongful identification and conviction. It was the lead story on the ten o'clock news.

The next day, Carly called and told me "Paul, there's something else. Grover died in prison in 1996."

Oh my God.

Jim and I planned another interview with Tim at Tamms that week. I fully intended on grilling him even more on the case. But our visit had to be postponed. Tim had pancreatitis that required surgery. Jim and Carl were once again concerned about ever getting Tim to Cape Girardeau to face charges.

Chief Mendenhall called as he promised. We had a fairly short conversation.

"I found the case and have reviewed it. I'm 100 percent sure that Grover Thompson stabbed Ida White and my department arrested the correct man for the crime," he said.

"Well, chief, I respectfully disagree. Why don't you send an investigator with me and Jim to interview Tim."

"We will be sending an investigator but only to talk about the rape cases he has admitted to doing."

I got a copy of the transcript of Grover's trial and took it home to read. It did not change my mind. In fact, it reinforced my opinion. Grover was born in Carthage, Mississippi, where he helped his father farm. He was one of eight children. He had been divorced twice and had one son. He left high school after the tenth grade but got a GED in New Albany, Indiana, while he was living with his brother. He served in the Florida National Guard, leaving after only six months with an honorable discharge. He worked various labor jobs his entire life, but he never held them long. For twenty years Grover was in and out of the Mississippi State Mental Hospital in Whitfield, Mississippi. Most of the medical reports described Grover as a quiet and well behaved individual. A report written by Dr. D. Davidson was typical of the way other doctors had described Grover through the years: "[Grover's] Memory is quite poor for both recent and remote events and he appears to be of dull normal intelligence. When seen by staff today, he is somewhat confused but is approximately, correctly oriented. He expresses himself with some difficulty and his memory is obviously quite poor for recent events."

Shortly after, his mother died. Shortly after that, he was diagnosed with schizophrenia. After his mother's death, he traveled from one family member to another, never having a home of his own. He was arrested in the state of Florida on charges such as sleeping on the sidewalks and trespassing. In 1975, a car hit him as he walked alongside a road and shattered one of his legs. It never fully recovered. Grover quit wearing shoes, saying in court that one leg was longer than the other and wearing shoes was painful. That same year he pulled a .22 caliber revolver and fired two shots at another patient whom he said had defrauded him. No one was injured and he was not charged criminally.

On the night he was arrested, he was wearing only socks and had been essentially homeless, traveling from one sister's home near Milwaukee, Wisconsin, on a bus headed back to family members in Mississippi. His medical problems allowed him to draw some SSI benefits but not enough to land him hotel rooms during his travels. He learned post office lobbies were a good place to crash. They were always open and always heated or cooled. When his bus pulled into Mount Vernon, he saw the post office just one block away. He had become uncomfortable on the bus that night and asked the ticket agent in Mount Vernon if he could catch the next bus in the morning. He found the bus station too noisy for the night, so he walked to the post office, a short distance away. There, he tucked his worldly goods, two small bags of clothing, on the floor underneath a table and laid down. He had found comfort.

I got in touch with Grover's defense attorney, Steve Swafford.

"I remember this case very well. Out of all the hundreds of cases I have tried through the years, this is the one where I always thought an innocent man went to jail.

Ida was a sweet, older lady—an Aunt Bea type. The jury wanted to convict someone
for what had happened to her and Grover was the man who was in the wrong place
at the wrong time. But Grover had a leg that had been injured and, in my opinion, he
was not physically capable of doing what the police said he did. The suspect had to
jump through a window, down into a basement apartment that was about half below
grade and then jump back up out the window to flee. We took a tour of Ida's apartment
during the trial and I just did not think Grover was capable of jumping down and then
back up. He had a difficult time walking because of the old leg injury. He also had a
difficult time in court comprehending what was going on around him."

I gave Steve the transcript in which Tim had provided details of the stabbing.
He said Tim's description of Ida's apartment was right on.

"For him to know the details so well, he had to have been there," he said.

The new information catapulted Tim's name back in the media. Chief
Mendenhall argued that Grover and Tim had both served time in the Menard Correctional Center's Psychiatric Ward together. It was true that two had been in the
same place with about 400 other inmates. Tim was temporarily housed there when
he came back from Pennsylvania in 1988. I found it doubtful that Grover could have
told Tim so many minute details and that Tim could remember them after this many
years. I also found it unlikely Tim would have befriended an older black man in
prison. Grover's family found it equally as unlikely that he would have talked to a
younger white man. In an article in the *St. Louis Post-Dispatch,* one of Grover's
nephews said his uncle had grown up in the Jim Crow south and likely wouldn't
have talked to Tim even if they had been in the same unit. One of Grover's only
surviving sisters was too emotional to talk to the newspaper about the situation, saying only that she didn't need her brother's conviction reversed posthumously, because
she always knew he was innocent. His nephew wanted it done.

Still, Chief Mendenhall maintained Grover's guilt. He told some media that
Tim was lying and questioned whether Tim was telling the truth in the Cape
Girardeau cases. He told the *St. Louis Post-Dispatch* that he would rather believe a victim and a witness over a psychopath and that Tim must have peeped into Ida's window to know the layout of her apartment as well as he did. This upset Carl, Jim and,
especially, Morley. But we were solid, I believed. Tim's confessions were backed up
by DNA matches in the Carbondale, Cape Girardeau and Pennsylvania murders.
We felt it impossible he had obtained in-depth knowledge about so many crimes
from other people in prison. Nonetheless, I felt strange defending a serial killer.

Chief Mendenhall then called my chief about the investigation. Chief Mendenhall did not know that Roger had approved the media release. Soon Roger called me,
agreeing to go along. Roger, like his chief, did not believe Tim was responsible for the

crime. Nevertheless, he agreed to go with me and Jim to interview Tim but would only consent to talk to him about the rapes.

"Grover did it and it's a closed case," he said stating his own opinion firmly.

"All right. I'll set up the interview when Tim feels better," I said.

I obtained a copy of the police report from another source. It was interesting. At 9:26 P.M. on September 7, 1981, Officer Dennis Baltzell was dispatched to an accident at 13th Street and Broadway. He arrived to find a stabbing scene there instead. Ida was lying naked across her bed and bleeding badly. In his report, the officer said that Nick, an off duty ambulance driver, told him that he and his wife and their infant son lived in an apartment that joined Ida's apartment. They were watching television when he heard her screams. They continued for several seconds before he forced open a common door and entered Ida's apartment and found her covered with blood. He said he also saw a man, "Reaching in from the bathroom window with about half of his body in the room." Nick said he grabbed the man by the shirt, but it ripped. "He described the shirt as very dirty and that it tore easy," the report stated. The ambulance driver described the suspect as black, five feet nine inches or five feet ten inches tall, very thin, with short hair and a rough complexion. The driver told the officer that he released the suspect to tend to Ida. He stayed with Ida when she went to the hospital. Blood covered the bathroom, bedroom and bed.

Officer Baltzell went outside and saw a window screen had been removed from the bathroom window. A woman noticed all of the police milling about the apartment and asked if they were looking for a black man. She told them there was one lying on the floor in the post office. There they found Grover, a thin black man with short hair, a rough complexion and a mustache and hair on his chin. Grover told them that he had just come into town on the bus. They found a pocket knife in his pocket and noticed a few specks of what appeared to be blood on the knife. Grover told the officer that he had cut himself trying to shave with the knife recently. Grover was wearing only socks and no shoes. Captain Andre McWilliams noticed the socks, because he had seen a fabric impression on the toilet seat in Ida's bathroom. He had collected the toilet seat and thought it might have been made by Grover's socked foot as he climbed out of the basement. There wasn't any blood on Grover's socks. They arrested him thirty-seven minutes after they had arrived at Ida's apartment. A booking photo revealed he was six feet two inches tall and 160 pounds. In the photo, Grover was wearing a black collared button-up knit shirt with a gold vertical strip along the button holes. After Grover's arrest, the officers brought Nick back from the hospital to the station. Grover was the only suspect in the room when Nick identified him as the suspect. It was enough to charge Grover with the crime.

In Captain McWilliams's report, Nick told officers that Grover's clothes were different than he remembered. While examining Grover, officers noticed the remnants of a red and grey colored shirt around his waist. The sleeve of the shirt was inside one of his bundles of clothing. It had no traces of blood on it.

Captain McWilliams interviewed Ida at the hospital. He asked her if the man who attacked her was the same man whom she had called the police about two days earlier. Steve Swafford later said Ida had called the police, concerned that she saw a black man near her apartment. She said she didn't know if it was the same man and wasn't sure if she could identify him.

Nick's story continued to change. In Sergeant Roy Payne's report, Nick said the black suspect had a partial beard and an ugly face.

Grover's case proceeded to a preliminary hearing on September 18, 1981—the same day Mount Vernon Officer Richard Grimes and I graduated from the training institute. A few parts of that transcript caught my eye, especially Officer Baltzell's testimony about the ambulance driver's initial recollection of his encounter with the suspect.

"The individual was half in. His upper torso of his body was extended from a window which is, the apartment is in a basement floor which the window is near ground level and the assailant was half in, face up to his waist, reaching back into the apartment," he said.

Nick told the officer that he struggled with the suspect while he was in the window and the suspect hit his back on the window. Right after Grover's arrest, officers found a mark at an angle across Grover's back near his shoulder blades. Grover told the officers it was from the table leg at the post office he had been lying against just before they arrested him. No pictures were taken of the mark. Captain McWilliams later testified that Ida described her suspect as a black male, thin, with a beard and ugly. He also testified that Nick denied ever seeing a knife in the suspect's hand during his encounter with him.

Judge Irish found there was enough probable cause and set the case for a jury trial. Steven Swafford later filed a motion to suppress Nick's identification of Grover at the police station, saying it was unfair to have just one suspect in a lineup and that officers had given Nick too much information about the arrest beforehand. The court heard that motion in November 1981. Officer Baltzell testified that Nick had described the suspect to him.

"His hair was not an afro type, it was close to his head and he had chin hair and the subject was dressed, he told me at that time, in a white or a light T-shirt, I can't be sure, and he was without shoes."

The prosecutor then asked the officer if he could refresh his memory by reading his notes. The judge asked if the information in the report was received directly from Nick and allowed the officer to read directly from his notes.

"According to my notes, the report says that the suspect was described as a male, black, five-nine, five-ten. Slight build, slim built, sparing beard, wearing blue jeans and a white T-shirt."

It was the first time the blue jeans and white T-shirt had been mentioned. The dispatcher log, containing information radiocd from the scene, reflected the blue jeans and white T-shirt description too. Tim had told me he remembered the crime had happened when it was warm out, because he was wearing a T-shirt.

Swafford was upset that the officers had told the ambulance driver how Grover was found and that he had been arrested before he identified him at the station through a one-way mirror. Grover was the only person in the room. Captain McWilliams said the driver needed about sixty to ninety seconds to identify Grover. He added that after the driver identified Grover, officers showed him the pieces of Grover's red and grey shirt and the driver identified them as what Grover had been wearing when Grover was in Ida's apartment.

Then it was Nick's turn to take the stand.

"Well, I saw someone in the window behind Ida and I ran past Ida to see just what was going on…The torso of his body was into the apartment and his legs and posterior were out of the window…I grabbed for the individual in the window and, at the same time, Ida was standing next to me and I saw her knees buckle and I released the individual to grab Ida, to administer first aid…I grabbed for him…and the shirt I had hold of was tearing and giving and Ida was collapsing, so I released the individual…we were face-to-face…Maybe a minute, maybe a minute and a half, I'm not exactly sure…"

The ambulance driver was asked how long it took him to identify Grover. His answer surprised me.

"Ten or fifteen minutes. I was making a positive identification, like I was told to, to be sure…I stated that was him, but they said you have got to be positive, so I kept on looking and looking and it was him, sir."

On cross-examination, the driver told the prosecutor that his struggle with the suspect was more of a tug-of-war. He was asked if he had any doubts that the individual he identified was the individual he struggled with in Ida's bathroom.

"No, ma'am, no doubt in my mind," he told the prosecutor.

Judge Irish denied the motion to suppress the driver's identification and moved the case onto a jury trial. The white T-shirt that the driver had initially told officers and his wife that the suspect was wearing was never discussed again in court. The focus now shifted to the remnants of the red and grey shirt that Grover had around his waist.

The results of forensic testing of the evidence in the case arrived just before the trial began. After Grover's arrest, the Mount Vernon Police Department sent the window screen, Grover's knife, Ida's toilet seat, the socks that Grover was wearing, the bag of socks in his possession and the red and grey shirt to the Illinois State Police

Crime Laboratory in Carbondale for examination. Experts determined that the blood on the knife was human, but there was not enough to provide a blood type. None of the socks Grover owned matched the fabric impression on the toilet seat. No blood was found on Grover, the clothes he was wearing, the long sleeve red and grey shirt or any clothes in his bags. No suitable latent fingerprints were found on the screen.

Grover's trial began on December 8, 1981, with jury selection. The first witness called to the stand was Ida. She told the court she was in her apartment by herself that evening and had been talking on the telephone just before undressing and going into her bathroom to take a bath. She said she pulled the shower curtain back and a man who had been in the shower stall grabbed her, put his hand over her mouth and showed her a knife. She said she began to scream and the man told her, "I will kill you and all the white people here." She said he then stabbed her in her stomach and "all the way around" several times.

"I got loose from him and I ran to the door, Nick's door, and they heard me and as I started to unlock the door, he [the ambulance driver] kicked it."

She told the court that before she got away from the attacker, she had grabbed the suspect's knife. The cuts on her hands required stitches. Ida said she did not know exactly how the suspect went out but remembered the ambulance driver laying her on the bed when she started to fall. She added that, "Nick got a good view of the suspect." She then clarified a point about how the suspect fled from her bathroom saying, "I thought he went out head first, but I guess he didn't." Ida said she was in the hospital for thirty days.

Steve Swafford cross-examined Ida.

"Now then, this individual jumped out from behind the shower?" he asked.

"He didn't jump all the way out. I could just see him from here down. I think he was colored."

"You saw he was a black man?"

"I saw he was a black man."

"You could not tell for sure who that man was?"

"I could not."

"So the gentleman was already on his way out the window when you screamed for Nick?"

"Well, he wasn't all the way out."

"But he was on his way out?"

"Yeah, he knocked the window out and Nick got to him real quick."

Steve couldn't figure out how the suspect would have started to climb out her below-grade bathroom window and then turn back around once he was outside and reach in the window to have the confrontation with the ambulance driver. Steve then tried to ask Ida about the confrontation she had with another black man a few days before her attack. The prosecutor objected. Judge Irish would not allow Ida to answer the question. Ida did not identify Grover in the courtroom.

On the second day of the trial, Officer Baltzell was the first to testify. The bulk of his testimony centered around the red and grey shirt and the mark on Grover's back. Nick also testified. This time he was asked to describe the shirt the suspect was wearing, the one that tore as the suspect was trying to flee his grasp.

"It was a printed shirt, printed on it, I believe orange on red was the colors on it. That is what stood out in my mind. It was kind of dirty and musty."

Grover took the witness stand to defend himself. Steve hoped the jury took note of his shuffle of a walk as he approached the witness stand, to see how he was physically incapable of pulling off such an attack and lifting himself out of a window. He explained why he got off the bus at Mount Vernon and why he went to the post office. He told the court that the remnants of the shirt he had around his waist were from an old shirt that tore easily when he pulled it off in a hurry to change before catching the bus to Mount Vernon. He said, once again, that the trace amounts of blood on the knife came from cutting his face while shaving.

In her closing arguments, the Jefferson County state's attorney told the jury that Grover was telling the truth about taking the shirt off in a hurry, because he had just stabbed Ida and he was trying to get rid of it. She argued that the socks he was wearing did not match the impressions on the toilet seat, because he had disposed of them. And she admitted the knife used in the attack might not be the one Grover had in his pocket, because he likely disposed of the real one too. The key to the case was Nick's eyewitness testimony.

Steve's closing arguments focused on how the state had not met its burden to prove Grover's guilt beyond a reasonable doubt. He pointed out that Ida could not identify her attacker. He reminded them that the ambulance driver's encounter with the suspect lasted a few seconds before the suspect fled out the window and he argued that the driver's identification of Grover at the police station was influenced by the way the officers conducted the lineup. Steve also pointed out that the doctor said Ida was stabbed three or four times and that her hands had been cut. He suggested that there should have been blood inside the knife that inflicted that many wounds, not trace amounts as found on Grover's knife. There should've been blood on Grover and his clothes if he did it.

The prosecutor had the last word. She reiterated that Grover had been found with a torn shirt, just as the witness had described. It was interesting that one of the last things the jury heard was the story about the torn red and grey shirt, or the orange and red-printed shirt as Nick had described, on the stand. It had become one of the most important pieces of evidence against Grover in the case. The initial description of the white T-shirt and blue jeans had been lost in the confusion. Tim had admitted, without influence, that he was wearing a white T-shirt and blue jeans the night he stabbed Ida. *What are the odds of that?* I wondered.

The all-white jury deliberated for three hours and thirty-five minutes before finding Grover guilty of attempted murder. He was later sentenced to forty years in prison. Steve told the *St. Louis Post-Dispatch* that Grover looked just as stunned and confused when the verdict came as he did the night he met him in jail. Grover's nephew told the newspaper that the family couldn't afford to attend Grover's trial, but never thought he would be convicted.

On January 28, 2008, a few more stories appeared in local newspapers about Ida's case that included some comments I had made. A *Southern Illinoisan* article read, "Who killed Ida White?" I frowned at the headline since Ida had not been killed. Bob came to my office and shut my door. *This won't be good.*

"Someone from the Mount Vernon City government has contacted our city manager about this. You're being ordered to back out of the controversy."

The muzzle had been officially placed on me. I would have no more public comments to make. But I did have more to say to Tim and wanted Roger to hear it. As soon as Tim got back to Tamms from the hospital, Roger took me up on the offer to go interview Tim. He and I rode together. Once again he told me he would not be interviewing Tim about Ida's stabbing, just the rapes. I told him that was fine with me, but I had questions about the stabbing, so he could just sit and listen. I told Roger that Nick had described the suspect's clothing as a white T-shirt. He discounted it, saying the dispatcher's log often contained errors. Jim met us at the prison. I introduced the two. Lieutenant Clark took us back to the interview room. As soon as Tim came into the room, he said he had heard about the controversy over who stabbed the lady in Mount Vernon on the news.

"That was me. The black guy was innocent," he said without prompting.

"Well, just hold on, Tim, and let us get started first," I told him, almost happy that he had brought it up even though Roger didn't want to talk about it.

I started the recording devices and laid into Tim pretty hard. I had stuck my neck out on this case and I really needed to make sure he was telling the truth.

"Okay. Let me just say this from the onset: you know we've talked to you about a lot of cases. I know you've confessed to several cases like Pennsylvania, Paducah, Cape Girardeau and Carbondale, all of these towns. And if you have lied about any of these, you have to tell me. You absolutely must tell me if you have made up any of these cases. And if any of these were not you, you have to tell me."

"I've told you no lies."

I once again had Tim go through the specific facts so Roger could hear how they just flowed from him. Tim did not have to sit and think about his story like a person who was trying to recall a conversation he had with another inmate. They came from a person who was drawing from a memory of being there. He explained how he went to post offices in Cape and Mount Vernon to expose himself and waited across the street from the post office near an apartment building for single women to arrive. While waiting for a woman that night, he noticed an older woman inside the basement apartment. He recalled her sliding screen window.

"Do you recall what the weather was at that time?" Jim asked.

"Warm. It was warm because I had a T-shirt on…I got blood on the T-shirt."

"You got blood on the T-shirt? What color was the T-shirt?" I asked to emphasize the point.

"White."

After removing the window screen, Tim said he went in headfirst and fell inside the bathroom. He said a toilet was next to the window and a steel shower stall stood in the corner. Tim said Ida was on the phone when he went inside. He said he waited about ten or fifteen minutes and she came in to the bathroom naked and sat on the toilet. He described Ida's physical size perfectly. Tim said he stepped out of the shower and accosted her. He remembered she did not have any teeth and he pushed his hand into her mouth telling her not to scream. But she wouldn't listen, so he stabbed her three or four times. He said afterward he jumped back out the window headfirst and ran back to his car, which was parked a few blocks away.

Roger sat patiently listening but eventually began to ask some questions. He asked Tim what time the crime occurred. Tim told him it was about nine or nine thirty at night. I then had Tim draw the area the best he could. He included the post office and apartment building across the street where Ida lived in his drawing along with the side of her house where the bathroom window was. He described the house as a white two- or three-story house, filled in where some shrubbery was back then and pointed to a Laundromat. He also drew a short retaining wall he remembered stepping over. He said he fled across a parking lot behind the building. Then I had Tim draw the floor plan of Ida's bathroom. Roger asked if the shower had a glass door or a curtain. Tim said he remembered it was curtain. Tim explained that the window was small and when he left the bathroom, he had to jump up, headfirst, to get back out of it. I told Tim that there was a witness who said he had grabbed the suspect as he fled out the window.

"He's …he's full of shit!" Tim said.

Jim and I could not help but laugh. But Roger failed to see the humor in it.

"This…this is where we're having problems, Tim," Roger said. "I believe you that you have told Paul a lot of stuff that you've done, okay? At this point, I think you may be confused on a lot of things too, because our victim and eyewitnesses tell us that they saw the person come in and he got stuck in the window. And through eyewitnesses, they grabbed a hold of the guy before he got out the window, okay? So now…if you think this is something that you've read…somebody's told you that they've done, okay, it's time to come clean with us now."

"Somebody's bullshitting you. I'm telling you the truth. Nobody grabbed me coming out that window. And the lady was sitting on the floor, facing the shower."

"Okay. Well, see…that does not match our…our evidence in what the witness and what the victim told us either, okay? That's why, I, from Mount Vernon, do not believe what you're telling right now. That you did this crime. I think we did get the right person. It was just a matter of minutes before somebody saw him going out… the eyewitness lived next door. He barged in. Had a confrontation with the suspect, okay? You did not have that. That's how we made our case. That's what I'm saying.

"I don't care what you tell Paul and I believe you're honest with him. You've told him a lot of crimes you've committed, but at this point I can't believe you, that you committed that particular crime in Mount Vernon, okay? There may be some other ones in Mount Vernon and that's what I want to get to also. You said there was…one behind the hospital and one behind the discount store, okay? Give you another opportunity, okay? My case, the transcripts, eyewitness accounts. You didn't do that. Maybe somebody in prison you talked to did it. Maybe you saw it on the news, okay? And I…I can understand you've been in prison a long time. You had a lot of people, you did a lot of crimes, you're trying to think about some ones you did. And maybe some you've talked about with other people. Maybe getting them mixed up a little. But that's…that's fine. I can understand that, Tim."

"That's not…that's not happening. You know…those…those, you don't make up those kind of stories. Why in the world, after all this time, would I make up a bullshit story like that?"

"I can understand, but like I've said, I've known people who have done crimes and they start talking to people and they try to embellish, well, 'Somebody did this. I'm gonna take credit for this, too.' Okay. I'm not saying that you do that."

With that, Roger was done. He asked that we move on to the other cases. He was not convinced. Tim then described in detail the two rape cases he had already told to Jim and me. He had burglarized one victim before going back to rape her. It was reminiscent of Myrtle Rupp's case. Roger took notes as Tim talked. In the middle of questioning, Tim told Roger that he would take a polygraph to prove he was telling the truth in the stabbing. It was a rare request: A person wanting a polygraph to prove his guilt. The Mount Vernon Police Department wasn't interested and never interviewed Tim again. Roger took notes as Tim talked, but if he ever found any rape reports matching Tim's descriptions, he never told me.

Later that night, I turned on the news. TV reporter Jackie McPherson aired a telephone interview with the ambulance driver, who no longer lived in the area. I listened closely to what he had to say. Much of what he told her I had already read in the court transcript. But he added one thing that I had not heard before.

"…The gentleman was standing behind her with the knife in his hand. He actually cut her once as I came through the door."

What? I thought. *Now he's saying he saw her get stabbed?* The driver also said he pulled Ida away from the suspect and the two men briefly struggled and that was when he grabbed the man's shirt.

"Do you remember being very confident that this was the man who had done this?" she asked.

"Yes!" he proudly exclaimed.

Morley, Carl and Jim decided to investigate further. They called the FBI and asked if they could interview the ambulance driver and his wife. Cape Girardeau FBI Agent Brian Ritter was assigned the task. He found the driver and his wife had divorced many years ago. In a phone interview, the driver's ex told Brian she remembered the night Ida was stabbed very well. She said she remembered her ex-husband told her that the suspect was a black man who was wearing a white shirt. When Brian asked her if she had any knowledge of her ex lying to the police, she stated that it wouldn't surprise her if he did.

Brian found the former ambulance driver in Eastern Tennessee and called him. He said he was willing to be interviewed. On March 11, 2008, Jim and Brian interviewed the former ambulance driver in Eastern Tennessee. He was still working for an emergency medical service, managing fifteen employees. Nick said he had experienced a stroke three or four years before and had had some memory problems but remembered the stabbing very well. He was in the Navy then and said he had come home to take care of his wife for a physical and mental condition. He said because of that, he became absent without leave (AWOL). After the stabbing he turned himself in and was put in a brig in San Francisco for sixty days. He said he was discharged and avoided a court marshal.

The driver said he learned about Tim's confession from Roger, who had called to check some facts with him. He said his mother, who still lives in Southern Illinois, had also called him about the case. Brian asked him to once again tell him what happened that night. There were a few differences in the version the witness told the two investigators compared with the version he told on the stand twenty-seven years before. He told them that when he came into Ida's room, the suspect was standing in the bathroom behind Ida. That was quite different than saying the suspect was hanging inside the window. He told them he feared the man would get to his family, so he ran past Ida and struggled with the man for a few seconds to a minute. He didn't remember originally telling Officer Baltzell that the suspect was wearing a white T-shirt and he had no memory of the color of the shirt either. He still contended that he grabbed the shirt and it tore. The investigators asked the driver about the statement he made in the television interview about how the suspect had cut Ida as he came in the door. He denied seeing the suspect stab or slash Ida and did not know why the media would quote him as saying that. The investigators reminded him it wasn't a quote; it was his own words and voice. After the two detectives discussed the new information Tim provided, Nick told them: "Knowing what I know [now], it must be possible the wrong guy was charged and convicted."

Like Tim, the witness offered to take a polygraph to validate his statements. He said that everything had happened so quickly that night that he never thought about whether Grover might have been in the wrong place at the wrong time. He told the investigators that if more than one person had been in the lineup, he never could have picked the suspect out, but he denied that he embellished the story or that the police influenced him to pick Grover.

"I'm not certain of anything now," he told them. "If a mistake was made, then it was me. I cannot put that on the police. I am 99.9 percent sure Grover would have walked away from it if four or five other people had been in that room."

The investigators asked the ambulance driver if it was possible that he identified the wrong man.

"I feel sick about this thing and knowing what I hear today, an innocent man may have gone to jail," he told them.

The FBI office in Knoxville contacted the ambulance driver on a couple of occasions after his interview to schedule his polygraph. He refused to take the test.

Grover's knife was recovered from the Jefferson County court file in 2008 and sent to the Illinois State Police Crime Laboratory in Carbondale to be examined for DNA. Unfortunately, no DNA was found on the blade. Earlier tests had consumed the small specks of blood. No physical evidence ever linked Grover to the crime. Ida lived for several more years after the stabbing and died a natural death. Grover died of natural causes in the Menard Correctional Center on June 28, 1996, almost fifteen years after getting off the bus in Mount Vernon to rest.

22

Power and Control

The Cape Girardeau City Council invited me and the chief to a meeting in early February 2008 to recognize us for our efforts in solving their town's most brutal string of attacks. Sheila and I rode with Bob and his wife to Cape. Jim was there with his girlfriend and his son. Most of the people there were interested in other city business on the agenda that night. But scattered among the crowd were a few family members of Tim's murder victims. Mayor Jay Knudson reflected on the day he learned about the break in the murder cases. He said it was a moment he'd never forget and remembered with emotion how Carl had told him the story. He then thanked Bob for his willingness to allow me to work with the Cape Girardeau Police Department and for all of our department's administrative assistant Lauren Rader's hard work in transcribing the interviews Jim and I had with Tim. He gave Bob a plaque.

Then the mayor thanked me for my involvement in the cases. He also recognized our wives and thanked them for being part of "what must have been a wild ride." He presented me with a plaque that read: "In appreciation for outstanding police cooperation and assistance in solving five cold case murders in the City of Cape Girardeau, Missouri."

After that it was Jim's turn. The mayor credited the city's public safety tax as the reason why Carl could appoint Jim as a full-time cold case investigator. He paid Jim respect for his efforts in investigating the cases and presented Jim with a plaque that read: "Honoring his commitment to the citizens of Cape Girardeau for his enduring investigation and resolution of five cold case homicides from 1977 to 1982."

Everyone in the room gave us a standing ovation. *Where's Moe?* I thought.

"On behalf of the entire city council, on behalf of the City of Cape Girardeau, thank all of you gentlemen for what you have done," the mayor said before asking us to come to the lectern and tell the council about the experience.

Bob stepped up first, saying that it was a great moment in our department's history. He said we must not forget the officers who investigated the cases and collected the evidence all those years ago, because they helped us solve the cases. Bob also told the crowd that the victims' families were our motivation to do what we did. Bob's choice of words was perfect. He had pretty much said it all.

I told the council that it was my privilege to have worked with Carl and Jim. I talked about how Carl and I were once classmates and how my heart was close to Cape, after having met my wife in the city. I bragged about Jim and his dedication to the cases and commended the original investigators.

Jim stepped up last. He talked about how he and his son liked to watch television shows about cold cases and how great it was to have been part of resolving some of those cases himself. He said he felt honored to have been chosen to investigate the cases and that his greatest reward was letting the victims' families know that their loved ones had not been forgotten and that their killer had been caught. And he, too, thanked the officers and investigators who came before him.

It was a flattering and moving evening. Jim and I firmed up our plans to conduct our final interview with Tim at Tamms. We had multiple follow-up questions for Tim. He had once said he that he was trying to figure himself out. We were trying to figure him out too. We wanted to know what made him tick. What made him be such a charismatic person on the surface yet so evil underneath. We wanted to take advantage of our rapport to dig as deep as Tim would let us.

When Lieutenant Clark brought Tim into the room and removed all the restraints, Tim sat down and immediately started talking to us. He was now very comfortable and had grown to trust us. It was a strange feeling to build a rapport with a serial killer.

First we chatted about his accommodations. He had been moved out of isolation and now spent one hour a day outside in an enclosed area surrounded by concrete walls. He was on a pod, where there were three or four other guys who had televisions inside their cells. Tim said he didn't care to have a TV, because he never wanted to see himself on one again. But his impending court date in Cape would soon change that. Tim asked Jim what was going on with his extradition to Missouri. Jim assured him it was only a number of days now before he would be brought to the Cape Girardeau County courthouse.

Once again, Tim wanted to talk about the Grover Thompson controversy. The guys in the other pods told him what was on television. Once again, he told us that the Mount Vernon Police had arrested the wrong guy and sent him to prison. He said he hoped Grover's family would find out that he was an innocent man. He was pleased to hear that they had. *I wish he had cared that much when it happened,* I thought.

Tim also told us that he had received some letters from women interested in dating him. He looked at me with a genuine look of concern on his face and said:

"Now that's weird." He also had some requests from media outlets and nationally syndicated shows for interviews. He wrote back and told them he wasn't interested.

Jim told Tim that DNA analysis of the pubic hair found on Margie Call's body had confirmed Tim was her killer. The hair still had a root, which yielded the STR DNA comparison. The statistical probability that it was Tim was one in almost five quadrillion. Tim seemed uninterested in hearing about the DNA match. It was a moot point now.

Tim told me he had seen an article about me in *Cosmopolitan* magazine. He said a guard handed it to him while he was being held in a mental health area. He thought it was a good article. It highlighted Deborah's case. Tim's mention of a guard reminded me of a time I heard one call him "Cracker Jack" at Big Muddy. Tim laughed and said some of the guards had started calling him that about four years ago after they had trouble pronouncing his last name.

Since my last visit with Tim, I had received multiple requests to ask him about other unsolved murder cases. Some were from Pennsylvania and some were from other states between Kansas and the East Coast. I asked Tim about each of them. He listened intently but denied all of them. He insisted that he had disclosed everything he could remember. I felt sorry for those families who would not get closure.

I also showed Tim a picture taken at a wedding the day after he killed Mary and Brenda Parsh. The groom was a fellow ambulance service employee who later posted bail to help Tim get out of jail in February 1979. In the photo Tim was wearing all white along with the rest of the groomsmen. I had sought out Tim's friend, knowing the photo likely existed, but he only let me copy the part that contained Tim. Tim was smiling in the photo. He said he remembered it well. The outdoor wedding was at the Giant City State Park. Tim remembered it was a morning wedding. Scrambled eggs and champagne were served. The night before, Tim was in Cape committing his first homicides—the Parsh murders. Tim said he had gone home and showered after the killings and then went to the bachelor party for his friend. I asked him what he was thinking when the picture was taken, seeing as though he had just killed a mother and daughter twelve hours earlier. He said he never thought about them after he did it. The wedding photo reminded Tim of his own wedding. He said he had often wondered what happened to his budding family.

I asked Tim how old he was when he had his first sexual experience. He told me he was thirteen. I was surprised by how young he was. Tim said he had hung around with three or four buddies and three or four girls all about the same age. He said they always had sex and changed partners. Tim said he never had any problems attracting girls and even when he was killing he had girlfriends. But he admitted his relationships never developed into what he hoped they would. His sexual relationships were not very good and he figured that was part of his problem. He said his sexual crimes were almost always satisfying.

"The power surge would, you know, would make the sex better or something. I don't know. But then it was brief, it…like, as soon as it happened, bam, it was over. And it was, like, a letdown and then it would build back up again and then you'd go out and do it again. All the stuff I did, it wasn't about the sex. It was about the power trip. The power and the control…By…by being in the house waiting for this person to come home, I'd be thinking what I'm gonna do. What I'm gonna make her do and she'll have to do this you know. And…and I think that was a…a lot of it."

Jim asked Tim what he was thinking as he waited for the victims to come in.

"You know, I could lay on her bed there and I'd masturbate or…Just thinking about what was gonna happen and it was like a rush. That's pretty much what rape is about, when you are talking to all different rapists, that's what they will tell you. It's about the power and control."

I told Tim that it was odd that he was taking lives, but as an EMT he was also helping people. Dottie and others who worked with Tim said he was very good at what he did. They mentioned that he had an uncanny ability to take control of a stressful situation. It was an eerie thing to hear, given I had read about how calm he was during his attacks in the police reports about his crimes. Doctors told him his efforts in treating people on the scene had probably saved their lives. He reminisced about some of his calls.

"I remember this one time we went and an old lady had broken her hip, you know, and she was screaming and hollering. I told her I was gonna have to hurt her a little bit more to put this splint on her leg, right? And as soon as we got it on and you put tension on it, it's called a Thomas half-ring. It relieves the pain because it pulls the muscle back into line, right? And then she just, uh, you could just hear her relax, you know. You get a pretty good feeling out of that."

Tim also said he did some teaching and some lectures about EMT work. He had signed a contract to teach at a local junior college, but his arrest in February 1979 cost him the job.

"I was going around giving guest lectures and he [a regional coordinator for EMS in Southern Illinois] was the one who got me the teaching job at Southeast [Southeastern Illinois College in Harrisburg]. He started the program down there at, uh…Vienna. And I was, like, I think I was in the second class that went through down there. And I was in the first group that went outside, you know. He had a lot of respect for my work…I heard from different people that he might've been grooming me to take his place."

I asked Tim about his experience when he went to Menard Psychiatric.

"Well, see, I was only eighteen. I'd never been locked up. I was pretty, you know, innocent more…more or less. And, uh…there's seven hundred people over there. I'd say a third of them were criminally insane. Straight out criminally insane…They had people off of death row who had said they were crazy, so they put them over there. They had every kind of sexual deviant you can imagine over there. In this…this, the rest of the five hundred were probably sexual deviates of one kind, type, or another. The place was loaded with transsexuals, queens and homosexuals and, uh…and when I went in there it was fight or fuck. The first day there, they put me on what they called two gallery. I'm in the cell locked in, right? They are serving lunch. Guys are walking by in front of the cell naked. Food all over them. Give me a cigarette, kid. Give me a cigarette kid. And this old man comes up to my cell and grabbed his dick and says, 'When you get out of here you're mine, motherfucker.' You know, this is my first day. And I don't know what's going on. I'm thinking, 'Jesus Christ! What's going on here?'

"And it wasn't all that bad, once I got out off two gallery. When I got off… and then, you know, like this one guy was bringing me candy bars and…I'm taking this stuff. I…I don't know what's going on, you know. So there, two weeks later, they sent me off two gallery and put me in population. Here comes this guy who was giving me candy bars. Wanted to give me something else. You know what I mean. And, uh…the first two years I was there it was fight…fight…fight…fight… fight. And I was lucky that I had a little bit of Irish in me, you know, even though, you know, I'd get my ass beat a couple of times, but, uh…it was hell.

"I was working in the kitchen, right. I stirred this big old pot of beans with a wooden handle. A guy came up behind me and grabbed a handful of my ass, you know. He wanted me to give him some. So I turned around and gave him something. I gave him the wooden paddle I had. Another time I had to chase a guy around the yard with a butcher knife. And they kicked me out of the kitchen," Tim said with a laugh. "Finally after about two years, they left me alone, but I was so insecure and so messed up in the head that, uh…I was letting a lot of homosexuals give me blow jobs. Stuff like that.

"And a…a lot of the guys in the camp, you know, were gamblers you know, and they had a little…a kid, you know. A punk. And…so I wanted to be like that, you know. So after a couple of years I became a gambler. I opened up a card game. And I ran my own card game. I lived off that card game for like three years. And I got my own little kid, you know, who used to suck my dick whenever I wanted, you know. I mean it was just not a place…to come out changed. I mean, it was the worst fuckin' place they could ever send a kid who had never been involved in anything like that. It was terrible. The only thing that saved me from really going off there was sports. I got involved with playing basketball and softball and that's pretty much what I did. Just stayed in that card game. Ran that card game for a few years and didn't get no money from home or nothing."

Then I asked Tim my last question.

"Tim, obviously you know, because of your sentences, that you are never going to be free. You can't get out. So you can answer this question truthfully now, where you probably couldn't have done that last year. If you were to get out today, had a car and a gun, would you be able to control yourself or would you likely go back to what you were doing?"

"I couldn't be sure."

With that, my last official interview with Tim ended.

23

The Hearing

Jim saw Tim again in mid-March when Cape Girardeau county sheriff deputies extradited Tim to the courthouse.

It was the first time Tim had been back to Cape since killing Mildred Wallace in 1982. The media interest in Tim began all over again. He spent two days in the county jail before he made his twenty-eight-second-long court appearance via video feed from the jail. The crowd of about twenty or so that filled the courtroom that day included mostly media. In the back, Cheryl Tyson sat quietly. She was disappointed that Tim had not appeared in person, but just seeing him on a television screen and hearing his voice again sent the fear rushing back. Tears rolled down her cheeks and she found it hard to breathe.

Jim visited Tim after the appearance to give him the Bible that Eunice Seabaugh asked *St. Louis Post-Dispatch* reporter Christine Byers to give to Tim. Tim also agreed to speak to Christine about the Grover Thompson case. He spent forty-five minutes on the phone with her from his jail cell, professing his guilt in the case. It was the first interview he had given to the media. He told the newspaper that he felt scared to be in Cape because, "I've done a lot of terrible things to this community and I imagine there is a lot of anger and hate here toward me. But believe it or not, I'm the type of person that likes to be liked."

Once again, he described Ida's bathroom and how the inside of her shower was metal. Chief Mendenhall again maintained that Tim and Grover likely shared the information when they were in prison together. Tim was quick to discount the chief's theory, saying, "I hung out with a select group. I was a good athlete and all my friends played on softball and basketball teams and were of a higher intellectual level." In other words, Grover wasn't part of his clique.

At the hearing, the judge set Tim's next appearance in Cape for April 4, 2008. Just a few days before, I was in Grand Rapids, Michigan, investigating another cold case I was working. On my way back home, I stopped at the Sheppards' home. It was the first time I had ever been there. As I stood on the front stoop, I thought of how the officers who were tasked with notifying the couple of their daughter's death had stood there twenty-five years before. It was the same house where Deborah was raised. Several photos of her adorned the walls and shelves in the two-level home. Bernie, Hazel and I drove to lunch and stopped at Maynegaite Park in Olympia Fields. There, the Sheppards proudly pointed out a beautiful towering spruce tree that the City of Olympia Fields planted in Deborah's memory after her murder. It was a living tribute to their beautiful daughter. I updated them on the investigations. They were happy to hear that something positive had come from their daughter's case. Hazel asked me to tell Brenda's sister that she would be praying for her, knowing she would likely be attending Tim's plea in court. Hazel knew what she was going to experience. It was great to see them.

Tim was expected to plead guilty to all five murders in Cape and Holly Jones's rape. A crowd also was expected, so they moved the hearing from the Cape Girardeau County Courthouse in Jackson to the Federal Courthouse in Cape Girardeau. I arrived before noon and met with Jim in Carl's office. Tracy, Roger and Morley were also there. Jim then brought Karen and her son to Carl's office. It was the first time any of us had met her. It was apparent that beauty had permeated the Parsh family.

Brenda's sister said it was extremely difficult for her to come to Cape for the hearing and didn't know how she was ultimately going to feel. She had left the town and all of its bad memories behind so many years ago. She thanked me and Jim for our roles in the investigation as we sat around the table in Carl's office. I couldn't help but think about the first time I sat at the table when all of this began. She recalled how guilty she had felt through the years about switching roles with Brenda that fateful night. I was touched by her sincerity and courage when she said her faith in God got her through the trying time. Jim pointed out Carl's window to the building where her father's aftercare home had been.

Morley told her what had taken place to get us to the plea deal. Karen's son began to tear up. Karen told us that she never told her kids about the murders until they were about sixteen years old. Karen's son said that when he was young, his mother told him and his two brothers that his grandmother and aunt had been killed in a car accident. She asked how we were able to get Tim to confess. I talked a bit of the Deborah Sheppard case and how that eventually led to our November interview and later Morley's letter. I told Brenda's sister that Deborah's mother was praying for her that day, which she said she appreciated. I gave credit to Lieutenant Schuler for helping me and Jim gather information about Tim from his prison buddies.

I felt heartsick for her when Morley told her about how Tim had initially missed shooting her mother and had gone back to finish her off after hearing her sobs. Jim had planned to tell her that privately, because we didn't want her hearing it for the first time in the media. We knew the revelations would be coming out, because Morley planned to release Tim's four-hour videotaped confession. The recording included all of the Cape cases and limited details on the Marion and Paducah cases. Morley said he was compelled to release the recording because of the Missouri Sunshine Law.

About an hour after our conversation began, Carl, Jim, Karen, her son and I rode over to the Federal courthouse. Brenda's sister mentioned how everything had changed so much in Cape since she had left. It took us a while to get through security, but finally we made it to the second floor. I looked around to see who was inside the old courtroom. I saw my sister. Brenda's sister and her son sat in the audience on the east side of the room. I saw Don Call and several of his family members. Teresa Haubold and her sister were there. Cheryl Tyson had come, too. Several federal marshals were positioned around the room. Jim and I sat at Morley's table on the west side of the room toward the front. FBI Agent Brian Ritter sat next to me. The courtroom was packed with spectators. Morley had mounted many of the eight-by-ten-inch crime scene photos on foam core boards. Several sets of DVD copies of Tim's confession were on the table, ready for the media. Carl sat in the juror's box with several police officers.

Tim was finally brought in under high security. A bright orange jumpsuit hung on his frail frame and concealed a bulletproof vest he was wearing. His hands and feet were shackled. A chain hung around his waist. Jim and I nodded at him as he sat directly across the room from us. He was still wearing the goofy looking glasses with the black plastic frames.

Everyone stood as Judge Benjamin F. Lewis entered the courtroom. The judge's bench was on the second tier, while the court reporters were on the first tier. The judge asked Tim and his public defender to step to the microphone. The judge spoke to Tim's defense attorney and some legal documents were signed. Tim then did the best he could to raise his right hand to be sworn. He was still handcuffed to a belly chain. Tim acknowledged that he was voluntarily pleading guilty and understood everything.

Judge Lewis read each of the charges against Tim. As he read each case, Tim had to acknowledge his guilt. Morley then added specific details of each crime, including the photos for the court to consider. The horrific list of brutal crimes went on for most of the nearly forty-five-minute hearing. There were thirteen criminal charges to go through. I cringed as every gruesome detail was revealed in front of many of the victims' families, but I knew they were finally getting the closure for which they had longed for so many years.

Then the judge invited the victims' families to make victims' impact statements during the sentencing phase. Seven people addressed Tim, including Don Call. He tearfully told the court that he and his now deceased brother had lived with guilt after their mother's death, because they weren't there to protect her.

"The overwhelming question we have asked is, 'Why was our mother murdered?'" Don said, pausing between tears. "Now we know she was murdered simply for being in the wrong place at the wrong time."

Margie Call's nephew told the court that even though Tim escaped the death penalty, he found comfort in knowing Tim someday will face judgment.

"And I hope you rot in the fiery walls of hell," he said as he glared at Tim.

A woman who was friends with Brenda Parsh in high school hobbled to the stand with a cane and tearfully told the court about how Tim had robbed the world of a beautiful person inside and out.

Cheryl Tyson, wearing a white button-down shirt and black pants, then walked to the microphone. She had taken the day off work to be there.

"Since '81 I've been living under this cloud that I cannot get rid of," she said as she wiped away tears. "Hopefully, today this cloud will rise. I'm not afraid anymore...Today is like a holiday, because it's clearing a hole that's been in our hearts and we know he won't ever harm anyone again."

At one point Cheryl told the court that Tim had pointed a gun at her son's head and threatened to shoot him if she didn't comply with his wishes. Tim violently shook his head, disagreeing with the point.

Judge Lewis then asked Tim if he would like to address the court. To my surprise, Tim walked to the microphone. He started to turn toward the victims. The judge admonished him and ordered him to look toward him. He thanked the victims' families for agreeing to the plea deal.

"I don't know if I could have been so generous if I were in the same situation. Thank you for sparing my life."

Krajcir told the court that therapy he had received in prison had helped him begin to understand the pain he had caused. For the first time, we saw the emotion Tim said he didn't have. His voice cracked. He wiped away tears.

"The first eight years of my incarceration I spent in intense therapy to learn the reasons why I did these terrible acts. I've learned a lot of answers, but there is more for me to learn. I would like to apologize to the victims, their families and the people of Cape Girardeau for the terror I caused."

He vowed to the victims and their families to counsel other sexual predators as he spent the rest of his life in prison.

"I will do everything in my power to help as many people as I can to prevent anything of this nature from happening again. I'm terribly sorry for what I've done. I can feel your pain."

Judge Lewis sentenced Tim to thirteen life sentences and court was adjourned.

Guards quickly whisked Tim out of the courtroom and took him back to Tamms. Brian shook my hand and congratulated me. I shook Jim's hand and told him congratulations. Morley shook my hand and held tight to it.

"You did a good job. It has been my privilege to work with you," he said.

Jim, Carl and I walked over to Brenda's sister and her son. Karen had been very strong, at least on the outside. I could not image what it must've been like to confront the man who killed her mother and sister. I knew time had helped, but it had not erased her feelings. As we waited for everyone to clear out, several members of the Call family came over and thanked me and Jim again. They invited us to join them for pizza, but we graciously declined. Karen talked about how she fought the urge to jump over the seats and attack Tim. I told her that Bernie Sheppard had felt the same way. She asked me to send her the Sheppard family's mailing address so she could send them a card. She hugged me and thanked me again. I felt so sorry for her. The terrible ordeal Tim had put her whole family through was unforgivable.

After we walked out of the courtroom, Jim introduced me to his older son who had been a police officer in Sikeston, Missouri, a few years before. When we got outside, several reporters were broadcasting from the courthouse steps and interviewing family members. I spoke briefly on camera. Jim and I rode back to the police station with Carl, Karen and her son. Karen hugged us all again. Her son shook our hands. Then they headed back to the St. Louis area. I doubted Karen would ever return to Cape.

It had been quite a journey. Finally justice was done and this was a day I'd never forget. I only hoped the victims' families received a measure of comfort.

24

Thank You, Deborah

As time passed, I was invited by various law enforcement agencies and community organizations to speak about the investigation. I was now getting the opportunity to share the inner workings of Tim's cases to educate future investigators as well as the public.

In May 2008, Jim, Carl, Morley and I were invited to the Cape Girardeau Evening Optimist Club, which is a civic organization that promotes a variety of community programs. About 100 people were in the crowd. My wife joined me at the dinner. Morley spoke and talked of our opposition to his push for the death penalty and the ultimate compromise that led to Tim's confession. He looked into the crowd and saw Jim's young son. He told both of us that someday our children would be proud of our accomplishments. That was something I had not really thought about. The club gave us plaques recognizing us for our efforts. The placemats at each table were decorated with the states of Illinois and Missouri. Stars marked the towns of Carbondale and Cape Girardeau. Five roses adorned the edge, one for each of the Cape victims. Later, I had one matted and framed and gave it to Jim as a souvenir of the night. We all stood in silence as they concluded the program by ringing a bell for each victim.

That same month, I did a presentation about Susan Schumake's case for the International Association of Identification, Illinois Division in Springfield, Illinois. I'm a member of the group of mostly forensic scientists and crime scene investigators.

Later, another DNA expert, Taylor Scott, reached out to me, telling me I had been invited to the 2009 FBI CODIS Conference in Reston, Virginia, to present the Tim Krajcir cases. It was quite an honor. Each year, the FBI sponsors a nationwide conference for DNA experts involved in CODIS and invites a few individuals from around the nation to tell how DNA resolved a case. Taylor said I could select a family member of one of the victims to come and address the DNA experts at the conference. I immediately thought of Don Call.

During our conversation, Taylor disclosed something else to me. He said my efforts in resolving the Deborah Sheppard case were more important than I may have realized. Tim's DNA was not in the national database in August 2007 as we had thought. Several years earlier, a legal loophole had prevented CODIS administrators from putting DNA profiles obtained from criminals deemed sexually dangerous persons and sexually violent persons in the national CODIS database, because those individuals were being held under a civil commitment, not a criminal charge. Tim's DNA had only been in the Illinois database. Taylor said that had Missouri or Pennsylvania searched their full DNA profiles against the national database first, they would not have identified Tim. It was only after Deborah's case that Tim became part of the national database. I now understood why Stacey Bollinger did not get a hit on Tim's profile when she ran the DNA from Mildred's case the first time. It reinforced the importance of Deborah's case and made Suzanne's find on Deborah's shirt even more critical. We realized that without our efforts it was unlikely that Tim would have ever been found and his crimes would likely have gone to the grave with him.

Before leaving for the conference, my son and I went to Cape Girardeau for a celebration of the police department's 150th anniversary. I had been asked to speak about the Cape murders and the ultimate resolution of the cases. I was the last speaker of what turned out to be a dynamic program held on the beautiful Southeast Missouri River Campus overlooking the Mississippi River. It started with a local historian who discussed the department's rich history. A Cape Girardeau Police Color Guard, adorned in full dress uniforms, took the stage to honor the department's fallen officers. Several retired police chiefs, along with Carl, had a sort of fireside chat about their experiences at the top. Several of the chiefs talked about the difficult times in 1977 and 1982 and how the murders changed life in Cape Girardeau forever.

I used a computer presentation with more than 100 slides and photos to take the group on a photographic journey though time explaining Tim's crimes, connecting Carbondale to Cape Girardeau, and how he was finally discovered. Jim was in the audience. I gave him credit for much of what was done and ended my presentation by dedicating it to the women who lost their lives at the hands of Tim Krajcir. The audience remained silent as the faces of each victim flashed across the screen. At that moment, I thought about the fact that just a couple of hundred yards from where I stood, the gun used to kill three of the women was lying on the bottom of the Mississippi River.

After the program, I had the opportunity to meet and take pictures alongside former Cape Girardeau Chief Ray Johnson, who had been chief when Margie and

Mildred were murdered. He shook my hand and thanked me for my work and congratulated me for a great presentation. It was an honor to meet Ray, who is now police chief in Chesterfield, Missouri, just west of St. Louis. A few former Cape police officers who worked during the murder cases introduced themselves to me. I congratulated them on the work they did years ago. David Warren, a former Cape Girardeau police officer, who now worked as a criminalist for the Missouri State Highway Patrol, greeted me. Jim had told me that Dave had helped process Margie and Mildred's crime scenes and later identified the partial palm print lifted by Officer Curt Casteel as Tim's left palm. Dave handed me a silver Missouri State Highway Patrol historical medallion as a token of his appreciation. I was flattered and will always treasure his gift. It had been a very exciting night and I was honored to have been part of such a historical event.

It was soon time for the big FBI CODIS conference. Don Call, his wife and I traveled to Reston, Virginia, to talk in front of about 400 DNA experts. In the audience that day was Suzanne Brenneke from the Missouri State Highway Patrol CODIS Administrator. She was Stacey Bollinger's supervisor at the lab in Jefferson City, Missouri. Stacie Speith from the Illinois State Police Crime Laboratory also was there. I thought about how two years before, Stacie had called me from the same conference in San Francisco to tell me about Pennsylvania's CODIS hit on Tim. At that time, Stacie told me I should present my case at the CODIS Conference. Her suggestion had come to fruition.

Taylor Scott and Peggy Moody-Kosman, assistant CODIS administrator for the Pennsylvania State Police, joined us on stage. Taylor began by explaining the basics of the case and then introduced me. I did a similar presentation to the one I had done at the anniversary celebration of the Cape Girardeau Police Department.

Peggy told the crowd about Myrtle Rupp's murder and how the evidence from her bedspread provided a DNA profile that was subsequently matched with Tim Krajcir.

Taylor explained the scientific parts to the group and how Tim had not been in CODIS because of his civil commitment as a sexually dangerous person. He told the DNA experts in the audience that they needed to make sure they did not have the same issue in their states.

After Taylor finished, I introduced Don Call to the group. Don, a retired school administrator, broke the ice by telling the group that he was used to standing in front of students and telling them to be quiet and he wasn't sure how to handle a group that had been behaving so well. The audience members chuckled before he worked toward a very serious subject. The room was silent as everyone paid close attention to Don's words. He talked about his mother and how her loss had affected the family. He thanked everyone for the jobs they did, saying closure was very important to families. Then he thanked the experts on behalf of all the families they had helped.

After Don finished, the crowd of experts applauded. The Calls were given a pyramid-shaped clear plaque that read:

> 2009 15th Annual CODIS Conference
> Our efforts are dedicated to the victims
> behind every case and the people
> who care for them.
> MARJORIE CALL

Amidst the appearances, I was still working behind the scenes to tie up a few other loose ends on Tim. I had discovered pictures of an African-American woman in Tim's scrapbook that had been taken inside his trailer. I was concerned she might have been a victim. Tim told me he had dated the woman in Carbondale. But again, I needed to confirm it. I found her living on Carbondale's east side. When I met her, she said she had been expecting someone would likely interview her. She had recognized Tim on television and in the newspaper. She told me she met Tim in 1982 when they worked at a Carbondale nursing home together. She described him as a good worker and fun to be around. They became friends and dated. On a few occasions, Tim took her and her son on picnics at the Giant City State Park. She said that she went to his trailer a few times and listened to music. The last time she saw Tim was during the summer of 1982. He had decided to return to Pennsylvania. The woman said it was almost unbelievable that Tim could have done what he had confessed doing.

Another follow-up involved a woman I considered a hero. Her name was Nichole Boyd and I found her name in police reports from Tim's indecent exposures in Carbondale. Just after lunch on December 5, 1978, Nichole decided to run an errand at a Carbondale discount store. Something caught her attention as she walked back to her car and passed a silver car in the parking lot. Sitting inside the car, she saw a white man masturbating with his penis exposed. I knew now that it was Tim. Nichole went back into the store and called the police. Officer Buddy Murphy arrived soon after and arrested Tim. He was issued a summons and released on his own recognizance.

On the afternoon of March 12, 1979, Nichole once again drove to the discount store. As she parked, she recognized a car in the parking lot. It was the same silver car driven by the man who had exposed himself a few months before. She even recognized the license plate number. Nichole wondered if he was up to his old tricks again. So she watched him. Tim stared at women as they came in and out of the store. She was concerned about what he might do, so she once again reported Tim to an employee inside the store. The manager got involved and decided they needed to see if the man was exposing himself before calling police. A female employee agreed to walk around the driver's side of Tim's car. As she did, Tim exposed himself to her. The manager called the Carbondale Police. Tim realized he had been seen and left the parking lot, but Officer Terry Mick stopped him a few blocks away. Tim was arrested and his car was inventoried and towed. Inside Tim's pocket, they found a blue bandanna. Tim was charged and released after posting 100 dollars as bond.

Nichole had since married, so finding her took a bit of effort. I was amazed to discover she was working for SIU and her office was only a couple blocks from mine. I knew she probably did not know the significance of her actions, so I hoped this meeting would be rewarding. I went to her office and introduced myself. She immediately thought something was wrong, so I put her at ease.

"Do you remember the incidents at that Carbondale discount store in 1978 and 1979 in which a man exposed himself to you?" I asked.

"Well, yes, I do remember, but that was a long time ago," she said with a puzzled look on her face.

"Do you remember seeing the news about a man who was arrested for a Carbondale murder and several murders in Cape Girardeau?"

Her eyes widened and she put her hand up to her mouth. Tears came to her eyes.

"Oh, my goodness," she said as she realized who Tim was.

"The day they arrested Tim, they took a blue bandanna from his right front pocket. That blue bandanna was a trademark of Tim's. He used it countless times to disguise his identity when he raped and murdered. Nichole, do you realize that your actions may have saved someone from being another one of Tim's victims on those days? You may have even saved a life. In my book, you are an unsung hero."

"My gosh," she said with a slightly shaken voice. "This gives me goose bumps!"

Just ten days after his arrest prompted by Nichole's keen observations, Tim covered his face with the blue bandanna and abducted, raped and murdered Joyce Tharp.

I finally boxed up all the reports associated with Deborah's case from my office and took them upstairs to be archived. It was like saying good-bye to an old friend. Taking a black marker I wrote, "Cleared by arrest of Tim Krajcir." My heart pounded when I did that. So much had happened since I found the report right after being promoted to lieutenant. In that large box of almost 2,000 pages of reports, the name

Tim Krajcir had not appeared until August 9, 2007. We had been that far off. I looked at how close we had come to catching Tim for other crimes, now knowing we had arrested him four times in 1978 and 1979. I found four examples of when Tim was a suspect or fled just before being captured.

One of those missed opportunities came during the Parsh murder investigation. My friend Illinois State Police Lieutenant Dick Evans had hand delivered several police reports to Cape Girardeau Police investigators that he thought might be related to the murders. Among them was the report about a burglary in Carbondale during July 1977 in which a gun was stolen from Don Strom's relative. It was the same gun used to kill Mary and Brenda and, three months later, to kill Sheila. Even though the report listed the make and caliber of gun Cape investigators were looking for, the report went unnoticed. It seemed unlikely at the time that a Carbondale burglary would be related to murders in Cape Girardeau.

When Tim raped Sarah two days after a blizzard hit Southern Illinois in 1979, Tim was out on bond and had just moved out of his trailer and in with a fellow ambulance service worker in the Carbondale Mobile Home Park. It was only about a mile north of Sarah's home. Investigators realized Sarah lived just a block away from where Tim had lived before his arrest. They interviewed Tim in his new trailer as a suspect in Sarah's rape. Tim told detectives that he had nothing to say and they could talk to his attorney. Investigators never spoke with Tim again about the case.

I wasn't even looking for it when I learned of another missed opportunity. I was shopping at a furniture store in Cape Girardeau when I met a salesman named John Cobb. As we spoke, I found out he was a former Cape Girardeau Police reserve officer. Our conversation soon turned to Tim Krajcir and the resolutions of the murders in Cape.

"I feel so sorry for the victims. You know, my grandmother, who has since passed away, also lived in Cape by herself during those years and she was terrified. One night, she came home to find her house had been burglarized. It had been raining that night, so she chose not to park behind the house where she normally parked. She parked down the street and walked up on her front porch. She immediately noticed that the glass on her front door was broken and the door was open. She went back to her car and drove to the police station and reported the break-in. When a police officer arrived, he shined his light toward the door. When he did that, my grandma told me someone inside fled out the back of the house. The officer gave pursuit, but the suspect got away," John told me.

I smiled at John. I had heard this story before. Tim had told me and Jim about a time he almost got caught and it perfectly matched John's story about his grandmother's break-in. Tim told us he broke in through the front door and fled out the back when the officer shined his light on the front door. John and his family had not considered it was the same person who had murdered the other women. They assumed it was just kids or a simple burglar. I later told Jim about my exchange at the furniture store. Now that we had a name, Jim had an easier time finding the report. Sure enough, it happened on December 20, 1981, just eleven days after Grover Thompson had been sentenced to prison and one week before Tim sexually assaulted Cheryl Tyson along the same street where John's grandmother lived. It appeared to me that Tim was likely waiting for the man's grandmother to arrive through the back door as she normally did.

"Your grandmother was a very lucky lady," I told John after confirming the report. I wrote to Tim in prison and asked him for more details. He confirmed it was him that night but denied that he was waiting inside to assault the older woman.

Tim's name surfaced in the media once more during his courtroom appearance on June 13, 2008, via a video link between the Tamms Supermax Prison and a Berks County Courtroom in Pennsylvania. Tim pled guilty to the murder of Myrtle Rupp. Judge Linda K.M. Ludgate accepted Tim's plea and, as expected, sentenced him to life in prison. Myrtle Rupp's nephew, who had asked investigators to reopen his aunt's case, made a victim's impact statement. Tim listened from 900 miles away.

"I'm not sure another life sentence for Timothy Krajcir really serves justice here. It really only prolongs the life of a career criminal who, in my opinion, deserves the death penalty. If he doesn't deserve the death penalty, who does? However, it is my hope that by prolonging his life in prison it affords the possibility that he encounters someone in the prison population exactly like himself, who one day arbitrarily decides to make Timothy Krajcir his victim. As that someone strangles the last breath of life from Krajcir's pathetic, repulsive existence, perhaps Krajcir will reflect on what he has done not only to Myrtle but also to all his other victims. That is precisely how Timothy Krajcir deserves to die. That would be justice. That is my hope for the outcome of this sentence."

Myrtle's nephew's comments were very powerful. They also made me feel a bit guilty for helping Tim avoid the death penalty. But I stood by what we did.

In our department, there were rumors of change. My boss, Calvin, was considering moving on. Bob told me to prepare for a promotion to deputy chief of operations if Calvin left. Bob even hinted that he would be moving on from his post as chief soon and I should prepare for that too. Thinking of leaving my investigations commander position was bittersweet. It had taken a long time to get back to investigations and do some of the things I wanted to do there, like reopen Deborah's case. There were still many other things I wanted to do. I hated that it took so long to get there. I knew if a promotion was offered, I'd take it, but I was starting to see the end of my career too.

When Bob retired, I was a candidate for the Carbondale Police chief position, but I was not chosen. A few months later, another opportunity came my way—one that I could not pass up. I was offered a full-time teaching position at Shawnee Community College near Ullin, Illinois. On August 14, 2009, I retired from the Carbondale Police Department after a twenty-eight-year career. Three days later, I started my new job. Leaving the department was very hard. I loved the excitement of my job and I loved being a police officer. It was the only full-time job I had ever had, starting at twenty-one years old. Yet the challenge of teaching new students intrigued me. I had been teaching part-time for the college since 1991 and, more recently, for Southern Illinois University. I was returning to the beautiful campus where I had played baseball over thirty years earlier. It was the same campus where I had watched Tim Krajcir walk across stage to accept his diploma in 1974.

Luckily, I had a free day when Tim's final court appearance came on March 25, 2010, in Paducah, Kentucky. He had been extradited from the Pontiac, Illinois, prison and brought to McCracken County to face kidnapping and burglary charges in Joyce Tharp's case. It was a rainy day, which probably was appropriate for the event. I went through metal detectors before I entered the old courthouse. One of the guards looked familiar and he recognized me too. It was Tom Emery, the McCracken County sheriff's deputy who had come with Paducah Police Assistant Chief Danny Carroll to Tamms on the day Tim confessed to Joyce's murder. We shook hands and smiled. I took the elevator to the second floor, walked through two large double doors leading to the courtroom and immediately saw Tim sitting at the defense table. He spotted me, smiled and nodded at me. I nodded back. I wondered if he was surprised to see me. Tim was dressed in a yellow jumpsuit. His head was shaved and he was still wearing the funny black plastic-framed glasses that he received while in Tamms.

The courtroom was cavernous. It was something out of an old Perry Mason movie, with lots of raised wood panels and old solid wooden chairs mixed with some modern chairs. I sat behind the area reserved for the court officers on an old oak bench seat. Cameras were allowed in the courtroom; it was the first of Tim's hearings to be videotaped by the media. I could hear the incessant snapping of one photographer's shutter. He had Tim locked in his telephoto lens. Two local television stations had cameras poised to record the hearing. Carly and her camerawoman were positioned and ready. She said hello to me. Since the Grover Thompson case we had become friends.

Eventually, Joyce Tharp's family entered and sat on the south side of the courtroom with the commonwealth attorney. Debbie Vaughn, Joyce's daughter, was there along with Joyce's sister. Tim sat on the opposite side of the courtroom facing the prosecutor's table. Tim's public defender, Audrey B. Lee, sat next to Tim.

The proceedings began as soon as Judge Craig Clymer came into the courtroom. Tim and his attorney walked to a lectern facing the judge. Just like in Cape, Tim did the best he could to raise his right hand, which was handcuffed to a belly chain, to be sworn in. Judge Clymer told Tim that he had been a Paducah police officer when Joyce was murdered but had not been part of the investigation. He asked Tim if he was okay with his being the judge who would impose the sentence on him. Tim told the judge that was fine.

Judge Clymer then read the charges to Tim, which included first-degree burglary and kidnapping.

"How do you plead?" he asked.

"Guilty, your honor," Tim said.

During the sentencing phase, Tim turned around and spoke to the Tharp family.

"I want you to know that I have not forgotten it and I spent ten straight years in heavy therapy trying to learn why I committed so many of these crimes. I haven't learned everything, but I have tried. And one of the things they really throw at us is trying to feel the pain of the family and put ourselves in that place so that we can feel their pain and their trauma. I know that I can't, because it's your relative and your family member, but I want you to know that I have tried to do that and I deeply regret what happened so long ago."

Tim's words were almost exactly those he told the families in Cape during his sentencing hearing there. Joyce's daughter told Tim that she was in court so she could see his face and tell him that he had robbed her and her family of her mother. She told him that because of what he did, Joyce's grandchildren would never know their grandmother. Like Hazel Sheppard, Debbie told Tim she would pray for him. She said knowing his identity did bring some closure for her. Debbie struck me as a very strong woman. Joyce's sister also addressed Tim.

"I am glad that there is some closure coming to this. You don't know what you did. You just tore my family so badly. And I'm going to try, really try, in my heart, because I'm a Christian, to try to forgive you if I can, because if I can't, then that means the Lord is not going to forgive me. I don't hate you, but I don't know. You just took a big part of my life from me, because like I said, it was my only sister and she's been gone now for thirty-one years. You took my sister, you took my niece's mother, you took my kids' aunt, you took my mother and father's daughter and it just tears me up. I can't say that I have forgiven you right now, but I'm so happy that there is some closure after thirty-one years and now maybe my mother and my father and also my sister can rest in peace. Thank you."

And with that, court was adjourned. Guards quickly removed Tim from the courtroom. I met with Debbie. She asked me to give their best to the other families. I thought of their faith and how it had gotten them through the difficult years since Joyce's murder. I thought of Hazel Sheppard and Karen Parsh and their faith. All of these women were very strong.

While Tim was being brought into Paducah, he pointed to the house where he had sexually assaulted a woman at gunpoint despite her warnings that she was someone important. Until then, the Paducah Police were unable to find the case. The woman had since died a natural death, but the mystery was now over. Tim was told the woman was someone important, but her identity was not revealed to him or the public.

As Tim rode back to the prison in Pontiac, I made my way back to the Shawnee College Campus. Spring was beginning to emerge in Southern Illinois. Life was everywhere. My thoughts were still with the Tharp family, who had just emotionally poured out their souls. I doubted they would see the life emerging around them that day. *Maybe tomorrow*, I hoped. I sat down at my desk that afternoon. It was quiet. I looked at a picture of Deborah Sheppard that was on a table beside my desk. I had brought the portrait from my office at the Carbondale Police Department. A lot had happened in the twenty-seven years since the night I heard the dispatcher send Margaret to Deborah's apartment. It was all over now. I had set out to resolve Deborah Sheppard's murder. As it turned out, Deborah had helped me resolve many others. *May God bless you, Deborah*, I thought. *May you now rest in peace.*

Epilogue

I continue to communicate with Tim Krajcir. There are several reasons: I want to learn what we could have done to catch him earlier and what future investigators can do to detect future brutal criminals like him. It would be naïve for us to think there will never be another Tim Krajcir. I also want to be able to ask him about other crimes that he might have forgotten. It is a rare opportunity to look into the soul of a person who has committed so many evil deeds. DNA is a great forensic tool, but, for the most part, it is a reactive tool. So, in addition to the forensic advances we have made, what can we learn now to prevent other Tim Krajcirs from victimizing our society? Through my correspondence with Tim, I have learned a lot. I have also found that there are no easy answers.

I wrote to Tim to tell him of my intentions to write a book and use the profits for a scholarship at SIU in memory of his victims. With that, he pledged to cooperate in this effort. Initially, the Illinois Department of Corrections withheld my letters, wanting to make sure that neither Tim nor his family would profit from the book. After a few months, the Illinois Department of Corrections senior legal counsel called and approved my correspondence with Tim. They released my letters to Tim and sent Tim's letters to me.

In the more than thirty multiple-page neat and articulate letters he has sent, he has been very open with me. I know some will be critical of me for including his words in this book. But because I am now teaching criminal justice students, I want to take advantage of my rapport with him and share this knowledge. What made this charismatic, athletic and intelligent man turn into a savage rapist and a serial killer? We may never know, but I would be remiss in not studying him and sharing this research with my students and the readers of this book. Here are some excerpts from his words that have really stuck out:

This is a chapter about me and what people don't know about me.
Yes, I am all those terrible things you've read about me. I have committed

terrible heinous crimes. I am a rapist, a killer of women, and exhibition-ist, a home invader, burglar; yes I am all these things [but] that is not all I am. I am also a conglomeration of various emotions. I am very fragile emotionally. But you say, you don't show any emotions, you don't seem to be remorseful. In prison, one of the first things you learn is not to show any emotions, you must be stoical, show no emotion. Look strong, be strong. If you show any weakness you will be run over, taken advan-tage of. So at eighteen, I was thrust into a den of vipers, murderers and sexual degenerates at Menard Psyche Center. Yes, I committed a rape and almost killed a woman [1963]. But it was the first time I had ever been locked up. It was a time with some psychiatric help, or good coun-seling, I may have been helped or could have been helped. Instead, I was sent to this den of evil. My family was told I was getting treatment, that I was seeing a psychiatrist on a regular basis, none of which was true. I was there almost five years. Seen a psyche once every six months. He'd ask how I was doing and that was my treatment. The only treat-ment I seen there was electric shock or hydro therapy, where they wrapped you in ice cold sheets or made you take hot baths. So I learned to hide my fear, I couldn't let anyone see how scared I was…A rage grew in me that had already developed in me as a youngster, moving place to place, never having a home. It was as if I had this core of anger deep within me. A rage that grew and smoldered for years until I was released in 1976.

…I've always had plenty of opportunities meeting and finding attractive and some beautiful women. But by this time, from 1975 to 1976 and on, my head was really screwed on wrong. Many of my romances were brief and didn't last long. Whether from psychological or emotional stress, my sex life was not good. Here I had all the willing partners, both beautiful and sexually attractive but very often became impotent at the onset of a sexual encounter, very often getting very angry at myself. I would then go out in the next day or so and look for victims and I found more sexual arousal in peeping and in situations where I got the power feeling. Having that feeling of power from con-trolling the situations and making them do what I wanted would briefly satisfy my need for instant gratification…In the time from 1974 until now, I have had maybe seven or eight affairs, three of which were on the serious level. All but two of them were while I was at Vienna and Anna [hospital] working for the [prison] ambulance service before my release in late 1976. Because of my early years, I believe I developed really low self-esteem, and as I grew older, I needed reassurance that I was cared for and loved. I think this need for continued reassurance from the women in my life may have ruined some of my relationships. I was always asking them if they loved me. I needed to hear it often. I remember one of my first victims, I think in Waukegan, I asked her to love me or let me make love to her, or told her to tell me she loved me. Something like that. In Anna [Union County Hospital], there were several women I became involved with; one becoming more serious and continuing when I got out in 1976. I think the women at both hospitals, Cairo and Anna, young women, older women, married women, all seemed to go crazy over the cons who were working at the hospitals. I assume the aura, or adventure, danger, the chance for a little excitement drove them. I know all the inmates, ugly or handsome, black or white had their hands full. It was amazing to me. We had light supervision and the full run of the hospitals. We worked in three-man shifts with one of us being the captain and designating what was what. I was the captain of my team. Only two of us would go on the ambulance calls and the third man would wait by the emergency room. We worked twenty-four hour shifts, living at the hospital again with little supervision. Forty-eight hours off and then another shift out. Plenty of opportunity for a little rendezvous. The second floor of the hospital was empty and those empty rooms were busy. I had four or five little adventures, then got real serious with one, who later came to see me in Carbondale. My mistake, she was married and promised she would get a divorce. We got along great, but I was trying to keep to the straight and narrow, and didn't like her sneaking around on her husband. So I put a little pressure on her to get a divorce and for us to get married. Well, she called one night, and out of the blue said goodbye. No explanation, nothing but goodbye. Right after that, I said to hell with things and made my first trip to Cape and assaulted Holly Jones there at [the discount store]. Probably the most stupid decision I ever made. My need for instant gratification again ruining my life…I knew once I made that decision, there was no turning back. I had crossed over that line.

Getting caught was never in my mind once I lost control. Like I said before, rationality went out the window. One of my favorite ways of describing myself to some of my friends at Big Muddy was to say "I'm Rationally Insane" and meaning it.

I do not believe in God as most people here do. I believe there may be something all powerful out there, but I don't believe Jesus was the son of God. Maybe a great teacher, healer, or philosopher, but the son of God? No.

I remember in the ninth grade, I went out for the Junior Varsity basketball team. The coach told me I had more talent than most of his players, but he wasn't going to use me because I wouldn't be there next year [because we moved around so much]. That happened more than once. I had a lot of nights where I walked home crying or went to bed crying. A young man full of dreams doesn't know how to handle that kind of intense pain. Then I couldn't talk to anyone about it. My stepdad and I had zero relationship and my mother and I had no close bond. So all the anger and emotion I had to internalize, no outlet for anger. So I began acting out. Those were not happy days for me…After I got kicked out of the house [in 1962], I came back about a week later and told mom I had to get out. I couldn't stand being around Bernie, my stepfather. Just too much anger there and I knew sooner or later one of us would hurt the other. Mom signed for me to join the Navy. Sent me to Great Lakes for boot camp. Enlisted with two friends so we would be in the same company. I wanted sea duty. But I got sick with double pneumonia and had to spend a month in the hospital. When I got released, they put me in a different company. Did well and I enjoyed the physical challenge. Loved all of it. After boot camp, instead of getting sea duty, I got stuck back on the main side of the base, working in the 1st Lieutenant's Department. We took care of guys coming and going from different assignments, it was like a transfer barracks. I fell into going to Milwaukee for liberty where I met [my wife] at the train station. We hit it off great and ended up getting married a year later. She became pregnant and I did the right thing. My trouble began with peeping, too much free time with nothing to do. I got a locker off the base, bought some civilian clothes and started peeping again. I just couldn't afford going back and forth to Milwaukee. Up to that point in time I never assaulted anyone. One evening looking in a doorway I saw this gal's husband leaving for work. I watched for a while, and why I don't know, but all of a sudden I went through a kitchen door and raped for the first time. A few months later, I got my orders to ship out on May 27, 1963. But I could not stop going out in the evening and peeping in windows. I saw another woman alone, back door open and I went in. This time the woman was not cooperating, giving me a hard time. Power and control, she wouldn't obey, fueling my anger. I did not consciously think of hurting her, but I did. I picked up a pair of scissors and stabbed her in the back. I guess [because of] the anger and rage. I remember thinking afterward, "Jesus Tim, how could you do that? Why? A wife, a baby coming?" I couldn't understand what was driving me. I know I cared for [my wife] and was looking forward to the baby coming. I remember the first time I felt the baby move, one of the nicest moments of my life. A few weeks after I got arrested for peeping, I confessed to the other two crimes, the rape and attempted murder. I often think how terrible it was for [my wife] during this time. I was thankful she was with her parents. The whole situation must have been both physically draining and devastating to her emotional well-being. Over the years I often thought how strong she must have been to make it there through that terrible time. Twenty-five to fifty years, thus began for me the most terrible and trying time of my life. That being five years spent at Menard Psychiatric Center, a hell on earth, and the last place a young immature emotionally disturbed teenager should have been sent...I spent many hours watching the river traffic passing by and wondering if I would ever see the outside again. It's made from large sandstone blocks that in the summer heat up so much that in the little yard, you can see the heat waves bouncing off the yard. It got so hot on the higher galleries that we would strip down to our underwear and some got naked, put water on the floor to stay cool. I don't know how many died over the years from the heat, but it was too many. The Psyche Center was closed off from the rest of the prison. I remember seeing this big gate on the day I arrived. We came around the corner of the cell house and some of the men were lined up by the door waiting for the fish line to come through. There were cat calls, whistles, threats, "Hey baby, you're gonna be mine," all kinds of wise cracks and smart remarks. To say the least, I was scared to death, never having been in that kind of environment. They took us fish on to two gallery, instant chaos and total madness. Naked men, crazies, some with food all over them, others partially dressed, just running all over the place. Took us and gave each of us a cell. Mattresses on the floor, blanket, and cockroaches everywhere. On the walls and on the floor...I was terrified of everything I was seeing, thinking this is my home for the next fifty years. I didn't know anything about good time or parole... They put me in the yard with a job in the dining room, and here come the predators. I was a young good looking dumb kid and they came at me from every direction. I was emotionally weak and easy taken advantage of. I was extremely lonely and was thinking maybe I should find someone to hook up with. I found a person and the first thing he wanted to do was to go to a room in the cell house and have sex. Like an idiot, I went along hoping to find some kind of comfort or care from this terrible place. Once in his room, he started making advances toward me and tried kissing me. Well, thank God for the Irish in me or the intestinal courage I found. I was instantly repulsed and said no way. I walked out of the room disgusted with the whole episode. But it had a terrible effect on me, because the person, to feed his ego, was telling everyone we had sex. Through the first two years there, I was in fight after fight trying to earn respect and gradually they left me alone. I became involved in sports almost from the start. Usually if I was playing ball they would leave me alone. So much free time I spent almost exclusively on the basketball court or the softball field. Eventually becoming one of the best athletes in the whole prison. But I was still growing up, started gambling, and began thinking I was a hot shot. Soon, the passive homosexuals started approaching me and, like an idiot, I let myself become involved with some of them. Because of my status as a gambler, athlete, politician, I started getting oral sex from some of the passive homosexuals. Along this time I met some people who I know had lasting effects on me. Both became serial killers later in life. We talked about one [Kenneth Paul Rogers], another was a guy who later killed some nuns. Both of these guys were athletes who helped me and taught me basketball and softball. I think I got programmed to kill during this time. I know they would talk about how to get away with crimes. "Hell, kill your victims, don't leave no witnesses, then you'll never get caught." I heard their stories over and over again. I kept getting better and better in the sports realm and soon was making all the all-star teams, winning basketball contests, championships, and meeting the guys from the general division. They would ask me when I was coming over to the general division. During my fourth year there, I really started becoming disgusted with the whole place. I realized all the gambling and homosexuals and being the big time politician wasn't what it was cracked up to be. I knew I had to get out of there and get my life in order. I put in for transfer and finally about late 1967 or early 1968, I left the nut house and went to the general division.

When I got to the general division, I found my reputation as an athlete had preceded me. I was met and welcomed with respect even by inmates I did not know, but had seen me play in the many all-star games I'd participated in over the past couple years. Especially by the white guys, as I was usually the only white athlete to make all the all-star teams. So I finally started feeling better about myself. I got into school, got my G.E.D. and enrolled in commercial school. Took bookkeeping and typing. Both beginning typing and advanced typing and advanced accounting. I was then asked to teach both and did for a while. After about a year, I enrolled full time in the college gang. At no time was there any treatment program for sex offenders. All they had was AA and NA— neither of which was ever a problem for me. The years from 1968 to 1972 were good for me. I matured as an athlete, got even better and was dominating both basketball and baseball. I played with the Menard Cubs in the Coal Belt league. Our coach, being an ex major leaguer, had contacts with the Cardinals and the scouts would come down occasionally and look us over. There were I believe maybe three of us who might have been able to play at a higher level, but I was doing fifty years, and my friend John was doing life. I've often wondered if I would have been able to hit major league pitching. I remember doing well against the pitchers from SIU who usually played us a couple games each summer. Who knows, thinking about it too much, about the what if's, just fed my internal rage. I got about as much as I could from the college game. I dropped out of it and then worked in the commissary for a year or so and finally left Menard in 1972 going to Vienna.

I got in the second EMT class there and was on the first crew that went out and worked in the community. Finally got into a therapeutic community of about twenty-five or thirty of us who all lived, worked, studied together. It was based on transactional analysis and a mixture of confrontative theory like Synanon (program). But by then, I had built a wall of concrete around my feelings and all the rage I had kept hidden. I wouldn't let anyone get inside, though Mike did try. Michael Dolan ran the program. He really started the SDP Program and helped make it what it is today. When he was at Vienna, I was his clerk and eventually became the Teaching Assistant Coordinator when Mike was not there. When I went back to Menard Psyche in 1979, he was there and had structured the program. But, like I said, I wouldn't let anyone get close to me. The next three years went by pretty quick. With me playing ball everywhere, working out on the ambulance in Cairo at PADCO (St. Mary's), and then working in Anna, going to Shawnee, I was a pretty busy fellow. I took care of the intellectual part of me, and did great in emergency medicine. I loved it. But in the emotional department, I was a bomb waiting to explode.

I got released in September 1976. I went to SIU on scholarship money and began working for the Health Service…I was then offered a job when Jackson County took over the Health Service duties and hired a professional crew…That was right after I moved into the little trailer on North Springer Street.

The job was going great, but in being honest, I think I behaved maybe a month after my release and started acting out, doing things I shouldn't. I was all right when I was around people, but when I started being alone too much, I couldn't handle it. I was alone so much of my young life, and then alone in prison, so I started going out in the evening.

The voyeurism started all over again. About the time my relationship ended [with a nurse from Union County Hospital], I made the most stupid decision of my life. While in prison, I had decided if I went back to crime, if I ever crossed that line again, there would be no going back.

It was all or nothing. I fantasized a lot in prison and decided I would and live these fantasies in the real world. This is when I made my first trip to Cape and met Holly at the [discount store] for the first time. And you pretty well know what happened from here on.

Why did I rape and kill? Difficult questions to answer. Before getting into that, I need to talk about one other thing, "the gun." When I burglarized that home [North Springer in Carbondale] where I found the .38 and a box of ammunition, I think I made the biggest mistake of my life. They say guns don't kill people, people do, but I wonder about that statement. I almost killed in 1963 but didn't. But I guess the intent was there. With that gun in my hand, I was infused with an unreal sense of power. Rape for me was secondary to the feeling of power and control you get from the anticipation of what you are going to do. The sex is usually a let down after the power and control is defused...Now I've got the gun, could I use it? Would I have the nerve to pull the trigger? With me, it was all about power and control. My whole life I had no control, no power to change anything...Now I had this gun and all the rage and frustration, my anger with my mother for never listening, never controlling things. From all these different emotions came the anger against women. Anger, rage at my step-father for never being the father I seen other kids have. So I took my anger and frustration out on my victims. Like I told you, I have never been able to dissolve the core and anger and rage that lives within me. When I did the [Parsh] killings in Cape, it was like I was numb, I didn't feel anything. I couldn't see them as caring loving human beings. I didn't know them. In prison, you learn to look out for yourself. Thinking of only yourself. The world revolved around you...I have worked on many of these issues [since] and finally got where I started caring for and respecting other people.

I can't understand how I could care so much for some people and nothing for others. I could risk my life trying to save a life and then turn around and take a life and think nothing of it. The thing about power and control is, you can't get enough. It consumed me. It is addictive, worse than drugs. I had to have it. Like I told you, rationality went out the window. Yes I knew it was wrong, but the need overrode the rationality.

...I'm thankful I had the opportunity to help so many people (with the ambulance service). There are many more stories, but too many to write about. Quite a contradiction, on one hand, risk my life to save a life, then turn around and take a life. It's almost as if I was two different people. Almost as if this blind would come over my conscientiousness and I would become this other person. I still don't understand how I can be so emotional on one hand, then so cold and unfeeling on the other. I can cry at a happy ending in a movie or a beautiful love story, I can see the beauty in a sunset or the beauty in nature, I love seeing people happy, I love children, yet ten minutes later after experiencing something wonderful I can kill someone and then forget about it the next day. Complex to say the least.

When in 1979 I went back inside [Menard Psyche], it was a little different. They had really cleaned up the place...Sex offenders had a couple counselors who held small sessions...It was easy for me to fool the counselor. Within one and a half years, I was released in June 1981. Back to school on scholarship. Finished my degree work. As long as it took me to get a gun and a car I was off again, raping, killing, causing havoc. It was the same all over again. Important, poor sexual relationships, so I needed the power, and off I went. After I graduated, I moved to Pennsylvania. But I could not stop. If anything, it got worse. For some reason, I stopped the killing, but kept up going out and raping. I couldn't wait to get off work and go out. I spent little time at home. I honestly believe I wanted to get caught. I started taking a lot of chances. Even the night I got caught, I had plenty of time to leave before the police arrived. What did I do? I slowly drove by the police, he took off after me and I was arrested again. I was glad it was over.

At Graterford [Pennsylvania] prison, I met Dr. Canal, a psychiatrist who worked with sex offenders. He and I did one-on-one's and group for five straight years along with additional therapy from a [treatment program] out of Philadelphia called St. Joseph's Institute, or something along those lines. Even though I learned a lot, I still kept myself hidden from the deep stuff. It was about here after five years of pretty good therapy, I started to think about keeping myself incarcerated. My five years were up, back to Illinois and Menard Psyche. In 1981, right before I left there, Michael Dolan was hired and started the SDP Program that evolved into what it is today. So I got involved, but by then I was pretty convinced I could not, under any circumstances, let myself be released. I did not want any more victims. So I withdrew from therapy telling Mike little but inferring a lot. I knew I could never be sure, no matter what I felt about myself. I must stay in prison. So, there I sat, year after year. At times, I struggled with that decision, but I knew it was right. I made peace with myself and the years rolled by. Until August 2007 when I met this guy named Paul [Echols]. Now another stage of my life began, and one I'm glad is almost over.

So you see, though there is much evil in me, there is also much good. I am deeply remorseful over the terrible crimes I committed. I continue, to this day, looking at the pain and heartache I've caused so many. I vowed to do anything I can to prevent other crimes of this nature from happening. All of this is me. I am good, I am evil, yes that's me.

Afterword

Tim now sits in a small cell at the Illinois Department of Corrections prison in Stateville, Illinois. Because of his status as an escape risk, dating to his attempted escape from a Pennsylvania jail in 1983, his liberties are very limited. Tim will be moved from one maximum prison to another about every year for the rest of his life. Tim is getting older, but he is in good physical condition. He still plays basketball as often as he can. "Cracker Jack," as some of the guards call him, typically defeats his younger opponents. When the "old man" beats the younger inmates, he earns their respect. Tim had many talents, but they were all wasted. His projected parole date is August 18, 2047.

Timothy Wayne Krajcir, with the persuasion of his cousin Donna, has offered to donate his brain and body to science when he dies. Maybe there are some physical explanations for what he did. Maybe not. But it's too rare of an opportunity not to try to find out.

Bernie and Hazel Sheppard still live in the home where they raised their three daughters. There are pictures and other artifacts of Deborah's life scattered around their home to never let her be forgotten. The couple now enjoys life through the eyes of their grandchildren. The marriage that almost ended under the stress of their oldest daughter's death is solid now.

Karen Parsh Chesser and her husband still live in the St. Louis area. They have three sons. Karen is looking forward to retirement soon and someday becoming a grandmother. She still feels guilt for trading places with her sister and always will. But she also realizes Brenda's sacrifice allowed her to bring three lives into this world. She still leans on her faith to get her through. The wounds left by Tim Krajcir run so deep, they will never heal completely.

Sheila Cole's parents died not knowing the truth. Her sister and brother survive and keep her memory alive.

A few months after her death, Virginia Witte's husband, David, grieving the loss of his wife, moved out of their house and back to St. Louis. The tough veteran of the D-Day invasion lived only three more years. Virginia's memory lives on with her two sons and grandchildren.

Joyce Tharp's daughter, Debbie, tells her children about their grandmother. While Debbie doesn't have many memories of her mother, she cherishes the ones she has.

Myrtle Rupp did not have any children and her husband had died a few years before her murder. Her nephew successfully lobbied police to find her killer. His aunt and uncle's memories live on with him.

Don Call and his cousins have never forgotten Margie. Their memories of her as a mom and Aunt Margie continue today. Several grandchildren and great-grandchildren have come along since her death. The close-knit families celebrate every Christmas with a family reunion and always share Aunt Margie stories. Don and his wife recently moved back to Cape Girardeau to be closer to family.

Mildred Wallace did not have any children and her sister and brother have since passed away. But her memory carries on in the hearts of Teresa Haubold and her elderly father, who was a close friend to Mildred. Those who joined her on various civic organizations still miss her dearly. Shortly after her death, an educational scholarship was established for business majors at Southeast Missouri University in her memory.

Grover Thompson's nephew is still pushing to overturn his uncle's conviction for the attempted murder of Ida White. He hopes this book may be the boost he needs.

Jim Smith continues to investigate cold cases for the Cape Girardeau Police Department. In 2009, with the assistance of prosecutor Morley Swingle, Jim arrested a suspect in a 1979 Cape murder. Unfortunately, the suspect died of natural causes before the case could go to court, but another cold case was cleared. The City of Cape Girardeau is lucky to have someone who cares so much about the victims and families in these old cases.

Carl Kinnison continues as Cape Girardeau's police chief. He is beginning to look forward to his retirement in a few years and plans to spend more time with his grandson and possibly teach. He also continues to follow the professional baseball career of his nephew.

Two of Tim's victims passed away in September of 2010, exactly one week apart. They were Pauline Brown, ninety-four, of Marion, and Eunice Seabaugh, eighty-eight, formerly of Cape Girardeau. They were truly brave women. May they rest in peace.

I continue to teach Criminal Justice full-time for Shawnee Community College and part-time for Southern Illinois University. My students seem to enjoy learning through some of my experiences. I find it very rewarding to teach what will be the next generation of police officers and investigators but miss the excitement of being an investigations commander. Occasionally, I volunteer my time in my old department as a fingerprint examiner and consultant. The department is made up of many good investigators and personnel. I have also joined a cold case team with the Williamson County Sheriff's Department in Illinois. Now I have the privilege of working with many retired investigators from Southern Illinois who are part of this team. In particular, I am working with retired Illinois State Police Captain Monica Joost, one of the original Carbondale detectives who investigated Deborah Sheppard's murder.

Most of the original members of the 1977 Jackson County Ambulance crew, which included Tim, have prospered. Several became doctors and others have climbed to the tops of their respective agencies and departments. They all remember the "good" Tim and are still trying to understand the dark side of his personality that he hid from them so well.

There are many prayers going out for Tim Krajcir every day. Some prayers ask that he be forgiven, while others pray for his death. Eventually, Tim will make one last court appearance, at the highest court possible. While nine angels watch, he will meet his maker. And the final verdict will come at the hands of God.

Acknowledgments

It has truly been an honor to meet the families of those who died at the hands of Tim Krajcir and the victims who survived his attacks. They are an impressive group of people who have somehow found a way to pick up the pieces and move forward in life.

I thank my wife, son and daughter, who supported my writing of this book and endured months of file boxes and folders scattered about our house. Without their support, my career and this book would not have been successful.

I want to thank Christine Byers, whom I asked to help write this book because of her talents in writing and her tenacity as a reporter. It was one of my better decisions. Thanks to her husband, Tony, who sacrificed countless hours with her while she wrote and edited.

I want to recognize Cape Girardeau Police Detective Jim Smith for his dedication and resolve in helping bring justice to the families of Cape Girardeau and beyond. Jim and I became lifelong friends throughout the investigation and resolution of Tim's cases. It was an experience neither of us will ever forget.

I also want to recognize Illinois Department of Corrections Lieutenant Harold Schuler. His assistance during the investigation was invaluable.

Thanks to attorney John Clemons for his legal advice in writing this book. Had a judge listened to John's arguments to keep Tim in prison in 1981, at least three lives would have been saved and many victims spared.

And last, I am grateful to all the police officers, police chiefs, prosecutors, crime scene technicians, forensic experts and investigators who worked diligently through the years to resolve these cases. They were resolved through a massive team effort and it was my privilege to be a member of this team. I have often used the analogy of a relay race when describing my role in these cases. I was just the last man across the finish line carrying the baton so many had carried before me. We are all winners.